REACHING ALL BY CREATING
TRIBES LEARNING COMMUNITIES

Taylor
Kennedy

*Reaching All
by Creating*

TRIBES
LEARNING
COMMUNITIES

JEANNE GIBBS

in collaboration with Teachers and Administrators Extraordinaire

CENTER
SOURCE
SYSTEMS

WINDSOR, CALIFORNIA

Published in the United States of America by

CenterSource Systems, LLC
7975 Cameron Drive, Suite 500, Windsor, California 95492

Library of Congress Cataloging-in-Publication Data
Gibbs, Jeanne
    Reaching all by creating tribes learning communities / by Jeanne Gibbs ;
    in collaboration with Teachers and Administrators Extraordinaire.
        p. cm.
    Includes bibliographical references and index.
    ISBN-13: 978-0-932762-41-2 (pbk.)
      1. Group work in education. 2. Classroom environment—United States.
      3. Academic achievement—United States. 4. Social learning. I. Title.

LB1032.G53 2006
371.3'6—dc22

                                        2006029506

ISBN 978-0-932762-41-2

Book Design: Lynn Bell, Monroe Street Studios, Santa Rosa, CA
Illustrations: Pat Ronzone, Sausalito, CA
Printing: Creel Printing, LLC, Las Vegas, NV

PRINTED IN THE UNITED STATES OF AMERICA
10   9   8   7   6   5

ONE LEARNS BY DOING THE THING,
FOR THOUGH YOU THINK YOU KNOW IT,
YOU HAVE NO CERTAINTY UNTIL YOU TRY.

—Sophocles

CONTENTS

PREFACE

The school that becomes a self-renewing
enterprise will shape its own future.[1]
—ROLAND S. BARTH

Throughout the years, the same inquiry is made—"Tribes? What is Tribes?"

Our response is never quite the same. It keeps changing as more and more schools report the impact that the process of Tribes, *Tribes Learning Communities*, brings to their students, teachers and whole school system. Over a period of time most discover that....

- ✦ the climate of the school becomes safe, caring and motivational for all— teachers as well as students

- ✦ participation in active learning groups (tribes) leads to higher student performance

- ✦ disruptive student problems fade away, giving teachers more time to teach

- ✦ respect among multicultural, multiethnic and diverse student populations increases, and

- ✦ teachers' professional competency, collegiality and collaborative responsibility for students' learning as well as whole school improvement increases.

Tribes is not a curriculum, not a program or a collection of activities. It is an on-going goal-oriented *process* based on sound *principles and practices* that maximize academic, social and emotional development and learning for today's children. The *principles* rise out of a synthesis of literature, research and studies from overlapping fields. They are identified in Chapter Three of this book, and are the conceptual foundation for Tribes Learning Community schools throughout many countries.

Principle based education means going beyond a myopic focus on narrowed down curriculum, high-stakes testing and so-called replicable curriculum and school reform models. The principles and process of Tribes go beyond "one-size-fits all" 19th century "schooling," rote instruction that no longer engages students of today....

- ✦ students who have been raised in this culture of technology, imagery, rapid communication, mobility and environmental complexity

✦ students who are proficient in acquiring information, concepts and data actively rather than passively

✦ students who are multifaceted, multi-tasked ….and creative.

Neuroscience studies tell us that the chemistry and cognitive brain structures of today's children have evolved, enabling them to learn in very different ways.[2] They are more likely to be reached through active experiential learning, collaboration with peers, meaningful problem solving, and working with interrelated images, ideas, music, words and movement. Whether we or they realize it or not, nature and culture have been preparing them well to live in this dramatically different 21st century world.

No longer can we ignore the big questions, such as….

"Where are our nations' schools in the midst of this unprecedented challenge?"

"Why are we teaching more of the same, in the same way? Only harder!"

"How do we reach and teach these learners of today? Especially, if we dismiss the need to be continuing learners ourselves!"

The purpose of this edition, *Reaching All by Creating Tribes Learning Communities,* is to highlight that a wealth of knowledge (sound principles, practices and a community building process) is available to transform education from what it has been—into what it can and needs to become. Countless numbers of schools are finding that the most effective way to achieve significant school improvement is to support and sustain school-site teacher learning communities. Teacher teams in schools using the process of Tribes are known as *Collegial Learning Communities.* Having the time to work and learn together increases their professional capacity to reach and teach in ways that correspond to how children and adolescents of today best can learn and excel.

Hundreds of experienced teachers, administrators, resource people, researchers, colleagues and certified Tribes trainers have helped to make the process of Tribes what it is today. Among the many has been Bonnie Benard, respected Senior Program Associate of the Health and Human Development Program at West Ed. Her new book, *What Is It About Tribes?* documents more than 400 literature references and studies that substantiate the principles and components of the process of Tribes.[3] Her research, writing and wisdom on the factors that nurture human development, resiliency and learning guide much of the Tribes "caring people process." Bonnie's collegial support has been invaluable.

We also particularly thank the teachers, trainers and administrators who are sharing their own experiences by writing articles for this edition of Tribes. Their learning is learning for all of us. It affects the emphasis, changes and new directions in which Tribes Learning Communities may go.

Once again we want readers to know that the quality and attractiveness of this book, as well as all TribesTLC® publications and materials are due to the expertise of two very creative people: Pat Ronsone for her lively and winsome illustrations; and Lynn Bell for her outstanding book designs, text layout and computer graphics. Pat and Lynn are appreciated and celebrated again and again with each new CenterSource publication.

Finally, more important than all…I welcome you as a new friend and colleague into the growing international Tribes Learning Community. May something herein lighten and brighten your days—and the futures of the children and youth who come your way. They are the ones that this process known simply as "Tribes" is really all about.

JEANNE GIBBS
DEVELOPER & AUTHOR

1

A New Pattern of Interaction

1 A New Pattern of Interaction

Who are these people? We're teachers, parents, administrators, business people, service organizations, and students who have come together to figure out how to change our school—so that everyone is excited about learning.

We're asking ourselves:

What if...

We created a safe and caring environment in our school?

Everyone respected individual differences and the diversity of our cultures?

Our teachers designed learning experiences to reach students who learn in different ways?

Students became responsible for themselves and each other?

We knew how to educate all of our students for success in the 21st century?

Our families became actively involved in the education of their children?

We could awaken a love of learning in everyone?

Pat Rincone

TOWARD A NEW PATTERN OF INTERACTION

"What if" questions like these are being asked by thousands of parents and educators throughout school communities. They recognize the need to prepare students with the knowledge, skills, and personal qualities to do well in a world of rapid change. They realize that they have much at stake, not just the health and well-being of their own children, but of all children. There are no easy answers, and certainly no single program or curriculum can revitalize a school. The complexity of change can only be met through an ongoing process that engages teachers, administrators, parents, community members, and students over several years of time. All must begin to relate, plan, and act out of a new pattern of interaction toward common goals on behalf of children. As you move through this book, you will discover a trusted process to use not only within classrooms but throughout the whole school community. It is a synthesis of concepts, agreements, and strategies woven into a new pattern of interaction to create caring environments for human growth and learning.

The first custom of the Tribes process, no matter where it is used, is to invite people to reflect upon and share their own experiences. This step is called "inclusion." In order to involve you, the reader, right away—we would like you to take a moment to reflect upon your own heartfelt experiences of being a student in school. The first question is, "When did you go to school? Was it in the 1980s, 70s, 60s, 50s, 40s, or 30s? What did you enjoy? What was difficult? What did teachers do? Did the days ever seem very long?"

The different decades of our experience really do not matter very much. Nine chances out of ten, most of us spent years hearing these or similar words:

> *"Be quiet."*
> *"Pay attention to the teacher."*
> *"Give the right answer."*
> *"Don't share your work with others—that's cheating."*
> *"Those with the right answer get A's."*
> *"Don't talk to your neighbor."*
> *"Work alone."*

We also heard teachers say:
> *"This is our classroom"*—but decisions were made by the teacher.
> *"You are in charge of yourself"*—but lots of rules were on the board.
> *"Everyone is special"*—but culture and ethnicity were ignored.
> *"No one is favored"*—but the smart kids were called on more.
> *"New Americans are welcome"*—but bilingual education was nonexistent.
> *"Creativity is important"*—but the approach was already defined.
> *"We live in a democracy"*—but not when in school.

The words, the structure, the roles, and the pattern of interaction between teachers and students have changed very little over the past 150 years. The

The way organizations are now is a product of how we think and interact. They cannot change in any fundamental way unless we can change our basic patterns of thinking and interacting so that learning can be a way of life.

—PETER SENGE

pattern, which also dominated the management of schools, is one of command and control. Its message to students has been that the teacher gives out information, students listen and speak only when called on, some people are smart and valued, and some people just can't learn. Most of all, people have to compete to be recognized, to have status and get rewards. The pattern, whether in traditional classrooms or school meetings, looks like this:

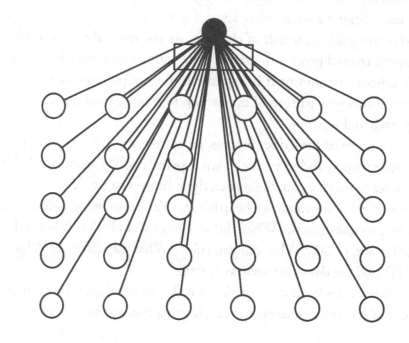

Pouring more money into the factory model of education is, for the most part, foolish. It does no more good to spend more money on teacher talk than it does to increase the amount of time that students have to sit in class listening to it. ...Schools clinging to this mode for learning are using a 19th-century model to prepare kids for the 21st-century world.

—EDWARD FISKE

The people-management pattern began in the 19th century to control factory workers at the beginning of the Industrial Age. When large numbers of people moved from farm areas to jobs in cities, the "little red school house" was relegated to the nostalgia of the disappearing Agricultural Age. With it went the caring, sharing, mutual support, and participation so longed for today. Factories needed workers who were punctual, could do repetitive tasks, and wouldn't make changes. Meeting the needs of the factory system became the role of schools. Students were seen as the raw material to be shaped into standardized products, out of standardized texts, taught by standardized teachers. The ability to memorize and repeat facts spelled success.

Although massive funds for school improvement, restructuring, and reform have flowed through school districts for more than 20 years, the traditional pattern of interaction between teachers and students has changed very little.

WHAT RESULTS ARE WE GETTING?

The question that is being asked by thousands of school communities is, What results are we getting from this model of education? Even a few sobering statistics help to overcome denial:[1]

68% of major business firms report educational shortcomings in their employees.

Only one in five 21–25 year-olds can read a bus timetable or draft a job application letter.

USA

80% of students entering school feel good about themselves. By the 5th grade only 20% do. Only one out of five high school students has positive self esteem.

THIS IS SERIOUS!

90% of U.S. students are dismally behind international averages in math and science.

36% of American companies spend an estimated $20 billion per year on remedial courses in math, reading, and writing.

More than 35% of high school students fail to graduate. Some high schools never graduate more than 50% of their students.

It is not enough just to look at the resulting data coming from traditional educational systems without facing the concurrent results on young people's lives. The CASEL publication, *Sustainable Schoolwide Social and Emotional Learning*, cites the following sets of figures.[2] A Center for Disease Control survey in 2004 reported that:

- 28% of youth reported feeling so sad or hopeless every day for two weeks or more that they stopped doing their normal activities

- 6% made a plan to commit suicide sometime during the last 12 months

- 28% had five or more alcoholic drinks in a row during the last 10 days

- more than 50% of students in some groups dropped out of school.[3]

At another level underlying the above statistics, Search Institute surveys indicated that:[4]

- 29% of youth see themselves as thinking through the results of their choices—but 71% do not.

- 35% see themselves as respecting the values and beliefs of people of different cultures—and 65% do not.

- 24% feel that their teachers really care about them—but 76% do not.

It becomes obvious that higher academic standards, more rigorous literacy and numeracy curriculum, and tests are not and will not prepare youth to meet with the complexity of challenges they face during their formative school years and future lives as adults. The emphasis on intellectual learning apart from individual human development is a misguided political solution that dismisses nurturing the social, emotional, physical and spiritual assets and wholeness of children. Fortunately, the tide is turning with various respected educators, researchers and organizations such as the Collaborative for Academic, Social and Emotional Learning (CASEL), the Association for Supervision and Curriculum Development (ASCD), the National Institute of Health (NIH), and educational laboratories urging national public policies to support the development of the whole child.

LETTING GO AND CATCHING ON

Few would disagree that improving the quality of education requires letting go of assumptions that no longer are working well. However, before letting go of a weak perch, it's good to examine the new one attracting your attention. The following chart points out the dramatic change taking place in many schools today.

Traditional Schooling	Progressive Learning
Emphasis on teaching	Emphasis on learning
Emphasis on parts	Emphasis on the whole
Isolated knowledge and skills	Integrated knowledge and skills
Student as passive recipient	Student as active constructor of meaning
Teacher as information giver	Teacher as co-learner and facilitator
Limited view of intelligence	Teaching to multiple learning styles
Sorting and weeding out of students	Equal access to instruction and content for all
Learning as an individual activity	Learning also as a social activity—collaboration enhances learning
Only teacher-directed learning	Also student-directed learning
Homogeneous grouping	Heterogeneous grouping
Emphasis on product and content	Emphasis on process, meta-cognition—learning how to learn
Primary emphasis on form	Primary emphasis on meaning
Learning decontextualized	Learning grounded in "real world" contexts
Language as separate skill—covered only in English	Reading, writing, thinking, communicating across the curriculum
One answer-one way, correctness	Open-ended, non-routine multiple solutions
Western bias	Multicultural, global views
Criteria, goals given by teacher; not explicit or public before instruction	Shared development of goals and criteria for performance
Tests that test	Tests that teach

In America's best classrooms, again, the emphasis has shifted. Instead of individual achievement and competition, the focus is on group learning. Students learn to articulate, clarify, and then restate for one another how they identify and find answers. They learn how to seek and accept criticism from their peers, solicit help, and give credit to others. …This is an ideal preparation for life-times of symbiotic work.

—ROBERT REICH

A NEW WAY OF LEARNING TOGETHER

The great news is that thousands of schools are making the big shift—learning how to create the new pattern of interaction and structures that support the emerging paradigm. The pattern of interaction in classrooms (and also faculty meetings) looks like this now:

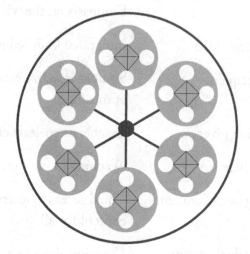

"What, you mean kids can work together on the same math problems?"

"That's right! They've always heard that many heads are better than one, but we never let them prove it to us before."

At best, the traditional structure may give each student five to ten minutes a day to speak about academic topics or respond to questions from the teacher. Dialogue with peers in groups can provide ten times that amount of "air time." At the same time, students are practicing an essential set of collaborative skills that people need in order to work well together. The ability to listen attentively, express ideas, solve group problems, resolve conflict, make decisions, research and analyze material, and encourage others are the democratic skills needed within families, work settings, government, and all organizational systems.

The new pattern of interaction changes the role of the teacher in a dramatic way. Teachers now see themselves as learners, facilitators, researchers, and designers of curricula. When teachers work in collegial groups their inherent isolation from each other disappears. No matter what the group approach may be called—cooperative learning, authentic instruction, student team learning, group investigation, co-op co-op, active learning, jigsaw, complex instruction, group work, or Tribes Learning Community—the benefits of cooperative instruction are documented by hundreds of research studies.[5] The traditional competitive system awards the few, but loses many. Students, even those considered to be slow learners, become motivated when able to work with peers.[6] At a time when school

At best, the traditional structure may give each student five to ten minutes a day to speak about academic topics or respond to questions from the teacher. Dialogue with peers in groups can provide ten times that amount of 'air time.'

failure is a critical problem jeopardizing the country's future, cooperative learning is heralded as one of the most promising instructional strategies to dramatically improve academic achievement.[7]

WHAT IS TRIBES?

Tribes? You smile and wonder when you hear the name. Thirty years ago, teachers in several northern California schools began to refer to the training groups that they were experiencing as "our tribes."[8] They were participants in a pilot project using small learning groups to increase participation and peer support. The purpose of the project was to call forth the unique potential of every student. The story of the ongoing development of the Tribes process is contained in the Resources section of this book.

Tribes is a democratic group process, not just a curriculum or set of cooperative activities. A "process" is a sequence of events that lead to the achievement of an outcome. The outcome of the Tribes process is to develop a positive environment that promotes human growth and learning. How does this happen? Can anyone do it? Yes! It requires learning how to build community through three stages of group development using four agreements among the students or adults with whom you are working.

Community Agreements

 ✦ Attentive listening

 ✦ Appreciation/no put downs

 ✦ The right to pass—the right to participate

 ✦ Mutual respect

Throughout the process people learn to use specific collaborative skills, and to reflect both on the interaction and the learning that is taking place. The Tribes process not only establishes a caring environment for cooperative learning, but provides structure for positive interaction and continuity for working groups whether in the classroom, the faculty, the administration or the parent community.

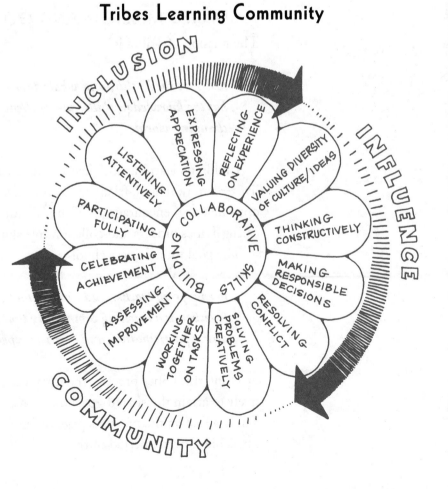

Tribes Learning Community

TRIBES IN THE CLASSROOM

Tribes are formed sociometrically to distribute boys and girls, students of high and low peer acceptance, and people of heterogeneous abilities. Although students have the opportunity to name others whom they would like to have in their tribe, the teacher determines who will be in each group. People are seated together in a small circle or square of desks, or at the same table. Unlike many cooperative learning approaches being used in schools today, Tribes stay together over a long period of time.

A tribe can consist of three to six students who work together each day throughout the school year. The size of the tribe varies depending upon the age of its members and its purpose. Preschool children, ages three to five, do very well when clustered in groups of three. Teachers using cooperative learning structures prefer groups of four, and high school/adult classes using the process for group projects or study groups prefer having the resources of five to six members.

The power of being included and valued by peers motivates students to active participation in their own learning. Positive expectations and support from an ongoing group of peers is the reason that students in Tribes Learning Communities (TLC) become excited about learning.

A SHARED MISSION AND GOAL

The mission of Tribes is

> *to assure the healthy and whole development of every child so that each has the knowledge, skills, and resiliency to be successful in a rapidly changing world.*

Children's learning and development are influenced by the key systems of their lives—family, school, friends, and community. Schools working toward this developmental goal encourage all of the systems involved in learning to use the same caring Tribes process and collaborative skills.

The goal for a Tribes school is

> *to engage all teachers, administrators, students, and families in working together as a learning community that is dedicated to caring and support, active participation, and positive expectations for all students.*

Using the Tribes process, the interactive systems have a way to work collaboratively to attain the shared goals they have for children in their circle of concern. The graphic on the previous page defines the outcomes that a school community can achieve over a period of time.

The power of being included and valued by peers motivates students to active participation in their own learning.

Students

who maintain long-term membership in classroom tribes will

+ Grow in social and emotional competency
+ Achieve greater academic performance
+ Communicate and work well with others
+ Value diverse abilities and cultural differences
+ Assume responsibility for their own behavior
+ Develop critical thinking and collaborative skills
+ Improve their sense of self-worth and mastery of academics

Parents

who become involved in the school community will report

+ Their children like school better than before
+ Positive behavior carries over into the home
+ Strengthening protective factors to foster children's resiliency
+ Appreciation of their involvement with other parents and the staff of the school
+ A new recognition of their own role in their children's education

TRIBES TLC®
A New Way of Learning and Being Together

Teachers

who are long-term members of collegial learning groups and fully implement the Tribes process in their classroom will

+ Spend less time managing student behavior
+ Have more time for creative teaching
+ Notice that students are retaining what they learn
+ Enjoy professional dialogue and supportive colleagues
+ Reduce their own levels of stress
+ Enjoy teaching more than they have before

Administrators

who use the Tribes process to organize and support their students, staff, and parent community will

+ Have fewer student behavior problems
+ Benefit from significant and supportive parent involvement
+ Over time, improve academic achievement
+ Achieve recognition for transforming the school to excellence

A Tribes school is a learning community where teachers, administrators, students, and parents all enjoy the mutual respect and caring essential for growth and learning

The essence of a "learning community" approach is described by Peter Senge, author of the book *The Fifth Discipline, The Art and Practice of the Learning Community*. In a recent interview Senge stated:

> *It's true that there is no substitute for individual caring and commitment, but I have come to think that the real generative point in moving toward a learning organization is in small groups that form around commitments. These are groups of people who are really committed to something larger than themselves and larger than their own personal desires. They support each other in the way that real friends support each other. They tell the truth to each other and they are continually in a mode of inquiry, knowing that nobody knows and everybody can learn continually."* [9]

HOW THE TRIBES TLC PROCESS CHANGES THE PATTERN

The process changes the traditional pattern in classrooms because

- The classroom is student-centered (people no longer relate primarily to the teacher, but work with peers)

- The teacher becomes a facilitator, using the proven group development process

- Everyone belongs to a long-term membership group and feels included and valued for their unique contribution

- Students themselves are involved in classroom management (defining agreements, problem-solving, choosing tasks, and sustaining the positive learning environment)

- Teachers use multiple strategies to reach and teach students of multiple cultures, intelligences, and abilities

- Students learn both critical thinking and collaborative social skills along with academic content

- Individual and group accountability is assessed jointly by students and teacher

- Inherent in the Tribes process are the protective factors that foster resiliency: caring/sharing, active participation, and positive expectations.

THE OPPORTUNITY TO PRACTICE DEMOCRACY

Critical in the shift to the emerging paradigm of education is the need to encourage active participation and give students more choice about what and how they learn. If we only chop up lesson plans for cooperative group learning and teach collaborative skills but fail to use democratic processes, everyone including our country as a whole will be short-changed. Moreover, we believe that cooperative learning will be seen as one more fleeting technique to teach academics. The important question is, after we announce that we are now practicing democracy, how much choice and control will we really give students? Alfie Kohn believes that "it is the integration of two values, community and choice, that defines democracy." He writes:

> It needs to be said that allowing people to make decisions about what happens to them is inherently preferable to controlling them. ...Apart from the skills that will be useful for students to have in the future, they ought to have a chance to choose in the present. Children after all are not just adults-in-the-making. They are people whose current needs and rights and experiences must be taken seriously. Put it this way: students should not only be trained to live in a democracy when they grow up; they should have the chance to live in one today.[10]

We teach reading, writing, and math by having students do them, but we teach democracy by lecture.
—SHELLY BERMAN

QUESTIONS TO CONSIDER WITH YOUR FACULTY

+ How can we help students formulate their own learning goals?

+ How will students take part in defining rules and agreements?

+ How can students help teachers design stimulating learning experiences?

+ How can they help to assess progress toward learning objectives?

There is much evidence that when children are given more opportunity to participate in decisions about schoolwork they miss school less, are more creative, put in more time on task, and complete tasks in less time.[11] Self-determination and a sense of self-worth and civic responsibility could well be the by-products of giving students authentic opportunities to use the democratic skills that they are being taught.

THE WHOLE SCHOOL COMMUNITY

Picture all of the students, faculty, parents, and support and resource people in your school community. (It takes wide-screen vision!) Everyone is included and involved in a group of their own peers—even those parents who are usually so hard to find. (Don't worry now about how to do it.) Picture all of the small groups: teachers with teachers of their same grade level, parents with other parents whose children are in the same classroom, students with other students in the same classroom, and so on. All of the groups are learning and using the same caring process and collaborative skills. All are developing ways to optimize the conditions that support the development of competency and resiliency for every student in the school community. It's as though a whole chorus once singing many different tunes finally is harmonizing and singing the same song! Impossible? No, it can become a reality once the old pattern begins to change.

2

Finding Our Way to the Future

Finding Our Way to the Future

The time is 7:30 p.m. and the meeting of the Middleton Middle School Restructuring Committee is called to order by Thelma Brown, the parent chairperson. "Friends, the purpose of our work tonight is to finalize the plan." Les Aldridge, principal, coughs. "First," he says, "I need to remind you of the District's mandate that our restructuring plan is not only to be innovative, but financially and organizationally sound as stipulated by the District's criteria." Heads nod. "Yes," says Thelma, "but now is the time you've been waiting for. Tonight we will select the immediate programs and policies to improve the school." The words are no sooner spoken than a flurry of hands begin to wave wildly.

Trudy Armstrong, teacher: *"Our test scores will go up if you all will finally vote to have the new math curriculum."*

Polly Crabtree, parent: *"No, teachers just need to give more homework, and we should go back to tracking."*

Donna Gonzales, parent: *"But that simply isn't enough!"*

Tony Salvatore, parent: *"I agree with Donna. What about upgrading computer equipment and doing more teacher training?"*

Les Aldridge, principal: *"My priority is to have guards on the play-ground, and a tougher discipline policy."*

John Pasquale, parent: *"Sure, and how about the dress code we discussed?"*

Jerry Lingo, teacher: *"We should consider school-site management, like some schools are doing."*

Trudy: *"No, what's important is just getting the new math curriculum."*

Parent (no one knows her name for sure): *"What about eliminating field trips?"*

Tony: *"Now you're talking . . . that's a good idea!"*

BEYOND THE QUICK-FIX APPROACH

If you have ever experienced a school planning meeting that in any way resembled this Middleton Middle School parody, and if you managed not to feel frustrated... there's really no use reading any further. Across America groups of dedicated, well-meaning people become caught in the quick-fix approach to school improvement, jumping to partial solutions rather than asking, what developmental outcomes do we want for our students? Ultimately, the principal or district administrators sort out the confusion and distribute a written plan that probably reflects little of the Planning Committee's influence...after all those meetings! Yet, the need for change remains.

WAVES OF REFORM

There are, however, clues that point a way. During the past ten years, American schools have moved through two waves of school reform. Following the release of *A Nation at Risk* in 1983 by the U.S. Department of Education, the focus of school reform was on such external factors as higher standards, competency statements, the strengthening of teacher certification, discipline policy, dress codes, and attendance rules. Five years later the next wave of reform, still current in many places, focused on changing the roles and interaction of adults: teacher empowerment, parental choice, school-site management, and the adoption of schools by local business groups. Attention shifted from mandated activities to collaborative efforts.

A NEW SET OF QUESTIONS

Centering on students rather than adults raises entirely different questions, which require new knowledge, research, and a richer discussion among school planning groups. Our friends from Middleton will have to ask:

+ What kind of world are we preparing kids for?

+ What knowledge, skills, and competencies do students need in order to do well in these rapidly changing times?

+ What are our children really like?

+ How do they learn? Do they all learn the same way?

+ What do **they** want to learn?

+ Should we have developmental goals beyond academics?

Unless these questions are seriously considered, child-centered goals supported by effective learning strategies cannot be well defined. Those many unrelated quick-fix solutions will continue to drive and sabotage the planning that needs to happen to prepare students for a 21st-century world.

LOOKING AT OUR CHANGING WORLD

If we are to plan how to educate kids for a future we're only beginning to imagine, it is important to look at some significant changes.

What we need today is a third wave that builds on the prior efforts, looking beyond both external factors and the roles of teachers, parents, and administrators. We need a comprehensive effort that places the students at the center of educational reform.[1]

—WILLIAM GREIDER

Let your mind wander and jot down some of the most important changes that took place during the last twenty, thirty, or forty years.

1.

2.

3.

4.

5.

6.

7.

8.

9.

10.

Now review your list and star the changes that you believe most affect how we educate kids. How many of the changes that you listed fall into the following major categories?

From	To
Industrial Age	Conceptual
Homogeneous culture	Information Age
Socialization by family	Multicultural diversity
Individualism	Socialization by media,
	peers, and school
	Community

FROM THE INDUSTRIAL AGE TO THE CONCEPTUAL INFORMATION AGE

It boggles the mind when we realize that there have been only two other times in the history of humankind when massive transitions totally changed the world: first, from the Age of Nomadic Hunter-Gatherers to the Age of Agriculture; then from the Age of Agriculture to the Industrial Age; and now from the Industrial Age to the Conceptual Information Age.

Conceptual Information Age

Industrial Age

Age of Agriculture

Age of Nomadic Hunter-Gatherers

Moving between ages means giving up hand-held plows for tractors, the abacus for calculators—the Pony Express for fax machines, cellular equipment, and satellite communication. Upheaval, chaos, and uncertainty inevitably accompany global change throughout every realm of society for many years. It is the process of letting go of old forms and creating new ones.

The Industrial Age of the past 150 years was based on a technology of centralized workplaces in which people worked on individual tasks without much influence over the end-product or service. It had time clocks, authoritarian management, and prescribed methods. To meet the needs of the Industrial Age, schools were organized to train people to be punctual, to do repetitive tasks, and not to make changes. Now as we move to the Conceptual Information Age we begin to realize that ever-changing data combined with rapidly changing systems and situations require critical thinking and collaborative skills. Even the military of many countries depend upon ground troops that can think critically...to analyze data flowing from computers, to synthesize a complexity of information, to relate it to the task at hand, to plan and to work cooperatively with colleagues as a team. There is no doubt about it—this is a high tech/high touch era.

A 1999 U.S. Department of Labor document, entitled *What Work Requires of Schools,* made the challenge very clear.[2]

When resources came out of the ground, the United States was a rich country. Now that resources come out of people's heads, we are a developing country.

—JOHN SCULLEY
FORMER CEO
APPLE COMPUTER

"More than half of our young people leave school without the knowledge or foundation required to find and hold a good job. These young people will pay a very high price. They face the bleak prospects of dead end work interrupted only by periods of unemployment."[3]

SCANS
U.S. Department of Labor Secretary's Commission on Achieving Necessary Skills

SKILLS FOR THE 21ST CENTURY

BASIC SKILLS

Reads, writes, performs arithmetic and mathematical operations, listens and speaks well

✦ **Reading**
 locates, understands, and interprets written information in prose and in document

✦ **Writing**
 communicates thoughts, ideas, information, and messages in writing, and creates documents such as letters, directions, manuals, reports, graphs, and flow charts

✦ **Arithmetic/Mathematics**
 performs basic computations and approaches practical problems by choosing appropriately from a variety of mathematical techniques

✦ **Listening**
 receives, attends to, interprets, and responds to verbal messages and other cues

✦ **Speaking**
 organizes ideas and communicates orally

THINKING SKILLS

Thinks critically, makes decisions, solves problems, visualizes, knows how to learn and reason

✦ **Creative Thinking**
 generates new ideas

✦ **Decision Making**
 specifies goals and constraints, generates alternatives, considers risks, evaluates and chooses best alternative

✦ **Problem Solving**
 recognizes problems, devises and implements a plan of action

✦ **Seeing Things in the Mind's Eye**
 organizes and processes symbols, pictures, graphs, objects, and other information

✦ **Knowing How to Learn**
 uses efficient learning techniques to acquire and apply new knowledge and skills

✦ **Reasoning**
 discovers a rule or principle underlying the relationship between two or more objects and applies it when solving a problem

PERSONAL QUALITIES

Displays responsibility, self esteem, sociability, self-management, integrity, and honesty

✦ **Responsibility**
 exerts a high level of effort and perseveres toward goal attainment

✦ **Self-Esteem**
 believes in own self-worth and maintains a positive view of self

✦ **Sociablity**
 demonstrates understanding, friendliness, adaptability, empathy, and politeness in group settings

✦ **Self-Management**
 assesses self accurately, sets personal goals, monitors progress, and exhibits self-control

✦ **Integrity/Honesty**
 chooses ethical course of action

SKILLS FOR THE 21ST CENTURY

The SCANS report emphasizes that schools must teach a new set of skills to prepare people to enter the world of work of today. Eight among the 16 necessary skills are social and emotional competencies. See if you can identify them in the chart. The Collaborative for Academic, Social and Emotional Learning (CASEL) defines social and emotional learning (SEL) as the process to:[4]

+ acquire skills to recognize and manage emotions

+ develop caring and concern for others

+ establish positive relationships

+ make responsible decisions, and

+ handle situations effectively.

If our schools graduate young people who are self-aware, can manage their emotions, are aware of others, have good relationship skills, and can solve problems effectively, we've given them a terrific start.[5]

—CASEL

FROM HOMOGENEITY TO MULTICULTURAL DIVERSITY

When the United States was originally founded to provide haven and opportunity to people from many countries, the metaphor of a cultural melting pot came into being. Now we realize that expecting all people to be assimilated into our dominant Western European culture has contributed to conflict, prejudice, and unequal opportunity for multi-ethnic populations. Our cities and the majority of suburbs already have rich diversities of people from many races and cultures. By the year 2000, white people will constitute only 55.9 percent of the U.S. population, down from 75.5 percent in 1980. Throughout the world by that same year 5 billion of the 6 billion people on earth will be people of color. The need for multicultural education, tolerance, and respect is apparent.

If we could shrink the earth's current population of 5.2 billion to a village of precisely 1,000 and all of the existing human ratios remained the same, it would look like this.

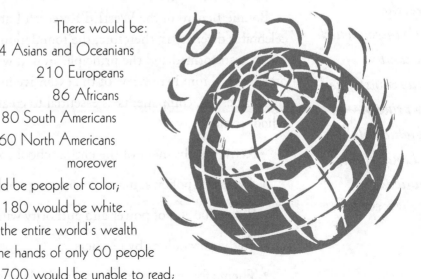

There would be:
564 Asians and Oceanians
210 Europeans
86 Africans
80 South Americans
60 North Americans
moreover
820 would be people of color;
180 would be white.
50% of the entire world's wealth
would be in the hands of only 60 people
700 would be unable to read;
500 would suffer from malnutrition
600 would live in substandard housing[6]

As a nation, we need to prepare young people to work and live in the realities of today's world. The challenge is articulated well by Mako Nakagawa, a multicultural educator.

> *If we are to succeed as a nation both in international trade and in leadership for democracy, we need to use the diverse cultural laboratory of our own country as a training ground for producing citizens who value differences, respect the validity of our own perspectives, understand the independence of people, and who have the interpersonal skills to effectively communicate across all spectra of ethnicity, nationality, language, culture, gender, values, and even political ideology.*
>
> *It is less important for students to learn to appreciate ethnic foods than it is for students to understand equal rights. Yet, much of what we have taught under the rubric of multicultural education has fallen into the trap of "Tacos on Tuesdays." That is, the trap of teaching about cultures and about cultural differences without teaching an understanding of how cultural differences, or gender, class, and other differences, contribute to the unified whole of a democratic nation.*[7]

If we want to give all kids a chance, we agree that schools across the nation need to embrace the concept of what Nakagawa calls "cooperative pluralism." It is a perspective that focuses on the linkages between and among people, coupled with the harmonious networking of all groups. It expands multicultural education from simply learning about a specific culture to learning about our whole system, how we interact, and how we can build everyone's skills and opportunities for active participation and power. Such a philosophy fosters unity and global harmony out of diversity.

Bonnie Benard of the WestEd Research Laboratory writes, "An attitude that celebrates diversity is, therefore, the foundation upon which a school can be culturally transformed and the principle around which all school change efforts are organized." From her review of the extensive literature on multicultural education, she defines five components as essential to creating a culturally transformed school community:

✦ Active involvement of the entire school community

✦ A mission policy/statement centering on diversity

✦ Redistribution of power and authority within the school and classrooms

✦ High expectations by teachers

✦ Theme focused multicultural curriculum, cooperative learning, respect for individual learning styles, and multiethnic, well-trained teachers.[8]

It is less important for students to learn to appreciate ethnic foods than it is for students to understand equal rights.

—MAKO NAKAGAWA

An attitude that celebrates diversity is, therefore, the foundation upon which a school can be culturally transformed and the principle around which all school change efforts are organized.

—BONNIE BENARD

The melting pot metaphor of assimilation grew out of the naiveté of two hundred years ago and is now an insensitive anachronism. Multiculturism is a reality and can become a great strength for this country due to the diversity of our people resources. We need to think in terms of alternative metaphors, such as an orchestra of many fine instruments or a salad bowl composed of many wonderful vegetables all contributing to the whole. The richness of the salad comes from the diversity of colors and flavors. The more the better! What holds it together? Of course, the dressing. It's called "inclusion."

FROM SOCIALIZATION BY THE FAMILY TO SOCIALIZATION BY PEERS

One of the greatest changes, of course, has taken place within American families. The average American family moves every two to three years, and each time loses whatever support systems it may have had. Twenty-five percent of American families are one-parent families. Of the remaining two-parent families, in 80 percent both parents work. It is startling to read in a national poll that the average family spends 27 minutes per day together. The one-time sense of family history, values, and expectations has largely disappeared. Grandparents, aunts, uncles, and cousins rarely live in the same area. A majority of families, due to various stressful situations, are no longer helping their own children to

+ Gain a sense of identity and self-worth

+ Learn shared cultural values

+ Bond to significant others.

Given the incredible stresses the family is now experiencing, school has become a vital refuge for a growing number of children.

—BONNIE BENARD

The dramatic changes in our families have caused youngsters to rely on peers for socialization. As they do so, a very different set of values and behaviors evolves. Of course, far too many are being socialized by television sets, more often than not filling the vacuum with negative social behaviors and values.

This leaves one more critical challenge up to the school since it is the system that has children for the greatest number of hours each day. Out of necessity schools must teach pro-social attitudes, principles, and skills. If for no other reason, so that students can learn how to read and write, and get along well with others. This fact alone calls for a new curriculum, a curriculum that develops identity, self-worth, social responsibility, and bonding to positive groups. You guessed it! This is especially what Tribes is about!

INDIVIDUALISM TO COMMUNITY

The Agricultural Age depended upon people helping each other. Images of a barn-raising, a quilting bee, and a town meeting spelled *community*. Things

With few exceptions, the solitary animal is, in any species, an abnormal creature... The dominant principle of social life is not the struggle for existence, but cooperation... If we would seek for one word that describes society better than any other the word is cooperation.

—ASHLEY MONTAGU

changed with the onset of the Industrial Age. People moved to cities to work in factories, families began to scatter, gold was discovered, the West and its natural resources were "conquered," and rugged individualism was heralded. Independence, competition, and domination were the cornerstones for survival in the 17th to 19th centuries to establish our independence as a new country. Extended into this century we became a "do it yourself" population...neighbors isolated from neighbors, freeways filled with solitary commuters twice a day, and people afraid to reach out to each other. Proud of our independence, we learned how to be competitive but not interdependent. We know how to operate but not cooperate. We have lost the basic *habits of the heart* of caring and sharing as a community.[9]

From all sides of the globe people recognize that survival now depends upon our capacity for cooperation, interdependence, conservation, and respect for a diversity of people and nations. It means

+ Negotiation rather than hostility

+ Cooperation, not just competition

+ Sharing and conserving resources

+ Community building through consensus

+ Decentralized rather than authoritarian management

+ Work teams and staff support groups

+ People coming together to help one another do what few can do alone.

Many believe that contemporary civilization is threatened by a loss of the sense of community that characterizes tribal peoples. David Maybury-Lewis, author of *Millennium: Tribal Wisdom and the Modern World*, points out that our emphasis on individualism has led to the isolation of individuals within mass society, and a deep longing for connection and community.

It has been the caring community that has assured personal and cultural survival throughout all of history. People giving each other support, respecting diversity, working in cooperation to achieve shared visions and goals. The slogans of yesterday may have been "I will take care of me" and "go

TOGETHER WE CAN!

it alone," but what about something like "together we can" for today and the world of tomorrow?

IMPLICATIONS FOR SCHOOLS

What conclusions can be drawn from these four major changes in our world? The explosion of information makes a fallacy of having students memorize facts and concepts from standardized curricula. Students (and teachers) need to learn how to access information relevant to interests, themes, and tasks at hand. Explorers together, they will become constructors of knowledge, using their own creativity to replace irrelevant curricula with meaningful learning experiences. No longer simply passive consumers, they will be producers, creating and contributing new

Change	Learning Experiences Need to Include:
CONCEPTUAL INFORMATION AGE	Critical thinking skills (reasoning and creativity) Collaborative/social skills Reading, writing, and mathematics Knowing how to learn (multiple intelligences) Seeing things in the mind's eye (visual/spatial learning)
MULTICULTURAL DIVERSITY	Knowledge of, and respect and appreciation for, a diversity of cultures Understanding cultural pluralism, ways to foster unity, communication, collaboration, and empowerment Group problem solving, decision making, and conflict management Knowledge of systems (group dynamics, systems change, Tribes group development process) Philosophy of mutual respect and cooperation
SOCIALIZATION BY MEDIA, PEERS AND SCHOOL	Pro-social skills Knowledge of the characteristics of resiliency How to develop active participation, peer groups, parent involvement
COMMUNITY	Community building Interdependence and individual accountability Cooperation and collaboration Individual and group creativity Pro-social principles: altruism, empathy, social support, and respect for diversity

ideas, knowledge, products, organizations, and systems. Since people no longer will work alone, but in groups composed of a rich diversity of cultures and skills, an understanding of cultural pluralism, cooperation, and human systems is essential.

Teachers will do more than teach—they will reach. They will call forth multicultural populations of students of multiple intelligences through multiple kinds of learning experiences. Static curricula will disappear.

Based on these major changes taking place, we need to ask, "What learning experiences should students have today in schools?" Here is a partial list for you and your school community to consider or revise:

The implications for educational systems are enormous yet very exciting. The basic 3 Rs, Reading, 'Riting and 'Rithmetic, may have been sufficient for an age gone by, but our entry into a high tech/high touch age requires the addition of 3 social Rs, Relatedness, Respect, and Responsibility. These are the basic habits of the heart so desperately needed throughout our schools, families, communities, nation, and workplace.

It's just a thought. But what if we all took off our comfortable old hats and launched out on our own to learn again? Yes, teachers, administrators, parents, and community leaders.

Good idea!
What do we need
to learn?

*How to help **all**
kids develop and
love learning!*

*It begins with
the next chapter on
the Developmental
Process of Tribes!*

3

The Research-Based Components
of Tribes Learning Communities

3 The Reasearch-Based Components of Tribes Learning Communities

ORIGIN AND DESIGN STAGES

The process, known simply as "Tribes," and now more specifically as "Tribes Learning Communities," was developed some years ago at a time when concerned educators in eighteen school districts of Contra Costa County, California, were seeking ways …

+ to prevent substance use and abuse, and other behavioral problems

+ to demonstrate improvement in academic test scores, and

+ to stem the tide of teachers leaving the profession.

Yes, and the same issues still are of great concern today.

*Now along with other big issues we see it as a need for **whole school reform**.*

The developmental learning process of Tribes has evolved through two stages of design that have led to the current Tribes Learning Community – whole school model.

INITIAL DESIGN: SUBSTANCE ABUSE PREVENTION

The goal of the first design was to prevent substance use and other youth behavioral problems. The twofold strategy was:

+ to develop inclusion, a sense of value and community for *all students* in every classroom, thereby to overcome isolation, alienation and acting-out behavior, and

+ to have well-trained teachers use small groups to teach the content of drug education curriculum in an active learning way.

Secondary students as "Youth Educators" and parent volunteers as "Parent Educators" also were trained in the group learning process to facilitate drug education curriculum in elementary schools, intermediate and high schools. During the 1980s more than 3000 parent volunteers were active in San Francisco Bay Area schools. For more than ten years the teacher, student and parent models were used in hundreds of schools and youth centers throughout the United States. The professional development was coordinated by the non-profit corporation, the Center for Human Development, which Jeanne Gibbs had founded and managed.

OUTCOMES: Schools reported...

+ significant decreases in student behavior problems

+ increases in student self-esteem and self-responsibility

+ improvements in school climate.

UN-ANTICIPATED OUTCOMES:

+ Teachers realized that they could also teach *core academic content* in small groups—thereby reaching and involving all of the students in a classroom.

+ Individual teachers and whole schools began to request training in *cooperative group learning*.

SECOND DESIGN: TRIBES COOPERATIVE LEARNING

Comprehensive studies on cooperative group learning, social development and group process were synthesized for the cooperative learning model. The approach trained teachers to build long-term small membership groups (tribes) for peer support and responsibility; to teach students essential democratic group skills; and to integrate academic concepts into cooperative learning strategies. *A positive culture* was built and sustained in classrooms by having students learn, practice and remind each other to honor the four Tribes Agreements....

ATTENTIVE LISTENING   APPRECIATION/NO PUT DOWNS

THE RIGHT TO PASS +   MUTUAL RESPECT

   THE RIGHT TO PARTICIPATE

Training courses emphasized transferring responsibility from teacher to student groups to support each others' learning, to problem-solve issues and to manage their work together.

OUTCOMES:

+ significant decreases in student behavior problems (average: 75% decrease in 3 months)

+ increase in teacher collegiality and parent involvement

+ improvement in teacher-student relationships

+ increase in students' liking of school and motivation for academic learning.

UN-ANTICIPATED OUTCOMES:

+ Teachers reported they did not spend as much time managing their classrooms, and that they had more time to teach subject matter.

+ More special education students could be mainstreamed into regular classrooms.

+ Teachers of separate special education classrooms began to report indicators of positive social and emotional development in their students.

+ Schools that had all teachers trained together and that set aside time for teacher learning and planning groups better sustained the learning process. Teacher collegiality increased.

+ The Tribes Cooperative Learning approach began to be marketed teacher-to-teacher, principal-to-principal and parent-to-parent across the country.

CURRENT MODEL: TRIBES LEARNING COMMUNITY

Ever-growing inquiries and training requests from schools throughout the United States and Canada led to the development of CenterSource Systems, LLC in 1995. The task of the new organization was: (1) to develop a research-based whole school model, and (2) to create a professional capacity-building training system—based on the long-standing philosophy and process of Tribes.

And here is what it's all about today!

PHILOSOPHY AND GOAL

We believe that:

+ The goal of education is to develop greatness in young human beings, active constructive citizens who are valuable contributors to society. To educate is to call forth all aspects of a student's human development—intellectual, social, emotional, physical and spiritual.

+ Intellectual, social and emotional learning is an interdependent growth process. It is influenced daily by the quality of the systems in a student's life.

+ Schools of excellence are student-centered. They have caring cultures, supportive structures and pedagogy that respond to and support the stages of development and the diversity of students' learning needs.

✦ School reform depends upon the whole system working together as a learning community—a school community committed to continual reflective practice towards improvement and educational excellence.

The philosophy and concepts above are the foundation of the dual mission and goal statement of Tribes Learning Community schools:

> The **MISSION OF TRIBES** is to assure the healthy development of every child so that each has the knowledge, competency and resilience to be successful in today's rapidly changing world.

> The **GOAL** is to engage all teachers, administrators, students and families in working together as a learning community that is dedicated to caring and support, active participation and positive expectations for all students.

THE DESIGN OF THE WHOLE SCHOOL MODEL

The design moves the four philosophy beliefs forward into a clear action plan framework for school reform. The four-fold philosophy and four-step framework are grounded in a synthesis of a wide-range of literature and research on human development, child and adolescent development, elements of ideal cultures for learning, resilience, cognitive-neuroscience theory, brain compatible learning, multiple intelligences, cooperative group learning, project learning snd constructivism, multicultural and gender equity, democratic group process, school climate, classroom management, reflective practice, system change, professional development and authentic assessment… approximately 17 research-based components for effective pedagogy and school reform.

THE DEVELOPMENTAL PROCESS OF TRIBES

The purpose of the graphic on the next page is to illustrate the research-based framework for the school renewal process. Brief discussions on the four strategies and the literature on which they are based follow.

STUDENT LEARNING AND DEVELOPMENT—RE-FOCUSING

Although the goal of the majority of schools today is to have higher student achievement on standardized tests, the promise of that happening depends upon the school community as a system: (1) becoming student-centered[2], and (2) learning how to reach and teach the diversity of students.[3] The primary focus of the Tribes school is not computer literacy, not a reading program or preparation for year-end tests—although all may be addressed and sequenced into the school's action plan. *The focus is on the students.* All policy, structures, decisions, curriculum and pedagogy depend upon the response to one question: "How and to what extent will 'this' support the learning and developmental needs of these students?"

Unless reform is child centered, children and society alike are going to be hurt— are being hurt.[1]

—JAMES COMER

Even to begin to know how to respond to the pivotal question, the Tribes school staff commits to working as an on-going collaborative "learning community." They up-date their knowledge and perspectives on children's development, resiliency, cognitive learning and multiple intelligences. Rather than teachers taking courses on their own, the whole staff learns together to better identify and respond effectively to the diversity of students' cultures and needs, and to use multiple ways to accelerate the inseparable interdependent triad: academic, social and emotional learning.

STUDENT DEVELOPMENT AND LEARNING

- Whole child
- Stages of development
- Resiliency

A CARING CULTURE

- Protective Factors
- Stages of community development
- Community agreements
- Multicultural and gender equity

THE COMMUNITY OF LEARNERS

- Small group structures
- Collaborative skills
- Reflective practice

RESPONSIVE EDUCATION—
STUDENT CENTERED ACTIVE LEARNING

- Group development process
- Cognitive theory
- Multiple intelligences
- Cooperative learning
- Constructivism
- Reflective practice
- Authentic assessment

A CARING CULTURE—RE-CULTURING

Given that the focus of a Tribes school is student-centered, the next question becomes, "How do we create an ideal culture for learning?" Comprehensive studies verify that the culture must be safe and caring.[5] The culture in Tribes school communities is based on the three well-proven principles that foster human resilience: caring relationships, positive expectations and beliefs, and opportunities for participation and contribution.[6] Its components are those of an ideal learning culture.[7] Namely, it is participative, proactive, collaborative, communal and given over to constructive meaning. The safe and caring culture is created and sustained by the students, teachers and the whole school community through daily use of the four previously mentioned Tribes Agreements:

ATTENTIVE LISTENING	APPRECIATION/NO PUT DOWNS
RIGHT TO PARTICIPATE +	
THE RIGHT TO PASS	MUTUAL RESPECT

The responsibility to honor and to monitor the agreements is transferred from the teacher to the tribes. Signs are posted throughout the school community, student groups and school meetings begin with reminders of "how we want to be while we work together." The agreements and the step-by-step community building process of Tribes assure that every student has inclusion (belonging to a small peer group), a sense of identity and value, and a community of supportive peers and adults.

THE COMMUNITY OF LEARNERS—RE-STRUCTURING

The culture is activated and sustained throughout the many small learning groups in which the students, teachers, administrators, support staff and parents are involved. All teachers belong to and meet regularly in small professional learning communities to study and move to research-based instruction, plan active learning curriculum and timely benchmark goals, to design authentic assessments and collectively identify how to help all students in their circle of care. A leadership team—composed of the principal, core teachers and the school or district's Certified Tribes TLC Trainers—coordinate overall action planning, implementation and assessment. They too are an inquiry group, raising questions and learning together. The same inquiry group process moves throughout teacher and parent groups. Training opportunities, courses and events are identified to the leadership team. As much as possible, just as with student tribes, integration and alignment of curriculum, problem-solving and decision-making is transferred to faculty and parent groups. District resource coordinators and the Certified Tribes Trainers participate and facilitate as needed. As learning areas are identified, the core leadership team are informed. Additional courses and special training are arranged by the school, preferably courses that their own Certified Tribes TLC Trainers are capable of conducting. The democratic

It is only by reculturing a school beforehand or along with any restructuring effort that meaningful improvement can be made.[4]

—MICHAEL FULLAN

The new model of school reform must seek to develop communities of learning grounded in communities of democratic discourse.[8]

—LINDA DARLING-HAMMOND

community-building approach based on the caring culture fosters collegiality, school spirit and achievement.

RESPONSIVE EDUCATION—ACTIVE LEARNING

"Responsive Education" is an essential pedagogy for academic achievement and school reform. It is the synthesis of artful teaching practices. It is based on understanding the critical developmental needs of a student age and cultural group. Its sole purpose is to enable more students to acquire knowledge in a lasting and meaningful way. Crafting a caring culture and trusting small active learning communities throughout a school gives all students the opportunity to excel.

The CenterSource Systems professional development courses and training of a school's own teachers as Certified Tribes Trainers assures continuous on-site learning for the instructional staff. It prepares all teachers, working in small teams, to be responsive to how the students of the school can best learn and grow socially, emotionally, spiritually (inner development) and intellectually—depending upon their respective stages of development, ways of learning and culture. It enables all teachers in a school to have students learn core academic content in meaningful ways via well-proven active learning strategies, project learning, group inquiry, research, composition projects, debates, team performance and peer assessment. Tribes materials provide teachers with approximately 175 strategies (or structures). Reflection *on what was learned and how it was learned* is an on-going practice after every group learning experience. Cognitive research validates that this maximizes the recall of information and concepts.[10] To a certain degree Tribes Learning Community teachers do use some direct instruction as well as active learning. However, once they recognize and experience the positive results of cooperative learning (validated by more than 1000 studies), the majority have students working in learning groups as much as possible.

"But," some say, "I gave up trying to use groups. Kids don't always work together well." Of course not! Nor can all adults. Time must be taken for all to learn some essential community building group skills that first are demonstrated, and then are woven into group curriculum tasks—one or two at a time as "social learning objectives." Having students themselves assess the social objective along with the content learning objective not only transfers teachers' responsibility but internalizes both the social and content learning. The partnership role of students and teachers consistently working together institutionalizes the ideal learning culture and "responsive education" pedagogy throughout the collaborative school community. Best of all, the caring culture, trust and energy significantly transforms a school system. Over time, it results in educational excellence and meaningful learning for all.

Rather than being powerless and dependent on the institution, learners need to be empowered to think and learn for themselves. Thus, learning needs to be conceived of as something a learner does, not something that is done to a learner.[9]

—CATHERINE FOSNOT

See the Resources section of this book for a summary of external evaluations on the developmental process of Tribes TLC.

4

A Perspective on Children's Development

4 A Perspective on Children's Development

A PERSPECTIVE ON CHILDREN'S DEVELOPMENT

What skills do our students need to be successful in the 21st century? That is the first question that a restructuring committee should discuss. Beyond that they need to ask, How do we go about developing the unique gifts and full potential inherent in each child? What do we know about the dynamics of human development? A shared philosophy and perspective are needed to guide an effective approach.

Many teachers and some parents in your community will have learned something about child development. They may be familiar with the stages listed on the following chart. These stages, however, do not tell the whole story. Children's development is not a neat, predictable path, but is affected by:

✦ The child's interaction in the settings of his/her daily life: family, school, community, and peer groups

✦ The cultural norms, languages, beliefs, and mores within surrounding systems

✦ The larger forces of institutions, government, economics, mass media, and religion[9]

Urie Bronfenbrenner, professor of human development and psychology, widened the perspective of our work with Tribes by stating that:

Human development is an ongoing trans-action between each of us and the surrounding systems. It is one's conception of an ever-widening world and one's interaction with it, as well as a growing capacity to discover, sustain, or change it.[1]

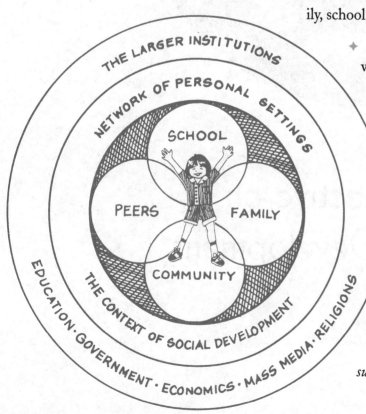

Looking at child development as a process that is interactive with the surrounding systems means that people in those child-rearing systems must learn how to challenge and support the child's ever-widening experiences, interests, and explorations in the world beyond self.

Think of it this way. A baby's world is limited to what sustains her physical well-being...a relationship with Mom, crib, and toys. Soon she is out of the crib, maybe in a playpen, then crawling about the house discovering, and most likely changing things. Her growing capacity to discover becomes more exciting to her and more challenging to Mom and Dad each day. She has begun her pattern of life-long learning. As a young child her world centers on "me" and "mine." But by seven or eight years she moves into a new mental world of ideas. The identification with her body, her things, and her ideas is a natural progression within the world of "me." Our mode of thinking and capacity to relate well beyond the smaller world of childhood depend upon moving from a "me" identification to a "we" identification with others and our common good.

Yet there are so many adult people living in worlds still narrowly focused on "me and mine." Persistent identification with our own bodies, objects, and ideas leads to misunderstandings, intolerance, conflict, nationalism, and war. It perpetuates the exclusion of those identified as different, or outsiders. Understanding human development from a systems perspective gives insight into pathological problems, alienation, violence, depression, alcohol/drug use... and hopelessness.

What was it that limited the worlds of so many kids in our country today? Were they the ones who were never challenged and supported to discover their own identification in a world of "we" as well as "me?" Did they find school irrelevant and restrictive? Did their teachers and parents fail to understand their unique ways of learning? Studies on pre-schoolers have shown that a child who, at an early age, can demonstrate that he is capable of changing a frustrating situation, later tends to be active and competent in grade school.[2] Those who stay passive, self-centered, and resigned to circumstances that they consider beyond their control have difficult lives. What if education were about this: truly calling forth every child's human development beyond just getting grades, a diploma, a job, or going on to college?

More than four decades ago, John Dewey also believed that a primary task of education was to enable people to influence their environment and to gain the insight needed to make choices beyond their past experiences.

We urge you to challenge the next planning committee in your school to *become a learning committee* or a *learning community*. Take the time to envision what you hope students in your school will become at their fullest potential. What characteristics and attitudes would they have? What capacity would they have to discover, sustain, or change the complexity of systems they will face in their lives?

THE STAGES OF DEVELOPMENT

Age/Grade	Key Systems	Cognitive Development
2–4 Preschool	Family	**Preoperative Stage** ✦ magical thinking ✦ circularity in thinking ✦ difficulty dealing with more than 1 or 2 causes ✦ concrete mental operations
5–7 Kindergarten to 1st Grade	Family School	**Preoperative Stage** ✦ magical thinking ✦ circularity in thinking ✦ difficulty dealing with more than 1 or 2 causes ✦ concrete mental operations
7–11 2nd to 5th Grade	Family School Neighborhood Peers	**Concrete Operations** ✦ begins to think relationally and to generalize ✦ becomes capable of integrating several variables (causes and relationships)
12–16 6th to 10th Grade	Family Peer group School	**Normal mental operations** ✦ capable of cognitive problem solving ✦ can think abstractly and hypothetically ✦ integrates multiple factors to understand concepts
16–18 11th to 12th Grade	Peer group School Work Family Community	**Relativistic Thinking** ✦ capable of synthesizing wide range of relational material

[3]This chart is based on a synthesis of stages described by child development theorists Jean Piaget and Erik Erikson.

in CHILDREN AND YOUTH

Social Development	Implications
✦ emphasis on self ✦ oriented to parents ✦ needs limits, secure environment ✦ developing motor skills	✦ build self-esteem ✦ support pro-social development (sharing, taking turns, asking questions) ✦ provide safe, caring environment
✦ emphasis on self ✦ identifies with own gender ✦ enjoys group play ✦ oriented to parents	✦ build self-esteem ✦ support pro-social development ✦ involve parents in activities, knowledge, social stages, and resiliency ✦ encourage sharing, caring behavior ✦ use cooperative learning groups
✦ oriented to parents ✦ enjoys group play and same gender peer relationships ✦ often competitive or has difficulties with peers ✦ often unaware of behavior effect on others ✦ impressed by older role models ✦ learns behavior from parent/peer role models ✦ more concerned about physical image than social	✦ train parents and teachers in development of resiliency ✦ teach collaborative skills ✦ use cooperative learning groups ✦ provide feedback on behavior ✦ teach decision making and problem solving
✦ oriented to present rather than future ✦ preoccupied with self-presentation, acceptance by peer group, physical maturity ✦ seeks initial sexual intimacy ✦ seeks peer role models ✦ motivated by social effects of drug use ✦ seeks independence in decision making ✦ differentiates between self and environment ✦ feels awkward in social skills	✦ oriented to peers ✦ teach collaborative skills ✦ peer role models teaching refusal skills ✦ use cooperative learning groups ✦ encourage responsible decision making ✦ promote peer leadership, peer helping programs ✦ involve in community service activities
✦ primary concern: individual identity, financial independence, deepening relationships, self-exploration, distancing from family and making own decisions	✦ provide opportunities for leadership ✦ involve in business ventures, community projects and drug-free alternative activities ✦ self-directed learning, inquiry with peers, and exploration of own emerging interests

AN ASSURANCE POLICY CALLED RESILIENCY

"But," as a teacher you say, "so many of these kids come from terrible neighborhoods and families with overwhelming problems. Poverty, unemployment, lack of health care, inadequate childcare, juvenile problems, community crime, divorce, alcoholism, drug abuse, and stress surround many of the kids in our classrooms." True, today's world has become a harsh one for America's children.

Yet, there are those who somehow live through deprivation, adversity, and stress more easily than others. Why does one child in a family, though raised in the same conditions as siblings, do well though the others fail? Why do some become competent and successful even though raised in the same overwhelming environment?

The answer is to be found in the exciting research on human resiliency, which (to the credit of Bonnie Benard) is being brought to the attention of schools throughout the nation.[4] Unlike the typical problem-focused, or "pathology," approach to identifying risk factors, the research on human resiliency identifies the protective factors that create competency, wellness, and the capacity to overcome stress. The lives of children who were considered to be at high risk (due to conditions of poverty, neglect, war, parental schizophrenia, abuse, physical handicaps, depression, alcoholism, and criminality) were followed by longitudinal studies. Throughout the years, a percentage of the high-risk children did develop various problems, but to the amazement of the researchers, a greater percentage became healthy and competent adults. Somehow, the larger percentage had become resilient enough to withstand difficulties and do well though they were raised under the same stressful conditions as others who developed problems. Profiles of the resilient children emerged.

The resilient children had the following attributes:

+ **SOCIAL COMPETENCE**: pro-social behaviors such as responsiveness, empathy, caring, communication skills, a sense of humor

+ **PROBLEM-SOLVING SKILLS**: abstract and reflective thinking, flexibility

+ **AUTONOMY**: an internal locus of control, a strong sense of independence, power, self-esteem, self-discipline, and control of impulses

+ **A SENSE OF PURPOSE AND FUTURE**: healthy expectancies, goal directedness, orientation to the future, motivation to achieve, persistence, hopefulness, hardiness, belief in a bright and compelling future, a sense of anticipation, and a sense of coherence

It was learned that the greater the number of these attributes, the greater a person's capacity to be resilient and invincible—even in the midst of severe stress. Resiliency is the capacity to survive, to progress through difficulty, to bounce back, to move on positively again and again in life.

Take time out now and think of those times in your own life when you were somehow able to move through a difficult situation or period of time, when you were able to face the stress and bounce back because of your own resilient attributes.

The question is, how did you develop such resiliency? The studies tell us an abundance of "protective factors" must have surrounded you. Protective factors are the positive (or health-enhancing) behaviors and conditions within schools, families, and communities that supported the development of those resilient attributes within you.

A consistent set of protective factors in the immediate care-giving environments has been identified. These factors are listed in the chart on the next page.

Learning about this research has been exciting because it indicates that the Tribes process is a good way for school communities to go about fostering resiliency in students. The Tribes process activates Benard's three categories. It promotes inclusion (caring), influence (participation and being valued by others), and community (positive expectations and support).

Resiliency is not a basic skill we can teach. It is what we do to change the human systems (families, schools, communities, peer groups, workplace) surrounding children. What better effort could schools and families work toward than to assure that all children in their care live within daily environments humming with an abundance of protective factors. Friends, it's the best way to give each and every child the capacity, the resiliency, he or she will need to meet inevitable life stress and to succeed in spite of it.

We must move beyond a focus on the risk factors in order to create the conditions that will facilitate children's healthy development.

—BONNIE BENARD

EVERYONE CREATING THE LEARNING ENVIRONMENT

Having a student-centered focus of human development and resiliency brings coherence to planning and the curricula of the school. Once all teachers, administrators, families, and community caregivers (the systems) appreciate the focus and learn some how-to-do-it knowledge, everyone can participate in creating healthy environments. School reform, restructuring, revitalizing...whatever we may call it, will not happen unless the systems determining children's development have a shared child-centered vision, and the courage to improve the systems themselves. Then, and only then, will the often quoted African saying "It takes the whole village to raise a child" become a reality in America.

Protective Factors

Family

+ Develops close bonding with child

+ Is nurturing and protective

+ Uses a high warmth/low criticism parenting style (rather than authoritarian or permissive)

+ Values and encourages education

+ Manages stress well

+ Spends quality time with children

+ Has clear expectations

+ Encourages supportive relationships with caring adults beyond the immediate family

+ Shares family responsibilities

School

+ Expresses positive expectations

+ Encourages goal setting and mastery

+ Encourages pro-social development (altruism and cooperation)

+ Provides opportunities for leadership and participation

+ Fosters active involvement for all students (whatever their learning style or capability)

+ Trains teachers in cooperative learning

+ Involves parents

+ Staff views themselves as caring people

Community

+ Provides opportunities for participation

+ Involves youth in community service

+ Provides supportive social networks

+ Leaders prioritize community health, safety, and quality of life for families

+ Provides access to resources (health care, housing, daycare, job training, employment, education, and recreation)

Bonnie Benard has summarized the protective factors into three helpful categories:

+ **caring and support**   + **positive expectations**   + **active participation**

DEFINING THE BASICS FOR TODAY'S SCHOOLS AND FAMILIES

The human experience of

- ✦ growing into ever-widening environments

- ✦ being capable of interacting beyond "me" to "we," to community, to nation, to the world

- ✦ having the resiliency to deal with it all

is what education can be all about. For the transactional model of human development to work well, all of the systems must communicate, collaborate, and cooperate. Not just schools alone, but all systems working toward their shared goal.

The more the school community understands and initiates many protective factors, the more it assures a positive future for all of the children within their care.

As one of the key systems, the school must examine its own environment, or climate. School climate is the spirit that prevails for teachers, students, administrators, resource people, and parents. It is the music underlying the words—an energy that either contributes to or inhibits learning. A positive classroom climate evolves out of

- ✦ an atmosphere of trust

- ✦ a sense of belonging and community

- ✦ involvement in decision making

- ✦ kindness and encouragement from peers

- ✦ the teacher's energy and morale

The more the school community understands and initiates many protective factors, the more it assures a positive future for all of the children within their care.

✦ the teacher's authenticity and nonjudgmental attitude

✦ clear expectations, goals, learning outcomes

✦ fairness and equity in participation.

Resiliency requires changing hearts and minds.[5]

—BONNIE BENARD

A positive climate is built through inclusion, sharing and caring, encouragement of participation, and high expectations for each and every child. In the same way, families need to zero in on these very same climate and protective factors. Everyone can finally learn to sing the same song.

It is not surprising that the attributes of human resiliency (social competence, problem-solving skills, autonomy and a sense of positive expectations and future) parallel the social emotional learning competencies needed for children's development. Having been defined by two well-researched human development fields and longitudinal studies, schools have positive proof of the important direction that needs to be taken. It is not a new curriculum to be taught. It is an on-going daily process in a caring culture and relationships to be lived in educational, family and community systems. Millions of children can move to promising futures as schools embrace social emotional learning and foster the development of resilience. Where to start? How to start? The Collaborative for Academic, Social and Emotional Learning recommends selecting and initiating an evaluated evidence-based school-wide program (or process) such as Tribes Learning Communities; and throughout the years tailoring it to the respective or unique student needs of the school. SEL evidence-based programs have two characteristics, each of which leads both directly and indirectly to better academic performance and other positive outcomes.[6] The CASEL recommendation of implementing Tribes TLC, one of the SELect Programs, may be found in the Appendix.

BACK TO THE MIDDLETON MIDDLE SCHOOL RESTRUCTURING COMMITTEE

It's 7:30 p.m. Three weeks later.

Thelma Brown, parent chairperson: *"I am glad we took these extra weeks to define our student-centered human development approach, and to agree that over the next three years we all will work together to foster resiliency for each and every student. Tonight we will hear from our cooperative learning study committee."*

Tony Salvatore, parent: *"We're so excited. We not only discovered that we're on the right track, but that a lot can be brought about through cooperative learning—using small groups in classrooms."*

Trudy Armstrong, teacher: *"And we realize that we already have eight teachers trained and using a cooperative learning process called Tribes."*

Tony: *"You'll be as excited as we are, once you hear about the hundreds of studies verifying what can happen for students. John Pasquale and Les Aldridge put this chart together and want to tell you about it."*

John began the presentation by saying that the information comes from the work of Drs. David and Roger Johnson of the University of Minnesota, who have summarized more than 600 studies reporting the significant benefits of learning through cooperation.[7]

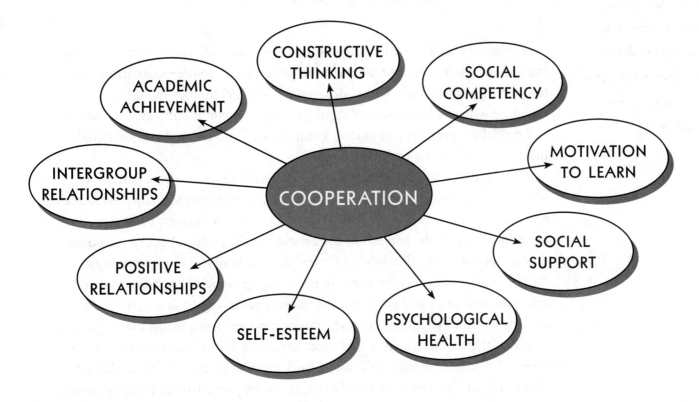

BENEFITS OF COOPERATION

The benefits of cooperation are:

✦ GREATER PRODUCTIVITY AND ACADEMIC ACHIEVEMENT

✦ CONSTRUCTIVE THINKING SKILLS: planning, inferring, analyzing, gathering data, and strategizing

✦ SOCIAL COMPETENCY: trust in others, perspective taking, sense of personal identity, awareness of interdependence, sense of direction and purpose

✦ MOTIVATION: high expectations of success and achievement; high commitment and persistence

✦ SOCIAL SUPPORT: constructive management of stress; high quality relationships that extend life and help people recover from illness

✦ PSYCHOLOGICAL HEALTH: the ability to develop, maintain, and improve one's relationships and situation in life; success in achieving goals

✦ SELF-ESTEEM: improved due to positive peer relations and to improved academic achievement

✦ POSITIVE INTERPERSONAL RELATIONSHIPS: acceptance of diversity; appreciation for peer contributions, skills, and efforts

✦ INTERGROUP RELATIONSHIPS: caring concern; acceptance of multicultural diversity; commitment to the common good.

*Our work is not about a curriculum or a teaching method...
it is about nurturing the human spirit with love.*[8]

—RON MILLER

These benefits are the healing components that build community and a caring democracy. We doubt that the many problems of youth—alienation, violence, drug abuse, gangs, school dropouts, suicide, delinquency, and despair—will ever lessen unless school, family, and community systems teach and model cooperation rather than competition. The isolated and alienated must be included, not excluded.

If you are trying to convince your school board, administrators, parents, or other teachers that cooperative learning works, we urge you to share the research on cooperative learning. Using the Tribes Learning Community (TLC) process not only can bring the benefits of cooperation to classrooms, but can introduce a new pattern of interaction into all groups of the school learning community.

The move to cooperative learning is an ever-growing phenomenon as more and more educators and parents realize that the learning environment must change. Martin Wolins asserts that schools need an environment that is "reclaiming...one that creates changes that meet the needs of both the young person and society."[9] Bronfenbrenner calls for "a curriculum of caring."[10] The resiliency studies highlight environments of caring/sharing, participation, and high expectations. Tribes doesn't just suggest what a positive learning environment should be...it makes it happen!

The best journeys begin with a vision, a knapsack, and some friends. So call up a few friends and grab your backpacks. This tribal community journey meets kids in a new way in the next chapter.

5 How Children Learn

5 How Children Learn

The busyness taking place in Mrs. Jones's 7th grade classroom this morning may at first look like a reenactment of Santa's workshop. Hearing the excitement, the principal has just slipped into the back of the room. Six groups of 7th graders are huddled together at tables filled with fascinating geometric designs. Some people in each group are measuring surface areas of the creations that people in their Tribes have made. Other pairs are estimating real-time construction costs. Architect workers are snipping, stapling, and taping poster board together. The best surprise of all are the three people in one corner who are trying out a song they have written. . . a song about "Polyhedraville."

"Ah, Mrs. Jones," the principal says, "is this the math lesson for today?" "Oh no," she answers, "Polyhedraville began three weeks ago, and it isn't just about math. Our theme is planning quality urban environments. The students have been designing a whole town...taking into consideration the many human, environmental, and facility needs. Each Tribe is working with budgets to design and construct their particular buildings for the town. The task depends upon each person creating a building and the tribes coming to a consensus on total costs for all of their buildings. Every person's creativity, participation, and skills are important. I'm the facilitator and the consultant on call as needed. The students are the ones planning the town and helping each other to learn."

WHAT MRS. JONES HAD TO LEARN

Two questions: First, What did Mrs. Jones have to give up in order to teach this way? And second, What did she have to learn in order to involve and excite this class of typically bored 7th graders? This note from the *Wall Street Journal* addresses the question of what she had to give up:

> *"Across the curriculum, up and down the grade ladder, a new wave of teachers is casting out textbooks, cursing standardized tests, killing drills and preaching a new creed of student engagement."* —*Wall Street Journal*, September 11, 1992.[1]

She also had to give up

+ Trying to pour standardized curriculum into the heads of nonstandardized students

+ Talking endlessly except to ask for right answers

+ Awarding just the kids who had the right answers

+ Praising boys more than girls

+ Having low expectations for students of different cultures

+ Teaching subjects in unrelated boxes

+ Wanting a quiet, orderly, straight-row classroom that she had to control all day long.

To make her classroom come alive, Mrs. J. had to learn what thousands of other teachers are learning today:

+ How to make classrooms student-centered rather than teacher-centered

+ How to use cooperative learning methods

+ How to reach and involve students of multiple learning styles

+ How to create and sustain a positive learning environment

+ How to design interactive learning experiences.

Developing resiliency and the potential of all types of children in our schools cannot become a reality unless teachers learn to make the critical shift from 19th-century methods to those that are effective with 21st-century people. If we acknowledge that the force feeding of textbooks and seat time has failed for too many children who simply do not learn that way, then it is time to find out how young people do learn. Once we're clear about that, environments and methods that support the development of all kids—no matter their culture, race, gender, or way of learning—can become a reality within a school.

MOVING FROM THE TEACHER-CENTERED CLASSROOM

It all begins for many teachers when they just get tired of talking to apathetic students. One day Mrs. J. really saw her standardized self and was startled with the emotion she felt. She was lonely. There seemed to be an impenetrable wall between her and the beautiful people sitting in rows in front of her. She had been noticing the wall ever since her faculty heard a presentation by a Tribes TLC® trainer several weeks earlier. She saw and heard about the diagram on the following page.[2]

Studies verify that when teachers depend upon "whole class instruction" they themselves talk more than two-thirds of the time, and more than 70% of their "teacher talk" is spent disciplining, lecturing, giving instructions, and asking questions. Students are expected to sit passively, to refrain from interaction with each other, and to listen to the teacher. When teachers use whole class instruction, only

30% of their time can be devoted to doing what the majority want to do...to praise, encourage initiative, give feedback, facilitate student communication, and help students.

Whole Class Instruction

% of All Teacher Communications

0	5	10	20	25%	
					Disciplines
					Gives Instruction
					Questions
					Lectures
					Praises
					Encourages Initiative
					Gives Feedback
					Facilitates Student Communication
					Helps

Traditional class structures cause students to be competitive more than cooperative. The illusion is that since this traditional approach was effective one hundred years ago it will always be effective though today's students, born out of many cultures, learn in very different ways. The failure of American education should be proof enough that teacher-centered classes, standardized textbooks, and competition perpetuates educational mediocrity and too many failures. Of course, several popular motion pictures exhort teachers to become dramatic actors like Robin Williams in *Dead Poets Society,* or tough challengers like James Olmos in *Stand and Deliver.* True, some students may become motivated, but these "sage on the stage" models are also teacher-centered rather than student-centered. Missing is

+ The transfer of responsibility to students themselves for their own learning

+ A realistic way to help each student develop his or her own unique set of intelligences and gifts

+ Opportunities for students to use inquiry, to construct meaning, and apply concepts learned

✦ A process to awaken each and every child to the joy of learning.

The "teacher talk" approach ignores the fact that we are social creatures stimulated and motivated by social interaction...which, of course, is ruled out in traditional classrooms. What if students discovered that learning was truly an exciting process when people entered into it together? What if school was not about who could get the most A's in the class, but how we can help each other to

✦ Listen

✦ Generate creative ideas

✦ Resolve conflicts

✦ Stay on task

✦ Synthesize information

✦ Conceptualize a drama

✦ Write a song

✦ Set goals

✦ Figure out a formula

✦ Think through a complex problem

✦ Care and share

Think about it...what if?

CREATING A STUDENT-CENTERED CLASSROOM

In contrast to the previous diagram, the same studies show that when classrooms are reorganized into student learning groups, "teacher talk" time lessens from 70% to 25%.[3]

INTERACTIVE LEARNING

Teacher as Facilitator

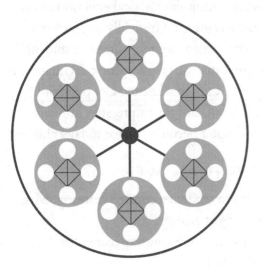

% of All Teacher Communications

Then 75% of the teacher's time can be spent in praising, encouraging initiatives, giving feedback, facilitating student communication, and helping students. The transfer of responsibility to student groups for gathering information, interpreting, and applying it makes the dramatic difference. When students become responsible to each other, accountability for performance and behavior is shared by the students and the teacher. The wall between teacher and students melts away. This is not to say that teachers should never use the lecture/question format, but if it is not integrated with interactive group learning, eyes will glaze over again.

Once a teacher changes his or her role to that of a "facilitator," meaning "one who makes it easy," the classroom becomes alive. The image of the classroom changes from austere rows to something like this:

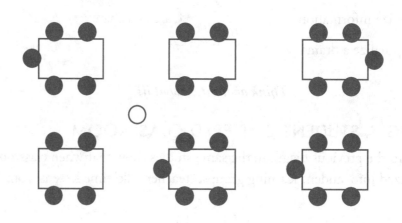

Tables often replace desks and desks become centered so that four or five students can face each other and work together. Altering the physical environment is step one toward making the classroom student-centered. Gradually, as cooperative learning tasks and much of the classroom management are transferred to students themselves, the teacher has time to encourage initiative, give feedback, facilitate student communication, suggest resources, help and praise students. Cooperation replaces competition and individualistic desk work, and the impressive, immense benefits of cooperation discussed in our last chapter become real for today's children.

GETTING BEYOND THE ONE RIGHT ANSWER

To switch from a teacher-centered classroom to student-centered learning, Mrs. Jones also had to give up asking for the "one right answer."

What grade are you teaching? Well, here's an interesting experiment to try. Someday, put a large dot on an empty chalkboard.

When students become responsible to each other, accountability for performance and behavior is shared by the students and the teacher. The wall between teacher and students melts away.

Then ask the class "What is it?" The book *A Whack on the Side of the Head* by Roger von Oech tells the story of a teacher of a sophomore English class who did this.[4] After she asked, "What is it?" the class just sat there and looked and looked in silence at the dot. Finally, someone said, "It's a chalk dot." The teacher looked rather sad and replied, "You know, I did this with a group of kindergarten children yesterday, and they said "It's an owl's eye, a cigar butt, a squashed egg, a pebble. They just went on and on." The important question is, What happened between the years of five to sixteen to kill expression and imagination?

Just think about the imprint of eleven school years—of being asked to repeat back or write down the right answer. The lecture/question format awards those who can call out right answers. And who wins? Right! The verbal/linguistic kids. The shy, low-self-image, and non-verbal learners lose. Gradually spontaneity and creativity, two qualities essential to our more complex, fast-moving information world, are killed off.

Stephen Schneider, MacArthur Award scientist, echoes our own concern:

> *Creativity isn't simply learning the textbook. It is finding new ways to think and act...Somehow we have to get kids participating creatively in the process of their education. Because if they continue to think that truth comes only from the front of the room, and that learning is a product that can be standardized, we are going to end up with sheeplike, uninformed citizens who are not capable of conducting public debate on difficult issues. And that will leave the "solutions" to the spin doctors, advertisers, elites, and lobbyists.[5]*

Instead of teaching kids to regurgitate right answers, teachers are learning to use open-ended questions, group brainstorming, student inquiry, and group investigation projects. They are cheering the diversity of ways that students within cooperative groups (tribes) handle a task or solve a problem.

CREATING EQUAL OPPORTUNITIES FOR ALL STUDENTS

Expression, creativity, self-image, and love of learning also are diminished between kindergarten and high school for students who are culturally different. Race, color, culture, gender, disabilities, and appearance all add up to being labeled and treated differently from the majority within a system. The pain of being called a name or ridiculed for being different is devastating. The exclusion of not being called on because you are not expected to have the "right answer" is damaging to self-image. The curriculum that does not accurately portray one's own culture or ignores it completely is an insult. The inner-city multi-ethnic or rural Native American school that still has a majority of white teachers, models institutional racism.

Admittedly, the exclusion and perpetuation of inequity is often unconscious on the part of teachers. For instance, studies show that teachers call upon boys more than girls when many hands are waving in a classroom.[6] To gain attention, many boys not only wave a hand but jump up and down to be called upon. They are five times more likely to receive attention from teachers. They are eight times more likely to call out in class, except when the teacher is a woman, and then they are twelve times more likely to speak out. Boys also receive more words of praise for responding. Boys out-talk girls in the classroom three to one. Jane Kahale, president of the National Association for Research in Science Teaching, refers to this behavior as "risk taking." Whether negative or positive, risk taking gets teachers' attention. Why do we wonder that girls, who are not as active in risk taking, are far less likely to volunteer responses in class?

Generalizations and labels also sabotage learning. How often have you heard

"You think like a girl."

"You throw like a girl."

"Black kids have rhythm."

"Girls have trouble with math; the boys do well."

"You're as wild as an Indian."

"He's just being a boy."

"Special Ed kids can't make it."

"The boys all have sloppy papers."

Comparisons like "the girls are working harder than the boys" or "the Asians are smarter than the Latinos in math" not only are hurtful put-downs but pit one group against another. "We" versus "they," the "in group" and the "out group," the "jocks" and the "nerds." Different expectations for behavior, language, and academic performance sentence some groups to years of unfair treatment. Bias and inequity are devastating to children's development and learning. They promote hostility, alienation, poor school performance, failure, and despair.

Equal opportunity for learning must begin with a recognition that multiculturism is a national reality in the United States. At its best it not only includes the experiences of particular individuals and groups but fosters interconnectedness between groups for unified action on shared interests and concerns.

Once teachers begin to use the Tribes TLC® process, which promotes inclusion and deep respect for individual uniqueness and diversity, classrooms are well on the way to equity for all students. There is a fine article, "How can we make multicultural education effective?" in Chapter 9 of this book. It was written for you by Gail Whang, a teacher in a multicultural city school, and it tells her experience in using the Tribes TLC® process with her students.

You can also

+ Awaken staff consciousness by having your faculty use the *Matrix for Achieving Equity in Classrooms*. See the next page.

+ Arrange training for the staff on multicultural and equity issues.

+ Make a plan that includes a review of current curricula and incorporates the five components suggested in Chapter 2, page 22, by Benard.

GIVING UP BOXES FOR INTEGRATED THEMES

Creativity is also sabotaged all day long in American schools through the factory model system of keeping things in separate curriculum boxes. Fifty minutes for English, fifty for math, then political science, history, biology, etc., all in chunks interrupted by clanging bells. Whose needs does this procedure best serve? Right! The school system's need for control, standardization, and convenience.

Yet our challenge is to educate people to understand and solve multi-disciplinary problems crossing multicultural, multinational, and multirelational boundaries. Issues such as peace, toxic pollution, urban violence, equity employment for women and people of color, integrated community services, conversion of defense industries, and educational change are not box topics! They are themes requiring integration of the sciences, mathematics, history, biology, composition, and the capacity to access and interpret information. We spend years teaching students about the boxes and then wonder why they have trouble synthesizing the diverse contents of the boxes when they are finally out in this world of complex issues.

Mrs. Jones's Polyhedraville project required student groups to investigate, research, discuss, and apply information from such subject areas as math, English, social science, science, and art. They were not only learning and applying subject area content, but living collaborative group skills of interdependence and individual accountability. Most important is the fact that each student got the clear message that they were needed and respected for their unique skills and contributions. One of the most exciting benefits is that the integration of disciplines into themes enhances the pattern-seeking operation of the brain, which in turn increases intelligence. The integration of curricula into themes has repeatedly been proven to energize student learning.

We're committed to equity for all students, but how do we go about implementing a gender equity/multicultural focus?

To control and sort young people for the sake of institutional efficiency is to crush the human spirit.[7]
—RON MILLER

Use a "kid-grabbing" theme.

MATRIX FOR ACHIEVING EQUITY IN CLASSROOMS

Use the following matrix to assess six forms of bias in a classroom or a school community. Strategies for reducing bias are included in each component.

	Linguistic Bias	Stereotyping	Invisibility/ Exclusion	Unreality	Imbalance/ Selectivity	Fragmentation/ Isolation
What To Look For	Language which is dehumanizing or denies the existence of females or males; e.g. Japs, mankind.	Members of a group portrayed in one role or with one characteristic.	The lack of representation of a group.	Misinformation about a group, event or contribution.	Single interpretation of an issue, situation or conditions.	Separating contributions of females and ethnic groups from the mainstream.
Policy What To Do	Review policy for biased language.	Ensure nondiscriminatory discipline policy.	Recognize teaching performance which fosters equity.	Design proactive mission statement which corrects past bias.	Earmark money for equity classroom materials and training.	Design staff evaluations inclusive of equity criteria.
Instructional Strategies	Pluralize subjects to avoid a gender pronoun.	Encourage males and females to express a wide range of feelings responses and sensibilities.	Encourage contributions from females and ethnic minorities.	Discuss controversial topics of discrimination and prejudice.	Engage students in analyzing and debating an issue.	Call on students equitably. Use cooperative learning.
Curriculum Content	Set expectations for students to use non-sexist language.	Select readings that have the females and ethnic minorities in responsible, exciting leadership positions.	Have students count the numbers of male, female and ethnic group members to determine the proportion in relation to a population.	Engage students in conducting research.	Introduce collaborative ways to solve problems and make decisions.	Stress that learning is the result of collaborative efforts and contributions by many.
Management (School and Classroom)	Engage all members in noticing and correcting biased language.	Intervene when slurs or jokes are made at another's expense.	Nurture cooperation among males, females and ethnically diverse students.	Facilitate shared decision making.	Create supportive climate for differing perspectives to be discussed.	Establish ways of integrating groups during free time.
Family and Community Involvement	Attend council meeting and have students present on the use of nonbiased language in newspapers, on road signs, etc.	Invite nontraditional role models to teach a lesson on their area of specialization.	Provide students with shadowing opportunities.	Examine the history of discrimination within local laws and history.	Establish community advisory groups that are balanced by sex, ethnicity and disability.	Solicit volunteers from diverse groups to work with students.

REACHING STUDENTS WHO LEARN IN DIFFERENT WAYS

Do you remember the story about the Animal School? It went something like this:

Once upon a time there was a school for animals. The teachers were certain it had a very comprehensive curriculum, but somehow all the animals were failing. The duck was the star in the class for swimming, but was flunking tree climbing. The monkey was great at tree climbing, but was getting F's in swimming. The chickens excelled in grain research, but disrupted the tree climbing class so much they were sent to the principal's office daily. The rabbits were sensational in running, but had to have private tutoring in swimming. Saddest of all were the turtles, who, after many diagnostic tests, were pronounced "developmentally disabled." Yes, they were sent to a special class in a remote gopher hole. The question is, Who were the real failures?

Like the animals in the story, each student is a unique creation...a person who has a different set of talents, intelligences, and ways of learning.

It is time to take seriously the fact that the predominant focus of American education favors students who are adept in verbal and logical/mathematical skills and those ways of learning, but discourages those who have different innate intelligences. One might ask, all are not tree climbers, but are great swimmers or runners doomed to failure simply because they are in a system designed solely for a different type of animal?

NINE INTELLIGENCES

The work of Howard Gardner and other scientists has identified nine intelligences that are common to all human beings and that vary in degree in each person. The multiple intelligences, ways of learning, and knowing, are as follows:[8]

Verbal/Linguistic

Thinks and learns through written and spoken words; has the ability to memorize facts, fill in workbooks, take written tests, and enjoy reading

Logical/Mathematical

Thinks deductively; deals with numbers and recognizes abstract patterns

Visual/Spatial

Thinks in and visualizes images and pictures; has the ability to create graphic designs and communicate with diagrams and graphics

Body/Kinesthetic

Learns through physical movement and body wisdom; has a sense of knowing through body memory

Musical/Rhythmic

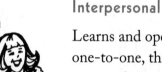

Recognizes tonal patterns and environmental sounds; learns through rhyme, rhythm, and repetition

Interpersonal

Learns and operates one-to-one, through group relationships, and communication; also depends on all of the other intelligences

Intrapersonal

Enjoys and learns through self-reflection, metacognition, working alone; has an awareness of inner spiritual realities

Existential

Is concerned with ultimate life issues—love, death, philosophy; learns in context with meaning

Naturalist

Loves nature and the out-of-doors; enjoys classifying species of flora and fauna

Remarkably enough, only two of the nine intelligences, verbal/linguistic and logical/mathematical, are developed in the majority of schools in the Western world. However, before our children enter school, they are usually busy developing the other intelligences. As a result, school can make many feel inadequate as they struggle to deal with the two less familiar intelligences. Their active, physical, rhythmic, imaginative, and relational selves must be anesthetized during school hours. This applies all the way through school for children coming from other than Western Caucasian cultures, namely: Native Americans, Asians, and Latino, Hispanic, Black and Aboriginal populations.

In infancy and early childhood children begin learning through what Gardner calls "raw patterning" to perform simple tasks as the foundation of a given intelligence. Walking, running, and jumping are the basics of body/kinesthetic intelligence; just as learning the alphabet is basic to verbal/linguistic intelligence. As children grow they move to greater levels of pattern complexity called "symbol systems," in which they may develop the ability to draw various shapes (visual/spatial intelligence) or make different tones (musical/rhythmic). Each intelligence has its own "notational language" that not only can be taught and can also be learned by others, but can also be recorded in some form, such as a musical composition (musical/rhythmic) or an understanding of group process (logical/mathematical). Finally, a stage is reached (generally in the secondary or college years) where an intelligence evolves into a "vocational or avocational" career path.

David Lazear writes:

> If we provide students the opportunity to develop the full range of their intellectual capacities and teach them how to use their multiple ways of knowing in the learning task, they will learn the things we are trying to teach more thoroughly than if we only permit them to learn in the more traditional verbal/linguistic and logical/mathematical ways.[9]

Lynn Stoddard, author of the very fine book *Redesigning Education: A Guide for Developing Human Greatness,* deplores the fact that "our fixation on curriculum development instead of human development is the enormous dam blocking educational reform."[10] It has caused us to ignore the work of those who reveal the individuality of human nature, how young (and even older) brains work, and how children learn.[11] Moreover, the discovery and development of each child's intelligences and gifts go unattended. In Chapter 10 we will revisit the multiple intelligences and look at many ways to support the development of all of the intelligences in students.

A PREFERENCE OF THE BRAIN: EXPERIENCING KNOWLEDGE

It is time to face a glaring reality! The majority of teachers today continue to "teach—teach—teach" and "instruct—instruct" in ways that are incompatible with how the human brain learns. How did we ever imagine that we knew how to reach and teach today's young people without knowing how they best can learn? It's like placing the cart before the horse. It's like looking up a recipe after taking the fallen cake out of the oven. It's like "testing—testing—testing" without knowing meaningful ways for students to acquire and retain learning as meaningful lasting knowledge.

Face it! 90% of what is 'taught' in a traditional way is forgotten in 90 days.

Traditional "schooling" treats knowledge as "a commodity" that is stored in teachers' minds and texts, and that can be "delivered" into the heads of students. Like other commodities the assumption is that it also can be itemized and measured. Students are required to listen attentively, complete assignments alone, remember facts and concepts—and one way or another return the same information to the teacher or a high stakes test. Disciplined students may take down information during a lecture hoping to keep it in memory until the next test, but the brain does not store memorized data for a long period of time. The assumption that knowledge simply can be transferred effectively into the minds of students by instructors is a fallacy that undermines meaningful long-lasting learning for students. It is critical that we understand why direct instruction is incompatible with how the human brain learns.

Years of impressive research on cognitive learning affirm that knowledge cannot be transmitted directly from one mind to another. Each person's storehouse of knowledge is a synthesis of what a person hears and reads—and interprets through previous experiences, familiar symbols and language. The human brain constructs and weaves all of the incoming data, information, concepts and experiences into its own continuous file system. It is a constructor of continually changing knowledge that is created and recreated between people doing things together. Moreover, acquiring knowledge is facilitated by working socially with others. It evolves out of group discourse, problem-solving and collaborative meaning-making. Students who have the opportunity to discuss, experience and apply information to real-life situations, problems and projects gain meaningful lasting knowledge for the future.

KNOWING HOW THE HUMAN BRAIN LEARNS

All information comes into the brain from the body's senses (sight, hearing, touch/feeling, smell, taste), and zooms into one of two possible pathways depending upon whether or not a sense of threat or danger is perceived. The body and brain work, one might say, in a co-dependent partnership—so much so that recent researchers are using the term "body/brain."[12]

Let's learn why this is so!

When there is no sense of danger the information travels on a slow pathway to a sensory relay station, called the *thalamus*, onward to the *hippocampus*, the center of learning and memory, and then to the *cerebral cortex*, the center of long term memory and thinking. However, when there is a sense of danger the sensory data *instantaneously activates* mechanisms for survival. The input goes directly to the *thalamus* relay station, which sends it to the *amygdala* which is the center of all fear, threat and passion where an internal regulator called the *hypothalamus* triggers the pituitary and adrenal glands to release a stress hormone called *cortisol*. The cortisol hormone activates fight or flight behaviors as it races through the body and brain via the bloodstream. The story doesn't end there! The rational cerebral cortex, center of long term memory, never has a chance to think things through because emotional balance is destroyed. With persistent stress, cortisol can be devastating to the learning and memory system and the internal regulator, the *hippocampus*.[13]

Knowing this, gives a better understanding of why the climate of classrooms must be safe and supportive learning environments. Somewhere in the novel "Dune" the frantic hero cries out, "Fear is a mind-killer!" Many kinds of fear kill minds daily in classrooms. There is the fear of asking a question, fear of not giving the right-answer, fear of being teased, called a name or ridiculed for one's culture, gender and diversity. Minds are killed through loneliness, hostility and exclusion by peers. For some it may be intimidation from a teacher, a reprimand that seems unfair, boys being called on more often than girls, or "the smart people" more than others. Whenever the body/mind becomes swamped with the stress hormone cortisol emotional balance is lost and rational thought and memory become unavailable. Repeated incidents inevitably result in a young person seeing him or herself as a loser….and giving up.

It verifies why neuroscience, human development and resiliency research concur that children's academic, social and emotional learning depend upon the existence of a safe and caring threat-free environment. It is the primary reason that the culture, small group structures, student-centered active learning and caring community process of Tribes leads to more lasting learning and greater achievement for students.

Understanding how the human brain acquires and constructs knowledge helps to explain the incongruity of traditional instruction. The principles are especially important for educators who are committed to overcoming the learning gap that

The illiterate of the 21st century will not be those who cannot read and write, but those who cannot learn, unlearn, and relearn.

—ALVIN TOFFLER

THE PRINCIPLES FOR STUDENT-CENTERED ACTIVE LEARNING[14]

COGNITIVE AND METACOGNITIVE FACTORS

PRINCIPLE 1. Learning is an active process in which meaning is developed on the basis of experience.

PRINCIPLE 2. The learner associates and links new information to existing knowledge in memory.

PRINCIPLE 3. Strategies for "thinking about thinking"—reflecting on learning—facilitate learning.

AFFECTIVE FACTORS

PRINCIPLE 4. Individuals are naturally curious and enjoy learning when in the absence of negative conditions and emotions.

PRINCIPLE 5. Curiosity, creativity and higher order thinking processes are stimulated by learning tasks of optimal difficulty, relevancy, authenticity, challenge and novelty for each student.

SOCIAL FACTORS

PRINCIPLE 6. Learning is facilitated by social interaction, discourse and collaboration.

PRINCIPLE 7. Learning and self-esteem are heightened when individuals are in respectful and caring relationships with others who genuinely appreciate their unique gifts and talents.

INDIVIDUAL DIFFERENCES

PRINCIPLE 8. Learners differ in their preferences for learning mode and strategies, the pace at which they learn, and their unique capabilities in particular areas.

PRINCIPLE 9. Each learner constructs reality and interprets life experiences in a different way depending upon prior learning, beliefs, culture and external experiences.

persists for many students coming from lower socio-economic populations, indigenous backgrounds and various cultures.

CREATING A POSITIVE LEARNING ENVIRONMENT

No, our friend Mrs. Jones didn't just start Polyhedraville out of the blue the first week of school. First she and her students created a Tribes TLC® (Tribes Learning Community) environment in the classroom. She knew that learning is a social phenomenon and that people not only had to know each other before working on tasks, but had to feel valued for the unique contributions they brought to their tribes and to the class.

So...Mrs. J. bought some books and attended Tribes TLC® training with teachers of her school, and together they began to focus on developing the gifts of each and every student in their school. Sounds complex? Not really. How they did it and how you can transform your classroom and school community is the content of the rest of this book.

Are you ready? Great! Grab your backpack again...we're heading down the Tribes trail!

6

What Tribes Are and
How They Work

6 What Tribes Are and How They Work

A Native American teacher, Paula Swift Robin, is talking with four other teachers at a conference in eastern Washington. "What is the most exciting thing you are doing in your classroom?" asks one of her new friends. Paula leans forward excitedly. "You'll never believe the gift that came my way. Two years ago I went to the annual used book sale at our town library, and my eye was attracted to a worn book called "Tribes." Must be about Native Americans, I said to myself. I bought it, took it home, and was so very surprised! It's about using small groups, called tribes, as a way to involve kids to help each other learn and to feel good about themselves. Our students took to it right away, and we wove in studies about our Native American tribes throughout the year. It's made amazing changes for our kids. It's the caring and challenge they long for...a lot like the closeness that our own people have depended upon throughout time."

When looking for a classroom program that was culturally compatible with First Nation beliefs and values, Tribes was recommended. It surpassed our expectations. Tribes honours the sacred circle in which all people come together. Tribes has helped us teach the children how to be kind and to own their responsibilities. It is helping us to talk and listen to one another, as the old ones still do.

—LAURA HORTON, NATIVE STUDENT RETENTION COORDINATOR FORT FRANCES-RAINY RIVER, BOARD OF EDUCATION, ONTARIO, CANADA

Yes, this is a true story. What Paula didn't realize was that the teacher at the table who kept beaming a big smile back at her while she talked was also a Tribes TLC® Trainer.

ABOUT CALLING THE PROCESS "TRIBES"

At times our Native American friends have asked why this interactive learning process is called Tribes. It's hard to remember exactly when it happened. Throughout the years people who experienced the caring, community-building process kept saying, "This is like being in a family...not a team but a tribe." People appreciated the social support, the respect for individual differences, and the sense of belonging that indigenous tribes seem to have. The process of Tribes seems to symbolize the affection and caring that so many of us in Western society long for today.

Ron Patrick, Native American Certified Tribes Trainer has graciously written the article that follows to give a perspective on the cultural values signified by the word "tribes," not only used by Native Americans but by indigenous people around the world. This new edition of the Tribes book is being used by First Nation, Inuit, Native American, Hawaiian, Australian Aboriginal, Micronesian, Dominican Republic and South American Certified Tribes Trainers and teachers throughout an ever-growing population of schools. Why? Many simply reply, "It's a people process."

Why the Name "Tribes"

The word "tribes" means very different things to people around the world. Indigenous people in the four directions of the world use "tribes" with special meaning and cultural significance. My tribe, the Eastern Band of the Cherokee, consider being part of the tribe a birth rite and not something someone can join. A person is born into this relationship. The formal definition of the word "tribe" is given in the Cambridge International Dictionary of English as "a group of people often of related families who live together, share the same language, culture, and heritage—especially those who do not live in towns or cities." Thus, from Africa, from Europe, to Asia, to Australia, to North America, to South America, and other parts of the world indigenous people consider the word "tribe" a formal word with special relational meaning often defining similarities and uniqueness. The values that most tribes hold focus around fairness, family, respect, responsibility, and positive relationships.

Due to a deep respect for the teachings and wisdom of native cultures around the world, the word came into use as the name for the developmental learning process developed by Jeanne Gibbs. This process is a way of being together helping each other teach our children to live a life based on time-honored values in caring, safe and supportive environments.

The word "tribes" also has been used in an "informal" manner. The informal definition (also from the Cambridge Dictionary) defines the meaning as "a large family or other group that someone belongs to." The process known as "Tribes" helps us to create "belonging" for children in schools and other organizations. It helps us as parents and teachers to teach the deep values of respect, responsibility, and relationship skills. No other word seems to come close to conveying the same hope and meaning. This process known simply as "Tribes" honors children. It seeks to make children's lives and their children's lives better.

As a person of native heritage I have been taught to always talk from my heart. I am honored to say that the Tribes learning process uses the word "tribes" with great respect. It is not a characterization, nor an attempt to steal an important cultural icon from our peoples. It comes from a place of deep respect and regard for both the word "tribe" and all indigenous people around the world.

May you walk in Beauty,
Asgaya Tawodi Digadoli
Ron Patrick

FROM A PSYCHOLOGIST'S VIEW

Ron Patrick, M.Ed.

Ron is an ecological/systems psychologist and a Tribes TLC® Trainer. He has worked with school and mental health communities for 33 years, most recently as Director of Psychological and Student Services. He also served as a consultant/ coach with the Mid-Eastern Ohio Regional Resource Center where he focused on primary preventive mental health, systems change, and literacy programs. As a Native American, Ron believes that the Tribes TLC® process honors his cultural values and the tradition of deep respect within native spiritual practice.

THE TRIBES AGREEMENTS—A NEW WAY OF BEING TOGETHER

Building the positive environment for a Tribes Learning Community, whether in a small group, a classroom, staff of whole school begins by replacing unspoken norms of the school with explicit positive agreements. All groups and organizations have tacit norms that affect behavior by conveying "this is how we do things around here." In a dispassionate impersonal school the norms may be:

Nobody listens anyway   *The more put-downs the more fun*
No one respects me or my things   *Don't ask for help!*
Never let on how you feel!   *Appreciation—what's that?*

There is no way to support, let alone reach and teach any age group of children, when negative norms are operant every hour of every day throughout a school.

Admonitions by teachers and attempts of outer control do not stop relational abuse. We have to engage students themselves to agree upon kinder new rules—agreements that they make and monitor with each other. Inherent in our goal of adolescent development is the encouragement of self-responsibility and the internalization of ethical social principles. It begins by transferring the responsibility of students to help each other live caring social agreements. It becomes intrinsic in behavior when kids' hearts as well as heads come to appreciate and commit to a better way of being with peers and others. The four agreements are:

What students can do together today, they can do alone tomorrow.[1]
—LEV VYGOTSKY

1. **ATTENTIVE LISTENING:** To pay close attention to one another's expression of ideas, opinions and feelings; to check for understanding; and to let others know that they have been heard

2. **APPRECIATION/NO PUT-DOWNS:** To treat others kindly; to state appreciation for unique qualities, gifts, skills and contributions; to avoid negative remarks, name-calling, hurtful gestures and behaviors

3. **RIGHT TO PASS AND TO PARTICIPATE:** To have the right to choose when and to what extent one will participate in a group activity; to observe quietly if not participating actively; and to choose whether to offer observations later to a group when asked to do so

4. **MUTUAL RESPECT:** To affirm the value and uniqueness of each person; to recognize and appreciate individual and cultural differences; and offer feedback that encourages growth.

Some schools or classes may want to add additional agreements beyond the four. For example, schools concerned with student violence have elaborated on the second and fourth agreements. Treat people as you want to be treated/no hitting or violence. It is important, however, that the list isn't longer than five agreements or students will be more likely to forget or overlook them and not reinforce them with each other.

Tribes agreements are very important and need to be posted in prominent places in classrooms and throughout the school. One dedicated leader, a bus driver of a Navajo reservation school, has the four agreements on the steps going up into his bus. He smiles and says now he is enjoying his riders, they all have a "new way of being" on the bus. The riders, of course, are the "agreement enforcers." Through practice and monitoring, and many strategies in classroom community circles, the new way or better way of being together begins to happen. Whenever the tribes begin work together, the teacher not only reminds everyone of the Tribes agreements again, but transfers the responsibility to the tribes to maintain them. Transforming the classroom or school into a positive, caring learning climate is dependent upon everyone internalizing these positive agreements.

A major difference between Tribes and some of the other classroom group methods is that people maintain membership in the same group for an extended period of time. This is based on research indicating that[2]

+ People perform better on learning tasks when they are members of "high cohesion" rather than "low cohesion" groups

+ Students who feel comfortable with their peers utilize their academic abilities more fully than those who do not.

The difference between using randomly organized task groups and creating on-going tribes looks something like this:

Random Learning Groups

The Tribes Learning Community

Random groupings produce a scattered energy, and since they do not provide ongoing inclusion (trust, safety, and a sense of belonging), it is more difficult for students to work together. The system of long-term membership in the Tribes process assures support for all members within each small group and within the classroom. This *intentionally created environment* supports development and achievement for students of all abilities.

STAGES OF GROUP DEVELOPMENT: THE TRIBES TRAIL

The strange map on the following page is one of the main secrets to the magic that happens in Tribes. OK, we know you think our map looks more like the cross-section of a gopher-infested garden! It really is our attempt to detail the important synchronization that takes place between the teacher-facilitator and the development of small groups. The success of any group's life together and the individual achievements its members can make depend upon the teacher-facilitator's knowledge and ability to orchestrate activities appropriate to the group's particular stage of development. It strikes us as sad that though all living takes place in groups, we seldom are taught how to make groups work well together. Families, labor unions, churches, parent-teacher associations, management staffs, faculties and classrooms...all are in search of positive participation and a reliable democratic process.

> "The meeting will come to order. Tonight's agenda was mailed to you. The secretary will read the minutes. The executive committee **has decided** that all members will..."

Ignorant of any group development process, a majority of organizations struggle in limbo somewhere between the Great Man theory of leadership and democratic process, waving Robert's Rules of Order to maintain control. As a member, you may never feel as involved as the leaders are. You may wonder why you are there at all, and how the group will ever really know what unique talents, skills, or resources you have to contribute. YOU, the real special "you," are seldom invited to express your expectations or opinions and may never become a possible resource to the organization. In time your interest wanes and you drift onward, hoping for more recognition, support, and a way to make a contribution in some other group.

The reason that people become drop-outs—whether from their families, staff, organization, or for that matter from other relationships is because they do not feel *included* and *of value* to the others. Paid employees (yes, even teachers and administrators) also manage to drop out, but in subtle ways, such as not following through on responsibilities, taking leave days, sabotaging a department's plans, caucusing with other disgruntled peers, manipulating meetings, or being apathetic. Students drop out by gradually moving to "flight or fight." Apathy, boredom, lack of participation, shyness, absenteeism, inability to complete tasks are some of the ways of taking flight. Those that fight, or initiate behaviors (such as

When one has no stake in the way things are, when one's needs or opinions are provided no forum, when one sees oneself as the object of unilateral actions, it takes no particular wisdom to suggest one would rather be elsewhere.

—SEYMOUR SARASON

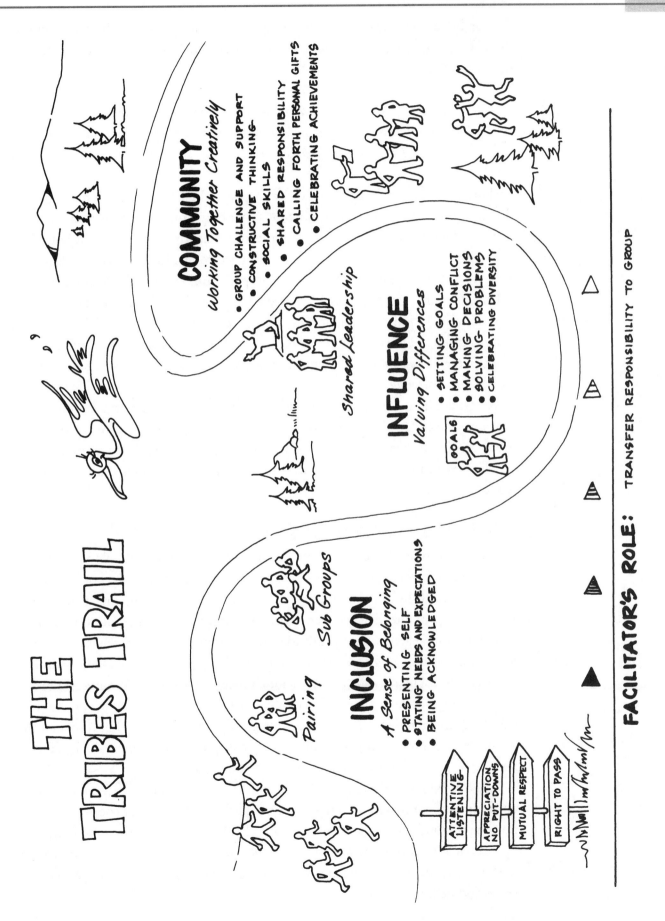

THE TRIBES TRAIL

COMMUNITY
Working Together Creatively
- GROUP CHALLENGE AND SUPPORT
- CONSTRUCTIVE THINKING
- SOCIAL SKILLS
- SHARED RESPONSIBILITY
- CALLING FORTH PERSONAL GIFTS
- CELEBRATING ACHIEVEMENTS

Shared Leadership

INFLUENCE
Valuing Differences
- SETTING GOALS
- MANAGING CONFLICT
- MAKING DECISIONS
- SOLVING PROBLEMS
- CELEBRATING DIVERSITY

GOALS

INCLUSION
A Sense of Belonging
- PRESENTING SELF
- STATING NEEDS AND EXPECTATIONS
- BEING ACKNOWLEDGED

Pairing *Sub Groups*

ATTENTIVE LISTENING

APPRECIATION NO PUT-DOWNS

MUTUAL RESPECT

RIGHT TO PASS

FACILITATOR'S ROLE: TRANSFER RESPONSIBILITY TO GROUP

teasing, hitting, stealing, using foul language, etc.), are delivering the same message: **"I don't feel included …nobody cares about me."** Few leaders are aware of a basic principle:

> *If a person does not feel included, he/she will create his or her own inclusion by grabbing influence—attracting attention, creating a controversy, demanding power, or withdrawing into a passive belligerence.*

This organizational *disease* is a veritable plague in any system still managed through top-down authoritarian methods that only provide inclusion and influence for the manager, principal, boss, or leader. Negatively outspoken teachers on the faculty or strident parents in the P.T.A. need to feel included and, lacking that, seek undue influence. We need to get past thinking of individual student behavior problems as hopeless, uncontrollable, or pathological. The majority are in need of inclusion and affection from teachers, family, and peers. *If school and family systems can learn how to help all kids feel included and of value to significant others in their lives, one of this country's major concerns, anti-social youth behavior, will be turned around.*

All guides taking people into a wilderness need a map so that the community of people traveling together arrives at their hoped-for destination. As a classroom group facilitator, it is essential that you understand some simple stages of group development and the major issues that are bound to arise as your students learn to work well in groups.

THE TRIBES TRAIL MAP

The Tribes Trail Map illustrates the sequential stages of group development that you, the teacher-facilitator, will lead your flock through. Notice the bottom line. It shows a gradual shift in your role from being directive, providing much structure, to becoming less directive and transferring leadership to tribes within the community. After initial activities that develop inclusion for everyone in classroom tribes, you will be encouraging students to assume leadership in their tribes and within the classroom. The net effect of this subtle process is that responsibility is transferred to students themselves. This is why the Tribes process is known as one that calls forth the potential talents and resources of group members. This provides the learning community or organization with a multiplicity of resources, and enables tasks to be accomplished by all in satisfying and creative ways.

It is this intentional transfer of leadership in the midst of a positive and caring environment that makes the Tribes program different from other cooperative learning methods. This transfer, this calling forth, is the big secret to building self-worth and motivation among people. No matter what the age level, it gives a loud and clear message—you are capable people who can indeed manage yourselves and help each other!

THE STAGE OF INCLUSION

Now let's look a bit closer at how this works. Notice on the Tribes Trail Map the separate individuals coming into a classroom, or into a staff or organization's meeting. As mentioned earlier, the scale at the bottom of the map indicates the degree of structuring that the leader, or teacher-facilitator, needs to provide for people as they come from their many separate paths. Each person entering the group is unique in his/her life experience and perceives the new classroom situation or meeting out of a personal complex of diverse needs and expectations. All newcomers to any group feel an initial anxiety and have many unspoken questions:

+ I wonder if I'll like this classroom.

+ Will the teacher and other kids like me?

+ How will they get to know me? I feel scared.

+ Why am I nervous?

+ What will we be doing?

+ I wish this were the end of the day, not the beginning.

Tribes is a process... the music for all of the words!

Knowing this, your responsibility is to live up to the name "facilitator," which means "one who makes it easy." If people stay immersed in these initial anxieties, they cannot learn and in time will demonstrate acting-out or dropping-out behaviors. Remember how the brain works? In fear or anxiety, the brain downshifts into a lower state and is not available to reason or learn. Immersed in anxiety, students will take to their own comfort zones...which may not be positive for either themselves or others. A student may simply show restlessness, shuffle papers, get a stomach ache, or in time become regarded as one more learning disability. A teacher who never feels comfortable in her faculty may be inattentive at

INCLUSION

In order to have INCLUSION, three opportunities must be provided:

1. Each person needs to be able to INTRODUCE HERSELF, not just by stating a name but offering a short description of her feelings, interests, resources, talents, or special qualities.

2. Each person needs to be able to EXPRESS HIS HOPES OR EXPECTATIONS for what will happen during the group's time together.

3. Each person needs to BE ACKNOWLEDGED by the group as having been heard, appreciated, and welcomed.

Invite the pelican that soars over the Tribes Trail to be your constant companion. Her name is Reflection. She will tell you, rather immodestly, that she makes the Tribes process work well anywhere. At times, you will want to ignore her calls: "timeout," "stop the action, teacher," "time to reflect," or "what's happening now?" Reflection knows that if you watch from the bird's eye view, classroom management goes more smoothly. Reflection is a wise bird who can describe just what she saw or heard while people worked together. You will find her questions on the pages of every Tribes strategy. Reflection clears up confusion and helps everyone soar to greater heights.

meetings, irritable with students, and simply suffer through to the end of the year.

In a classroom it may take several days or weeks for all students to present themselves to the total class or within a small group. In organizational settings (like faculty meetings), initial **inclusion** means gaining adequate recognition and the same opportunity to present oneself prior to tasks and agendas. It means **balancing persons and tasks.** This is what makes the big difference in how people finally are able to work together.

As soon as possible the facilitator begins to model and discuss the basic four agreements that make the Tribes process work well. By having people first meet in small temporary groupings (pairs or triads), initial anxiety is alleviated and inclusion begins to happen. Observe any organization of more than six people. People very naturally sub-group or arrive at a meeting with one or two others in order to feel less anxious. The intentional use of small temporary groups (sometimes called "trial tribes") early in a meeting makes it easier for all to feel included at least with a few others before relating to a larger group of people. Using our process, leaders of large conferences sub-group hundreds of people early in the gathering just to guarantee that no one is isolated. Agenda items can even be submitted from all of the small groups in order to include everyone's expectations.

Inclusion is a basic human need, and unless it is met people feel vulnerable and defensive. The saying "a camel is a horse designed by a committee" most certainly refers to a committee whose members attempted to undertake a task without first having achieved inclusion together. Time spent up front, building inclusion and trust is the most valuable commitment a group can make. Although it takes a bit longer at first, the pay-off in achievement makes all the difference!

THE STAGE OF INFLUENCE

As mellow as the stage of inclusion can be, in time a very natural restlessness will be seen throughout the community. The restlessness is a good sign, because it means people do feel included and are ready to work together. You will begin to notice that

 ◆ Members are taking more initiative and speaking up to you; they may be making suggestions, asking confronting questions, and even criticizing the current leadership

 ◆ People are discussing or questioning group goals, ways to work together, and how decisions are being made

 ◆ People are not being as polite or as patient with each other

 ◆ Conflicts are beginning to arise.

Rather than panic and decide that groups just don't work, recognize these indicators as positive signals. The new restlessness means that the time spent in building inclusion, trust, kindness, and a sense of belonging has been achieved. People are now ready to really work on tasks together...the stage of influence has arrived. Congratulations!

The **influence stage** centers on these questions:

To feel "of influence" is to feel of value.

+ How can each person influence the goals, tasks, and decision-making process of the group?

+ How can members assert their individuality and value in the midst of the group?

+ How can leadership be shared so that the resource and potential of each member is called forth?

To feel "of influence" is to feel of value (worth, power, individual resource to the group). To the extent that each person does not feel important in a classroom or organization, commitment and motivation decrease.

INFLUENCE

Rather than allowing group members to wrestle for ways to have influence, the skilled facilitator provides a selection of strategies that help people to

+ Express diverse attitudes, opinions, positions, and personal feelings

+ Put forth ideas without others passing judgment; help people to respect individual differences

+ Use participatory methods for decision making so that all members feel they are influential and of value to the group

+ Help members share leadership responsibility.

THE ROLE OF THE TEACHER-FACILITATOR is also to provide methods for resolving the inevitable different issues and concerns. Conflicts and misunderstandings are a natural part, a vital dynamic, of the process and cannot be ignored. They can be resolved through a variety of strategies, such as

+ Reflecting on and discussing the incident or situation that is happening

+ Helping people to state their feelings clearly

+ Assisting the group to give constructive feedback

✦ Facilitating problem-solving methods

✦ Role-playing, using role-reversal techniques

✦ Negotiating the priorities of individual members.

If issues are ignored, the energy of the group is deflected away from its capacity to accomplish tasks together!

The sensitive classroom teacher recognizes that continuing to focus on subject matter in the midst of interpersonal or group issues is neither academically nor emotionally helpful. Having people meet in their tribes to resolve a disruptive issue not only transfers responsibility to the class, but promotes a sense of value for the students. Once the conflict has been resolved by students, people will go back to their work on tasks with renewed energy.

During the **influence stage** the facilitator supports the tribes to work as much as possible on their own. Maintain contact with the groups by requesting periodic reports and circulating among the tribes to determine whether assistance is needed. If the facilitator sits down within a group, the dynamic changes immediately. Group members will once again center on the teacher and cease to participate with each other. As the influence stage progresses and issues become resolved, shared leadership begins to emerge from group members. What a delight it is to see the shy child of the class lead an activity in her tribe! And what a relief it is to see the dominant member sit back as the others in the tribe demonstrate their unique skills and talents. Some folks have called the Tribes process **magic**... but we call it a reality that can be achieved by any committed teacher.

THE STAGE OF COMMUNITY

Who does not long for a sense of community in the midst of a city, an organization, a staff, a school, the classroom...the impersonal crowd? The deep human longing is our need to be known, to belong, to care and be cared for. Community is the esprit that happens when many minds and hearts come together to work toward a common good. Community happens through inclusion and the appreciation of individual differences. One can tell when community has become a reality. It is the delightful surprise one day that those we are with (no matter what the difference in age, gender, race, culture, intelligence, or talent) are indispensable and beautiful.

The possibility for community, whether in a classroom, school, or any organization, depends upon the assumption that interdependence and connection to others is key to human development, learning, and the accomplishment of task.

You will know that you are in a community if you often hear laughter and singing. You will know you are in an institution or bureaucracy if you hear the silence of long halls and the intonations of formal meetings.[3]
—JOHN MC KNIGHT

FIVE INDICATORS OF COMMUNITY

John McKnight, author, points out five indicators:[4]

CAPACITY: Communities are built upon recognizing the whole depth, the strengths, weaknesses, the unique capacities of each member.

COLLECTIVE EFFORT: They share responsibility to achieve goals for the common good, and engage the diversity of individual talents and skills to do so.

INFORMALITY: Transactions of value are based on consideration; care and affection take place spontaneously.

STORIES: Reflection upon individual and community experiences provide knowledge about truth, relationships, and future direction.

CELEBRATION: Activities incorporate celebration, parties, and social events. The line between work and play is blurred as people enjoy both at once.

At this point in the Tribes process, the classroom, faculty, or school community needs to ask itself the following:

+ How well do we know the unique strengths and weakness of each of our members?

+ Do we share responsibility for accomplishing goals for the good of the whole community using our diverse talents and skills?

+ Are we freely expressing our caring and consideration for one another?

+ Do we take time to tell stories and reflect on our experiences together?

+ Do we laugh, play, and enjoy each other as we create new approaches or solve old problems together?

+ How well do we recognize contributions and celebrate our community accomplishments and shared traditions?

The caring community we long for doesn't just happen; it can be intentionally developed. It depends upon any group of people deliberately creating *inclusion* for all members, and working through the nitty-gritty issues of *influence*.

COMMUNITY

Creating community requires

* Dedication to resolving rather than avoiding uncomfortable problems and conflicts that begin to separate members

* Learning and practicing the skills that enable collaboration

* Agreements about how we will treat each other

* Time to reflect on how well we are doing.

Once a group has gone through adversity together, its members become filled with confidence that they can handle whatever comes their way. This is the path to resilient relationships, creativity and outstanding results!

THE SPIRAL OF RENEWAL

The repeated sequence of inclusion, influence, and community enables the group to experience increasingly more profound interaction the longer they are together.

Each time the members of a learning community or classroom tribe come together they need some type of inclusion activity before they begin to focus on task; and influence issues will always need to be addressed. A helpful way of visualizing the continuing growth and evolution of a tribe is to imagine an ascending spiral that moves up through the levels of inclusion, influence, and community as it rises. One full "loop" represents a group meeting, so that each time the spiral completes a cycle it goes through the three stages again. But each time a tribe meets, though it still needs to begin with inclusion, it moves on to a slightly higher level of positive interaction. The spiral is continuous and a never-ending process. Graphically, it looks something like this:

Although we have been experimenting and evaluating this process for many years, there is still so much to learn. It is gratifying to hear students, teachers, administrators, and parents say that they emerged a bit more **special in their own self-worth** because they had the opportunity to be part of a tribe somewhere. It does take a commitment and time to integrate the Tribes cooperative learning process into a classroom or school community, but a surprising array of benefits do come about whenever **inclusion** leads the way.

7

Creating the
Learning Community

7 Creating the Learning Community

Here they come! Twenty-six 3rd, 4th, and 5th graders are entering their class-room this snowy day in November. Teacher Brad Allen observes the chaos as hats, coats, gloves, and boots find their way to shelves and racks. Every snowy day Brad wonders again why he didn't take that job in the sunshine of San Diego, and the same answer keeps coming back to him: It's these kids...this bunch of kids from this community. One by one the waiting circle of chairs is filled. The 5th graders, who have had two years with Brad, are helpful with the younger 3rd graders. They keep the positive energy going. "There's hardly a put-down anymore, no teasing, pushing, or shoving," Brad muses. He raises his hand, and one by one people raise their hands and the chatter stops. "Good morning and congratulations," Brad says. "We're all here in spite of the storm. To build our community inclusion today, let's go around the circle and share anything amusing, crazy, or special that happened to you this morning. We'll just do one-sentence stories so that everyone has a turn. Remember, you have the right to pass if you would rather not share at all." One by one people begin to speak:

"I found my lost skateboard under a bush when my dad and I were shoveling a path to our car this morning."
"My grandma came out and out-shoveled my mom."
"I brought that pulley that our tribe needs for our project."
"I dropped my lunch in a snowdrift and found it except for one banana."
"I got to wear my brother's boots today."
A few say they would like to pass. No one pressures them to participate. Everyone is listening attentively to those who do share. Brad nods, comments, and laughs now and then. The day has begun.

Why is this community circle so important each morning, each day? Brad Allen would say there are three big reasons:

+ I want to help these students make a transition from whatever has gone on in their lives outside of school to the classroom.

+ I want to have them feel included in the classroom community before working on tasks.

+ I want to involve them in creating and sustaining a positive learning environment.

THE COMMUNITY CIRCLE

The special spirit of community doesn't just happen in a classroom or organization by having people work in small groups, or by using randomly selected cooperative learning activities. Building community is a deliberate process that a teacher or leader facilitates over a period of time. It begins by creating inclusion for every person within the intended learning community and by practicing the set of positive Tribes agreements:

+ Attentive listening

+ Appreciation/No put-downs

+ Right to pass/Participate

+ Mutual respect

It takes several weeks for all students within a new class to be able to know everyone else. The purpose of the time is to give students many opportunities to present themselves in positive ways. During this time, the teacher not only will be selecting many of the Tribes inclusion strategies from this book, but will be teaching collaborative social skills and engaging students in honoring agreements. She will also be modeling the skills and agreements.

Experienced Tribes teachers may have students meet several times each day in a community circle for sharing, discussions on curricula, learning collaborative skills, reflecting on the day, and celebrating.

The daily community circle is step one in implementing the essential protective factors that foster resiliency: caring and sharing, participation, and positive expectations.

At the same time that a teacher begins to help students become familiar with the community circle process, he also begins to have people get together in pairs, triads, and groups of four or five, as an additional way to promote inclusion and to begin working together on academic topics.

> **INCLUSION EXAMPLE:** *"Find two people you still do not know very well and for five minutes share your favorite summer outdoor activity."*

> **ACADEMIC EXAMPLE:** *"Turn to a neighbor and for a few minutes discuss what you would have done if you had been Rosa Parks in her situation."*

This use of temporary small groups helps to make the transition to long-term Tribes membership groups. It also gives the teacher an opportunity to see how different combinations of students work together.

When I first heard about Tribes, I said, 'Good. It's about time that non-native people realize how much Anishnoabe people have to offer.' The community circle is like our Healing Circle. It allows everyone a chance to be seen, to speak, and to be heard. Each of us has a different way of looking at things. We can learn from each other. It's good to listen and watch. When you watch, you see everything. You learn to give to other people and you see different ways to deal with problems.

—ANNE WILSON,
OJIBWE ELDER,
MANITOU RAPIDS
FIRST NATION,
ONTARIO, CANADA

GETTING STARTED

So there you are with twenty-six faces looking up at you expectantly. How do we get started? Remember the Tribes Trail Map? Yes, here in the beginning it is up to you to be directive...to help all become comfortable and feel included. Your primary responsibility is to make it safe for people to share and for you to affirm how glad you are that they are part of the learning community. The quality of the classroom environment is strongly influenced by your personal style, the behavior that you model and expect from your students. What is talked about during a community circle session is usually less important at this point than how the group interacts together.

Here's an example of the community circle experience. You have chosen the strategy "Five Tribles." First, be sure that all people are sitting in a circle large enough so that each person can see all the other faces. Your students will probably chatter among themselves while the circle is being formed. Be patient and observe their interactions. Soon they will settle down and you can get started.

Tell them, "This year our class will be working together in some new ways—in small groups, so that people can help each other learn and learn from each other. We will meet often as a whole class, talking together in a community circle like this."

Somewhere during this first introduction, raise your hand and tell the class that this is how you will ask for attention. It is a non-verbal signal. Whenever people see the teacher's raised hand it means that everyone also raises his or her hand and stops talking. You might state that using the signal means they will never have to hear you shout.

"Now how many people would like that? (Ask for a show of hands.) It is also a great test of our awareness, or consciousness. Are the same people the first to notice?"

GIVING INSTRUCTIONS

Describe the activity or task that the community will be doing, and give the purpose for doing it. For example: "Look at the faces of these five little creatures, called "Tribles," and choose one that seems to be what you feel like this morning. It is important for us to hear how everyone is today before we begin to work together." Manage the time by asking students to make their statements in one or two sentences, a phrase or word. Some initial strategies, other than the "Five Tribles," that may be appropriate for your students are Community Circle Topics, Zoo-Animals and

JOY. Check the Tribes Strategy Grid in Chapter 13 to make selections for age, grade level and population groups. The primary purpose of Tribes active learning strategies is for teachers to use them as structures (formats) for the active learning of academic material.

INITIATING SHARING

The teacher-facilitator initiates sharing by saying something like, "This morning I feel like the middle Trible, quiet but not excited. I think that is because I was up rather late last night." Then, "Let's go around the circle starting with you Jennifer." Remind everyone they have the right-to-pass. When someone does pass, openly acknowledge the person with a nod or smile to convey that it is all right. After going around the circle once, facilitate a second go-around to give those who hesitated to speak the first time a second opportunity. It is often helpful to pass a physical object such as a feather, bean bag, "talking pencil," stuffed animal, etc., from speaker to speaker. This helps younger children and special learners, who may have shorter attention spans. It also works well with those folks of any age who cannot stop talking even if no one is listening. Set a time limit for holding the physical object.

KEEPING THINGS MOVING

It is best not to repeat, paraphrasing or comment on anyone's contribution. Make mental notes on things you want to bring up later. However, if someone gets put down by the group (derisive laughter, groans, etc.) deal with the incident in a direct but matter-of-fact way. "People, remember the agreement that we made about not putting anyone down." Or, ask the group, "Which agreement do we seem to be ignoring?" And let the class identify it rather than you.

LEARNING AND PRACTICING TRIBES AGREEMENTS

The second purpose of the community circle is to teach and practice the Tribes agreements and other basic social skills. Announce the skill to be practiced for a certain time: "Class, we will be practicing attentive listening during our ten minutes of sharing." Be sure that the time is well within your students' abilities. Begin by transferring responsibility to the class by asking one or two people to keep track of the time, and later have them ask, "How well did people listen to each to other?" The class can also discuss and post "Spotlight Behaviors" that time-keepers select and look for during circle time. At the close of the circle discussion the time-keepers can identify people who demonstrated a "Spotlight Behavior." The rest of the class can guess which behaviors were spotlighted. Kids love this, and try to demonstrate all of the behaviors during circle time.

Thank you to Teri Ushijima, Ed.D., who submitted the Daily Pledge when she was a 5th grade teacher at Mililani Elementary School, Central Oahu District, Hawaii.

Teri is now a Complex Area Superintendent in Central Oahu School District, Hawaii. Her photo and biography accompany her article, "Tribes in the High School?," which appears in Chapter 11.

The Daily Pledge of Fifth Grade Class D203

The democratic group process of Tribes has provided us with a systemic approach to creating a climate where the responsibility for learning is shared with all members of the class. In our classroom, we have a "constitution" that is displayed and recited in unison every morning. It is a pledge to honor the Tribes agreements. After determining what we wanted out learning community to be like for the year, the document was written by the students. We used the Tribes strategy, "An Ideal Classroom" to gather everyone's ideas. As I continue to use the Tribes process in my classroom, I know that the constructive social skills my students are gaining enable them to sustain community in our classroom every day. I believe that meaningful learning will allow them to create and sustain democratic group learning communities throughout their school years—and well into their future adult lives.

Our Classroom Constitution

We the people, in order to form an ideal classroom and establish attentive listening, mutual respect, appreciation, no put-downs, participation, the right to pass, and safety, do ordain this Constitution for our class.

Article 1: Attentive Listening
We will listen with our eyes, ears and heart.

Article 2: Mutual Respect
We will treat people the way we want to be treated.

Article 3: Appreciation/No Put-Downs
We will speak kindly to others and think of other people's feelings.

Article 4: Right to Participate/Pass
We have the right to pass in certain activities, and to know that the more we participate the more we gain.

Article 5: Safety
We will always think of safety first.

DEFINING COMMUNITY AGREEMENTS

It is important for the students in your classroom to enter into a discussion of what they need in order to feel safe, or trusting, in a group. Take the time to do this rather than simply posting the Tribes agreements. This can be done as a brainstorm in small groups or as a community circle discussion. Typically, people will say things like

> *"I don't like it when people call me names."*
> *"I don't want to get pushed around."*
> *"I don't want to do something just because everyone else does."*
> *"I don't want our group to fight and hassle all the time."*
> *"I want people to like me."*
> *"I want people to listen to me when I talk."*

After the brainstorm, synthesize and summarize similar statements that are as close as possible to the basic four Tribes agreements introduced in the last chapter:

✦ Attentive listening

✦ Appreciation/No put-downs

✦ Right to pass/Participate

✦ Mutual respect

It's OK if the class feels it needs one more agreement. However, since the purpose of these agreements is to build a positive learning environment and to have students become responsible for sustaining the agreements, the list should be brief—actually no more than five. It must not become just another version of school or teacher rules. The agreements are relational, defining how we want to relate to each other. *Such rules as No Running in the Halls or No Pushing in the Bus Line are not what is meant by relational agreements.* In time such behaviors will lessen due to the agreements of mutual respect and no put-downs being internalized by students. The point is to have your students "own" the agreements as much as possible. Even though you may have a beautiful graphic of the agreements ready for posting, save it for the next day or have the class make posters after this important discussion.

Of course, this initial activity may not be possible with younger children or all populations. In that case, do your graphic ahead of time, and have it posted in a prominent place in the classroom. Tell the class that these agreements help people get along well together and create a classroom that everyone will enjoy.

Your own modeling is absolutely the most essential factor in teaching the new Tribes agreements. Modeling comes through to kids as authentic when it is

No matter what my voice and eyes are saying, if my heart isn't present, I remain separate from my students and they will know it.

—VICKI STEWART

congruent and heartfelt. Vicki Stewart once said, *"No matter what my voice and eyes are saying, if my heart isn't present, I remain separate from my students and they know it."* Creating the Tribes environment begins with you, the facilitator, owning and living the agreements yourself. It also means

- Setting aside a lesson plan long enough to tune into a student's concern or pain

- Being non-judgmental, patient, and caring even with the more difficult ones

- Avoiding subtle put-downs in the midst of frustration or stress

- Standing on your own rights...to pass, to state your feelings, to say "No, I choose not to do that. It would not be good for me."

- Affirming through warm eye contact or a gentle touch on the shoulder

- Laughing at your own mistakes; conveying your own fallibility and commitment to lifelong growth and learning.

It means being there in an authentic way, consciously present in the existential moment...touching, speaking, and listening with head and heart.

听

you

eyes

ears

undivided
attention

heart

ATTENTIVE LISTENING

Attentive listening is probably the most important social skill to be taught and practiced by everyone in the learning community. Unfortunately, for many students (and adults) the experience of being listened to in a caring way rarely happens.

Attentive listening is a gift to be given. It depends upon

- Acknowledging the person who is speaking with full attention and eye contact

- Withholding one's own comments, opinions, and need to talk at the time

- Paraphrasing key words to encourage the speaker and to let them know they have been heard

- Affirming through body language that the speaker is being heard

- Paying attention not only to the words but also to the feelings behind the words.

Too often we half-listen to each other, running the words through our heads that we want to say as soon as it is our turn. Most teachers assume that kids have learned at home how to listen. Most adults assume that we all do it well—though we may never have been taught the principles.

The skill of attentive listening needs to be considered a priority within every school's curriculum because it affects children's ability to learn academic material. This is especially important as classrooms move toward cooperative educational methods. Some of the listening skills that should be practiced include:

- Attending (listening silently with full attention)

- Non-verbal encouragement (nodding "Uh-huh")

- Paraphrasing ("What I heard you say was...")

- Reflecting feelings ("You sound angry...")

Begin with these strategies:

- Teaching listening

- Teaching paraphrasing

- Reflecting feelings

APPRECIATION/NO PUT-DOWNS

If one of our main objectives is to develop a sense of self-worth and self-esteem in children, school systems and families must find ways to eliminate the scores of derogatory and negative remarks that bombard young people each day. Unfortunately, put-down remarks are a basic form of communication among children and adults themselves; at times they are used in families to convey affection: you goof-off, you jerk, you crazy kid. Though off-hand or flippant, they not only damage self-esteem but undermine the level of trust within a group. A positive climate that builds self-worth cannot develop unless you, the teacher-facilitator

- Challenge students themselves to prohibit put-down remarks

- Encourage students to exchange statements of appreciation (positive regard and recognition).

Eliminating put-downs can be a tedious process until students themselves begin to object when they hear one. When calling attention to a put-down, remind people that the class has made an agreement not to use them.

One way to encourage your class to confront put-down statements is to teach them to respond with I-Messages: *"I feel sad when I'm called 'stupid,' Aaron. It's a put-down and hurts!"* The next chapter contains instructions for teaching I-Messages.

Minimizing put-down statements is half of the step toward building student self-esteem. Put-downs need to be replaced with statements of appreciation. You might want to tell the class that as we quit hurting people with put-downs, we will discover that just as a coin has two sides, our put-down agreement has a secret on its other side that will help everyone feel great. It's called *appreciation*. Helping people of any age to express appreciation often can feel like swimming against a strong current. It is a sad commentary on our society that in the course of a day we make five times as many negative comments as statements that affirm how we value each other.

It is a sad commentary on our society that we make five times as many negative comments in the course of a day as statements that affirm how we value each other.

Statements of appreciation are invited after every strategy and are modeled by the teacher throughout the day. It is very important that you search for truths to say. Kids know when something doesn't ring true—is not sincere and honest. To help people begin making statements of appreciation, use such sentence starters as these:

"I liked it when...(describe the situation)."
"I felt good when you..."
"I admire you for...(describe the quality)."

After completing a group activity, write the sentence starter on the chalk board and invite people to make statements. Your own modeling encourages the sharing of positive statements perhaps more than anything. It is important that you model being both a good giver and a good receiver.

EXAMPLES:
"I appreciate your kindness, Joel."
"The ideas that you came up with, Sandy, made our project special."
"I felt honored when you gave me a copy of your own poem."

THE RIGHT TO PASS—THE RIGHT TO PARTICIPATE

The right to pass means that each person has the right to choose the extent to which she or he will share in a group activity. It is the essence of our democratic system not to be coerced, to have a right to one's privacy, and to take a stand, if necessary, apart from the majority. Without such guarantees, individual freedom within a group is not protected. Choosing the right to pass means that the community member prefers not to share personal information or feelings, or to actively participate in the group at the moment. It may be their choice to remain quiet and to be an observer for a short period of time. This right must be affirmed repeatedly by teachers and peers: *"OK, you do have the right to pass. It's just fine to do so."* Being a silent observer is still a form of participation and can also lead to greater learning.

This protective agreement is essential within all organizational and group settings because it provides control to members. It encourages students to be self-determining and responsible for their own well-being among peers. It gives members the practice and courage to stand back from situations that are uncomfortable or contrary to their own values. Drug abuse prevention programs for secondary students have emphasized the teaching of refusal skills, and the slogan "Just Say No" has become popular over the last few years. However, we are convinced that the teen years are a bit late to begin learning refusal skills: By this time admonishing kids to just say "No" is somewhat simplistic. They need to be able to assert their right to pass throughout all their developmental years. To be "me" and to know that "I" do not have to go along with the crowd is an essential resiliency strength for life.

Many teachers are anxious that if this agreement is used in classrooms, students will pass on learning subject matter. First of all, the agreement does not apply when individual accountability is required on learning tasks. Students do not have the right to pass on homework, taking tests, responding to the teacher, etc. They do, however, have the right to pass on peer-led interaction. It is important to keep in mind that

+ Temporarily withdrawing from activity does not mean a student is not learning

+ You can count on the tribe, or peer group, to draw the person who usually passes back into an active working role.

Healthy human development and resiliency depend upon young people becoming inner-directed rather than remaining dependent upon outer control from others.

MUTUAL RESPECT

The purpose of the mutual respect agreement is to assure everyone that their individual cultural values, beliefs, and needs will be considered and properly honored. It also means respect by adults for children's rights, needs, and differences. The rich multicultural diversity of our population is an invaluable resource for this country's future. Within a school community this agreement means respect for

+ Others—no matter what their race, gender, age, color, or learning ability

+ Newcomers from other cities, states, or countries

+ Teachers, parents, and other caring adults

+ Personal property and individual privacy

+ Individual skills, talents, and contributions.

This new agreement for the Tribes process was expanded from one once called "confidentiality/no rumors-no gossip," which we regard as one of the important aspects of mutual respect. Students will continue to need assurance of confidentiality—to know that others in their group will not disclose personal confidences. For students in classroom tribes, "No Gossip" does not mean that a student should not go home and tell her parents what she said or did in her tribe. It does mean that she does not have group members' permission to disclose what someone else may have said.

One way to teach this part of the agreement is to have each tribe make lists of how people feel when someone gossips about them. Help them to see that it is OK to share your own secret elsewhere, but not another's. Example questions:

> *"How did you feel when someone told Amy what you were going to give her for her birthday?"*
> *"Was a surprise ever spoiled for you due to someone's sharing?"*
> *"Do you think gossip always hurts people?"*

BUILDING COLLABORATIVE SKILLS THROUGH STAGES OF GROUP DEVELOPMENT

The Tribes process with its sequential stages of group development—inclusion, influence and community—is a pathway for the development of the essential collaborative skills that students (and all of us) need in order to live, love, play, and work well together. Collaborative skills don't just happen, even though we may use cooperative learning groups in classrooms, or have the intent to collaborate with others on a work project. The skills must be taught and practiced over and over in relation to others who share a common purpose and meaning in their lives. This could be a class, faculty, a work team, a board of directors, a neighborhood group, or city council. Whenever human systems do not work well or fall apart, these vital human skills are missing. Collaborative skills are the constructive thinking and social skills set forth in the U.S. Secretary of Labor's report as necessary skills for the 21st Century. Business leaders say that more jobs are lost due to the inability to work well with others than due to a lack of knowledge among American workers.

The graphic on the next page illustrates the twelve skills taught and strengthened during the sequential stages of group development in a Tribes classroom. Inclusion skills prepare the class to handle the influence stage. The essential collaborative skills learned in the influence stage become the foundation for a vital community...working together with others from diverse backgrounds, solving problems, assessing for improvement, and celebrating their achievements. The ongoing practice of these key collaborative skills creates a classroom with high levels of participation on the part of all students and establishes a positive climate for teaching and learning.

Placing socially unskilled students in a learning group and telling them to cooperate obviously will not be successful. Students must be taught the social skills needed for collaboration, and be motivated to use them.

—DAVID AND ROGER JOHNSON

TRIBES LEARNING COMMUNITY

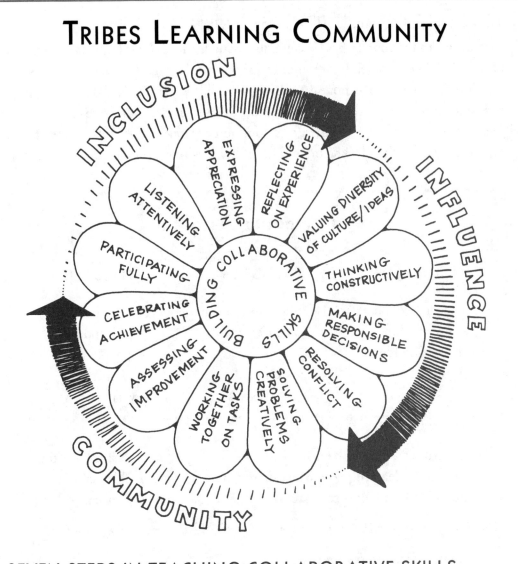

SEVEN STEPS IN TEACHING COLLABORATIVE SKILLS

1. Engage students in identifying the need for the skill (using discussion, role-play, story, or situation).

2. Teach the skill (using the Looks/Sounds/Feels-Like structure or other strategy).

3. Practice the skill regularly, and have students give feedback on how well it was used.

4. Transfer the responsibility to the tribes to remind each other to use the skill.

5. Ask reflection questions about the use of the skill in tribes, the class, the playground, at home, etc.

6. Point out times when you notice people using the skill well.

7. Notice and celebrate when the skill is "owned" as a natural behavior in the classroom or school.

TEACHING COMMUNITY AGREEMENTS

In addition to the four Tribes agreements, many faculties (and families) choose a universal collaborative skill each month for the whole school to work on. These are human values such as honesty, self-responsibility, truth, unselfishness, kindness, and justice. A good way to teach these (as well as the four Tribes agreements) is to call students together in a community circle. Pre-sketch or sketch the following grid on the blackboard and have the class fill in the specific examples:

Agreement: Listening		
LOOKS LIKE	**SOUNDS LIKE**	**FEELS LIKE**
heads together	talking one at a time	great
eyes looking	encouragement	I'm important
people nodding	good idea	people care
leaning forward	uh-huh	I'm smart
smiling	yes!	we're friends

1. Invite discussion on the need for the skill or agreement. Remember the cooperative learning way: Meet them where they are. Don't lecture or talk at them. Invite students to share what they already know and then add to it.

2. Ask people to call out words for the grid: *"What does listening look like?"*

3. Then: *"What does it sound like?"*

4. And: *"What does it feel like?"*

The four agreements should be posted in a prominent place and reviewed whenever the community circle or tribes meet. When learning the Tribes agreements, affirm the behaviors whenever you see them happening, and in time ask students to do the same.

> Example: *"I can tell the Zoomer tribe is listening well to each other... people are talking one at a time and their heads are together."*

Now and then you may inadvertently overlook one of the agreements yourself. Do encourage the class to bring this to your attention. Accept such reminders graciously and without defensiveness. Kids can be great agreement and social skills reinforcers. You can count on them to monitor and help sustain the Tribes learning environment for the class.

ASKING REFLECTION QUESTIONS

The activity alone is not enough! This phrase is the key to moving beyond just using small-group strategies and expecting them to make a difference in student learning. Cooperative learning strategies need to be followed with reflection (or process) questions so that students can focus on the interaction or learning that has happened. Research studies as well as the experience of hundreds of teachers verify that the time taken to ask reflection questions can double the retention of the facts and concepts learned in an academic lesson.[1] See Chapter 14 for an article on the exciting results of a cooperative learning study on the impact of "group processing," or reflection.

In Tribes TLC® we prefer to use the word "reflection" rather than "process" in order to

+ Distinguish the after-strategy questions from the Tribes group development process

+ Teach and emphasize that reflection is a skill critical to doing well in a complex world of information and relationships.

Reflection questions can double the retention of the facts and concepts learned in an academic lesson.

You'll find examples of each type in the Learning Strategies section of this book.

Three Types of Reflection Questions

CONTENT/THINKING QUESTIONS are focused on the content of the lesson, and on the thinking skills that were used in order to work with the content. The content consists of facts, concepts, and information.

COLLABORATIVE/SOCIAL QUESTIONS focus on the interaction that happens within a tribe or learning group and on the collaborative skills that were used.

PERSONAL LEARNING QUESTIONS focus on what the individual has learned or felt.

Here are examples from two classes using the Tribes process. The first is a kindergarten and the second is a class of high school seniors.

The activity alone is not enough!

BOB HOLLOWAY'S KINDERGARTEN CLASS

The kindergarten tribes have been learning about cooperation by having each tribe prepare a fruit salad together.

1. **CONTENT:** *"Which fruits did your tribe put into your salad? Tell me what they were."*

THINKING: *"What did you have to do to get the different fruits ready for the salad?"*

2. COLLABORATIVE: *"What did your tribe do when some people started to eat the cherries instead of putting them into your tribe's salad?"*

3. PERSONAL: *"What did you learn?" "Why did you like doing this?"*

JILL LANGLEY'S SENIOR LITERATURE CLASS

The class has been reading a Dostoevsky short story, "A Gentle Creature."

1. CONTENT: *"Why did the shopkeeper and the woman begin to quarrel?"*

   THINKING: *"What steps did your group take to analyze the main theme?"*

2. COLLABORATIVE: *"Looking back at how your group worked together, what did various people do to help the group complete the task?"*

3. PERSONAL: *"What emotions did you feel?" "How do you feel about your participation in your group?"*

You need not ask all three types of reflection questions after a strategy, but do use at least two of the different types. Base your choice on what you believe will make the content memorable and the learning experience meaningful for the majority of students in the class.

Time out for reflection develops the capacity of introspection...to learn from experience and understand the working dynamics of groups and systems. It supports this definition of human development: to discover, sustain, and alter "situations"—to move into ever-widening realms of knowledge and experience.

The questions suggested for each strategy in this book may not be the best ones to ask your own class. There simply are no sure-fire questions that are appropriate for all cultural populations and age levels. Your own intuition, creativity, and judgment are needed to draw out the most important learning from the group strategies that you use.

ENCOURAGING APPRECIATION

As pointed out earlier in this chapter, in our discussion of Tribes agreements, much of the power of the Tribes process comes from the practice of giving students opportunities to express appreciation to each other after working together. To be able to hear one's peers acknowledge special qualities, skills, and contributions to the group is much more meaningful to most students than periodic affirmation from a teacher.

People also need to be encouraged to appreciate themselves, to be proud of a job well done or a special contribution. It's OK to brag! Some strategies that you might try are

Boasters   *I'm Proud*   *Personal Journal*

To believe in oneself is to have high self-regard...to feel empowered, competent, and confident of doing well in tomorrow's world. It is an essential component of resiliency.

MANAGING DISRUPTIVE BEHAVIOR

Teachers have learned that there are several good ways to manage energetic people who disrupt the community's time together.

1. Before students come to the community circle, give them a topic to think, write or draw about at their desks.

2. If any students become extremely disruptive, call out "Freeze" and ask everyone to "run the movie backward, in your heads, and recall what was happening." Keep the descriptions as objective as possible by not using names. An alternative is to send people to their desks and have them write or draw what happened in the group. After discussing the disruptive behaviors, you can:

    ✦ Ask the class to suggest one thing that they could work on the next time that they meet in a community circle

    ✦ Have each person jot down in their journals or share with their tribe one thing that they will do to improve circle time.

3. Use an I-Message: *"I feel sad when people are so noisy that we can't hear the person who is speaking."*

4. Give students time out: *"Juan and Leslie, I would like you to go to your desks and return to the circle just as soon as you can commit to listening to other people and taking your turn to talk."*

5. The key to a successful community circle is to use more structure and less time if people are having difficulty. As students learn to respect the Tribes agreements and manage their own behavior, lessen the structure and increase the time.

Keep in mind that it's all about caring support, encouraging participation, and communicating positive expectations. Trust the process— It works!

USING TEMPORARY SMALL GROUPS TO BUILD COMMUNITY

If you look at the Tribes Trail Map again, you will notice that pairs, triads, and temporary groups are also used to build inclusion in the community before people become members in long-term tribes.

While your students are working together in these "trial tribes" you can observe how people get along with others. This serves as valuable information when you are ready to move students into long-term tribes.

The major disadvantage of the large community circle format is that each student must spend more time listening than talking, which leads to restlessness.

BUILDING COMMUNITY CREATIVELY

Please do not feel limited to the strategies and energizers in this book in order to develop a sense of community among all your students. Use your teacher ingenuity to create whatever will best reach your students.

An abundance of good inclusion activities exists in other books, many of which are listed in Chapter 14. The criteria for a good community building activity are:

+ It has a win-win rather than a win-lose outcome—cooperation rather than competition

+ It provides inclusion for everyone—all can participate

+ It draws upon and highlights the contributions that people make in the course of the activity

+ It is fun!

A SAFE PLACE

By Gilbert Rees[2]

*I*n a safe place
I am wanted.
Me, all the edges
And the angles
And the hidden
parts that are me.

And no one says,
"You just won't do.
You'll never be
The things I want
You never will."
No one says that
In a safe place.

And no one comes
With sudden anger
Or a "What am I
going to do with you?"
Look…in hopeless eyes,
Not in a safe place.

For there
If I reach my hand out only a little
If I gently touch someone,
Then someone reaches back
As gently,
As softly.

And on one breaks
apart our reaching
And no one tears
apart our silence
In the safe place—
We make together.

8

Building Tribes

8 Building Tribes

People are fidgety in the community circle this morning. Renata Berger smiles to herself, knowing that the excitement centers on one question in the mind of each 3rd grader: Who's in my tribe? No use waiting. The big day is here. "Are we ready to get into tribes?" she says. "Yes!"..."Sure!"..."Can we do it now?"..."How do we know who's with us, Mrs. Berger?"

Renata explains that she has hidden the pieces of six puzzles around the classroom and that each piece has someone's name on it. "Find your own puzzle piece and then find the four or five other people whose pieces fit together with yours to make a complete puzzle." Twenty-seven wide-eyed, giggling kids scurry around the room. Within five minutes six groups are huddled around completed puzzles. They're excited to belong to a group, ready to be together in the fine Tribes tradition.

Yes, after building community inclusion and getting your students familiar with the agreements of the Tribes process, the time has come for students to become members of long-term learning groups—tribes. The material in this chapter will enable you to do just that. You will learn how to

+ Determine when your class is ready for tribes

+ Introduce your class to the Tribes concept

+ Balance members in tribes sociometrically

+ Build tribal inclusion

+ Lead strategies in tribes

+ Teach I-Messages

+ Facilitate the transfer of responsibility to the student groups

+ Resolve group issues and conflicts that commonly occur.

IS YOUR CLASS READY FOR TRIBES?

After several weeks of community strategies, you may start asking yourself in the wee hours of the night whether the time has come to take the next step. Your class is probably ready to be in tribes when you can say "Yes" to the following questions:

Readiness for Tribes

1. Do students understand and respect the agreements?

2. Do they know one another's names?

3. Can you identify the leaders, the less popular students, the particular friendships, the possible behavior problems?

4. Have the students had many successful experiences in various trial tribes, or practice groups?

5. Do you feel ready? (Of course you do, after getting this far!)

INTRODUCING THE CONCEPT

One day when you are feeling good and things are going smoothly, take a few minutes to talk about everyone's experience of being together, not only in the large community circle but in many small groups. Tell your students that the class is ready to become members of long-term learning groups. Of course, they will all begin to wonder who will be in their tribe. State that each person will write the names of several people they would like to have in their group, and assure them that one or more of those named will be in their tribe. Explain that the purpose of being in an ongoing group is to help one another learn important skills and curricula together.

You may want to spend some time talking about what it is like to be a member of a group, club, family, or team; perhaps have your students discuss the purpose of various social systems:

> *"Why do you think people need to learn how to work together?"*
> *"Why do people join different groups?"*
> *"Have you ever been in a club or group with a few people who became very special to you?"*

You don't need to "sell" the concept. It is your decision as their teacher to use cooperative learning groups this year. Tell your students what they can expect, and answer their questions. Your attentive listening skills will let them know you are hearing their concerns. Some may feel excitement at this point, others apprehension about a new way of learning together. Do what you can to help them become invested in the idea of belonging to a learning group and working together rather than on their own.

SOCIOMETRY MADE EASY—HOW TO BUILD TRIBES

The guidelines for assigning people to tribes are important:

1. Assign an age-appropriate number of people to each tribe as follows—

Preschools use groups of three
Kindergarten: groups of three and four
Elementary and middle school or junior high: groups of four and five
High school and adult classes: groups of five and six

2. Balance the number of boys and girls in each learning group.

3. Distribute leaders among all the tribes.

4. Distribute the less popular (shy, less social, disruptive, etc.) among all groups.

5. Be absolutely certain that each person has at least one chosen friend in his or her tribe.

Here is a step-by-step process that you can use to achieve a sociometric balance in your classroom groups, without using any cumbersome instruments. Give yourself enough time to do this.

Seven Friends

1. Give each person a 5 x 8-inch index card. Have people print their names in the center of the card.

2. Ask each person to print the names of seven other people they would like to have in a tribe. Ask for at least 3 boys and 3 girls. (Kindergarten and 1st grade children will need help.)

3. Collect all the cards. Remind your students that they will each be in a tribe with at least one identified friend, but not with all of those listed.

4. Assuming that you will have six tribes, select the cards belonging to six leader types, those who have been named the most by others and who also enjoy learning. Spread these cards out on a table.

5. Select the cards of six students who exhibit quiet or less positive behavior. Place one of their cards next to each of the leader's cards.

6. Add the remaining cards to each group, making sure that each card has a name requested by someone in the group.

7. Make any adjustments necessary to achieve a balance of boys and girls.

8. Check once more to be sure that each card is still matched with a friend.

9. Congratulations! You have just formed your tribes!

The "Seven Friends" method of building tribes enables you to match or separate students to achieve the best mix of skills, cultures, and relationships. It has the added advantage of allowing your students some influence in determining who will be in their tribe.

FORMING TRIBES

Once you have determined the composition of the tribes, set a date when everyone will move into the groups. Advance notice builds great anticipation. When "T Day" arrives, choose an exciting way for people to discover who is in their tribe. Here are the directions for the strategy used by the teacher in the beginning of this chapter:

People Puzzles

1. Begin with sheets of poster board, one for each tribe.

2. Sketch a design on each sheet so that you can cut as many puzzle pieces as the number of students you want in a particular tribe.

3. Print a student's name on each piece. Make sure that all the members of a tribe are included in the same People Puzzle.

4. Hide the pieces around the classroom before school, or during lunch or recess.

5. Tell the class to look for their own names and to find people with matching pieces.

When everyone has found their tribe, assign the groups to different areas of the classroom. Desks and chairs need to be rearranged so that tribe members face one another. Tables may be used for high school and adult groups, and small rugs are great for preschool "tot tribes."

Once the tribes have settled down, ask reflection questions. Examples:

PERSONAL: *What did you feel when you were trying to find other tribe members?*

CONTENT/THINKING: *What made this strategy a good way to find your tribe?*

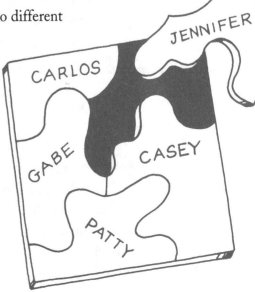

You can, of course, invent other ways to form tribes. "Barnyard Babble," in Chapter 13, has become quite popular even with adult groups. It provides a hilarious experience worth videotaping when teacher groups are doing it!

After the tribes have done some initial inclusion strategies, tell the class that people will remain in these groups for at least one month. Then the whole class will evaluate how their tribes are working and whether any changes need to be made. This defuses the inevitable remark, "I wanted to have someone else in my tribe!" Once we did a survey to learn how many new Tribes teachers actually had to alter the membership of the tribes. Those who had students stay in the same tribe for at least three weeks never felt the need to make any membership changes. The secret is that after that much time, the inclusion strategies, group process, and positive agreements have created a sense of belonging, caring, and trust. People have forgotten about wanting a particular friend—they have made several new close friends whom they like and do not want to leave.

BUILDING TRIBAL INCLUSION

Remember that Tribes Trail Map and discussion back in Chapter 6? Well, here is where your understanding of it really moves into application. Although you did many inclusion strategies with the whole class to build community before forming tribes, the need for inclusion continues. Each time a new group forms, people sense the same "stranger anxiety." If this issue is not addressed, it limits the ability of a group to work well together. Inclusion must happen all over again with the new tribes.

As a facilitator of this group process, you need to select a series of inclusion strategies that will help people present who they are, what they do well, and what their expectations, hopes, and needs might be. Taking the time to do this during the first days in tribes makes all the difference in managing the class and integrating other cooperative learning methods. People are not ready to work together on curricula unless inclusion and trust have been developed within their learning groups. Disruptive behavior in classrooms happens whenever students do not feel included and recognized. If you remember the discussion in Chapter 6, you'll recall that

"A way to become included is to grab influence."

That's what plagues teachers throughout the day and school year. Anti-social behavior gains attention, meaning someone notices "me" and cares. It is a way to feel included and important in the midst of many others. The Tribes process decreases behavior problems in schools simply because everyone is included.

On the day before the new tribes are to be announced, invite people to bring something special from home to share at the first meeting of their new tribe. The item should have special meaning, perhaps an award, a gift, or something they have made. Sharing such treasures on the first day helps each person to talk about himself or herself and it develops positive energy in the group.

STRATEGIES THAT BUILD INCLUSION

Though we have said it before and will say it again, it is important that you select inclusion strategies geared to the interests, age level, and culture of your particular class. Do read the preface to Chapter 13 Strategies section before leaping into using them.

Hopefully, you are involved in an in-service training conducted by one of CenterSource Systems' qualified Tribes TLC® District Trainers. If so, you will experience many good initial strategies that can be easily adapted to your class. Some of the favorites are

Name Game   Wishful Thinking
Spider Web   I'm Proud Circle
J.O.Y.   What's Your Bag
Kitchen Kaper   Campaign Manager
Interview Circle

One teacher advises, "You need to be as flexible and creative as you are with all other curricula!"

TRANSFERRING RESPONSIBILITY

One of the major objectives of tribes is to call forth positive leadership qualities and self-responsibility in children. This means that an intentional transfer of control needs to be made from the teacher to the tribe, and from the tribe to its members. As a sensitive teacher you can look for opportunities to have the tribes increase their capacity to function independently. Here are some of the ways in which responsibility can be transferred:

✦ Intervene only as necessary while the tribes are working together

✦ Encourage members to remind one another about the agreements

✦ When students ask you a question, refrain from answering immediately; turn it back to the class or tribe, asking "Who can help to clarify the instructions?" "What ideas do other people have?"

✦ Ask tribe members to assume helpful tasks and roles

✦ Have tribes keep attendance, make contact with people who are absent, and help returning members to catch up with the tribe and class

✦ Have the class make a list of classroom maintenance tasks, and have the tribes assume different ones for a period of time

✦ Have the tribes plan parties, field trips, parent involvement, and other class activities

✦ Ask tribes for suggestions to improve lesson plans, academic projects, and the learning environment

✦ Have them give feedback to you as the teacher.

The process of transferring responsibility to students increases participation—and, if you recall, participation, caring, and high expectations contribute to the development of resiliency.

Here's my bird's eye view.

The First Days of Using Tribes

1. Commit to begin and end each day with a community circle.

2. Ask students to review the class agreements.

3. Use an inclusion strategy for the whole community. Ask reflection questions. Give an overview of the day's schedule, work, and any announcements.

4. Have people move to their customary tribe's areas.

5. Explain the activity or task that the tribes will be working on and what skills and content people will be learning.

6. Give the directions one step at a time, using as few words as possible. Write the steps on the chalk board of there are several.

7. If clarification is needed on instructions, ask that the group confer among themselves before asking you.

8. State how much time there will be to complete the task or strategy. Ask each tribe to make sure that every member participates. If using group roles (to be discussed in Chapter 10), clarify the roles.

9. While the tribes are working together, observe their progress. Intervene only if absolutely necessary.

10. Signal when time is up, and have each tribe report progress by responding to appropriate reflection questions. Reflection questions can be handled either in community circle on in tribes.

11. Invite statements of appreciation.

OBSERVING THE PROCESS

Admittedly, it can feel strange to be in the background while your tribes tackle a challenging, engrossing task or strategy. This, however, is not a time to sit idly by, or to catch up on correcting those arithmetic papers! During these periods when your busy tribes cease to need you, you become the process observer, looking for the new skills and behaviors to be affirmed and noticing the dynamics within the tribes. On the next page is a list of some of the dynamics that you can observe while your tribes are working together.

FACILITATING THE PROCESS

What happens when you observe breakdowns in the process? Let's use an example. You have given your 7th grade tribes the strategy "Brainstorming," so that they will learn the process and use it later in a history lesson. One recorder in each tribe is furiously attempting to write down all the ideas being voiced by tribe members. While observing the behaviors in each tribe, you notice that Tanya, one of the recorders, is really having a hard time getting all the information down on paper. People are saying things like, "Hey, you left out my idea!" "Slow poke!" Your impulse is to stride over to the group and take charge. Instead, you take a deep breath and reflect on all that is going on. You observe that only two students, Heidi and Jamal, are really "into" the strategy. They're leaning forward and putting forth many ideas. The other tribe members are sitting back rather apathetically, waiting for the time to run out.

What are your alternatives, other than intervening directly?

You could do nothing, in which case the situation would either

1. Stay the same.

2. Get better—someone might remind others of the agreements, or volunteer to help Tanya.

3. Get worse—an argument might erupt.

What do you see, hear and feel right now?

A better alternative is to stop the action anytime things seem strained or get a bit crazy. Simply call out, "Freeze," "Time out," or "Stop the action!" Wait patiently until order and silence fill the room. Then simply ask "What's happening?" Ask everyone to *look and listen* back to what was going on in the classroom or tribes. With young children, teachers can ask, *"If you had been flies on the ceiling during the last few minutes and looked down, what would you have seen and heard?"* Or suggest that they *"run the movie backward"* in their heads, and describe what people were doing. You may want to list some reflection questions on the board, and give people thinking time. The first question for each person to answer should be *"I saw myself..."* (Describe your own behavior, not that of others.) *"I felt..."* (Describe your own feelings during the interaction.) Then ask for descriptions of specific sounds

Process Observation Checklist

1. **HOW ARE PEOPLE SITTING?**

   ✦ Are they in a neat circle, or are some people sitting back?

   ✦ Are they leaning forward attentively, or are they slouching, sprawling, or lying back?

2. **HOW ARE PEOPLE PARTICIPATING?**

   ✦ Are a few doing all the talking or work? Is participation balanced?

   ✦ Are people lively and animated, or lethargic and tentative?

   ✦ Is everyone focused on what is happening, or are side conversations taking place?

   ✦ Are people passing?

3. **HOW ARE PEOPLE TAKING CARE OF ONE ANOTHER?**

   ✦ Are they listening to one another?

   ✦ Are put-downs happening? (If so, are they being confronted by group members?)

   ✦ Are disagreements being resolved in satisfying (win-win) ways?

   ✦ Are kindness and cooperation being demonstrated?

   ✦ Is appreciation being expressed?

   ✦ Is the group drawing in the quieter people?

4. **HOW ARE PEOPLE FEELING AND BEHAVING?**

   ✦ Are they smiling and/or laughing?

   ✦ Is your intuitive response one of warmth and relaxation, or anxiety and tension?

5. **ARE THEY WORKING WELL ON TASK OR CURRICULA?**

   ✦ Who has assumed leadership?

   ✦ Are the slower learners included?

   ✦ Do they seem mindful of the goal to complete the task on time?

6. **WHAT IS HAPPENING FOR YOU?**

7. **OTHER**

and actions. Following the Time Out Reflection Cycle below, help the class decide what everyone can do to improve things.

Time Out Reflection Cycle

+ Stop the action—ask *"What's happening?"*

+ Give everyone time to reflect—don't start diagnosing the situation yourself. Wait until people begin to speak up.

+ Ask for descriptions of specific sounds and actions.

+ Ask how people felt and how the behavior or situation affects the class as a whole.

+ Invite or brainstorm ideas to change the situation.

+ Have everyone decide what to do to improve things.

DECIDE   STOP   LOOK

DESCRIBE   LISTEN

The repeated practice of reflecting on group and community interaction helps people to become aware of the impact of their behavior on others and the dynamics of groups. Reflection is emphasized in Tribes TLC® because it is essential for learning and development.

If you do not choose to take time out, be sure to have everyone reflect on the situation after the strategy or task is completed. You exclaim, "Why make all the tribes go through this when only one tribe had the problem?" Good question! In this case, the time out might accomplish the following:

+ Tanya's tribe, in addition to exploring their own behaviors, would learn from the other tribes how they dealt with the same or similar issues

+ The other tribes would benefit from discussing the same questions and reflecting on their own interaction

+ In listening to the responses of Tanya's tribe, you would have additional data to use in deciding what specific work may need to happen with this tribe alone.

Of course, if Tanya's tribe does not report on the behavior that you observed, you should comment on it. Not to do so would be interpreted as an indication that you were not paying attention, or that you did not think it was important.

I'm a meta-cognitive symbol! Wow!

KEEPING YOUR PURPOSE AND ROLE IN MIND

The Tribes process, the positive environment, agreements, and all of the cooperative learning strategies have but one overall purpose:

to assure the healthy development of every child in the school community so that each has the knowledge, skills, and resilient strengths to be successful in a world of rapid change.

The Tribes strategies are not time fillers for rainy days in the classroom, but are meaningful experiences to teach children how to reflect upon and learn to manage their own lives.

This interactive approach to human development and learning makes the "here and now" of each day a laboratory. Through group interaction, this generation of children will be able to move from a singular focus on "me" to "we"—and to a concern for our community, our nation, and the future of our world.

Your role is to make the cooperative learning process easy, exciting, and effective. You are the caretaker of the positive learning environment. The Tribes cooperative learning facilitator is more than a teacher. Now the profession can call forth the best within each and every child. Teachers need a new title—something like "learning and human development facilitators." Do send us your ideas on this!

One of the most important collaborative skills for today's students and teachers to learn is how to manage conflict—a dynamic that inevitably arises within any group of people working, playing, or living together. Denial or avoidance of a conflict ultimately undermines relationships, the group environment, and its ability to work well together. There's a saying, "There is no way around—only a way through."

Conflict is a natural part of life because as individuals we differ in what we want, need, and think. Conflicts occur over these differences. But conflict itself isn't the problem—*it's how we deal with it*. Most people have not learned how to manage conflict constructively. The adults in a child's world must learn to resolve conflict before they can teach the process to children.

Within each conflict there is an opportunity to gain new knowledge. If our intent is to learn, we will seek to understand why the conflict happened. In the process, each person discovers more about his or her own perceptions and unspoken assumptions, as well as those of other people. As a result, relationships will be more satisfying.

The capacity of teachers and students to work well together in cooperative learning groups is dependent upon how well they learn to solve problems and manage conflict. When a group has the commitment and skill to resolve all conflicts, individuals feel free to contribute ideas, explore one another's assumptions, and raise questions. This is essential in the process of becoming a learning community.[1]

Resolving conflict needs to begin with the assumption that a "win-win" solution is possible. Strong feelings often make defining the problem difficult, and what appears to be the problem is identified and agreed upon, it becomes possible for people who have been in opposition to work out a solution that will be fair to both of them. For further discussion, turn to page 405 in the Resources section of this book where you will find the article, "Preventing Conflict through Dialogues of Discovery" by Ron Patrick.

Gail Whang of Oakland Unified School District recalls how learning the Tribes process and a conflict resolution process affected their school staff at Hawthorne Elementary.

Conflict resolution brought people out of their classrooms and together. Tribes built on that power. Not only were we involved together in a schoolwide program, but because of the nature of both trainings, it brought the staff closer. We got beyond griping about students in the lunchroom and began talking to each other about what we valued and who we are. We began to change the culture of our school.

TEACHING I-MESSAGES

An I-Message is a statement of the speaker's feelings in response to the behavior of others. Unlike a You-Message, an I-Message does not convey judgment, nor is it a put-down. Notice the difference between the following examples:

YOU-MESSAGE: *"Kim, you dummy, you ruined my chance to be the pitcher. You make me angry."*

I-MESSAGE: *"Kim, I feel angry whenever a catcher isn't paying attention."*

In the first example, Kim was rudely put down and blamed for the situation. In the second example, the speaker took responsibility for his feelings, stated them in strong terms...but did not put the blame on Kim. He defined the behavior that he perceived.

I-Messages	You-Messages
✦ State and own the speaker's feelings	✦ Hold another person responsible for the speaker's feelings
✦ Describe the perceived behavior or situation; not a personal judgment	✦ Blame others; judge and put people down

A Conflict Resolution Curriculum

The outstanding school curriculum *Conflict Resolution*, developed and published by the Community Board Program of San Francisco, recommends a set of "building blocks" for the effective resolution of conflict:[3]

✦ Awareness of conflict in our won lives and how we respond to it
✦ Appreciation for the differences between people
✦ Understanding of important feelings
✦ The ability to talk clearly to another person about a conflict
✦ The ability to listen to a person with whom we have a conflict

A specific sequence of steps is suggested for use whenever tow students become involved in a conflict:

STEP 1: Both students agree to the ground rules
"I agree not to interrupt, not to call a name, and I agree to work to solve the conflict."

STEP 2: One person tells his/her side of the story using I-Messages, saying how s/he feels about what happened, and what s/he wants. The other person listens attentively and restates the problem.

STEP 3: The second person restates what the problem is for the first person. Suggestion" begin with *"So, the problem for you is…"*

STEP 4: Steps 2 and 3 are repeated, with the 2nd student speaking.

STEP 5: Both people suggest possible solutions.

STEP 6: Both work to agree on a resolution that is:
   ✦ specific
   ✦ balanced—both people will be responsible for making it work
   ✦ realistic—and will solve the problem

Many Tribes schools not only use the Community Board Program within their elementary and secondary classrooms, but also train groups of students in the schools to be Conflict Managers who are available on the playground, and in classrooms, halls, and neighborhoods to help students resolve differences peaceably.

> *To create a classroom where students feel safe enough to challenge each other—and us—is to give them an enormous gift.*[2]
>
> —ALFIE KOHN

The purpose of an I-Message is to communicate feelings in such a way that the other person is not forced to defend herself or avoid the situation. The impact of the You-Message blames, shames, or intimidates the other person. It causes the other person to become resistant. The recipient of a You-Message hears the message as "you are bad or wrong," and is less likely to consider resolution of the difficulty. Worst of all, You-Messages escalate conflict.

You-Messages can also masquerade as I-Messages: *"I feel that you are always a nuisance"* is a disguised You-Message because

1. No feelings are stated or owned, even though the speaker says "I feel" (he really means "I think" or "I believe").

2. The phrase *"You are always a nuisance"* is a judgment, implying that the person is bad or incapable of being different.

In teaching people how to use I-Messages, it is helpful to write this formula on the board:

I feel_____(name the feeling)
when_____(describe the situation or behavior).

Give examples:
"I feel confused when people shout at me."
"I feel sad when I hear someone has hurt an animal."
"I feel scared when anyone threatens me."

I-Messages are also a good way to communicate positive feelings:
"I feel happy when I receive a compliment."
"I feel excited when we meet in tribes."
"I feel great when everyone participates."

The I-Message is a tricky concept to master, even though it seems quite simple at first. This is another instance in which you need to be an appropriate role model. It may take some time, but with daily practice your students will begin to use them.

KNOWING WHEN TO TAKE CHARGE—YOUR CRITERIA

Yes, there are those crisis times when I-Messages just won't work—for instance, when you encounter one child hurting another.

"Stop that this instant!" is much more appropriate for the moment than *"I feel unhappy when you hit Aaron."*

Handling antisocial or inappropriate behavior depends upon thinking through in advance what your own criteria will be:

✦ When to use additional inclusion activities

✦ When to encourage students to use I-Messages with one another

✦ When to use an I-Message yourself

✦ When to use group problem solving (see the next chapter)

✦ When to be directive and take charge.

RESOLVING GROUP ISSUES

The social climate in your classroom and your success with the Tribes process will be greatly influenced by the way in which conflicts and angry feelings are routinely expressed and resolved. As a Tribes teacher, your willingness to acknowledge, discuss, and resolve group issues in a caring, process-based manner will result in growth and learning for you and your students. All groups of people living, playing, or working together experience many predictable interpersonal issues. The chart on the following page gives an overview of typical questions that come up in a group's development, and it gives suggestions on how to resolve many situations.

As you begin to use the Tribes process you may hear statements that indicate group issues:

✦ "I pass!"

✦ "I don't like my tribe."

✦ "What about the new kid?"

✦ "Hey, that's a put-down!"

✦ "Let's form new tribes."

1. "I PASS!"

Early in the tribe-building process, some people may be passing all the time, and others may not be participating. This type of behavior is usually an indication that some people feel unsafe with their groups. Suggestions:

✦ Discuss the reasons why some people are not participating, and then have the small groups discuss what to do.

✦ Have people work in pairs. Match a shy person with a more confident, outgoing one.

✦ Make sure that you are using appropriate inclusion strategies. (Try "Interview Circle" in tribes.)

TRIBES ISSUE CHART

ISSUES	QUESTIONS/FEELINGS	YOU, THE FACILITATOR, NEED TO
INCLUSION Presentation of Self	*"Will I like this group?"* *"How will they get to know me?"*	Be directive and provide structure; use many inclusion activities that permit each person to share who they are; what feelings, skills, qualities, and resources they have.
	"I feel nervous with these new people." *"Will they listen to me?"* *"Will they put me down?"*	Have people work in pairs and triads; it feel less threatening. Teach listening skills. Make sure that people respect the Tribes agreements, especially "No put-downs."
Expectations and Needs	*"Will we finish by 3 o'clock?"* *"May we work outside today?"* *"Can you help me with a problem?"*	Provide opportunities for each member to state wants, needs, and expectations for the time the group is together.
Acknowledgments	*"Will they like me?"* *"Do I dare tell someone I think she is a nice person?"*	Be a good role model by giving and receiving appreciation easily. Provide opportunities for people to exchange statements of appreciation and good feelings.
	"Does anyone else feel the way I feel?"	Ask reflection questions that encourage people to share thoughts and feelings about coming together as a group.
INFLUENCE Me vs. the Group	*"Will my opinions be respected?"*	Provide activities that help people share individual differences and cultural strengths.
Goals	*"What are we to accomplish together?"*	Introduce techniques that elicit input from each member in defining group goals. Model and encourage acceptance of all ideas before choosing group goals.
Decision Making	*"How can we reach agreement?"*	Introduce techniques for consensus decision making.
Conflict	*"How can we work this out?"*	Introduce conflict resolution techniques, (active listening, I-Messages, role reversal). Assist group members in reaching win-win solution. Teach collaborative skills.
Leadership & Authority	*"Do we need a leader?"*	Encourage rotation of roles. Urge natural leaders to draw out more passive members.
	"I resent it when someone tries to tell us what to do."	Ask reflection questions that help members discuss and resolve leadership problems. Use conflict resolution techniques as needed.
COMMUNITY Creativity	*"I feel good about my abilities."*	Recognize individuals for unique achievements and self-direction; encourage group members to do so with one another.
Cooperation	*"Our group really works well together."*	Assign group tasks that require innovation, cooperation, and creativity.
Achievement	*"We did a great job!"*	Assign projects: All group members receive the same grade or reward.
	"What shall we tackle next?"	Use groups for peer teaching, problem solving, planning, and fun! Be alert for inclusion/influence issues; support groups in resolving them.
Celebration	*"I really like our tribe and community."*	Take the time to celebrate—for whatever big or small reason!

✦ Spend some time with the habitual passer. Learn his special interests and talents; encourage him to share them with the tribe.

✦ Assign the passer a role or task in the tribe.

✦ Make sure that the agreements are being honored so that the environment is safe.

2. "I DON'T LIKE MY TRIBE."

A person who feels uncomfortable in his group may say things like:

"I don't like the people in my tribe."

"I get bored in my tribe."

"People in my tribe are dumb."

"I want to be in Sarah's tribe."

Rather than trying to talk a student out of a complaint, use your listening skills to find out what is really going on. Suggestions:

✦ Enlist the help of the tribe to give the person more inclusion.

✦ Gear some activities to her learning style and interests.

✦ Ask the person to "hang in" with the tribe for two or three weeks; by this time things usually work themselves out.

✦ In some extreme cases, it may be advisable to transfer a student to another tribe, or to provide her with something to do alone while tribes are meeting. These are last-resort measures, only to be considered if all else fails.

3. "WHAT ABOUT THE NEW KID?"

When a new person enters your class after tribes have been formed, it is important to give her a special welcome.

A new girl named Robin shows up at school on Monday. She is given a short tour of the school; then she is introduced to her new teacher and classmates. The teacher may enlist the help of one or two students to explain to the newcomer what tribes are all about. Later in the morning, Robin experiences the Tribes Adoption Ceremony.

During this activity, build inclusion with Robin by interviewing her, letting her know a bit about tribes and that it will be her choice as to which tribe she'll join. The choice may be limited to those tribes having fewer people. If you prefer to assign the newcomer to a tribe, you can still ask your tribes to come up with creative ideas for helping the person feel welcome and included. Hundreds of parents have expressed their great appreciation to tribes schools that use this ceremony. In a very transient society, it is wonderful to have your child come home the first day and say, *"I belong to a group already, and the kids were real nice to me!"*

Adoption Ceremony

1. Introduce Robin and then ask the class how many people have ever moved to a new school, like Robin is doing.

2. In tribes, ask people to share their newcomer experiences. Transfer the time for sharing; five minutes is enough. Meanwhile, visit with Robin.

3. Then ask the question, "What ideas does your tribe have to help Robin feel welcome and included in our class?"

4. Ask each tribe to make Brainstorm lists of some positive, caring things its members could do. Allow five to ten minutes.

5. Have the tribes take turns reading their lists to Robin.

6. After all the tribes have done so, ask Robin to choose which tribe she would like to join.

---

4. "HEY, THAT'S A PUT-DOWN!"

If you find that in spite of your most heroic efforts, people are still using many put-down statements, you may need to take some remedial action. Suggestions:

+ Have each student write on a card something someone said to them that really hurt. Put all cards in the center and have each draw one and read it without comment. Then discuss how it would feel to receive them.

+ Initiate an "anti-put-down" campaign.

+ Challenge the put-down experts to create statements of appreciation that they would like to receive.

+ Provide lots of opportunities for statements of appreciation. Strategies like "Campaign Manager" and self-esteem cards are especially useful. With young children (K-3), you can use the "Warm Fuzzy" story and the related activity.

+ Be a good role model, both in giving and accepting statements of appreciation. Just make sure you are honest at all times—kids can spot a "plastic fuzzy" a block away!

They drew a circle that shut me out,

Heretic, rebel, a thing to flout,

But love and I had to wit to win,

We drew a circle that took them in.

—EDWIN MARKHAM

5. **"LET'S FORM NEW TRIBES!"**

If your students begin agitating to change tribes, it is probably an indication that you need to do more full-group community inclusion and intergroup strategies. Suggestions:

✦ Remind your students that they will remain in the same tribes for at least three to four weeks before any changes are made.

✦ Combine two tribes for a strategy like "Interview Circle."

Membership in tribes needs to remain as constant as possible. The long-term membership factor develops cooperation and peer support for individual achievement.

There really is no way to anticipate and address all of the issues that may arise as you initiate cooperative learning groups in your classroom. The next chapter, "Calling Forth Power and Self-Worth," presents ways to handle issues of influence and problem solving. Do get together with other teachers who are using the Tribes process, so that you can share ideas, generate your own appropriate strategies, and enjoy ongoing membership in supportive tribes of your own. Chapter 12 contains ideas for staff support. After all—teachers are students too and, just like students, love school when in a tribe.

Burnt out

So what if he can't read
Teach him how to love
Himself? Me? Others?
Lost in a stack of paper
That good guy note he needed

> *I needed the look in the eyes*
> *When you finally dig it out*
> *The eyes say For me? From you?*
> *A warm moment on a cold day*
> *It passes math time*
> *You forget—they remember.*
>
> —JOE RHODES, A TEACHER

9

Calling Forth Power
and Self-Worth

9 Calling Forth Power and Self-Worth

The meaning of the high cyclone fence around the inner-city school is two-fold. It keeps unwanted intruders out, and reminds everyone on the inside that they're a community of people who care for each other. The parents of the 1,446 middle school students speak 39 different languages and there is a 36 percent turnover within the transient student population each year.

"But we have to reach each and every one of them," teacher Joe Cimono says in the faculty planning session. "You're right," Principal Norma Terry says. "I'm certain that if we just keep using this Tribes cooperative learning process throughout the school, a sense of self-worth and mastery will happen for these kids."

Saul Bromberg adds, "We've done a lot of inclusion. Must be we need to recognize their need for influence, draw upon their diversity, and get them into decision making. They need to experience a sense of power over their lives."

"O.K., that's where we are! Let's get back to our faculty tribes and go to work. We just need to apply all we've been learning!"

This glimpse into one school staff meeting illustrates how a faculty is transforming its approach to teaching. The development of every student is their new focus. They are moving from the impersonal factory model of standardization to designing an approach that will reach all of the unique students in their school community. They're excited because they are learning to have the students help manage classroom behavior, to use the Tribes strategies for teaching academics, and to awaken self-worth within their students.

The material in this chapter will help you to

✦ Understand the dynamics and issues in the stage of influence

✦ Develop a sense of value and power for students through multicultural education, decision making, and problem solving

✦ Integrate academic content into the Tribes process.

ACKNOWLEDGING THE NEED FOR INFLUENCE

You thought you had it made. Your students had been in tribes for over a month and things were going great. No more agitating to change tribes. Almost no put-downs. And talk about working independently...one afternoon when they were working you realized that you could have gone home at one o'clock and nobody (except perhaps the principal) would have missed you!

Then one morning your lovely, smooth-running tribal classroom began to get a little out of hand. Some of the people you counted on as positive role models began acting up. During Tribes activities you noticed many subtle and not-so-subtle indicators that disagreements were happening. I-Messages and attentive listening were forgotten. It seemed like a terrible setback. You said to yourself, "Forget teaching with groups!"

Congratulations! Your class is now ready to really go to work! The inclusion, or "honeymoon," stage of the Tribes process has run its course, and the stage of influence has arrived! The new restlessness is a sign that your students are comfortable with the group process—they feel included and safe enough to speak out, even those shy ones.

THE STAGE OF INFLUENCE

The stage of influence is not about fighting for control or power over others. It is an organizational stage in which people want to contribute value to their group or community. Take a few minutes before moving further into this chapter and review "The Stage of Influence" in Chapter 6.

It's important to remember that if groups ignore the underlying issues of the stage of influence rather than working through them, their capacity to work well together will suffer, and they will never come to appreciate the diversity of group members. There is no way around—only through! Your job as a process facilitator is to recognize the restlessness as a sign of progress, and use strategies that help people express their individuality. A sense of value and positive power then becomes a reality. As soon as that happens, your class (or staff or organization) will be a strong learning community in which everyone participates, shares leadership, and leaps ahead in learning.

There are five ways to empower people at this stage of group development. Indeed, they are the objectives for this stage:

+ Provide many opportunities for people to state their differing opinions, values, and beliefs openly

+ Make multicultural education and cultural pluralism a focus in your classroom and school

+ Teach strategies for individual and group decision making

+ Teach strategies for individual and group problem solving

+ Allow time for students to define individual and group goals.

Cooperative structures create the conditions for reversing inequity, producing egalitarian social structures and caring relationships where diverse people can work together toward common goals.[1]

—MARA SAPON-SHEVIN AND NANCY SCHNIEDEWIND

LEARNING TO STATE OPINIONS

It takes courage and trust to take a stand in the midst of peers and say, "I feel differently about this than the rest of you do." The more that students are given opportunities to state diverse beliefs, the stronger they will be to do more than parrot back the words "Just say no."

Let's say you have a 9th grade history/civics class this year in which you've been using a theme such as "Self and Society" or "Contemporary Issues." You've been building class community and have seven classroom tribes, each composed of five students. Throughout the inclusion stage you also started to use some of the Tribes strategies as structures for lesson topics. You have yet to formalize all this into a lesson plan, but expect that will happen in time.

Today you have decided to tackle the first steps of the stage of influence. To do this we suggest that you begin with the four influence strategies listed below. Tailor the language and topics to fit the grade level and cultures of your students. The strategies are:

- Thumbs Up/Thumbs Down
- Where Do I Stand
- One, Two, Three
- Put Yourself on the Line

Follow the directions as written, and remember: the strategy alone is not enough! Allow sufficient time for reflection questions so that in-depth learning happens. These four strategies could take several hours to do thoroughly. Work on them over several consecutive days. The first time that you use the strategies, use topics of personal interest.

Then use them again, but this time ask a controversial question from whatever material the class is studying.

Examples using the strategy "Put Yourself on the Line:"

"The only way to have a safe school is to have more rules, monitors and metal detectors."
Where do you stand?

"The age that you can vote and drive should be substantially lowered."
Where do you stand?

Ask several types of reflection questions. Although example questions are noted for the Tribes strategies in this book, craft your own special questions for the content of the lesson and your students.

The "Put Yourself on the Line" strategy can be followed up with many other learning opportunities.

Follow-up ideas:

1. People who agree on a position can form temporary new study groups to research and prepare a defense for their position.

2. The people on the extreme ends, who differ the most, can get together in debate and dialogue groups.

3. Students who learn through rhythm/music, visual/spatial, or body/kinesthetic intelligences may want to illustrate the various positions through role play, music, diagrams, or drawings. The next chapter discusses multiple learning styles and has many ideas to use.

The creative controversy that can evolve out of Tribes influence strategies can not only produce a wealth of learning in lesson content, but can also challenge students' critical thinking and collaborative skills. Best of all, different opinions are affirmed and valued.

MULTICULTURAL EDUCATION AND CULTURAL PLURALISM

Learning respect for different opinions during the stage of influence leads to the next important component, respect for multicultural diversity. Celebrate the fact that public schools are finally making a significant shift, from cultural assimilation to cultural pluralism.

Even though we're in the "How to Do It" section of this book, we would like you to keep reading back to the theory sections on the same topics. Take a few minutes now to look at

+ Chapter 2, on "Multicultural Diversity," page 21.

+ Chapter 5, "Creating Equal Opportunities for All Students," page 54.

Begin to plan with other teachers, parents, and administration how to initiate the five components considered essential to creating a culturally transformed school community. Again, they are:

1. Active involvement of the whole school community

2. A mission statement/policy centering on diversity

3. Redistribution of power and authority within school and classes

4. High expectations by teachers

5. Theme-focused multicultural curriculum, cooperative learning, a respect for individual learning styles, and well-trained multiethnic teachers.

FROM AN ADMINISTRATOR'S VIEW

Gail Whang, M.A.

Gail is an educational consultant and former Executive Director in the Department of Student, Family and Community Services, Oakland Unified School District in California. At the time of this writing, she was a fifth-sixth grade bilingual teacher and leader at Hawthorne Elementary School. As a long-time Tribes TLC® Trainer, Gail has used the Tribes process as a foundation for promoting diversity education and creating positive school and organizational environments.

How can we make multicultural education effective when race relations are at an all-time low?

With the diversity among populations growing at unprecedented rates, cultural clashes and conflicts are inevitable. Often the conflicts become violent, as we saw in Los Angeles. It is essential that our schools and communities learn not only how to help children of different cultures, races, and ethnic groups get along with each other, but also how to create environments in which children of one culture can assert their pride in who they are and are excited to learn about the cultures of others.

The staff of our school realized a few years ago that Tribes provided an absolutely critical process to ensure the success of our multicultural efforts. While Tribes does not explicitly teach about stereotyping, or prejudice, the Tribes process should be in place before one attempts to teach this sensitive topic. By consistently implementing the agreements of Tribes and creating the caring safe environment, the Tribes teacher can be assured that students will respect each other's cultures. Often times when children talk about their culture, or a particular custom that is very different from those of the other students, a typical reaction is to laugh or make fun. With Tribes it not only is easy for the teacher to remind the class about "no put-downs" and the value of diversity,

but it is easy for the students to share personal feelings. Teachers often need to stop teaching the curriculum in order to deal with a conflict arising from a racist or sexist remark. Unless the teacher feels comfortable doing so, these remarks often go unnoticed or are handled only on an individual basis. In our Tribes classroom the environment is in place to resolve conflict as well as to seize the teachable moment and confront issues of racism or sexism.

Every morning we have a Tribes community circle. In one morning circle activity each person shares how he/she is feeling. Quite often during this sharing session feelings of anger come out as a result of a child being called a racial name. One time, some of the Asian students were angry because they were being called "Chino" by Latino students. Chino means Chinese in Spanish. "But," they protested, "we are not Chinese." At this time one Mexican student spoke up and said that maybe the Latino students were not putting the Asian students down. He went on to explain that in his culture, friends would sometimes call each other by name depicting a physical characteristic. "We call one friend 'Panson' because he was a little fat." This was a wonderful opportunity to share differences within cultures.

Once I was having a disagreement with a Mien student about a conflict she had with another student. During the discussion, she never once looked at me. Instead, as she spoke, she looked down to the side of me. I found myself feeling angry because I thought she was not listening to me. At this moment I realized we had two very different approaches to speaking and listening. Again, in the Tribes circle I raised this point for discussion. Many Laotian and Mien students shared that at home it is considered rude to look their parents in the eye when speaking to them. Looking down is a way of showing respect to their elders. As we discussed eye contact, a Mien student shared that some teachers say, "Look at me when I'm talking to you," and how it makes her uncomfortable. Through the discussion she realized how eye contact shows respect and that you are listening attentively in some cultures. With this knowledge Laotian and Mien students become aware of the differences as they go from one culture to another on a daily basis. The other students also learn that if a Laotian or Mien student isn't looking directly at them, it does not mean they are not listening.

With so many cultures living together in one school, it is inevitable that what is considered polite in one culture could be considered rude in another. It is impossible for teachers to know the characteristics and values of all the different cultures represented in her class. Inadvertently, children will offend others from a different culture. That's why a supportive Tribes environment facilitates learning about other cultures. Children feel free to express any emotion.

The Tribes classroom is **empowering for students.** Not only do students share how they are feeling, but we discuss what we can do to change a bad or difficult situation. An instance in which students were empowered occurred last year. Many students complained about a teacher in the school who they felt was being disrespectful to them. One student complained that the teacher called him a racial name. Another student said that teacher made fun of how short he was. Again, in the Tribes circle we discussed the problem openly. Going beyond how we felt about this, we brainstormed what we could do about changing the situation. Students suggested that a meeting be called with them and the teacher to express their concern. This was done while another teacher mediated. It became clear that the students had misinterpreted what the teacher had said. Positive suggestions were made by the students and the teacher on how to improve the situation and prevent future misunderstanding.

As you can see, Tribes doesn't explicitly teach about multicultural understanding, but without the Tribes process, multicultural understanding cannot take place. Tribes must be in place for rich lessons to be learned about other cultures.

6 STEPS TOWARD CULTURAL PLURALISM

Essential Commitments

1. **BUILD STAFF AWARENESS**
   - Examine the current curriculum
   - Clarify misnomers and misinformation
   - Examine racism/bias: what does it look like?

2. **DEVELOP CURRICULUM FOR TEACHING TOLERANCE**
   - Conduct training in existing anti-bias curriculum
   - Develop additional curriculum
   - Identify levels of readiness

3. **CELEBRATE MULTICULTURAL DIVERSITY**
   - Use themes to integrate cultures rather than just studying one particular culture
   - Utilize parents and community resources
   - Include people with special needs
   - Utilize staff's multicultural talents

4. **INTEGRATE CLASSES**
   - Define how to maintain integrity to bilingual program and integrate classes
   - Pair up classes of different languages to work together
   - Focus on inclusion of special needs students

5. **BUILD SELF-CONFIDENCE AND SELF-WORTH**
   - Create and maintain a supportive and collaborative environment through the use of the Tribes process
   - Teach and practice conflict-resolution skills
   - Encourage student-initiated projects

6. **INVOLVE PARENTS**
   - Arrange cross-cultural workshops and support groups
   - Sponsor family picnics, potlucks, and other events

Gail Whang and her fellow staff members spent time defining what they believe are the essential components for multicultural education in their school, and they made a commitment to focus on these areas for two years.

Admittedly, it will take time to create a culturally tranformed school community, but you are already well on the way because the Tribes process helps to initiate all of the components.

Develop your own multicultural curriculum with the help of your students. Use some of the Tribes strategies to help people talk about their different countries, cultures, customs, languages, and uniqueness. No matter what strategies or activities you use, be sure to follow them up with Tribes reflection questions.

Create all-school activities, such as:

+ Celebrating multicultural diversity

+ Multiethnic fairs

+ School family events

+ Parent and grandparent story hours

+ Multicultural movie night

+ Staff awareness and training

+ Parent involvement initiatives

+ Classroom parent tribes.

In cooperative classrooms heterogeneity and diversity are not simply tolerated, they are nourished and valued.[2]

—MARA SAPON-SHEVIN AND NANCY SCHNIEDEWIND

Help your students understand that each time the tribes reflect on their collaborative skills, the dynamics of their tribes, the resolving of conflict, and problem solving, they are learning the skills for living in a pluralistic world. Help them to become familiar with the concepts underlying intergroup education, and to generate their own activities based on these concepts.

1. Every person needs to have the sense of belonging to a group.

2. Ethnic groups have both similarities and differences.

3. Segregated people develop myths, prejudices, and stereotypes about other cultures.

This perspective on linkages between and among people, coupled with the harmonious networking of all groups, fosters unity out of diversity and promises the harmony so desperately needed throughout our communities and world.

TEACHING INDIVIDUAL DECISION MAKING AND PROBLEM SOLVING

Have you ever wondered why schools limit student choices to the extent that they do? Everything is so predictable for kids for twelve years—the classes one must take, the way the system works, the competition, the tests, the workbooks year after year. The opportunity to make choices is next to zero in traditional schools.

If we truly want students to become self-directed and gain a sense of autonomy, learning how to make responsible decisions is essential.

The distinction between decisions and problems is an important one:

✦ Decisions are judgments made concerning information as perceived by an individual or a group.

✦ Problems are dilemmas, intricate issues, and predicaments that need to be analyzed in order to reach resolution.

The difference between the two defines the sequence that Tribes uses to teach decision making and problem solving.

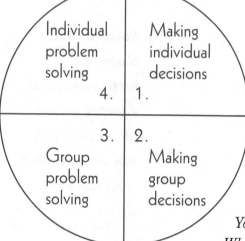

MAKING INDIVIDUAL DECISIONS

Three of the four strategies you used to help students express different opinions now can help them practice making individual decisions. Use topics appropriate for your class.

Thumbs Up/Thumbs Down

Your high school career tests suggest that you would be a good engineer. What decision would you make?

Someone tells you that you don't have to put on a seat belt in their car. What decision would you make?

One, Two, Three

If you were to take a vacation next week and money were no object, would you prefer to go to:

Disneyland

London for a week of theater

The World Series

Where Do I Stand?

Our class will be working on four issues about the Civil War during the next three weeks. Stand by the sign of the topic you want to work on.

1. Roles of European countries

2. The Emancipation Proclamation

3. Lincoln's personal and political dilemmas

4. Economics in the South and North

Individual decision making can be practiced throughout the teaching day by using many influence strategies and reflection questions. Reflection can happen in tribes or through writing in personal journals. Individual decisions can also be made with the help of trusted tribe members, teachers, and parents through the Tribes strategy "Let's Talk."

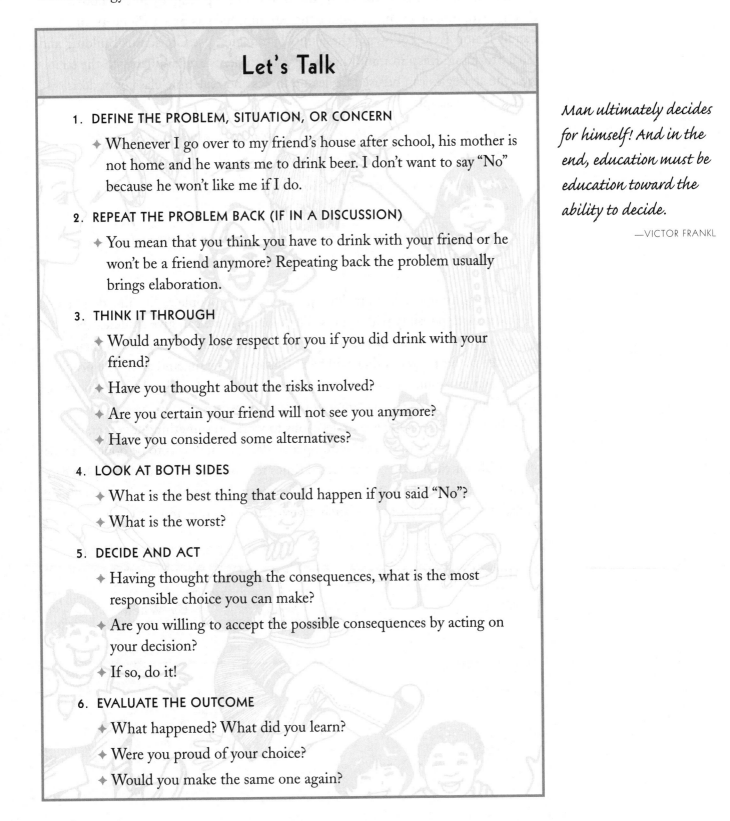

Let's Talk

1. **DEFINE THE PROBLEM, SITUATION, OR CONCERN**
   - ✦ Whenever I go over to my friend's house after school, his mother is not home and he wants me to drink beer. I don't want to say "No" because he won't like me if I do.

2. **REPEAT THE PROBLEM BACK (IF IN A DISCUSSION)**
   - ✦ You mean that you think you have to drink with your friend or he won't be a friend anymore? Repeating back the problem usually brings elaboration.

3. **THINK IT THROUGH**
   - ✦ Would anybody lose respect for you if you did drink with your friend?
   - ✦ Have you thought about the risks involved?
   - ✦ Are you certain your friend will not see you anymore?
   - ✦ Have you considered some alternatives?

4. **LOOK AT BOTH SIDES**
   - ✦ What is the best thing that could happen if you said "No"?
   - ✦ What is the worst?

5. **DECIDE AND ACT**
   - ✦ Having thought through the consequences, what is the most responsible choice you can make?
   - ✦ Are you willing to accept the possible consequences by acting on your decision?
   - ✦ If so, do it!

6. **EVALUATE THE OUTCOME**
   - ✦ What happened? What did you learn?
   - ✦ Were you proud of your choice?
   - ✦ Would you make the same one again?

Man ultimately decides for himself! And in the end, education must be education toward the ability to decide.

—VICTOR FRANKL

MAKING GROUP DECISIONS AND ACTION PLANS

The stage of influence calls into question how tribes can make decisions together. Reaching agreement even on simple things (such as, who will report for our tribe?) often proves to be difficult.

First, teach the tribes how to use the Brainstorming strategy in this book. Practice working on group decisions that are fun, such as Space Pioneers, or Family Camp Trek. Following these initial strategies, use Consensus Building and Goal Storming. Keep in mind that once your students are familiar with the strategies, the strategies can be used for lesson topics and real-time classroom decision making. For example:

> ✦ *We only have four kick balls to last us the year. How can we make sure that we don't lose any between now and June?*

> ✦ *How can we make sure that the plants get just the right amount of water each day?*

> ✦ *How can we share responsibility for feeding Benjamin Bunny and cleaning his cage?*

Practicing group decision making prepares young people to live in a democracy—to work responsibly with others. The more that we can give students the opportunity to reflect upon and analyze the dynamics that take place in their tribes, the better prepared they will be to "discover, sustain, and alter" the properties in their environments and systems (to quote the human development perspective of Tribes). This is the meaning of personal power.

If the tribes have made group decisions to work on something together, you may want to have them create "action plans" designating tasks to be done, persons responsible for each task, and expected times for completion. The action plan can be posted, reviewed daily, and revised if necessary. Action plans are "group contracts," which remind people of their accountability to one another.

TRIBAL ACTION PLAN Tribe Name:		
What	**Who**	**By When**

GROUP PROBLEM SOLVING

The maxim is so simple, yet so difficult for adults to put into practice. Our immediate reaction is to suggest solutions, and then become aggravated when students care little about carrying them out. Our basic goal of preparing this generation to do well in today's world depends upon helping kids become responsible citizens. For this reason Tribes trains teachers to transfer responsibility to student groups as much as possible. Having tribes rather than adult personnel solve classroom or school problems is also the key to sustaining a mellow environment. Let's look at two problems in need of student solutions.

Problem #1:

A few 6th grade students of the school have been seen spraying graffiti designs on the outside wall of the gym on weekends. Some of the offenders may be in your 6th grade class.

Strategy: Tell the class about the problem. Then lead them through this "Step-by-Step Process for Group Problem Solving."

STEP-BY-STEP PROCESS FOR GROUP PROBLEM SOLVING

1. Ask the tribes to discuss how they feel about people spraying paint on the wall of the school. Allow 3 to 5 minutes.

2. Pass out large sheets of paper and ask the tribes to brainstorm some ways that they could help solve the problem. Remind them of the rules for Tribes Brainstorming.

3. Ask each tribe to select their three best ideas or solutions to the problem. This can be done by consensus or by having each person write "1, 2, or 3" after three items of their choice. Stickers of three different colors may also be used. In this case, each student selects his/her top choices by placing a blue sticker on the first choice, red on the second choice, and yellow on the third choice. The totals on each suggested solution are counted (blue stickers 15 points, red stickers 10 points, yellow stickers 5 points).

4. Have two people record the three ideas from each tribe on the blackboard as they are read to the class.

5. Combine any duplicate or similar solutions.

6. Have all of the students approach the board, tribe by tribe, and vote for one solution.

7. Ask for two volunteers to add up the sticker points for each item. The solution receiving the most votes will be the one that the class will carry out.

What is remarkable in this example is that the identity of the 6th graders causing the problem is never discussed. They may, in fact, have participated (somewhat silently) in the problem solving.

Behavior problems can easily be handled whenever peers are given the opportunity to express how they feel about a disagreeable behavior. Have your tribes brainstorm "behavior that bugs me." Count on the power of peer feedback! Just going through the process of identifying conduct that is not approved by peers can cause a behavior to disappear rather quickly.

Problem #2:

You notice that the tribes are having various interaction problems. You want them to learn how to resolve group problems or issues.

The more that students are involved in defining a solution to a problem, the more likely they are to accept the responsibility to make the solution work.

Strategy: Ask the class if they have noticed that people are having difficulties in working together. After hearing their replies, tell them that you also have observed some interaction problems, and that you would like them to figure out how to resolve them.

Then lead them through "Tribes Resolving Group Issues."

Tribes Resolving Group Issues

1. Ask each person to reflect upon the group's interaction in recent work together, and using a 3 x 5 inch card jot down any difficulties that kept the tribe from working well together.

2. Have each tribe place its cards face down in a pile.

3. Collect the stacks and exchange them among the tribes so that no tribe has its own.

4. Give the tribes 10 minutes to identify one issue from the cards and make suggestions on what a tribe might do to resolve the problem.

5. Have each group share suggestions with the whole class. The tribe being discussed may remain anonymous.

INDIVIDUAL PROBLEM SOLVING

There is an understandable concern about students sharing personal problems within groups in educational settings. We have always taken the position in Tribes that it is inappropriate for educational groups to deal with any personal problems that border on the psychological, and that only qualified professionals should do so. Tribes are educational, not therapy, groups!

It is inevitable, however, in these times of severe stress among children that family-oriented psychological problems become evident. The advice we give Tribes teachers is the same as that which their districts probably give. If you notice or hear anything that indicates a serious disturbance in a child, it is your responsibility to refer that student to the professional designated to handle such problems for the school.

Help your students understand that it is not the purpose of their tribes to deal with personal or family problems. Tribes may, however, help people think through concerns related to their school work, career questions, future goals, skill development, roles among peers, and friendships.

Here are three strategies you can use to help students sort out individual problems.

1. Practice the "Client Consultant" strategy, using educational, career, or personal interest topics.

2. Have people keep personal journals, sharing only what they would like peers to help them think through.

3. Use the strategy "Let's Talk."

If you do sense that an inappropriate personal problem is being discussed, intervene and determine the appropriate assistance for the student.

IMPORTANT! Should you ever hear anyone say that cooperative learning or Tribes TLC® groups are therapy groups, respond with vehemence—and share this material. *The purpose of all cooperative learning groups is the social and academic development of young people within school settings.* The benefits of cooperative group learning are too valuable for the process to be disparaged by unfounded assumptions.

SETTING GOALS AND MAKING INDIVIDUAL CONTRACTS

Social development also means helping students to become self-controlled and self-directed. Provide the time necessary for students to learn how to define positive goals—a key attribute of resiliency.

One way to start working on positive goals is to have students do the "Goal Storming" strategy independently. Ask people to choose something about themselves that they would like to improve (social or academic skills, attitudes, or behaviors) during the next weeks. Short time durations are better than long ones. As a way to model the activity, you might share your own list:

Teacher's List of Short-Term Goals

1. To exercise for ten minutes each morning this week.

2. To give up drinking coffee for at least one month.

3. To phone my friend tomorrow and apologize for forgetting her birthday.

Influence is the sense that I am of value and have power over my life.

Students may wish to share their goals with other Tribes members and write personal contracts, which can be signed by peers who agree to give encouragement and support. There is a form for the personal contract in Chapter 13 of this book. Positive peer support can work wonders!

Goals also can be recorded in personal journals, so that students can continue to reflect upon their experiences, document progress, and record changes. Personal journals are respected as private documents that are shared only if a student chooses to do so.

Designing and Implementing Learning Experiences

Designing and Implementing Learning Experiences

10

The teachers of the Middletown Middle School now meet in grade level groups (their own tribes) for planning and to support each other. Like their students, they have also chosen names for their tribes, and they begin each meeting with inclusion. Margery Burnett of the Red Zingers has just facilitated the strategy J.O.Y.

After reflecting on their sharing, Jerry Carroll exclaims, "OK, let's go, Zingers. How do we keep reaching all of our 7th graders these next weeks? It's time to whip out another set of history-based learning experiences that reach them all."

"I've been thinking a lot about what we're doing," Joe Santini says. "Now that we're weaving themes and concepts into Tribes strategies and other interactive structures, even those apathetic kids are participating well. Learning is now more like a journey of meaningful discoveries that friends make together. And I've been meaning to tell you, I like teaching now and I'm not going to leave you guys at the end of the year."

Cheers go up! Then the Zingers gather around the table to continue their planning. Before leaving, Joe quietly tacks a colorful new sign up on the faculty room wall. Its message is heartening:

TEACHING MEANS REACHING
AND MIDDLETOWN IS DOING IT!

What students understand does not correspond directly to what they have been told or have read in authoritative texts.

Scenes like this one are taking place in schools throughout the country. **Teachers have become learners,** and the more that they learn about how kids learn, the more excited they become about designing learning experiences for their students.

ACHIEVING ACADEMIC EXCELLENCE

Now is the time to get the word around your school and district that if, indeed, we truly want to improve students' academic learning, our instructional practices can be—and need to be—based on sound learning principles and practices such as in the process of Tribes TLC®. Essentially, the comprehensive studies compiled by the Collaborative for Academic, Social and Emotional Learning (CASEL),[1] and the hundreds of studies on cooperative group learning,[2] if implemented faithfully and well within a caring culture, achieve higher levels of academic learning for students. CASEL's research "demonstrates that social and emotional learning is integral to learning" and that "the nature of learning is fundamentally social."[3]

Children who succeed in school are:

+ Engaged in active social and intellectual interactions with their peers and teachers

+ Active participants in learning rather than passive recipients of knowledge

+ Able to communicate effectively and ask for help when needed. [4]

—CASEL

Rather than diverting schools from their primary academic mission, improving the social and emotional competence of students and the climate of schools advances it."[5]

How do we know the process of Tribes TLC® is promoting academic achievement? News like the following examples are coming back from schools throughout the country. Student scores on the SAT9 test at a school in Arizona were normally 15–25, and moved upward to the 40–50's in a bilingual class. The same district is heralding a teacher where the normally low scores became 60–70's in a regular class. An on-going study in a Wisconsin school reports that the consistent application of the Tribes process is resulting in significantly higher CTBS reading scores. Call CenterSource Systems for additional information on the results of using the process of Tribes TLC®.

Modifying the predominant practice of whole class teacher-centered instruction requires that teachers and parents, understand how human learning takes place. They need to decide whether they want students just to continue memorizing material for tests, or become constructive thinkers and problem-solvers for real life issues. More than 30 years ago respected educator Paulo Freire also pointed out the fallacy of didactic instruction. He was convinced that what students understand does not correspond directly to what they have been told or have read in authoritative texts.[6]

Numerous cognitive learning research studies now affirm Freire's conclusion. Understanding incoming information, facts and concepts depends upon the meaning given to the information by the human brain.[7] The brain continually seeks to understand new information by linking it to previous patterns of knowledge in the mind. Each student's understanding depends upon a synthesis of what he or she has heard and read, as interpreted through previous experiences.

Familiar symbols, language and culture also affect individual understanding. Thus the term: "the brain is a meaning-maker." It is also known that meaningful knowledge is created and recreated between people as they explore, apply and do things together.[8] Group discourse and collaboration on conceptual problem-solving and the design of projects lead to greater academic achievement. It is time to dismiss the idea that a teacher's knowledge simply can be transferred into the minds of students. Some few determined students (probably those seeking all A's to get into prestigious universities) will take down lecture notes to memorize for a next test. Deep down most also know the facts and concepts heard or read will not be lasting. Knowing this aspect of cognition more than justifies moving from passive direct instruction to ways of active learning in cooperative small groups. Admittedly, we have a long way to go since it is estimated that 85% of teachers within 17,500 school districts in the U.S. use the traditional teacher-talk minimally effective approach.

STAGES ON THE CONTINUUM TO EXCELLENCE THROUGH GROUP LEARNING

The chart on the adjacent page illustrates the continuum of change in teaching practices that thousands of teachers are making to reach and teach students more effectively—and to improve test scores! The continuum moves from traditional whole class instruction to active learning groups. Wherever you and your faculty are now on the continuum is truly o.k. What is important is that teachers support each other, coach each other and reflect upon their progress along the way. Change takes time, but once the direction is clarified, it builds the spirit of community, collegiality and excellence in learning throughout a school.

Oh, good, there's a chart on that page!

STAGES TOWARDS EXCELLENCE THROUGH GROUP LEARNING

Whole Class Instruction	Whole Class Tribes Community Circle	Cooperative Learning in Tribes	Discovery Learning in Tribes
TEACHER: directs lectures facts and concepts asks questions seeks correct answers assigns desk work manages behavior tests for facts STUDENTS: learn alone	TEACHER: directs initiates activity asks questions affirms multiple answers manages behavior builds inclusion STUDENTS: use agreements learn collaborative skills work in collaboration reflect on interaction learn together	TEACHER: plans initiates strategy TRIBES: discuss and work on task or problem seek ideas and report solutions to class manage task and interaction build inclusion and influence monitor agreements use appreciation reflect on learning and group interaction assess for knowledge and learning learn together	TEACHER: selects topic/problem engages students through inclusion makes connections to past + present learning experiences lays groundwork for group task STUDENT TRIBES: 1. ENGAGE define inquiry questions and process each tribe selects a question to explore (teacher acts as resource facilitator) 2. EXPLORE implement activities to explore inquiry manage and assess group interaction 3. EXPLAIN articulate observations and ideas share and clarify terms/language with facilitator (facilitator determines misconceptions & levels of understanding) present learning/project to whole class or parents justify conclusion based on academic knowledge 4. ELABORATE expand on concepts make connections to real world 5. EVALUATE reflect on performance outcomes share appreciation students (and teacher) assess learning

Turn back to page 51 to recall the student-centered classroom study.

ABOUT THE STAGES

As pointed out in earlier chapters, as soon as teachers of a school have become trained in the basic Tribes Learning Community course, they are ready to implement the process by engaging students daily in a Tribes community circle. The objective of this first stage is to build inclusion, to learn to use the four Tribes agreements and to teach students to assess their participation and learning through group reflection. The community circle is teacher-centered—all eyes and ears on the teacher while he or she introduces topics, asks questions and controls behavior. Unfortunately some few teachers assume that they "are doing Tribes" because they have their class meet in the circle configuration.

The community circle stage used consistently, does develop a caring community climate and social skills, but it is only the launching pad to the next stage, Tribes Cooperative Learning.

As soon as students are familiar with the Tribes community process and collaborative skills to work well together, the teacher and students organize tribes for cooperative learning.

The classroom becomes student-centered, filled with new energy, as the teacher's style changes from didactic instruction to facilitating active group learning. Gradually increased responsibility is transferred to students to learn academic material, to monitor the agreements and to manage the interaction of their tribes. The transfer from teacher to students not only is motivational but meets their developmental needs. This is especially true for middle level and high school adolescents. No longer do teachers spend 70% of their time lecturing, asking questions, giving instructions and disciplining. As facilitators of cooperative learning, teachers then have that much time to give support and encouragement to students. Best of all they have time to know their students and tailor learning experiences to their interests and needs.

The move to Tribes Discovery Learning adds even a more significant dimension and promise for the education of today's children. The Tribes Discovery Learning process is based on decades of learning about teaching by such eminent leaders as John Dewey, Jean Piaget, Jerome Bruner, Howard Gardner, and Lev Vygotsky, to name but a few. Even back to the 18th century a Neapolitan philosopher, Gambattista Vico, asserted that humans can only understand what they have themselves "constructed." Today the concept has become known as constructivism, and is gaining ever-increasing validity from recent evidence in the brain and biological sciences.[9] the approach engages students in social dialogue to define questions for inquiry, research, problem-solving, and to challenge hypotheses, design projects, test/defend solutions and evaluate their collaborative results. It transforms academic concepts for young learners into meaningful real-world possibilities.

Most teachers have learned the hard way that placing socially unskilled students in a learning group and expecting them to cooperate will not be successful.

They must have learned essential social skills for collaboration. This is the reason many teachers give up cooperative learning—students do not know how to work well together.

Tribes is the glue that holds it all together . . .

Sure, and that happens with adult groups too!

. . . and makes group learning successful!

Tribes Discovery Learning is an integration of two frameworks:

1. the Tribes group development process of inclusion/influence/community, and the collaborative skills and agreements

2. a constructivist model, developed for the biological Science curriculum Study, Roger Bybee, Principal Investigator, Miami Museum of Science, and known as the "Five E's" standing for **E**ngage, **E**xplore, **E**xplain, **E**laborate, and **E**valuate.[10]

The complimentary frameworks make planning easy for teachers who want students to gain meaningful real-life learning experiences.

CONNECTING THE ESSENTIAL ELEMENTS OF COOPERATIVE LEARNING THROUGH THE TRIBES PROCESS

Among those who have done so much to advance the cooperative learning field are Drs. David and Roger Johnson of the University of Minnesota. In response to the inevitable question, "What is cooperative learning?" they have identified five basic elements that are considered essential to all cooperative learning groups. These essential elements are shown in the following graphic and described on the next page.[11]

Tribes creates a context on community agreements and the collaborative skills students need to be successful in

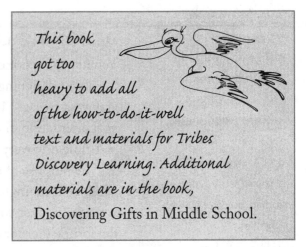

This book got too heavy to add all of the how-to-do-it-well text and materials for Tribes Discovery Learning. Additional materials are in the book, Discovering Gifts in Middle School.

POSITIVE INTERDEPENDENCE
People undertake a group task with a feeling of mutuality, each person contributing, doing his or her own part, knowing "we sink or swim together."

FACE-TO-FACE INTERACTION
People help each other to understand the task, check comprehension, and reflect on what was learned.

INTERPERSONAL AND SMALL GROUP SKILLS
People learn interactive skills, manage conflict, develop trust and respect within a group.

INDIVIDUAL ACCOUNTABILITY
Group members take personal responsibility for learning the material, contributing to the group, and assessing both individual and group achievement.

GROUP PROCESSING
Members reflect upon and analyze group effectiveness, and define ways to improve group work together.

cooperative learning groups. If this foundation is simply taken for granted, teachers are often frustrated by their students' "inability to work together." Each student needs to feel a sense of inclusion, to feel of value to the group, in order to participate fully. Strategies and structures alone are not enough to assure the success of group learning.

Essential Elements of Cooperative Learning through the Tribes Process

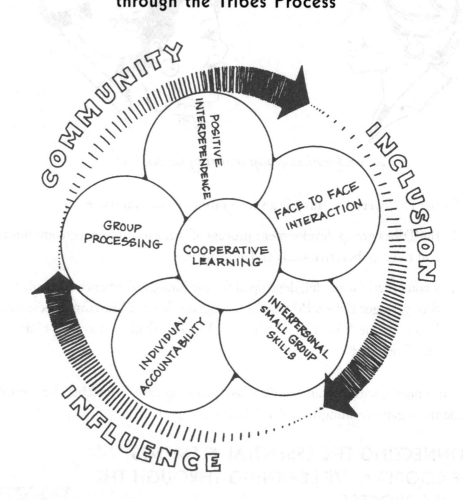

DESIGNING LEARNING EXPERIENCES—THE TLC® PLAN

You may have noticed that instead of talking about designing curricula, we're talking about designing learning experiences. Of course, it's up to you which phrase you want to use. Most Tribes teachers agree that "learning experience" conveys a goal orientation, the intentional selection of strategies to achieve objectives, and real-time discovery for students.

The purpose of the Tribes TLC® example plan on the next page is to help you organize meaningful learning experiences for your students. A blank form that you can copy for your own use is contained in Chapter 14, Resources. You can use the form either for integrating academic content into a single Tribes strategy, or

| EXAMPLE | A Tribes TLC® Learning Experience | GRADE: 4–8 |

1. PROVIDE FOR INCLUSION—A QUESTION, ACTIVITY, OR ENERGIZER.

Energizer: Knots, page 381

2. IDENTIFY THE CONTENT OBJECTIVE TO BE LEARNED AND THE COLLABORATIVE/SOCIAL SKILL OBJECTIVE TO BE PRACTICED.

Content Objective (write): *To learn and apply knowledge of geometric terms*

Collaborative Skills: (check)

- ☑ Participating fully
- ☐ Listening attentively
- ☐ Expressing appreciation
- ☐ Reflecting on experience
- ☐ Valuing diversity of culture/ideas
- ☑ Thinking constructively
- ☐ Making responsible decisions
- ☑ Resolving conflict
- ☐ Solving problems creatively
- ☐ Working on tasks together
- ☐ Assessing improvement
- ☐ Celebrating achievement

Social Skills:

- ☐ Sharing
- ☑ Listening
- ☑ Respecting
- ☐ No Put-Downs
- ☐ Empathizing

Other:

3. IDENTIFY THE STRATEGY(IES).

Give Me a Clue, page 255: Have class in groups or tribes. Remind students of agreements. Clarify roles: facilitator, reporter, encourager. Follow directions in book.

4. ASK REFLECTION QUESTIONS ABOUT WHAT WAS LEARNED.

Content: *What terms did you have to clarify to come to a solution? What comments from your tribe or group members helped to open up your thinking?*

Collaborative: *What skills did you use?*

Personal: *On a scale of 1–5 what was you level of participation? (Hold up fingers.)*

5. PROVIDE AN OPPORTUNITY FOR APPRECIATION.

"It was helpful when (name) (behavior)."

"I appreciated…"

for writing a more comprehensive sequence of interactive strategies and cooperative learning structures. An example plan is on the next page.

The **Tribes TLC® Plan** form is headed by five important sections that you need to think about before selecting any strategies:

1. Stages of group development—appropriate inclusion activity

2. Learning Objectives—Content and Collaborative/Social Skills

3. Sequence of Strategies and Structures

4. Reflection/Accountability

5. Appreciation

Stages of Group Development

What stage are the tribes in now?

+ Has inclusion been developed sufficiently in the classroom?

+ Do people know and honor the Tribes agreements?

+ Do they all known each other?

+ Have they gone through the issues of the stage of influence?

+ Are they making decisions together? Voicing different opinions?

+ Do they respect the diversity of their members?

+ Are they working on tasks cooperatively?

OBJECTIVES

What academic content is to be learned? Of course, this depends on where your school is in preparing students for the 21st century, and what the district requirements are.

You may want to look back at Chapter 2 (page 25), to review the list of learning experiences needed to prepare today's students for the 21st century. Because the list goes beyond the teaching of separate disciplines, it is important for school communities to generate a framework that integrates what they consider important for students as a meaningful whole. Marion Brady suggests four areas, based on their "probable contribution to human survival," and a synthesizing component to weld the four into a single discipline:[13]

+ Learning about our physical environment

+ Learning about the humans who occupy the environment

+ Understanding states of mind that underlie human action

+ Understanding how assumptions and beliefs manifest themselves in human behavior

+ Synthesizing all these study areas into meaningful themes on national and global issues affecting humankind.

Brady writes:

> If we are to survive as a society, we and our students need comprehensive answers to the question, What's going on here? We are not going to get those answers from the random, ethnocentric images of reality provided by the traditional disciplines. We need to look at reality freshly, and, if we are to put what we see in perspective, we need the means for seeing it as a whole...To send students out into the world without a conceptual framework for organizing experience is to fail them in the most fundamental sense possible.[14]

Which Thinking Skills?

The constructive thinking skills needed by young people in today's world may also be considered as *collaborative* skills in every sense of the word. The ability to contribute to a learning group or a work team depends upon clear thinking and expression. Academic content is the vehicle to develop higher order (constructive) thinking skills. Two challenges become evident: (1) Which thinking skills should be emphasized? (2) How do we help students learn about their own thinking processes?

Students today need to know how to:

1. **Access information** from a wide array of resources

2. **Infer and interpret** its meaning

3. **Synthesize and link** it to existing knowledge

4. **Plan and apply** it to a real-life issue or problem

5. **Evaluate and refine** it for ongoing application or conclusion.

The list is influenced by our belief that students need to be able to seek out and construct their own knowledge—not simply learn current knowledge, but know how to access relevant information at any time in life, whether from a data bank, a library, or any other source. It is startling to read that only one in five young adults (under 22 years old) can read and interpret a bus, train, or airline schedule. The capacity to plan and evaluate is essential for an era in which the rate of change is accelerated well beyond the stability of former decades.

Some Strategies to Develop Constructive Thinking Skills

ASSESSING INFORMATION	✦ Using group investigation and inquiry
	✦ Learning to use the library, computers, data banks, and public records
	✦ Conducting surveys and interviews
	✦ Using the "Jigsaw" process
INFERRING AND INTERPRETING	✦ Using graphic organizers, displaying data on graphs or charts
	✦ Debating; discussing; drawing; dancing
	✦ Writing; using role play and music
SYNTHESIZING AND LINKING	✦ Summarizing previous knowledge
	✦ Comparing and integrating concepts and resources
PLANNING AND APPLYING	✦ Analyzing relevance to a problem or situation
	✦ Using problem-solving strategies
	✦ Designing and creating applications
	✦ Implementing action
EVALUATING AND REFINING	✦ Reflecting
	✦ Monitoring; measuring; interviewing
	✦ Reporting; judging

Which Collaborative/Social Skills?

David and Roger Johnson emphasize that two types of instructional objectives need to be articulated in cooperative learning lessons: an academic objective and a collaborative skills objective. The latter designates the interpersonal and small-group skills that will be learned or practiced during a cooperative learning lesson. Each school community needs to choose the collaborative/social skills important to their own cultural population. On the next page are some of these skills inherent in the Tribes process. It is helpful to have people practice the same skill for many days at a time, or for the whole school to focus on one skill for a month.

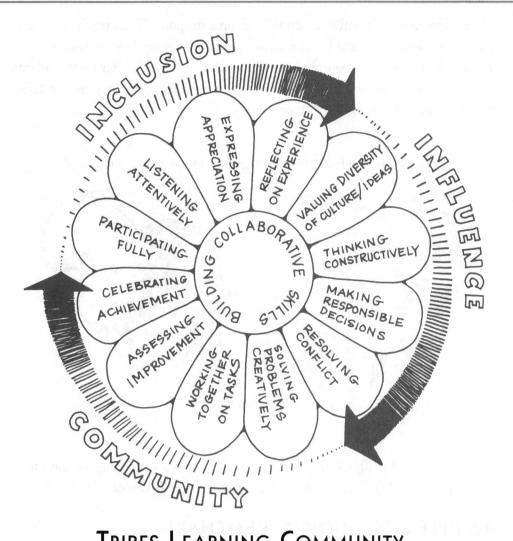

TRIBES LEARNING COMMUNITY

SELECTING STRATEGIES AND STRUCTURES

The Tribes strategies and/or cooperative learning structures that you select to carry the lesson content need to support the observed stage of group development. For instance, you would not want to use "Where Do I Stand," a strategy for the stage of influence, if tribes still need inclusion. Moreover, if they are to work on a task involving controversial issues, they should already have practiced a number of influence strategies. The exciting thing about the majority of the Tribes strategies is that they can be used over and over again as interactive formats for academic content.

REACHING STUDENTS OF MULTIPLE LEARNING STYLES

Picture nine students sitting in a semicircle in front of you. They all have different learning styles because they all have different intelligences. Yet the traditional classroom reaches only two out of the nine, the 20 percent that learn through verbal/linguistic and logical/mathematical methods. National statistics tell us that at least three out of the other seven will become dropouts if not reached academically in the elementary and middle school years. One thing is for certain—they are not stupid kids! They simply have ways of knowing that differ from students with verbal/linguistic and logical/mathematical intelligences. They are not failing—their schools are failing to reach them.

I certainly can't create nine different lesson plans every day!

Of course not!

> *The good news about teaching with multiple intelligences is that it is not an "add on" to an already overfilled curricula.[15]*
>
> —DAVID LAZEAR

The Multiple Intelligences Idea Chart summarizes a wide range of ways to help you achieve that big goal of reaching each and every student.[16 & 17]

MULTIPLE INTELLIGENCES IDEA CHART

EXISTENTIAL

Engage in reflection and self-study

Read books on the meaning of life

Attend some form of worship

Watch films on big life questions

Record thoughts in a journal

Listen to inspirational music

Study literature, art, philosophy

Discuss life-human issues in a group

Record dreams and mystical events

Paint while listening to music

Create a private "centering" space

NATURALIST

Keep a journal of observations

Collect and categorize data

Make a taxonomy of plants or animals

Explain similarities among species

Study means of survival

Examine cellular structures with a microscope

Illustrate cellular material

Take out-of-door field trips

Visit an aquarium

Camp outside to identify stars

VERBAL LINGUISTIC

Write story problems

Create TV advertisements

Compile a notebook of jokes

Debate current/ historical issues

Play "Trivial Pursuit"

Explain a situation/problem

Create poems

Impromptu speaking/writing

Create crossword puzzles

Teach "concept mapping"

Learn a foreign language

Write instructions

Read stories to others

Describe an object for another to draw

Make up a story about a piece of music

Describe the steps to a dance

Write a role play/drama

Keep a personal journal

LOGICAL / MATHEMATICAL

Create a time line

Compare/contrast ideas

Predict the next events in a story

Define patterns in history

Follow a recipe/instructions

Rank-order factors

Analyze causes and effects

Learn patterns

Analyze similarities/differences

Classify biological specimens

Create outlines of stories

Create computer programs

Use a story grid/creative writing

Create a "paint-by-number" picture

Read/design maps

Solve math problems

Teach calculator/computer use

Decipher codes

Compose music from a matrix

VISUAL / SPATIAL

Make a visual diagram/flow charts

Illustrate a story/historical event

Design/paint murals

Imagine the future/go back in time

Play "Pictionary"

Teach "mind mapping" for notetaking

Write/decipher codes

Graph results of a survey

Create posters/flyers

Create collages on topics

Draw maps

Study the arts of a culture

Make clay maps/buildings/figures

Create visual diagrams/machines

Illustrate dance steps/physical games

Teach Tribes energizers

Learn spatial games

Draw from different perspectives

Draw to music

MUSICAL / RHYTHMIC

Create "raps" (key dates, math, poems)

Teach songs from different cultures and eras

Play musical instruments

Make simple musical instruments

Learn via songs and jingles

Learn through drum beats/rhythm

Make up sounds and sound effects

Practice impromptu music

Create interpretive dance to music

Lead singing (songs from different cultures)

Write to music

Reduce stress with music

Teach rhythm patterns/different cultures

Compose music for a dramatic production

Teach dance steps

Identify social issues through lyrics

Illustrate different moods through dance steps

Lead physical exercise to music

Clap a rhythm for the class to repeat

BODY / KINESTHETIC

Lead Tribes energizers and cooperative games

Practice physical exercises

Lead students in stretching to music, deep breathing, tai chi, and yoga poses

Learn dances of different cultures and periods of history

Practice aerobic routines to fast music

Measure items of distances with thumbs, feet, or hands

Illustrate geometrical figures (parallel lines, triangles, rectangles, circles) with arms, legs and/or fingers

Conduct hands-on experiments

Act out scenes from stories of plays

Design role plays

Invent a new household tool

Prepare a food or snacks

Simulate various situations

Learn alphabet through physical movement

Learn/teach sign language

Make up a cooperative playground game

Create human sculptures to illustrate situations

INTERPERSONAL

Role play a historical/literary or class situation

Analyze a story

Tell stories

Read poetry using different moods

Teach arithmetic, math, computer games

Review a book orally

Act out a different cultural perspective

Design and act out dramas/role play

Help tribe come to a consensus or resolve a problem

Facilitate participation in the tribe

Coach peers and/or younger children

Teach cooperative games

Help people deliver appreciation statements

Solve complex story problems

Discuss/debate controversial issues

Analyze group dynamics/relationships

Learn to sing and lead rounds

Plan and arrange social events

Find relationships between objects, cultures, situations

INTRAPERSONAL

Keep a personal journal or feelings diary

Analyze historical personalities

Write on personal learning experiences

Evaluate personal and group strengths/weaknesses

Analyze thinking patterns

Understand group dynamics

Use, design, or lead guided imagery

Write an autobiography

Analyze literary characters and historical personalities

Define personal reflection questions

Imagine and write about the future

Dance different stages in life

Lead Tribes personal inclusion activities

Practice relaxation techniques

Imagine self as character in history or story

Illustrate feelings/moods

Listen attentively

Draw self at different periods in life

Share how music affects feelings

Observe self (metacognition perspective)

REFLECTION QUESTIONS

The most important part of any TLC learning experience may be the reflection questions that you ask your students, because:

1. Asking good reflection questions within cooperative learning groups can double the rate of knowledge retention[18]

2. Students understand that they are not just learning information, but also higher-order thinking, social, and personal skills—competencies critical to their futures

3. Well-chosen reflection questions are an immediate way to assess how well your learning objectives were achieved.

What questions will you ask so that your students realize what they have learned? As mentioned earlier in Chapter 7, three types of reflection questions are used in Tribes:

 ✦ **CONTENT/THINKING** questions are focused on the content of the lesson and on the thinking skills that were used in order to work with the content. The content consists of the concepts learned.

 ✦ **COLLABORATIVE/SOCIAL** questions focus on the interaction that happens within a tribe or learning community, and on the interpersonal and collaborative group skills that were used.

 ✦ **PERSONAL** questions focus on what the individual has learned.

Now you'll especially see why I am so prominent in this book and in Tribes schools!

Plan the questions you will use, and jot them down on the TLC Lesson Plan form. Of course, there will be times when you will want to change them due to events that happen during the class experience. Ask questions that will be most relevant and underline the key learning experiences.

APPRECIATION

Last but hardly least, opportunities need to be provided for people to express appreciation to those with whom they have worked. Never let a group finish work together without allowing time for statements of appreciation. It might be helpful to review "Encouraging Appreciation" in Chapter 7.

The more that appreciation happens, the more cohesive the tribes will be—the more comfortable they will be to keep working together, the better they will accomplish learning tasks, and the greater will be every student's sense of self-worth.

Lesson plans are not the whole answer, of course, to encouraging student learning. Your skills in presenting the learning experience are equally important. Reaching and teaching all students means personalizing the lesson, asking productive questions, and ensuring cooperation in learning groups.

ACCOUNTABILITY: INDIVIDUAL AND GROUP

The Tribes TLC teacher can use a variety of ways to determine the degree to which the three typed of learning objectives are being achieved by tribes and individual members. The objective are:

Collaborative skills—both thinking and social interaction

Content—curricular content and integrating themes

Collaborative skills

In Chapter 14 there are four forms that may be used to assess how well your students are learning and practicing collaborative skills. Form A is to be used by the teacher or an another observer (such as a parent volunteer) to assess attentive listening within tribes of as demonstrated by individual students. Each time that a behavior listed in the vertical columns is observed, place a check mark in the corresponding box. Totals may be added up at the end of the observation time. Be sure to tell the students beforehand what will be observed. Let them know their progress over time and make suggestions on how their tribe or the class can improve the ability to listen attentively. Other collaborative skills may be observed in the same way by listing the behaviors of a skill and keeping a tally.

The other three forms may be used by students to reflect upon and assess their own participation in their tribes, the quality of their working together, and their use of various constructive thinking skills.

Form B is used by individual students to reflect on their own participation in their tribe. They can monitor how well they are using certain skills, based on their personal observations over a period of time. The form can become part of their portfolios, recorded in personal journals, shared with their tribes, or shared with you.

Form C can be used either by individual group members or by the whole tribe to reflect on how well they worked together during a learning experience. If done by individual members, the tribe can total and average all of the ratings for a group score. In addition, the reflection questions that you ask throughout all learning experiences will indicate how well the collaborative objectives are being achieved by your class.

The first level of assessment on thinking skills is done through the reflection questions that you ask throughout the learning experience. Students can also help to evaluate the extent to which they used various thinking skills by using the fourth form, form D. This assessment can by used individually or by the tribe

Form A

TEACHER
OBSERVATION
*Assessing
Collaborative
Skills/Listening*

Form B

STUDENT
ASSESSMENT
*Participation
In My Tribe*

Form C

STUDENT
ASSESSMENT
*Our Tribe's
Work Together*

From D

STUDENT
ASSESSMENT
*My Constructive
Thinking Skills*

after the tribes have worked together to solve a problem or accomplish a difficult learning task. If the assessment is made by the whole tribe together, allow students sufficient discussion time to cite specific examples of how various thinking skills were used. This can be a very rich learning experience.

Content

You and your faculty need to determine and generate ways to evaluate the learning of academic content. The scope can vary and include:

- Reflection questions

- Project presentations (speeches; role play; video; oral reports)

- Portfolios

- Individual or group testing

- Written reports

- Video and audiotapes

- Teacher interviews with groups

- Student-to-student interviews.

Assessment of the Tribes TLC® Process and Outcomes

All Tribes school communities will want to know the impact of the Tribes process on various outcomes such as a decrease in behavior problems, increase in academic achievement, attendance and other long term goals the school may have. Research on group learning indicates that the greater the extent that the process components of Tribes are used, the greater extent targeted outcomes will be realized. The Northwest Regional Educational Laboratory designed an Assessment Kit to help your school strengthen its use of the process and assess outcomes. Phone CenterSource Systems for information on the process and instruments.

Implementing a Tribes Learning Experience in Five Steps

1. **INCLUSION**
   Introduce the learning experience (as people sit either in the community circle or in tribes) with an inclusion strategy (content linked to lesson topic) or a "YOU" question.

2. **OBJECTIVES**
   Tell the students what content objective and what collaborative skills are to be learned or practiced.

3. **IMPLEMENTATION OF STRATEGIES**

   - Explain the task, group roles, and time available.

   - Ask, "What questions do you have?"

   - Observe and monitor the dynamics of the tribes working together, intervening only if they cannot resolve a situation or problem.

4. **REFLECTION/ACCOUNTABILITY**
   Ask reflection questions. Use written tests for individual and/or group accountability.

5. **APPRECIATION**
   Invite statements of appreciation.

PERSONALIZING THE LEARNING EXPERIENCE

Earlier we discussed how learning happens—how the human brain seeks out and catalogues patterns, linking new information to prior knowledge and experiences. Moreover, learning is accelerated when this happens. It becomes obvious that if we want students to learn new content, we need to connect it to previous experiences at the introduction of a lesson.

One way to do this is to initiate the lesson with personalized YOU questions, which also serve as inclusion activities for the class community or tribes.

Example: The lesson content is about the California Gold Rush. Begin the learning experience with a YOU question.

✦ Have YOU dreamed of finding a lost treasure? What was it?

✦ If YOU found a priceless treasure, what would you do?

✦ If YOU had to work out of doors in a remote place for a very long time alone, what would you take with you in order to survive?

The YOU question

✦ Is addressed directly to the student

✦ Is relevant to personal experiences, interests, feelings, or previous knowledge

✦ Evokes interest, recollection, opinions, and energy

✦ Appeals to the imagination

✦ Is shared prior to the introduction of lesson content.

Responses to YOU questions are best shared in tribes, pairs, or triads. The questions can be used in a writing activity such as an imaginary letter to a friend, or recorded in the students' personal journals. YOU questions can be structured into these Tribes strategies or Cooperative Learning structures:

Think/Pair/Share　　　　　　*One, Two, Three*
Think/Write or Draw/Pair/Share　　*Community Circle*
Tribes/Brainstorm/Record/Report　　*Open Forum*
Chain Reaction　　　　　*One-Minute Biography*

Asking Inviting Questions

Teachers ask questions! Yes, all kinds of questions. However, real learning depends upon the kinds of questions asked. Here's a short list of questions that are less than productive.[19]

STUDENT: I want to study about the Great Barrier Reef.

TEACHER: Do you have a library card? (Question is irrelevant and does not encourage student.)

TEACHER: So how come the Pilgrims had to make friends with the Indians? (pause) No one knows? Well, it's because they needed their help in learning about the new land. (This is a teacher monologue question and gives students no thinking time or opportunity to answer.)

TEACHER: What were the causes of World War II? (The question is too big and complex for a clear verbal response; may be intended only to showcase the brightest student.)

TEACHER: Is the theme of the book "War and Peace" complicated? (The question calls for a "yes" or "no" answer, and closes off response.)

No doubt you can think of many others that keep classrooms from being student-centered and are unproductive. Step number one for teachers committed to moving to a new pattern of interaction with students is to ask open questions which invite richer responses.

This is the difference between open and closed questions:

CLOSED QUESTIONS—	OPEN QUESTIONS—
Ask for Yes or No Answers	Invite More Complete Answers
Did you...	*How did you...*
Would you...	*Why would that...*
Can you...	*Tell me how...*

Productive questions are open-ended and provocative, and challenge higher levels of thinking. They are clearly stated and focus on the big idea, the content issue of the lesson, or the thinking and interpersonal skills that were used.

Examples:

✦ What is your understanding of the events that led to the Vietnam War? (assessing/interpreting)

✦ What's different about each of the three little pigs? (analyzing)

✦ Which of the characters in the play *As You Like It* would you have wanted for a friend?

✦ What data from the play supports your choice? (accessing, analyzing, relating, strategizing).

QUESTIONS THAT ARE AFFIRMATIVE[20]

Questions can be used to affirm positive behavior, constructive thinking skills, and multiple intelligences.

Examples:

✦ How did you ever guess that our class would have such a great time signing and beating out rhythm to your Brazilian tapes, Ricardo?

✦ Carly, what make you decide to invite your whole tribe?

✦ Andy, how did you manage to continue your sketching with all of the confusion going on around you?

✦ Tell us how your tribe decided to help the kindergarten children on the playground.

EXTENDING STUDENT THINKING

Teachers can help students to extend their thinking in a variety of ways when implementing Tribes learning experiences.

PRACTICE "WAIT TIME:" Provide at least 3 seconds of thinking time after a question and after a response.

USE "THINK/PAIR/SHARE:" Allow individual thinking time, and discussion with a partner, then open up for class discussion.

ASK FOLLOW-UPS: Why? Do you agree? Can you elaborate? Tell me more. Can you give an example?

WITHHOLD JUDGMENT: Respond to student answers in a non-evaluative fashion.

ASK FOR A SUMMARY: Could you please summarize John's point?

SURVEY THE CLASS: How many people agree with the author's point of view? (Thumbs up-Thumbs down)

ALLOW THE STUDENT TO CALL ON SOMEONE: Jason, will you please call on someone else to respond?

PLAY THE DEVIL'S ADVOCATE: Ask students to defend their reasoning against opposing points of view.

ASK STUDENTS TO "UNPACK THEIR THINKING:" Describe how you arrived at your answer. Think out loud.

CALL ON STUDENTS RANDOMLY: Don't limit yourself just to those with raised hands.

CUE STUDENT RESPONSES: There is no single correct answer for this question. Please consider many alternatives.

Tribes is...an Attitude

As I travel around the country sharing the Tribes philosophy with educators, students, parents and community members, I feel compelled to make sure people understand that Tribes isn't "something else" they have to squeeze into their already-busy lives. I have come to the conclusion that the process of Tribes is more of an "attitude" – of respect, caring and acceptance. I have seen so many examples of positive change as the Tribes process begins to permeate the environment of a school community.

A few years ago, I had the opportunity to facilitate a Tribes training at an urban school in the East, one which had seen tremendous decline over the past several years. This school at one time had been seen as a "state of the art facility" but now was suffering from economic and demographic challenges as well as a downward shift in morale. The staff had experienced a significant number of administrative changes over the past several years.

Although the current principal had expended great effort in providing numerous opportunities for staff development, she had expressed a great deal of frustration due to the lack of positive change resulting from the various learning experiences. Cynicism and a defeatist attitude greeted me as I entered the school environment, and felt like I had my work cut out for me.

It was obvious within the first hours of the training that there was hope in this school for a new way of learning. There were, however, dynamics that needed to be addressed openly and honestly. For example, as I began the first day of training, I was confronted by several seasoned teachers who had the "arms crossed," "what are you possibly going to tell me that I don't already know" attitude. Undaunted and convinced that the Tribes process can truly effect change, I began the process of building inclusion. By the end of the first hour, the transformation had begun. I heard comments such as, "Boy, I've taught next door to this person for the last 20 years and never knew how special he is." Or, "We've had a lot of staff development in cooperative learning and team-building before, but now it's all starting to make sense!"

A highlight for me personally was seeing one particularly reluctant male participant (of the "folded arms" camp) demonstrate an incredible shift in attitude by bringing flowers to all of his female colleagues and food for the whole group on the final day of the training. He admitted that it is still difficult for him to communicate openly, but now he feels much more comfortable doing so in this more accepting environment. He also stated that he doesn't feel so isolated any more and can ask a colleague for help or ideas instead of doing everything "on his own."

FROM A SCHOOL PSYCHOLOGIST'S VIEW

Nancy Lindhjem, Ed.S. Nancy is a school psychologist and a Tribes TLC® Professional Development Consultant who has worked for more than twelve years in public school settings in Indianapolis, Indiana, using the Tribes process as the foundation for a wide range of middle and high school peer programs. Her shift to private practice with Children's Resource Group allows her the flexibility to work as a CenterSource Systems Professional Development Consultant, sharing the Tribes philosophy and process with educators across the country.

The more we help children to have their wonderful ideas and to feel good about themselves for having them, the more likely it is that they will some day happen upon wonderful ideas that no one else has happened upon before.[21]

—ELEANOR DUCKWORTH
"THE HAVING OF
WONDERFUL IDEAS"

It was truly inspiring and exciting to witness the beginning of growth in these dedicated professionals. It was especially moving to see how the once-disenchanted administrator had begun to understand that Tribes is a process and real change takes time. At a brief follow-up about six months later, I was elated to hear her say, "I never thought Tribes would be happening in my building, but it's happening *all over* this building!" The former discipline plan had been replaced by the Tribes agreements which were gradually embraced by the teachers, administrators, and initially-wary students. Referrals to the office were cut drastically as were suspensions and expulsions. After experiencing a year of the Tribes process in her building, this administrator has now expressed interest in becoming a Tribes trainer to continue to promote the process in her building and raise the level of awareness in her district.

When I returned to this school for the follow-up after six months of implementation, I felt an entirely different atmosphere than what I had experienced upon my initial arrival. People were more open, more relaxed. They laughed more and listened intently to one another. They were able to immediately work cooperatively to complete tasks. Their relationships to one another had obviously been heightened. There are still issues to be dealt with, to be sure, but it seems this staff has been able to develop the necessary climate of respect, caring and acceptance of one another which will allow the continuation of positive growth and change.

The Tribes process is a powerful tool to promote change and improve the climate, whether it be within the school, home, community, or within ourselves. I feel very fortunate to have these opportunities to spread the work about Tribes, and if one needs to cop an attitude, let it be a "Tribes" attitude. It works.

ENSURING INTERDEPENDENCE

There are many ways to ensure cooperative interdependence in tribes or learning groups. Three important ones are to:

1. Develop bonding and group trust

2. Use group roles

3. Structure content areas.

Develop bonding and group trust

Teachers who use the Tribes process realize that the promotion of inclusion, safety, and trust produces close bonding after several weeks of inclusion strategies. This factor in itself develops the cooperation and interconnectedness among group members that all cooperative learning groups need in order to work well together on task. Groups that have experienced the Tribes process demonstrate thoughtfulness, and take care that everyone participates. The trust level also assures participation. Many teachers believe that the Tribes environment is an intrinsic rather than extrinsic way of assuring interdependence, and in time using group roles is optional.

Use group roles

Complementary group roles do help students learn to cooperate and count on each other's contribution and participation. Roles can be assigned by the teacher or selected by people within the tribes. It's important, of course, that roles are rotated, so that Dave isn't always the recorder, Heidi the encourager! Define roles that will be helpful to the completion of the task. Some of the roles used in cooperative learning groups are

FACILITATOR: Gets group started; makes sure directions are clear; encourages everyone to participate; calls the teacher if no one in the group can help

RECORDER: Records group's work and shares with the community what the group has discovered

ENCOURAGER: Cheers people on; invites participation

CHECKER: Invites explanations from all members; checks materials

ACCURACY COACH: Checks for mistakes and the following of directions

SUMMARIZER: Restates major conclusions; paraphrases agreements and disagreements

ELABORATION SEEKER: Asks people to relate material to previous material

TIME KEEPER: Helps group decide how much time will be needed; tells

group how much time remains for task completion; gives
5 to 10 minute wrap-up warning.

The roles can be combined in any way to help the tribes work on tasks well.
Make certain that the responsibilities of the roles are clear each time people begin
to work together. You will notice that roles are not written into many of the Tribes
strategies. Roles are probably more helpful when working with academic tasks
than when learning social skills. We have left it up to each teacher to decide when
to use roles.

Structuring content areas

The content can be divided into as many sections as there are members in the
tribes, so that each student has part of what is needed to complete the task.
"Cooperative Squares" is also a good strategy to use initially to teach the importance of interdependence and introduce the slogan "Together We Sink or Swim."

Research on the very popular "Jigsaw" process, designed by Elliot Aronson, has
repeatedly proven that lower achieving students alter the academic image they
have of themselves as they experience being "experts," teaching a part of the lesson
to peers within their cooperative learning groups.

At the secondary or university level, the use of "Group Inquiry" (see Strategy
section) is a great way to involve students in researching and studying part of an
academic topic over a period of time, and then teaching the content to their learning group. The richness attained by many people collaborating can exceed the
amount of data and information disseminated by any one instructor.
Collaboration also prepares people for the workforce of today and
tomorrow—to work cooperatively as team members.

If You Sense They Are Not With You

There are those inevitable times when you realize your students have tuned you out. They are no longer listening, have a glaze in their eyes, and are drifting—beyond caring about what is going on in the classroom. You may have been working hard in your move to have a more participatory classroom, and are baffled whenever things seem to slip back. Not to worry…it is a signal to take time out, diagnose what has happened, and take positive action. This checklist may help you to determine why your students' attention is waning.

1. Are you connecting the topic or lesson to their personal experience and previous learning?

2. Are you getting off the topic or talking too long?

3. How long have your students been sitting or working without much physical movement?

4. Have you identified their stage of development and group issues so that you select appropriate strategies?

5. Are you using enough group strategies to maximize participation?

6. Are you hovering over the tribes, rather than giving them responsibility to help each other with the task?

7. After an activity are you asking personal or social reflection questions before asking content questions?

8. Is there a disturbing event that needs to be aired or resolved before learning can be resumed?

9. Are you sensitive to the loss-of-energy dynamic when it begins to happen?

10. Do you "stop the action" and ask students what is going on?

11

Working With People Big and Small

11 Working With People Big and Small

There's no doubt about it! The Saturday flea market in our town is an important community meeting place. A few weeks ago, Barbara Marshall, Principal of our middle school, waved wildly across a pottery table to the author of this book. "Jeanne," she said, "do you have time for coffee? I have something to ask you about Tribes." We wandered over to the coffee stand, and after I set down the pink bird cage and old desk lamp I had found, we talked for an hour. Barbara asked a familiar question. "How can we help school board members, parents, and other district people understand what the Tribes process is all about in our school? It's hard to convey the big difference that it is making at all grade levels and with the staff."

"Aha," I thought to myself, "it's time for the Flatlands story again."[1]

I asked Barbara if she knew the story. She said she would like to hear it.

The story begins just as most stories do. Once upon a time...there was a country that had just two dimensions, length and width, but it had no third dimension, height. The people of Flatlands had to inch their way through space...around corners, along streets, and into their flat houses. It was very frustrating. They had no perspective.

One day a Flatlander bumped into a strange object and then heard a voice say, "Come with me. Up here...come up here with me." "Up? What's up?" said the Flatlands man. Then he felt a tug on his arm and was pulled in a direction he had never before explored. Later he would learn the word "ladder." The friendly person at the top smiled and said, "Look at your country now."

The Flatlands man was amazed! Flatlands was beautiful from this new perspective. He could see an easier way to go from his house to his office, and wonderful undeveloped areas that people could live in and enjoy. He was so excited that he thanked his new friend and slid back down the ladder to tell people what he had seen. But no one could understand. "Up? Down? Height? Ladder?" they asked. At first they considered the Flatlands explorer a bit crazy, but then people began to wonder and even hope that the new perspective was real. Finally, the Flatlands man realized that his words alone would never be enough. He too could only say "Come with me—see and experience the difference yourself."

The postscript to this story is that Barbara Marshall got the message and did the same. Her school is now a Tribes demonstration school with a welcome sign out to anyone who wants to see Tribes at work at different grade levels, with special education classes, with staff and parent groups. Understanding a new way means experiencing it a bit with those who set out earlier into a different dimension.

The purpose of this chapter is to provide a peek into some applications of the Tribes process with populations other than the elementary level. We asked some teachers, trainers, and principals to describe what the process looks like in their school communities. So put down your backpack...(or pink bird cage), and come along. You will learn how Tribes is used with the following groups:

+ Kindergarten and pre-school

+ Special Education

+ Middle school

+ High school

KINDERGARTEN AND PRE-SCHOOL

The use of the Tribes process for little people began many years ago when some pre-school Montessori teachers in Seattle wanted 3- to 5-year-olds to learn pro-social behaviors as well as the individual responsibility that Montessori emphasizes. There, as well as in other pre-schools and kindergartens, it was learned that:

+ The community circle should be used many times during the day, that the tribes should consist of no more than three people for 3- to 4-year-olds and four people for 5-year-olds.

+ Each tribe needs to have a space designated just for them...a small rug or table of their own is essential. Just doing that much within a kindergarten or pre-school provides security for each child. Much of the aimless energy (running about) is an effort to find a safe and familiar place in the midst of many people. The atmosphere changes when small children can relate more closely to two or three others, who become caring friends. They love to name their tribes and feel proud of their tribes' accomplishments.

+ Young children enjoy helping each other and learn from one another. Those who can tie shoes can help others. Pro-social behaviors modeled and affirmed by teachers and aides are quickly learned.

+ First teach the skill of listening. During community circle time, pass an object such as a feather, ball of yarn, stuffed animal, or puppet to help people focus on who is speaking. Teach children a signal such as hand cupped to ear or the thumbs-up sign, to let speakers know they are being heard. Provide a purpose for listening. Example: *"We will be making clay animals today and there are three things you must remember."* Ask people to repeat the directions

FROM A PRINCIPAL'S VIEW

Brian Jones

Brian has worked creatively as a Kindergarten teacher, an Instructional Strategy Consultant, a motivational speaker, and as Course Director for the Faculty of Education at York University in Canada. He is currently the Principal of a Tribes School in the Durham District School Board, Ontario. Brian has been a Tribes TLC® Trainer since 1993 with over twenty years of teaching experience. Brian's knowledgeable experience with children in the formative years has proven to be invaluable in his work with teachers of all grade levels.

How Can We Use Tribes in Pre-School and Kindergarten?

Brian Jones' eyes sparkled when he talked about using the Tribes process with 3 to 5 year-olds. Laughing at himself, he said—

Yes, I had to learn that what worked on Monday, might not work on Friday. But I do know what these little people are like:

They love to talk

They love to touch, feel and manipulate objects

They are egocentric

They play beside each other before playing with a partner

They enjoy the element of fantasy

They love praise, positive reinforcement

They mimic and model behavior

They talk spontaneously

They want to be heard

They like choices and situations they can control

They want to share, and

They are honest.

As a principal, the Tribes process gave me the structure we needed. The biggest improvement has been having these very early learners reflect upon their experiences and feelings.

As a teacher, each day I would discuss the agenda in our community circle and share what would happen in various blocks of time known as morning circle, the 8 intelligence centers, and "study-buddies" (tribes).

Community circle topics of interest promote participation...especially those that give advice to the teacher. We would pass a teddy bear around the circle. Whoever had the bear was the speaker and the others were listeners. Some great topics have been:

 ◆ Today is going to be a good day because...

 ◆ I know someone loves me when...

 ◆ What's your favorite fairy tale? Why?

 ◆ If a hockey stick wasn't a hockey stick, what else could it be?

 ◆ What would be a good name for a new dinosaur? Donut-o-saurus? Sing-a-saurus?

 ◆ What do you think I should get my wife, Mrs. Jones, for her birthday?

Social skills are a vital part of every lesson. I would constantly refer to Gonzo. This puppet oversees all social skill T-charts. Here are a few modifications to some of the Tribes strategies for 3–5 year-olds.

 ◆ TWO-ON-A-CRAYON: (p. 361) becomes two-on-a-paper at first!

◆ **JIGSAW:** (p. 267) Tell a few (2–4) students how to complete a learning activity so that they become the "experts." Have small groups sit with these experts to learn the expectations.

◆ **GALLERY WALK:** (p. 254) Have students stand beside their art masterpieces, and answer one question and acknowledge one appreciation statement that observers may ask.

◆ **PEOPLE HUNT:** (p. 307) Use pictures.

◆ **BRAINSTORMING:** (p. 218) Whole class brainstorming with teacher recording in words or images. Popular topics included:

Build a super-duper sandwich

Build a best dinner

Build a better bedroom

Build a better bathroom

◆ **KITCHEN KAPERS:** (p. 270) Give partners or tribes a bag of junk. They can make anything they want to as long as it is all attached.

◆ **LIFE MAP:** (p. 271) Change this to "day map."

Example: *Got up, had breakfast, brushed teeth, combed hair, etc.*

◆ **BARNYARD BABBLE:** (p. 215) Give students a small plastic zoo or farm animal to hold while they move around the room making the animal sound.

◆ **AM I NAPOLEON?** (p. 210) Tape pictures and/ or an alphabet letter on the backs of people.

◆ **WHERE DO I STAND?** (p. 376) Give small people only two choices.

Examples: *Who is braver: Jack in the Beanstalk or Little Red Riding Hood?*

Should the world have weapons? Yes/No?

◆ **APPRECIATING OTHERS:** (p. 213) Have two hats available in the classroom; one labeled "Praiser" and the other labeled "Encourager." People who wear these hats have the job of circulating throughout the room, finding out what peers are doing and giving appreciation statements.

In preparing lessons I would read an activity and then re-think it through the eyes of kindergarten students. I'd ask myself how can I modify it to meet the children's developmental level and at the same time use it as a vehicle to teach the Ontario Provincial Curriculum Expectations. The Tribes process helped me to survive a full day program with 25 3–5 year-old students and no classroom assistant.

My tribe are my friends—we work together and like us lots.

—SARAH, 4 YEARS OLD

I know it's working when my students go to each other as a source of help and learning. It makes my class size almost manageable to be able to have them in small groups working together so that I can devote my focus to a few children at a time. But the overall message is that they can seek in each other the skills and know-how to accomplish wonderful things.

—KINDERGARTEN TEACHER, SAN FRANCISCO

that you have given. Have the children identify sound effects (crinkling cellophane=a lively fire; shaking a cookie sheet=thunder). Have buddies take turns telling each other how to draw an object or animal. Use continuing stories, each person adding a sentence. Also have children in tribes tell each other stories and then relay the stories heard to other tribes. Above all, model attentive listening and affirm it in your students as it happens.

◆ Since young children love to enforce rules with each other, the Tribes agreements (once illustrated and practiced daily) easily become part of the classroom environment.

◆ Managing the kindergarten or pre-school is easier and behavior problems lessen as teachers (just as with older students) learn to involve the tribes in problemsolving. These little people love to give advice; they are creative and honest whenever suggesting how to improve the classroom or Tribes interactions.

THE WIDER CHALLENGE FOR MIDDLE SCHOOLS

Middle schools across the country have been scrambling to initiate different ways "to recapture millions of youth adrift." They are introducing interdisciplinary teams, block schedules, advisory programs, exploratory projects, integrated study themes, and curriculum focusing on problem-solving. Yet, the curriculum still may not be reflective of what is known about the needs of the early adolescence;[2] and the pattern of interaction has not been altered to meet the disparate needs of the population.

This time in a child's life is a dramatic one of personal and social change. It is a time or experimentation with new roles and values, and a time to discover identity. *Who one is* depends upon *who one is with*. A sense of acceptance and power among peers is central to young adolescents' sense of self-worth, thus central to their motivation and learning. Their major concerns seem to be more connected to coping, surviving and adjusting that to success. A recent survey of 9 to 16 year-olds found that:[3]

◆ 66% need guidance in understanding how to get along with others

◆ 42% want to know how to communicate with and relate to their parents and teachers

◆ 33% need help in dealing with loneliness of grief

◆ 25% want assistance in dealing with alcohol and/or other drug-addicted parents.

Middle grade schools— junior high, intermediate, and middle schools—are potentially society's most powerful force to recapture millions of youth adrift and help young people thrive during early adolescence. Yet all too often these schools exacerbate the problems of young adolescents.

—TURNING POINTS: PREPARING AMERICAN YOUTH FOR THE 21ST CENTURY, 1989

James A. Beane, author of *A Middle School Curriculum: From Rhetoric to Reality,* makes the point that the developmental concerns of early adolescence must be addressed along with the social issues that these young people are facing. He writes:[4]

"The middle school ought to be a general education school, and its version of general education ought to be based upon personal and social concerns."

In recognition of the fact that the need for identity, belonging, and power among peers is not being net by the traditional middle school structure, especially in large middle schools, the 1989 Carnegie Council Task Force Report urged schools to provide membership structures, "communities of learning."[5] The committee envisioned that these communities could help students:

✦ gain the skills, knowledge, and attitudes necessary to create strong families, work groups, and communities

✦ and acquire cognitive and relational skills.

The suggestion was heard, and since then many schools have created school-within-a-school, or "house," structures of teachers and students working together. The smaller units often consist of four teachers with 100 students. However, many are finding that students still have difficulty in relating to each other and developing close bonding with peers. Smaller groups are still needed. Ongoing membership in learning groups or four to six, and the use of the Tribes community building process are ways to structure the inclusion and identity that all students of this age group especially need. When teachers and students within the "house" learn and use the same collaborative skills, positive agreements, can caring process, a new way of learning together can happen.

FROM A TEACHER'S VIEW

Mary Palin, M.A.

Mary is a Tribes TLC® Trainer and Professional Development Consultant for CenterSource Systems, and is certified by the National Board for Professional Teaching Standards. She has been a teacher of grades K–8 in the South Lake Tahoe Unified School District, where she also taught a middle school Challenge Class—"for kids who are a challenge or need one." Mary enjoys working with adolescents because of their spirit, creativity and energy—which coincidentally are qualities well matched in Mary. She currently enjoys training, curriculum and program development, and applying the Tribes process to everything possible.

What Happens When Tribes Is Used with Middle School Students?

After years of training staff in the Tribes process, and then watching a teacher's reaction when she bounces into a secondary school classroom and tries a strategy like "J.O.Y." and gets little or no response from her students—some tips for the process are important.

Typically, middle school adolescents are very egocentric. They love to talk about themselves, and their many opinions. However, respect for those outside their peer group or sharing the spotlight with peers is difficult. For the secondary student, a clear expectation of behavior and a "reason for doing this" should precede any activity.

Establishing trust in the classroom is essential and adolescents know enough about life to not give their trust easily. They have an uncanny sense of what is fair and what is not. The Tribes agreements are most important to the security of the classroom. The teacher/facilitator must be a positive and consistent model, establishing and modeling the agreements as a baseline for a positive classroom climate. When introducing or reviewing the agreements at the beginning of an activity, stress that the purpose of the "right to pass" is to assure people that it is their option to participate or not. I have found it effective to present the right to pass in terms of the right to

participate. This gives middle school students a positive expectation for behavior without minimizing the importance of their right to pass. Tribes strategies and other activities that are low risk and encourage all to participate will be most successful.

Most adolescents possess a sharp wit and tongue. Their brand of kidding more often than not can include many put-downs. Acknowledge their sense of humor, but raise their consciousness on how put-downs hurt people. Some ways to do this are:

✦ Have students view excerpts from a favorite television show, and count the put-downs. Reflect on how the characters must have felt receiving them.

✦ Have them do a survey for one week, tallying the put-downs that they receive and their reactions to them. Make a grand tally for the whole class. Repeat this several weeks later and compare results.

✦ Have students in tribes brainstorm how to eliminate put-downs in the class, among younger children—even on TV programs.

Attentive listening, a collaborative skill, can be taught as an objective right along with academic objectives. Once students know that they might grade each other or be graded on how well they listen, they begin to practice it to perfection. Do teach them the elements of good listening first. The agreement of mutual respect, which also assures students of confidentiality, is perhaps the most honored and accepted of the agreements among middle school students. They feel good about sharing when they can count on their group's trust and support.

In choosing strategies for secondary students, there are some definite criteria to consider:

1. **SECONDARY STUDENTS NEED A MIX OF COMPETITIVE AND COOPERATIVE ACTIVITIES**...an interesting situation since, typically, adolescents are proficient at neither! On some days, one may focus on inclusion; on others, influence; and more times than not, the class will want both. Adolescents desperately need to feel valued (influence), but they sometimes lack the self-confidence and self-respect (inclusion) to properly seek recognition. The structure that the Tribes process provides, allows for constant reuse, or repeating, of different strategies and integrating different learning content. Some favorites include: Put Yourself on the Line, Brainstorming, Tower Building, Outlines, Life Map, and What's My Bag.

2. **REFLECT ON THE ACTIVITY OR STRATEGY BEFORE, DURING, AND AT THE END.** This keeps the limits and learning objectives well-defined, keeps communication flowing between the teacher and students, and provides on-going assessment of what is happening. Remember the phrase "the activity alone is not enough?" With secondary students, the point is moot; their participation and ways of learning demand constant reinforcement, assessment and reflective practice.

3. **FACILITATORS MUST PARTICIPATE!** Your behavior and life experience are most interesting and secondary students will not perform without good reason and showmanship. Do not ask your class to do anything that you would not do first.

The path of the Tribes process through middle school may not always be predictable, but the returns are high and come in unexpected packages. After weeks of making small steps with a class or group, a strategy or reflection question will magically open new doors. However, prepare yourself for the day when those fun-loving sixth graders suddenly become shy and skeptical seventh graders—and a favorite energizer like "I love you, honey" gets a very different response.

Trust the process... it works!

THE TRIBES PROCESS WITH SPECIAL EDUCATION STUDENTS

The realization and legislation (Public Law 94–142) that students with mild disabilities should spend at least part of each school day in regular classrooms has been a challenge to many teachers. Teachers using the Tribes cooperative learning process report that the inclusive Tribes process is the best way they have found to mainstream these students because their regular students, so accept individual uniqueness and diversity, that the special learners are simply considered part of "our community." Margery Hadden, in Park City, Utah, told us about a teacher with a student who was in a wheelchair. "Within a few weeks my fifth graders even seemed to forget about the chair and just took it for granted that John would be part of every activity."

Research has more than verified that all students achieve more in cooperative learning than in traditional (competitive or individualistic) classrooms, and that "this finding held for all age groups, ability levels, subject ages, and learning tasks."[6] Studies just on the achievement of handicapped students verify that not only do they have higher achievement, but that individualistic instruction may be detrimental to their development.[7] The Tribes process has been recognized as a particularly good way to teach special education students social skills since it assures the caring and accepting environment so essential to their relational needs.[8] Learning, whether within the realm of academic content or social skills, simply does not happen for them unless the classroom is inclusive, safe, and affectionate. Like all students, they need a place to share their feelings, concerns, and hopes. They need ongoing opportunities to make decisions, solve problems, assume leadership, and relate to peers in positive ways.

How Does the Tribes Process Work with Special Education Students?

The Tribes process creates the positive social climate so critical to the needs of the special education student. Typically, special ed classrooms are populated by multiple age groups of multi-ability-level students. With some modifications, Tribes can be implemented with these classes as well as in regular classes that have mainstreamed special needs students. Here are some tips to special education teachers:

◆ Follow the same group development sequence as described in this book.

◆ Introduce the Tribes agreements one by one; make sure that students understand the need for each agreement and how it will be helpful to the class and to themselves; post visuals (posters, pictures, and written instructions) of the agreements and refer to them often; practice each one in many ways (auditory, kinesthetic, musical) over an extensive number of days until they become "the way we are together."

The community circle is the most important strategy to develop in special education classrooms. It gives you the opportunity to gather everyone together; to practice the agreements; to experience inclusion strategies, address problems, and make group decisions. Be sure to give clear directions as well as visual cues for whatever topics are being talked about. Always model a response first yourself to be certain that directions for the strategy are clear. Trust built through regular use of a community circle enables reticent students to express themselves and to find commonalities with peers. Use many affirmative reflection questions, such as, "Terry, how did you decide that everyone would enjoy learning about fly fishing?"

Such reflection questions, repeatedly used, can help to move students to higher thinking skills and also build self-esteem. Just as in all classes using the Tribes process, an invitation to peers to give appreciation statements needs to follow every activity.

Most of the Tribes strategies can be used as written or with the modifications shared above. A valuable resource for implementing Tribes in special education classes is the book *In Their Own Way,* by Thomas Armstrong. Armstrong was a special education teacher who saw that the application of Howard Gardner's work on seven intelligences would be of immense value in working with students with special needs. The

FROM A TEACHER'S VIEW

Michele Cahall, M.A.
Michele has worked as a special education teacher of communicatively handicapped middle school students for more than 20 years. She currently serves as a Speech-Language Pathologist for preschool and middle school students with El Dorado County Schools in California. She is a Tribes TLC® Trainer and Professional Development Consultant for Center-Source Systems. Michele has been deeply involved in the development of Tribes TLC® training and materials. In the midst of meetings, she can be counted on to remind everyone of her own primary purpose—"to improve the lives of kids and their families."

book helps teachers and parents to understand that students may be stronger in other intelligences than in those traditionally used in schools. Teachers having a clear understanding of the seven intelligences can provide their special students with choices on how they can share their knowledge of the material. The Multiple Intelligence Idea Chart in Chapter 10 and the description of the intelligences in Chapter 5 can help you to enrich the ways in which you work with your class.

Tribes energizers (contained in the Strategy section) are also a great way to involve special learners, especially the kinesthetic youngster who has a difficult time sitting for long periods of time doing tasks that do not require physical activity. In order for these children to reclaim their energy for learning, they need to be involved periodically in complex movements in the large muscles of the arms, legs, and torso.

Energizers lend themselves to classroom use with a minimal amount of preparation time.

A management technique that is very helpful is "Stop the Action." Whenever a lot of disruptions are happening, simply call out "freeze" or "stop the action." Then guide your students to identify whatever was happening, and the behaviors that would be more helpful. Ask them to share ways they can help the class accomplish the desired behaviors. This helps them to recognize their own responsibility and the positive contribution that each one can make to the community.

The following strategies and energizers are easy to implement in special education classes because they require little or no modification:

Community Circle

Two on a Crayon

Fuzzyland Map

Creative Storytelling

Warm Fuzzies

Warm Fuzzybag

Five Tribles

Brainstorming

Sharing from a Sack

Bumper Sticker

Spider Web

Life Map

Kitchen Kapers

Cooperation Squares

One, Two, Three

Thumbs Up–Thumbs Down

Where Do I Stand?

Put Yourself on the Line

Peer Response Huddle

Love My Neighbor

I Love You, Honey

Zap!

Snowball

HIGH SCHOOL GROUPS

Investigative or inquiry groups are most helpful and stimulating for students at the upper grade levels, college and adult classes. There are several different effective strategies:

1. **COOP-COOP**, developed by Spencer Kagan, calls for selecting a main topic of study and then sub-dividing it into mini-topics. Each student selects a mini-topic, studies it and then shares the information with his group. The group compiles all information and presents it to the class. Evaluation covers the student's work in the group and individual papers.

2. **GROUP INQUIRY** emphasizes interdependence among groups. An area of study is selected by the teacher. Student groups then select a topic related to the area that interests them. The teacher and the groups decide how to investigate the topic. Each member carries out an individual investigation, the group then summarizes findings and prepares an interesting presentation for the class. With younger children, work-stations can be set up in the classroom where research is conducted.

3. **JIGSAW**, developed by Elliot Aronson, works well for on-going tribe groups. Again the main topic of study and mini-topics are selected by the teacher. Students number off within the tribes and join mini-topic groups to research and become experts in one aspect of the topic. In time, they return to their tribes and teach their peers the content learned.

These methods are particularly helpful in practicing higher level thinking skills, such as analyzing synthesizing and applying. The groups also learn that achievement depends upon their effective use of collaborative skills. The instructions for Group Inquiry and Jig Saw are contained in the Strategy Section of this book.

The high school years give educational systems the final opportunity to develop the essential resilient attributes young people need in order to do well in their lives. We need to ask what really the priorities are and what will most awaken the innate potentials within each young person who comes our way.

I want to instill in them a hunger for knowledge, truth, and justice. I see teaching as the opportunity to light the fire that will send them on a quest for lifelong learning and for justice.[9]

—DAVID CHRISTIANO,
HIGH SCHOOL
ENGLISH TEACHER

FROM AN ADMINISTRATOR'S VIEW

Teri Ushijima, Ed.D.

Teri is the Complex Area Superintendent of the Central Oahu District Southside Schools in Hawaii. Her wealth of experience as an elementary school teacher, school counselor, high school vice-principal, superintendent, and certified Tribes TLC® Trainer underlies the sound principles and practices that Teri provides as a highly respected school leader.

Teri is the 2006 recipient of the Milken Family Foundation National Educator Award for the State of Hawaii. She is a past President of the Hawaii affiliate of the Association for Supervision and Curriculum Development (ASCD). She is also co-author of the book **Engaging All by Creating High School Learning Communities** with Jeanne Gibbs.

Tribes in the High School?

"They don't respect me, so why should I respect them?
"They were saying things about me..."
"My teacher doesn't like me."

As a high school vice principal, these were familiar cries I often heard when listening to students who were sent to my office. What I found to be true in most cases was that problems stemmed from not feeling connected, a perception that the teacher didn't like them, a belief that others weren't respectful towards them, and reactions to "he said, she said" rumors.

What if... all students had a strong sense of belonging in all their classes?

What if... all students were highly engaged in their lessons?

What if... all students knew their teacher truly cared about them as a person?

Recently, there has been heightened awareness of the need for the traditional high school institutional model to change. Recent sources cite the drop out rate ranging from roughly 30%–50% if it is measured by the number of freshmen students who do not graduate by their senior year.[10]

High schools around the nation are taking a closer look at *Breaking Ranks II*, a document published by NASSP that gives recommendations for reform.[11] It is no surprise that this report identifies personalization of the high school as one of three major focus areas that require significant attention. Students need to learn in an environment where they are safe physically and emotionally, and feel a sense of belonging.

So how does Tribes fit in for the high school? It fits in throughout the system. At our high school, the Tribes process was first used to design a comprehensive teacher-centered professional development program. Teachers work in professional development groups and inquiry groups as part of a larger learning community to refine their teaching practices. Teachers new to the school attend an intensive orientation where they are engaged in building community among themselves and experience the Tribes process as they learn about the school's culture, operations, and school initiatives. Once experiencing this support and comfort with colleagues, teachers are given the opportunity to attend a full Tribes training where they learn how to deliberately create community amongst learners in their own classrooms. Referrals from these teachers are rare and few.

What might it look like with students? In a high school Tribes classroom, you will find students who know and understand the Tribes community agreements. As students engage in cooperative learning strategies and work on collaborative tasks, students are expected to live the agreements. You will see small groups—in science class it may be lab groups; in history it may be inquiry groups; in band it may be sectional groups; in English it may be literature circles. Despite what the groups are called, there are high expectations of all students and tasks are designed to be relevant and authentic. In the school, you will also see permanent advisory groups that meet weekly where students may work on developing collaborative skills, discover their own interests, monitor their success towards graduation, and prepare for goals after high school. Co-curricular activities play a major part in further personalizing the high school experience by having students pursue an area of interest. Whether it is a service group, drama club, marching band, or athletics, these opportunities enable students to further develop their gifts and gain a sense of positive participation and contribution to the school.

So, Tribes in the High School? Absolutely!

Just a Teacher

Today I was a nurse binding a hurt with the white bandage of compassion,
A doctor healing a small broken world,
A surgeon suturing a friendship together.

Today I was an alchemist seeking gold in base metals,
A scientist answering endless whys,
A philosopher pondering elusive truths.

Today, I was an entertainer, refreshing young minds with laughter,
A fisherman dangling learning as a bait,
A pilot guiding youth away from ignorance.

Today, I was a general campaigning against intolerance,
A lawyer speaking out for brotherhood,
A juror weighing right and wrong.

Today, I was a philanthropist sharing the might of the past,
A mother wholly giving love,
A humble follower of truth.

Mine are such varied occupations.
How can they know me?
Just a teacher.

—author unknown

12

Bringing It All Together

Bringing It All Together

Remember us? We're the people who were asking all the questions, back in Chapter 1 of this book, on how to improve the quality of education for all of the kids in our school. We've been looking forward to this last chapter because it describes how to involve the whole school community in collaborative action to achieve the developmental goals that we have for students. Participation just doesn't happen—it must be structured so that everyone feels included, acknowledged, and valued. That's what it takes to create a learning community.

✦ *Now every person belongs to a tribe (a small group of peers)—students with students, teachers with teachers, parents with parents, community resource people and administrators with one another.*

✦ *Every person understands and uses the same inclusive Tribes process, positive agreements, and collaborative skills as taught to our students.*

✦ *Every person is involved in strategizing how to bring about the healthy development and resiliency of all students and quite possibly ourselves! The "new way of learning together" within our many peer groups has given us an authentic sense of community, which makes collaboration possible.*

INNOVATION HAPPENS THROUGH PEER LEARNING COMMUNITIES

The Tribes process is an innovation that, like any other, challenges people to adopt new ways of perceiving, relating, and acting. Invariably, new methods are met with varying degrees of enthusiasm and persistence. Here at Tribes headquarters, we are

Pat Rincone

sometimes asked how long it takes for a majority of teachers in a school to make the TLC process their own, or how long will it take to develop a TLC school community. Our reply is that it depends upon the rate of movement through the following stages:

1. KNOWLEDGE: Some decision makers or leaders gain an understanding and perceive the benefits of the new process or method.

2. PERSUASION: The early adopters (peers) tell others.

3. DECISION: People agree to participate in an activity that leads to making a choice (that is, hear a presentation, discuss with peers, watch a video, visit demonstration classrooms).

4. IMPLEMENTATION: People take steps to learn (training, support, and peer coaching).

5. CONFIRMATION: People give each other support and reinforcement.

Most people evaluate an innovation not on the basis of scientific research by experts, but on the subjective evaluations of near peers who have already adopted the innovation.

—EVERETT ROGERS

Everett Rogers, who has written extensively about the adoption of innovations and defined the stages above, emphasizes that it is the activation of peer networks that leads to "take off."[1] This is why school restructuring efforts need to begin with the formation of small membership groups of peers: students, teachers, parents, administrators, and community resource people. Peter Senge, author of *The Fifth Discipline, The Art and Practice of the Learning Organization*, says:[2]

> *"Virtually all important decisions occur in groups. The learning units of organizations are 'teams,' groups of people who need one another to act."*

Although the concept of school "learning communities" is blanketing educational journals and conference speeches these days, how to structure such communities and how to create a collaborative environment within them has remained vague. In other words, most people agree on the vision but are searching for a way to make it happen. Once a staff learns how to use the Tribes group development process in classrooms, they also can organize the faculty, parents, and resource people into learning groups (tribes), and plan across groups for network action. This makes the school learning community a reality.

Then all of the peer groups can discuss common issues, solve problems, and make collaborative decisions. They can investigate and design supportive strategies for the school community. Their new collegial structure supports learning just as it does for students in classrooms. The integrated school community can acquire knowledge, collaborative skills, and resources.

Parents and teacher tribes can learn about the protective factors that build resiliency, and they can implement a wide range of activities for students of

It is social support from and accountability to valued peers that motivates committed efforts to succeed.[3]

—DAVID AND ROGER JOHNSON

different grade levels. The essence of the protective factors (caring and sharing, participation, and positive expectations) catalyze action throughout the school community system. Integrated through the Tribes group process of inclusion, influence, and community, the school learning community not only has a new way of learning together but a new way of being together.

SUCCESSFUL IMPLEMENTATION

Successful implementation of the Tribes Learning Community process depends upon….

1. Recognition by school leaders, teachers and parents of the school community that the Tribes approach will accelerate learning and development for students of the whole school.

2. A widely held desire for the school to become an active learning community.

3. Designation of sufficient time for the training of the instructional staff by qualified Tribes TLC district or CenterSource Systems trainers.

4. Leadership that is visionary, democratic and supportive.

5. Teachers' commitment to continuous professional learning and quality implementation over a significant period of time.

6. Formation of parent learning groups also using the community building process of Tribes, and that are facilitated by parent leaders.

7. Commitment of the whole school community (teachers, students, school leaders and parents) to on-going reflective practice.

8. Assessments that are designed to check on-going progress.

9. Celebrations that happen regularly.

WHAT SCHOOL LEADERS CAN DO

As a school leader, you need to be clear about the potential payoffs of working in a new pattern of interaction throughout the school community. If you have some questions about what the Tribes process can do for your students and school, give us a call at CenterSource Systems so that we can put you in touch with other principals and administrators who have been using the process for some time. There are benefits not only for classroom management, but for the school as a whole. Once a faculty becomes familiar with using the Tribes process in grade or departmental level small groups, shared decision making and school site planning become collaborative and satisfying.

Just as with other new programs, you need to identify the following resources that will be needed over time:

- ✦ Experienced and qualified trainers
- ✦ Initial training and release time
- ✦ Materials
- ✦ Coaching and follow-up time for the faculty
- ✦ Assessment tools.

The full implementation of the school community Tribes process takes time. A staff will go through predictable stages as they increase their skill and confidence in using the tribes process and integrating it with curriculum in a variety of ways. Progress takes a big leap whenever a principal uses the democratic process (teacher tribes) for staff meetings and school improvement planning. Whether solving a parking problem, establishing new grading policy, or revising curriculum, the collaborative "people skills" and caring environment make management and change easier. Nothing makes collaboration clearer than the principal's willingness to become a learner too.

You can't improve schools without good teachers, but you can't get good teachers unless you treat them as professionals.[4]
—MARC TUCKER

A sense of community is a perception that members have of belonging and being important to each other.[5]
—FLORIN AND CHAVIS

STOP, LOOK, AND LISTEN! KIDS ARE LEARNING HERE!

FROM THE VIEW OF DISTRICT LEADERS

Annette Griffith, M.Ed.
Linda Reed, Ed.D.
Marilyn Sumner, M.Ed.

Annette, Linda and Marilyn organized the initial Spring Branch ISD implementation of Tribes in 1994. Tribes TLC® Trainers since 1995, they have most recently worked with CenterSource and Nancy Latham to develop the new training, Collaboration—The Art Form of Leadership, which is designed to support leadership teams in Tribes Learning Community schools.

Annette has been a teacher, counselor, and district-level administrator. Currently, she is an independent consultant working with school districts to help increase the leadership capacity of both students and adults.

Transforming a District into a Caring Community

We often hear the question: "Why have schools in your district chosen to use Tribes?" Our original goal was to transform classrooms into interdependent, inclusive learning environments that would increase success for all students. By using the Tribes process and common language as a framework, we would begin to align other instructional initiatives across grade levels and subjects.

Less than two years after the first Tribes 24-hour trainings, we realized that the impact of Tribes would be bigger, more systemic and more powerful than predicted. As teachers and other staff began to use Tribes, vivid success stories telegraphed from teacher to teacher and school to school. Without a district mandate and with limited funding, Tribes grew from two schools to implementation in all elementary schools and a quarter of the middle schools.

Campus commitment was critical to Tribes implementation. Administrators and teaching staff demonstrated commitment by incorporating training, resources and follow-up activities into their campus plans. The district allocated resources for CenterSource materials and training for a cadre of Certified Tribes District Trainers with the goal of having two per campus. A collaborative district network supported trainers with study group meetings to discuss progress of implementation.

Leaders' commitment was a key to implementation. Administrators were urged to involve the entire community of students, parents, and staff in learning and using the Tribes process. Principals and facilitators modeled the use of Tribes in faculty meetings. Opportunities were created for staff to share successes, reflect on their learning, and plan collaboratively.

Assessments have helped to improve support of Tribes each year. Observable evidence illustrated that behaviors and attitudes were changing. Schools realized that many discipline approaches previously in use failed to transfer responsibility to students. In a district evaluation, teachers who had implemented Tribes indicated that they spent less time managing student behavior, and students reported that they got along better with others. The most exciting stories describe youngsters who changed from "dropped out but present" to full participation. Group behaviors changed even at bus stops as students became more responsible for their behavior.

Regular evaluations have been critical to maintain community and administrative support and to plan further integration. In 1999, 55 classroom teachers and their students responded to an evaluation survey. Data indicated that in Tribes classrooms mutual respect was consistently evidenced. Teachers indicated that they had more time for creative teaching, and students saw new learning as "fun."

Various departments began to identify ways that Tribes related to their work. The most effective meetings look similar to the Tribes TLC® lesson components incorporating inclusion, objectives, interactive strategies, energizers, reflection and appreciation. Work teams often comment on the emerging sense of community and positive energy.

After several years of implementation, application of Tribes began to erode as the state created more mandates, and other initiatives competed for time. We knew that the longevity of the Tribes initiative was a result of building a strong link between Tribes and new initiatives such as character education and developmental assets. To increase the integration of Tribes, a federal grant was written and awarded. Project HEART is a Partnerships in Education grant designed to integrate character education with the state mandated curriculum. It provides all new teachers with the opportunity to be trained in Basic or Middle School Tribes. Teachers at four schools are part of the research component that involves additional coaching by Phyllis Wells, the Character Education Facilitator and current district leader for Tribes implementation. Project HEART is helping sustain the SBISD commitment to Tribes by broadening our understanding of the connection between social-emotional and academic learning.

Spring Branch schools are still in the midst of their Tribes journey. CenterSource has been an important partner providing leadership and additional training. In 2004, Spring Branch had a ten-year anniversary celebration to honor the positive impact of Tribes! Jeanne Gibbs, Board members, administrators, staff, parents and students participated through stories, interactive strategies and a celebration community circle. Currently, Tribes school leadership teams are taking advantage of the new *Collaboration: The Art Form of Leadership* training.

Our current superintendent, Dr. Duncan Klussmann is a staunch supporter of Tribes and what it has accomplished. "As accountability for academic performance increases, it becomes even more important that we make sure that we are addressing the 'whole child' so that our students learn social and emotional skills as well as the academic skills needed to be successful. Tribes provides Spring Branch educators a process that develops well-rounded, creative, critical thinkers with a strong foundation in ethics and character."

Our schools face daunting challenges that require new ways to reach and teach all students. SBISD's commitment to Tribes is weaving an amazing, stronger human fiber to improve the way we "do school." Please accept our invitation to join us in this journey that truly brings joy to learning and relationships.

Linda has worked as an elementary school principal, Interim Superintendent, and Assistant Superintendent. Currently, a private consultant, she recently completed her Doctor of Education with a research emphasis on implementation.

Marilyn has worn many hats, including teacher, curriculum coordinator, and district administrator. Currently, she is an independent consultant with a focus on improving work, learning and leadership through collaboration.

FROM A PRINCIPAL'S VIEW

Carole Freehan, Ph.D. As a Tribes TLC® Trainer and former principal of Pearl Harbor Kai Elementary School in Honolulu, Hawaii, Carole trained in-service and pre-service teachers, clerical, and support staff to create a school community that supported increased student learning. She earned her doctorate in Leadership Studies and currently teaches Educational Leadership courses to doctoral students, modeling the Tribes process for future educational leaders.

Transforming a School

Transforming any school into an excellent school involves everyone working hard. It takes the commitment of parents, teaching staff, paraprofessionals, clerical, cafeteria and custodial staff to create an exceptional learning environment for children. As educators, we need to improve and strengthen our teaching strategies while school is in session. We are under unbelievable pressure from a multitude of constituencies: parents, boards of education, community, and society. The stakes are constantly being raised.

How can the transformation of a school take place? I believe it comes when everyone knows what excellence looks like, feels like and sounds like. It comes when we can collaborate to seek out the hard issues of what is important for children to learn. It happens when the re-culturing of the school ensures that all the constituents' voices are heard and included.

Historically, Pearl Harbor Kai Elementary has regularly scored in the average or slightly above average on standardized tests. As a staff we were struggling with making changes by implementing programs. We were hoping that the next *program* would be one to help us rise above mediocrity and transport us to a higher level of excellence. As part of the change process, I put teachers into groups and asked them to work together on school-wide professional issues.

While some groups functioned very well, others were less successful. I arranged and rearranged groups of teachers by interest and expertise. The end result was a scattering of many good ideas that did not lead to a coherent workable structure for school improvement. Individually the teachers were excellent teachers, but working collaboratively as a group was a very different and underdeveloped skill.

As much as I rationalized this whole process, I knew that I was missing something—a something that could really affect change in the staff. The lightning bolt of discovery hit me when I went through my first four-day Tribes TLC® training with half of my staff. I realized that my teachers and other staff members were not a learning community or *any* type of community, even though many of them had worked together for over a decade! Just as a teacher has a classroom of children who come with diverse talents and gifts, I had the same situation, although my *students* were adults in the school. A few months after I completed the Tribes TLC® training, I was able to provide another four-day training for the rest of my staff and a two-day program for my classified staff and parent leaders in the school. Training everyone at the school was the first and the easiest step we need to take.

Tribes TLC® is not that *next program;* rather it is a philosophy and process that is critical to creating an environment in which everyone is both a teacher and a learner. One of my roles as the principal is to model the process for the teachers. Teachers need support when they are trying something new or different. They too need to be supported to use the caring Tribes agreements, to experience strategies and take time for reflection questions that are critical to learning. We all know that experience is the best teacher!

So how has the process of Tribes helped us? Well, as we continue to work to become an excellent school, we find that our efforts are not as frustrating as before. All of the teachers, paraprofessionals, classified staff, and students speak the same language. We have a common understanding of the Community Agreements. This understanding is extending to our parents. We are traveling the journey to transform ourselves. Along the way we are creating community, a community that is caring and supportive and learning. Pedagogical differences among the teaching staff are to be expected. Immersion in the process of Tribes has helped us to deal with the differences and see them as opportunities

for professional growth. Now that we include everyone in a respectful and supportive environment, the teachers are more willing to take risks. I see a staff that works daily with their colleagues. I hear student and teachers speak respectfully with each other reducing conflicts. I feel the support that radiates from students, teachers and staff to each other.

Tribes TLC® is not the panacea to a school's problems. Just spending four days going through the training will not, by itself, change anything. We have to live the process every day. As the Principal, I know that I am responsible for carrying the torch for the school. Are we at the top level of excellence yet? Of course not! Have our standardized test scores improved? Yes, they have! As the school travels the Tribes trail together, I see the synergy of the teachers learning from each other and creating exciting opportunities for our students. There are still areas of instruction and assessment we need to define, study, align, update, and improve so that we increase student achievement. Knowing how to work and learn together, we are able to pass over any barriers that block out way towards consistent success. Now that we are a community, I find there are many hands carrying that torch now.

After ten years as a principal I finally figured that out—and I found a life again!

STAFF DEVELOPMENT AND ONGOING SUPPORT

Time out for a question. How many times have you participated in "staff development, in-service, or an educational course" that sent you back to your classroom with some great activities that you whipped through, and then said to yourself, "Now what?" Effective training provides the WHY, the WHAT, and the HOW. The WHY is the theoretical basis for the teaching approach or method. Unless we understand the rationale, some of the research, and why a process or method is appropriate for a population or the times, WHAT to do and HOW to do it are limited.

Quality in-service training and ongoing support are essential. Research (also common sense) tells us that teachers not only need to have knowledge of the theoretical basis or rationale for the teaching method, but they need to be able to:

+ Observe demonstrations by persons who are well versed in the TLC classroom process

+ Practice and be given feedback under controlled conditions (such as trying out the strategy with one another before using it with students)

+ Coach one another as they begin to implement the process, and to

+ Reflect upon and evaluate their own progress.[6]

Demonstrations can happen any of these ways. You can:

+ Visit some Tribes classrooms in you area

+ Invite a qualified Tribes TLC® District Trainer to do demonstrations in classrooms of your school

+ Or you can encourage any of your own teachers who may have been using the process for a period of time to have others observe their students working tribes.

Be sure to take the time to reflect with those demonstration teachers on what you observed.

We urge all Tribes schools to arrange for ongoing meeting time so that teachers' grade level and planning groups can meet regularly. Teacher tribes need to:

+ Support and coach each other

+ Design integrated learning experiences (lesson plans)

+ Identify appropriate materials and resources

+ Assess programs toward learning objectives, and

+ Plan training for the parent facilitators of classroom parent groups.

It takes the realization at the district level that teachers as learners and planners are a school's best bet toward improving education for students. Some schools add days to the teaching year so that their teachers have two hours every week to work together. Others add monthly in-service days, and even paid meeting and sabbatical time. As helpful as periodic in-service days may be, ongoing learning/planning/coaching groups are the most effective way to assure year-long support.

BUILDING A PARENT NETWORK

Although studies have more than proven that there is a direct correlation between family/school collaboration and gains in student achievement,[7] how to involve a majority of parents has been an ongoing puzzle. Getting out to evening meetings at the school after a long day of work, needs to be something more than an obligation. Parents are people too! They have the same human need for attentive listening, appreciation, and a sense of community.

Unfortunately, typical school meetings follow a traditional "we'll-tell-you-what-you-need-to-know" format, and are not structured for inclusion and active participation. Tribes schools have a big advantage! Knowing the TLC process, their teachers can facilitate a school-wide support system for hundreds of parents. The system is based on *parents reaching parents rather than teachers reaching parents*. Here's how it works! Have each teacher identify two parents of students in his or her class. The two parents identified from all of the classrooms are invited to become facilitators of parent groups (tribes) in their child's classroom. The parent volunteers participate in an initial two hours of training to learn and practice how they will lead the first classroom meeting. Back-to-School-Night is a good time to have parents begin meeting in their own small groups. The two parents in each classroom who have been trained to facilitate the parent tribes invite, by phone or letter, the other parents in the class. A phone call from another classroom parent is more effective in terms of getting a response than a notice or letter from the school. The first class meeting is one hour long. The teacher introduces the parents and shares the purpose of the hour: to have parents meet each other and experience some of the process being used in classrooms. The teacher states that he or she will talk about current curricula and the cooperative learning process during the last 10 or 15 minutes of the meeting.

The parent facilitators lead the meeting as detailed in the plan contained in the Resources section of this book. At the end of the hour, reflection questions are used within the groups and a feedback card is filled out. The important question asked by the facilitators at the end of the meeting is, "How many of you enjoyed having time to talk with other parents?" And, "How many would like to meet again using this process to define ways we can support learning for our students?" Names and phone numbers are jotted down within each tribe, and given to the parent facilitators for duplication and mailing back to the members of each parent tribe. People in each tribe can make phone calls to invite their parent tribe members to learning

We sent invitations to all of the parents of our 948 kids to come to the meeting, and 23 came.

—A TEACHER

We had to create a school where people understood the developmental needs of the children and could establish a relationship between home and school that would enhance them.[8]

—JAMES COMER

events and celebrations throughout the year. The gatherings during the year continue to use the TLC process with parents staying in the same groups to build a sense of community.

Learning groups throughout the year can help parents to

+ understand their children's current stage of development

+ learn about resiliency and protective factors

+ discuss how to strengthen protective strategies within their families

+ learn and practice the same collaborative skills in their homes that are being taught in the classroom

+ and support the learning goals and objectives of the class and school.

Why is this an effective way to get parent involvement? Come on, we bet that you know by now. Inclusion, caring, and participation happen just as in classroom tribes. Influence is invited, and commonalities experienced, building a sense of community throughout the year. The approach gives the parent learning community its own support system to help make real the beautiful perspective expressed in the African motto, "It takes a whole village to raise a child."

MORE WAYS TO ENGAGE PARENTS

There are a variety of ways to share the Tribes process with parents. Michele Cahall suggests that on Back-to-School Night teachers have an hour or more to involve the parents in several inclusion strategies. They discuss how the Tribes agreements establish a positive classroom environment to improve academic learning.

Even though intermediate and high school teachers often have as little as ten minutes to present information to parents, many share the important Tribes agreements, and invite parents to share their names and a positive characteristic of their teenager. Regardless of the time available, parents gain an appreciation of how the research-based developmental process is being used in the classroom.

Celebrations of Learning, short presentations of student learning, are scheduled throughout the school year. This gives students an opportunity to demonstrate their newly acquired knowledge and skills. Celebrations can be scheduled during the school day or in the evening. The format is flexible and is best chosen and planned by students themselves. It can be a play, literature reading, inclusion strategies, cooperative learning structures, or hands-on activities in which the parents participate. Celebrations of Learning are a wonderful way for parents to experience first hand the benefits of the Tribes process for their children. The TLC process is also used within parenting classes and parent support groups. Classes emphasize family meetings, agreements, effective communication techniques, decision-making strategies, problem solving, and win/win conflict resolution. The intent is to transfer the same supportive process to families so that a deeper level of caring and sharing touches them too.

The system is based on parents reaching parents rather than teachers reaching parents.

Transforming Environments Rather Than Kids

For two consecutive years, I had the opportunity to travel across the United States as an instructional facilitator for a well-known educational research project. The majority of the numerous schools that I worked with were in very impoverished neighborhoods with populations of "at risk" children. While most of the teachers at these schools had never heard of what we call the caring Tribes process, they too believed in the importance of enhancing human development through kinder school environments. All were convinced that their children needed to learn the social and collaborative skills that not only would help them survive, but move beyond the difficult environments in which they were growing up. It comes at no surprise that daily interaction with these needy children drains the energy and enthusiasm from too many good teachers. Though they give their all, they simply burn out.

I came to realize that even in this world of constant transition and challenge, education is a tough profession. Yet teachers are a resilient

group! By training teachers in Tribes, no matter where they teach, we give them the bolster, on-going support and ability to "hang in there." Once they have the tools to achieve the goals that called them into the teaching profession...they can help their students become healthy well-adjusted beings in an ever changing world.

A Tribes training is the license for a staff to laugh and learn together, to compliment each other, to share concerns and to care for each other. It transforms the teaching experience knowing there is an opportunity to share ideas and ask for suggestions. In my own district, teachers who have been through the Tribes training enroll to take the course again and again. When asked why, they most assuredly reply that it is their "shot in the arm." After the first day of a training, one teacher told me, "I always knew how I wanted my classroom to be. I just didn't know how to get there. Now I do!"

Schools committed to lasting change or reform provide on-going Tribes training and support to teachers by establishing "teacher tribes,"

FROM A TEACHER'S VIEW

Betty White

Betty has contributed to the world of education as an expert teacher of many grade levels, a schoolwide reading facilitator at the Central Canyon Elementary School in Caldwell, Idaho, a national trainer traveling for two years for the John Hopkins University reading curriculum Success for All...and a Tribes TLC® Trainer and Professional Development Consultant for CenterSource Systems. Wherever Betty goes her competence and caring become long remembered as gifts to all.

and allocating regular weekly time for the staff support system to work together. Once this staff restructuring happens, a noticeable climate of enthusiasm, togetherness and high energy changes the school community. In such schools you will find staff, students, and parents all working together with the same common goal of creating a safe and caring learning community... a place where everyone looks forward to coming to school each day!

This is my message and dream for all those schools exhausted with trying to fix, control and teach children "at risk." It's not the children, it's the "at risk" environments that must be transformed.

The Tribes TLC® process over time can indeed transform the culture of a school system, and quality training for staff is the way to bring it about. Unlike many training approaches which become dependent upon "outside consultants and trainers," CenterSource Systems has defined a capacity building model of professional development which prepares teachers and administrators themselves to conduct training in their own schools. Check out the page on CenterSource System's Professional Development opportunities in the Resource section. It's step one in starting your school on a whole new way of being and learning together.

THE TRIBES SCHOOL

The Tribes School

+ is student-centered

+ actively involves the staff in participative management

+ welcomes parents and community involvement in the same process of learning

+ everyone has a tribe of their own— students, staff, even parents and community

+ at home, families learn to use the same communication skills to strengthen family bonds.

Where students, staff and families work together to create a learning environment for healthy human development

And that, my friends, is a Tribes
Learning Community!

13

Active Learning Strategies and Energizers

Active Learning Strategies and Energizers

ACTIVE LEARNING STRATEGIES

Tribes strategies are designed to create a culture for a community of learners; and the strategies are ways to achieve learning objectives, as well. In most cases, it is recommended that one uses the strategy, as written, for the social advantage. Then, after reflecting and realizing that the participants are perceptive to the strategy/process, follow the suggestions in the Options section, which includes formats for subject content. Tribes strategies can be used in combination with Spencer Kagan cooperative learning structures and other notable/creative learning structures that effective teachers acquire through experience.

The Strategy Index Grid that follows these introductory pages is alphabetized and coded so that you can select appropriate strategies and energizers. Each strategy contains the following notations:

1. Objectives

2. Suggested grade levels

3. Grouping: community circle, tribes, sub groups

4. Approximate time required

5. Materials needed

Following the instructions are three kinds of suggested reflection questions: content/thinking, collaborative/social skills, and personal learning. Next, every bit as important, are invitations for appreciation. Follow-up reflection questions and statements of appreciation not only enhance learning for students, but sustain the positive environment. Last, options for using the strategy in content areas are suggested. Remember, if your students liked "Milling to Music" as an opportunity to move and talk about themselves, why not use the strategy as a curriculum learning experience?

Many of the strategies have been adapted from other sources, some familiar to you. The Appendix section following this chapter contains listings of many collections. Some of the best, however, have been contributed by creative Tribes teachers.

Strategies need to be selected carefully, and tailored to fit the ethnicity, culture, age level, interests, language, and socio-economic status of the students in your class. A strategy that is not sensitive to community culture undermines the teaching process. Following are some obvious examples of this:

✦ Using the names of Christian holidays but not those of other religions.

✦ Urging Native Americans, Latinos, and indigenous populations to make personal statements during the inclusion stage. The opportunity first to share about their culture, family, or group is traditional for them, and therefore more comfortable and inclusive.

✦ Ignoring the economic realities of a community (i.e., using examples of luxury items in a low-income area).

✦ Urging Cambodian and Thai students to demonstrate eye contact during attentive listening (when in their own culture averting one's eyes denotes respect).

It also is very important to plan and implement strategies well. The chart on the next page will give you a quick summary for implementing Tribes strategies.

ENERGIZERS

In the midst of any time together groups of people will periodically experience lower energy within their environments. Concentration becomes more difficult; boredom and sleepiness can set in and will be counterproductive to accomplishing the task at hand. Students, especially, become restless. They are likely to withdraw or even create a disturbance. The remedy? A quick five-minute physical activity to revitalize the group with an "energizer."

Energizers are satisfying because they engage many of the multiple intelligences primarily: body/kinesthetic, musical/rhythmic, interpersonal and visual/spatial.

Six outcomes can be achieved through the use of energizers:

1. The energy of the classroom or group is revitalized.

2. People's attention can be drawn back to the classroom after a time away (recess, lunch break, or some other interruption).

3. Different types of academic learning activities can be bridged, renewing energy and concentration.

4. People can feel connected again with one another and the whole community.

5. Multiple intelligences can be reached and are engaged.

6. They add to the fun of learning and being together!

The pages that follow contain a collection of some favorite Tribes energizers. Some are more physical than others, and as with other activities in this book it is up to you to select the most appropriate ones for your students. Much depends upon the level of trust within the class at any one time, and the age level of your students.

Know that energizers can also be extended into content/subjects areas. For example, "Two Truths and a Lie" can easily be applied to writing true/false statements about a subject of study, to review or assess learning. And, asking reflection questions is always recommended, to ensure significance within context (listed above as outcomes).

The Tribes Energizer Box contains an additional 101 energizers, and is available from CenterSource.

SUMMARY: FACILITATING TRIBES STRATEGIES

1. Remind students about the Tribes agreements:

   ✦ Whenever appropriate, ask the class or tribe to review the agreements.

   ✦ Have the agreements posted at all times.

   ✦ Respect and model the agreements congruently yourself.

2. Give the instructions:

   ✦ Select and tailor an appropriate strategy or series of them to achieve your learning objectives.

   ✦ Tell your students what the objectives are (what they will learn).

   ✦ Give instructions simply and concisely; do not get off the track or use too many words.

   ✦ Tell students how much time they will have to complete the task.

3. If students are in a community circle:

   ✦ Initiate the sharing yourself.

   ✦ Let the students know who will be next—which way you'll go around the circle.

   ✦ Ask people to speak directly to one another.

✦ Withhold your own comments on what students share.

✦ Encourage people to use first names.

✦ Make it okay to pass.

✦ Deal with put-downs or a lack of attentive listening.

✦ Give people a second opportunity to share if they pass the first time.

✦ Ask appropriate content, social, and/or personal reflection questions.

✦ Wind things up when people feel bored or restless.

4. If students are working in tribes or small groups:

✦ Follow suggestions noted above in sections two and three.

✦ If using roles, discuss them, assign them, or have students choose them.

✦ Describe the task to be accomplished (materials, resources, and time for completion).

✦ Ask students to clarify the task to you or each other.

✦ Observe their interaction and assist only as needed.

✦ Ask reflection questions.

✦ Assess (or have students assess) and evaluate outcomes.

5. Invite statements of appreciation:

✦ Suggest sentence starters.

✦ Be a good role model.

6. Celebrate class, tribe, or individual contributions and achievements.

7. REFLECT. Remember, "the activity alone is not enough!" It's appropriate and effective to reflect before, during, and/or after the strategy/learning experience.

STRATEGIES MATRIX

STRATEGY TITLE	Page	INCLUSION	Presenting Self	Social Skills	Agreements	INFLUENCE	Decisions/Problem Solving	Resolving Conflict	Goal Setting	COMMUNITY	Energizer	Celebration	ACADEMICS
Abstract Painting Of Feelings	208	●	●	●		●	●						●
Ali Baba	384									●	●		
All In The Family	209	●	●	●									●
Alligator Attack	382									●	●		
Alligators	382									●	●		
Am I Napoleon?	210	●	●			●				●			●
Animal Triads	211				●		●	●					●
Appreciating Others	213	●		●						●		●	
Barnyard Babble	215	●											●
Boasters	216	●	●	●	●								●
Brainstorming	218	●	●			●	●	●		●		●	●
Bubble Gum	382									●	●		
Building A Time Machine	219	●		●		●	●	●					●
Bumper Sticker	220	●	●	●						●		●	●
Bumpety-Bump-Bump	388									●	●		
Campaign Manager	221	●	●							●		●	●
Career Choices	222	●	●			●	●						●
Celebrity Sign-In	223		●			●	●						●
Chain Reaction	224	●	●	●						●		●	●
Changes	385									●	●		
Clap-Slap	386									●	●		
Client-Consultants	225	●		●		●	●						●
Community Circle	226	●	●	●	●					●		●	●

STRATEGY TITLE	Page	INCLUSION	Presenting Self	Social Skills	Agreements	INFLUENCE	Decisions/Problem Solving	Resolving Conflict	Goal Setting	COMMUNITY	Energizer	Celebration	ACADEMICS
Community Circle Metaphor	228	•	•	•						•		•	•
Confrontation	229	•		•		•		•	•				•
Consensus-Building	230	•		•		•	•	•	•				•
Cooperation Squares	231	•		•		•	•	•					•
Creative Storytelling	233	•	•							•			•
Current Events Debate	234	•			•	•	•						•
Dear Abby	235	•	•			•	•	•					•
Do After Me	387									•	•		
Dream Quilt	236	•	•	•		•	•		•	•			•
Electricity	388									•	•		
Extended Nametags	237	•	•	•									•
Family Camp Trek	239	•		•		•	•			•			•
Family Changes	241	•	•	•									•
Find The Word	242	•		•		•							•
Finding All We Have In Common	243	•	•	•									•
Five E's	244			•			•			•			•
Five Tribles	246	•	•										•
Flies On the Ceiling	248	•		•		•		•	•	•			•
Fold the Line Reading	249	•		•		•		•					•
Fork and Spoon	384									•	•		
Funeral For Put-Downs	250		•			•	•	•					•
Fuzzyland	252	•	•	•	•	•	•	•					
Fuzzyland Map	251	•		•	•								•

STRATEGIES MATRIX

STRATEGY TITLE	Page	INCLUSION	Presenting Self	Social Skills	Agreements	INFLUENCE	Decisions/Problem Solving	Resolving Conflict	Goal Setting	COMMUNITY	Energizer	Celebration	ACADEMICS
Gallery Walks	254	●	●	●		●				●		●	●
Give Me A Clue	255	●		●		●	●						●
Goal-Storming	257	●		●		●	●						●
Graphing Who We Are	258	●		●		●	●						●
Group Inquiry	259	●		●			●	●		●			●
Group Problem-Solving	261	●		●		●	●						●
Hagoo	386									●	●		
Hug Tag	386									●	●		
I Like My Neighbors	386									●	●		
I Love You, Honey	386									●	●		
I Sit in a Chair with My Friend	262	●	●	●	●					●	●		●
I Used To Be; We Used To Be	263	●	●	●	●	●							●
I'm Proud Appreciation Circle	264	●	●	●									●
Ideal Classroom	265	●	●	●		●	●	●	●				●
Interview Circle	266	●	●	●		●	●						●
Jigsaw	267	●		●		●	●						●
Joy	269	●	●	●									●
Kitchen Kapers	270	●	●			●	●	●					●
Knots	381									●	●		
Lap Game	387									●	●		
Life Map	271	●	●	●									●
Line-up	384									●	●		
Live Wire	272	●	●	●									●

STRATEGY TITLE	Page	INCLUSION	Presenting Self	Social Skills	Agreements	INFLUENCE	Decisions/Problem Solving	Resolving Conflict	Goal Setting	COMMUNITY	Energizer	Celebration	ACADEMICS
Look At Me!	273	●	●	●									
Making a Choice	275			●		●	●						●
Me Book	277	●	●	●									●
Meet Someone Special	278	●	●	●									●
Milling To Music	279	●	●	●									●
Mirror...Mirror	280	●	●										●
Mirrors	380									●	●		
Monkey, Elephant, Palm Tree	387									●	●		
My Favorite People and Things	282	●	●	●									●
My Name In Print	285	●	●	●									●
Name Game	286	●	●	●									●
Name Wave	388									●	●		
Newspaper Scavenger Hunt	287	●		●		●	●						●
Novel in an Hour	289						●			●			●
Now I Am	290	●		●									●
On My Back	291	●	●										●
One Special Thing About Me	292	●	●	●									●
One, Two, Three	293	●		●		●	●						●
One-Minute History	294	●	●	●									●
Open Forum	295	●	●	●		●	●						●
Our Treasury	296	●		●		●	●						●
Our World Is Changing	297	●		●		●			●				●
Outlines	298	●	●	●									●

STRATEGIES MATRIX

STRATEGY TITLE	Page	INCLUSION	Presenting Self	Social Skills	Agreements	INFLUENCE	Decisions/Problem Solving	Resolving Conflict	Goal Setting	COMMUNITY	Energizer	Celebration	ACADEMICS
Pantomime	301	●	●										●
Paper Toss	381									●	●		
Paraphrase Passport	302	●		●	●								●
Paraphrasing	303	●		●	●								●
Partner Introduction	305	●	●	●									●
Peer-Response Huddle	306	●		●		●	●						●
Pen Pals	389									●	●		
People Hunt	307	●	●	●									●
People Machine	388									●	●		
People Patterns	382									●	●		
People Puzzles	311	●		●									●
Perception and Transmission	312	●		●		●		●					●
Personal Contract	314	●		●		●	●	●	●				●
Personal Journal	315	●	●										●
Poem By Our Tribe	316	●	●			●	●			●		●	●
Problem Solving...Appreciative Inquiry	318					●	●						●
Put Down the Put-Downs	319	●	●		●	●		●					●
Put Yourself On the Line	320	●		●		●	●						●
Rain	387									●	●		
Reasons and Alternatives	321	●		●									●
Reflecting Feelings	322	●		●		●		●					●
Resentment/Appreciation	324	●		●		●		●					●
Roles People Play	325	●		●		●		●					●

STRATEGY TITLE	Page	INCLUSION	Presenting Self	Social Skills	Agreements	INFLUENCE	Decisions/Problem Solving	Resolving Conflict	Goal Setting	COMMUNITY	Energizer	Celebration	ACADEMICS
Self-Esteem Cards	328	●	●	●									●
Shaping Up with Blocks	329	●		●									●
Sharing From A Sack	330	●	●	●						●		●	●
Shoe 'n Tell	331	●	●	●									●
Shuffle Your Buns	385									●	●		
Silhouettes	332	●	●	●									●
Singing the Blues	333	●	●	●									●
Skin the Snake	388									●	●		
Slip Game	334	●	●	●									●
Snowball	389									●	●		
Snowball I-Messages	336	●		●									●
Something Good	337	●	●	●									●
Something I Cherish	338	●	●	●									●
Space Pioneers	339	●		●		●	●						●
Special Friend I Know	341	●	●	●									●
Spider Web	342	●	●	●						●		●	●
Stand Off	380									●	●		
Stand Up	380									●	●		
Student-Developed Lesson	343	●		●		●	●						●
Suggestion Circle	344	●		●		●	●	●					●
Taking A Closer Look	345	●		●		●	●						●
Teaching Agreements	347	●		●	●	●	●						●
Teaching I-Messages	348	●		●		●		●					●

STRATEGIES MATRIX

STRATEGIES MATRIX

STRATEGY TITLE	Page	INCLUSION	Presenting Self	Social Skills	Agreements	INFLUENCE	Decisions/Problem Solving	Resolving Conflict	Goal Setting	COMMUNITY	Energizer	Celebration	ACADEMICS
Teaching Listening	349	●		●									●
Teaching Paraphrasing/Feelings	350	●		●									●
Ten	389									●	●		
That's Me—That's Us!	351	●	●							●		●	●
Third-Party Mediation	352	●		●		●	●	●					●
This Is Me	353	●	●	●									●
Three Ball Pass	383									●	●		
Thumbs Up, Thumbs Down	355					●	●						●
Tower-Building	356	●		●		●	●						●
Traffic Jam	380									●	●		
Tribal Peer Coaching	357	●		●		●	●						●
Tribe Graffiti	358	●		●									●
Tribe Mimes/Role-Play	359	●	●			●		●					●
Tribe Portrait	360	●	●	●									●
Trust Walk	380									●	●		
Two On A Crayon	361	●		●		●	●						●
Two Truths and a Lie	383									●	●		
Unfinished Fantasies	362	●	●			●		●	●				●
Urgent!	363	●		●		●	●						●
Vehicle	390									●	●		
Warm Fuzzies	364	●			●								
Warm Fuzzy Bag	366	●			●								
Week In Perspective	367	●	●	●									●

STRATEGY TITLE	Page	INCLUSION	Presenting Self	Social Skills	Agreements	INFLUENCE	Decisions/Problem Solving	Resolving Conflict	Goal Setting	COMMUNITY	Energizer	Celebration	ACADEMICS
What Are You Doing?	389									●	●		
What Feelings Do You Have?	368	●	●										●
What Will Happen Next?	369	●		●		●	●						●
What's In A Name?	370	●		●									●
What's In My Name?	371	●	●	●									●
What's In Your Wallet?	373	●	●	●									●
What's The Tint of Your Glasses?	374	●		●		●		●					●
What's Your Bag?	375	●	●	●									●
Where Do I Stand?	376	●	●	●		●	●						●
Why Is This Word Important?	377	●	●			●	●						●
Wink	381									●	●		
Wishful Thinking	378	●	●	●									●
Zap	385									●	●		
Zoo Stories	379	●	●	●									●
Zoom, Zoom, Brake!	383									●	●		

STRATEGIES MATRIX

Abstact Painting of Feelings

GRADES
K–3

TIME
30 minutes

GROUPING
tribes, subgroups

MATERIALS
12 x 18-inch
paper, paints,
and brushes

Objectives
1. To build inclusion
2. To express feelings by using colors

Instructions
1. Ask the students to meet in tribes or form groups of three to five.
2. Give each tribe member a sheet of paper and a brush.
3. Have each tribe choose three colors.
4. Ask each tribe member to paint a picture using the color that represents how he or she is feeling (refer to the chart made in the previous activity, "What Feelings Do You Have?").
5. Invite the students to share the feelings they painted.

Suggested Reflection Questions
CONTENT/THINKING
  ✦ What were the different feelings painted by your tribe members?
  ✦ How did you know what colors to use?

SOCIAL
  ✦ How did this activity help you get to know your tribe members?

PERSONAL
  ✦ Did you discover anything new about yourself?

Appreciation
INVITE STATEMENTS OF APPRECIATION:
  ✦ "I'm a lot like you when..."
  ✦ "I admired your honesty about..."
  ✦ "I liked it when you..."

Options
Choose characters in literature or history, current events, or social issues at school.
Illustrate feelings about those topics.

All In the Family

Objectives
1. To build inclusion
2. To promote awareness of how other family members feel

Instructions
1. Ask the students to form groups in different parts of the room according to their birth positions in their families: (eldest, youngest, in-betweens, only child).
2. Have each student share with the other members of his or her group:
   + How does it feel to be [*firstborn, etc.*]?
   + What are the responsibilities he or she has?
   + What are the advantages he or she has?
3. Merge the groups so that the eldest are with the in-betweens, and the only children are with youngest (or mix the groups together whichever way you want).
4. Now ask these groups to share:
   + Who do you think has the most power in your family?
   + How do you feel toward other siblings?
   + Who gets attention in your family and how do they get it?

GRADES 2–adult
TIME 20 minutes
GROUPING subgroups
MATERIALS none

Suggested Reflection Questions
CONTENT/THINKING
   + What did you learn about birth order and power in a family?
   + What generalizations can you make about birth order?

SOCIAL
   + What social skills did you use to make this activity successful?
   + How well did you participate?

PERSONAL
   + How did you feel when you were with others in the same birth position as you?
   + What did you feel about those in the same birth position/different birth position?
   + What did you learn about yourself?

Appreciation
INVITE STATEMENTS OF APPRECIATION:
   + "I'm a lot like you when..."
   + "I felt good when..."

Options
Have students research facts about historical figures including the birth order of those people. Make a graph of the class results of birth orders researched (or the birth orders of students in the class, or the responses to reflection questions).

Am I Napoleon?

GRADES
K–adult

TIME
20 minutes

GROUPING
community

MATERIALS
3 x 5-inch cards,
pins, crayons or
felt pens

Objectives

1. To build inclusion
2. To identify and learn about famous people in history, politics, science, or some other academic content

Instructions

1. Give each person a 3 x 5-inch index card, a pin, and a pencil.
2. Ask each student to print on the card in large block letters the name of some famous person, living or dead. (With young students, use pictures of animals, plants, or fruits.)
3. Ask each student to pin his or her "famous person" card onto the back of another student, without letting that student know the name on the card.
4. Tell the students to find out who they are by milling around and asking other students questions that can be answered "yes" or "no." Students may ask only one question each time they talk to another student. Continue the process until everyone has identified his or her famous name. Simple hints from other students or the teacher may be given to help those having a difficult time.

Suggested Reflection Questions

CONTENT/THINKING

◆ Who were some of the famous people?

◆ What kind of questions did you ask?

◆ What do you know about the person whose name was pinned onto your back?

SOCIAL

◆ How did you help each other successfully identify your famous people?

PERSONAL

◆ Do you identify with your famous person in any way?

◆ What kind of questions will you ask next time?

Appreciation

INVITE STATEMENTS OF APPRECIATION:

◆ "I liked it when..."

◆ "I'm a lot like you when..."

Options

Use historical figures, vocabulary words (practice definitions: Am I the word that means "talkative"?), or numbers (for example, practice simple equations or order of operations).

Animal Triads

Objectives

1. To encourage influence
2. To increase awareness of animal families

Instructions

1. Lead a community discussion about cooperation. Emphasize:
   + Each student wants all the people in the group to do well.
   + Each student believes that he or she can help the others.
   + Everyone must understand the task.
2. Ask the community to meet in tribes. Explain that the activity is to put a puzzle together, and that it can be solved only if everyone helps each other (cooperates).
3. Pass out an "Animal Triads" set to each tribe.
4. Read the following directions aloud: "Each tribe has an envelope containing twelve or fifteen triangles with the name (or picture) of an animal on each triangle. The triangles are blue, red and yellow. The task is complete when each tribe member has arranged three triangles with animals from the same family on them in a row. While doing this, follow the rules which are:
   + No one may speak
   + No one may signal for a triangle
   + You may give triangles, but you may not reach over and just take any."
5. Ask each tribe to distribute the triangles equally among tribe members giving each person, one of each color, but not in the same "family" (For example: fox, dolphin, and koala).
6. The remaining member(s) are to be "Observers," who remain silent during the activity, and share their observations after the task is completed.
7. Each tribe works until the task has been completed.

> **GRADES**
> 2–5
>
> **TIME**
> 20 minutes
>
> **GROUPING**
> tribes, subgroups
>
> **MATERIALS**
> Animal Triads sets

Suggested Reflection Questions

CONTENT/THINKING
+ What did you learn about animal families?
+ Why is it important to follow the rules in this activity?

SOCIAL
+ What did you learn about communication skills and giving to others?
+ What did you learn about cooperation?

PERSONAL
+ What was frustrating about this activity?

Appreciation

INVITE STATEMENTS OF APPRECIATION:
+ "I liked it when..."
+ "I felt good when..."

Options

Use other lesson topics for categorization, such as geography, arithmetic, parts of speech, or history.

Animal Triads

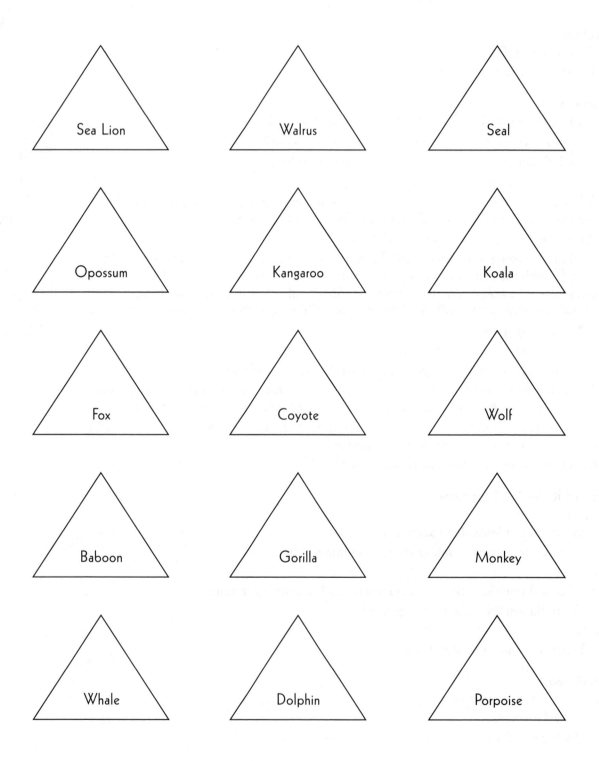

Appreciating Others

Objectives

1. To increase awareness of importance of stating appreciation
2. To practice the norms
3. To provide for initial inclusion

Instructions

1. Pass out "Appreciating Others" worksheet to all class members.
2. In the front of the room post a large visual of the worksheet from which you can work as a model.
3. Ask each student to fill in the boxes with positive statements, one to self, best friend, Mom and/or Dad, and a classmate. Suggest that they use some of the positive statement forms noted on the bottom of the worksheet, if they need to.
4. Ask the students to meet in tribes to share their positive statements.
5. Have one member of each tribe record all the core ideas that are included on the tribe members' worksheets.
6. Ask the recorder from each tribe to report the summaries to the community.
7. Suggest that students tell one of their statements to the person it was written to.

GRADES
2–adult

TIME
45 minutes

GROUPING
community, tribes

MATERIALS
"Appreciating Others" worksheets, pencils, large paper, felt pens

Suggested Reflection Questions

CONTENT/THINKING

+ Why did you learn to give statements of appreciation?
+ What were three statements shared by your tribe members?

SOCIAL

+ How can making statements of appreciation help a tribe work together better?
+ Why is it important to make statements of appreciation to friends, family, and others?

PERSONAL

+ How do you feel when you receive a statement of appreciation from someone else?
+ Which of the statements you wrote would make you feel good?

Appreciation

INVITE STATEMENTS OF APPRECIATION:

+ "I liked it when..."
+ "Thank you for..."

Options

Ask how many students would commit to using at least one appreciation statement every day. Have tribes write contracts to do so. Post the contracts and review them regularly.

Appeciating Others

Self	**Best Friend**
Mom/Dad	**Classmate**

Suggested positive statement formats:

_____, I liked it when you…

_____, I appreciate it when…

_____, I'm glad you…

_____, I want to give you a warm fuzzy for…

_____, thanks for…

Barnyard Babble

Objectives

1. To build community inclusion
2. To divide people into tribes or random groups
3. To have a hilarious time

Instructions

1. Prepare a small slip of paper for each student. Depending on the number of tribes that the community will divide into, select names of that many noisy animals. Examples: horse, cow, chicken, pig, sheep, donkey, mouse, rooster, dog, cat.
2. Write the name of an animal (or use a picture) on each slip so that the students in the "horse" tribe all have slips labeled "horse" and the students in the "chicken" tribe all have slips marked "chicken."
3. If you are assigning students to specific tribes, write the name of the student on one side of the slip and the name of the animal on the other side.
4. Before distributing the slips, tell the students that they are not to let anyone else know what animal names are on their slips.
5. Have the community circulate with eyes closed, making the noises of their animals.
6. When all the students with the same animal names find each other, have the "animal tribes" sit together and discuss and reflect.

Suggested Reflection Questions

CONTENT/THINKING

+ What do you think of this way of finding tribe members?
+ What made this an exciting way to divide into tribes?

SOCIAL

+ How did it feel when you found each other?

PERSONAL

+ How did you end up finding your tribe?
+ How do you feel now?

Appreciation

INVITE STATEMENTS OF APPRECIATION:

+ "I was [*feeling*] when..."
+ "Thank you, [*name*] for..."
+ "I liked it when..."

Options

Have the community divide into tribes by humming or singing nursery rhymes or familiar tunes. More mature groups may enjoy using different dance steps or acting out career descriptions, historical events, topics of study, or foreign language phrases.

GRADES
K–adult

TIME
15 minutes

GROUPING
community

MATERIALS
name slips

Boasters

Objectives

1. To make statements of appreciation to self and others
2. To build self-esteem
3. To build inclusion

Instructions

1. Prepare posterboard or construction paper cutouts similar to the one on the next page for each student, or have each student prepare one for himself or herself.
2. Ask the community to meet in tribes.
3. Have each student write his or her name in large, colorful letters on the head area of his or her cut-out.
4. Instruct the tribe members to pass the cutouts around the tribe so that each tribe member can write a positive statement on each other tribe member's cutout.
5. Have a discussion about complimenting yourself and how it is different than bragging. Then ask each student to write a positive statement about himself or herself on his or her own card.

GRADES
2–adult

TIME
30–45 minutes

GROUPING
tribes, subgroups

MATERIALS
12-inch-high cutouts of student profiles

Suggested Reflection Questions

CONTENT/THINKING

✦ Why is it important to be able to make positive statements about others?
✦ What are two positive statements that you made to others/they made to you?

SOCIAL

✦ How can making positive statements to each other help us work together better?

PERSONAL

✦ How did you feel when you knew someone else was writing on your card?
✦ How did you feel when you read the comments on your card?
✦ Do you ever compliment yourself?
✦ Make a plan for complimenting yourself at least once every day.

Appreciation

INVITE STATEMENTS OF APPRECIATION:

✦ "I'm glad you notice that I..."
✦ "I felt good when..."

Options

Use as a "book report" format, where students review the literature through one of the characters, using the historical figures' attributes, opinions, or accomplishments.

Boasters

Brainstorming

Objectives

1. To energize a tribe
2. To promote inclusion and influence
3. To experience the fun and creative power of brainstorming as a decision-making or problem-solving technique

Instructions

1. Ask each tribe to appoint a recorder to jot down all the ideas on paper, chalkboard, or newsprint as fast as ideas are called out. (With very young students use an aide or older student.)
2. Instruct the tribes on the "DOVE" rules that they need to follow in order to "brainstorm."

   D defer judgment

   O off beat, original

   V vast number

   E expand, elaborate

3. Have the community meet in tribes. Explain that each tribe will have five minutes to call out and write down as many ideas as possible on a subject. Examples:
   + "How could we design a better bathtub—one for more enjoyment, efficiency, and comfort than ordinary tubs?"
   + Other possible subjects: better bicycle, bedroom, car, school cafeteria, school
4. Stop the brainstorming after five minutes. Ask each recorder to read his or her tribe's list. Lead applause after each tribe's creativity.
5. If time allows, have the tribes draw their creations. Find a way to include everyone in the tribe.

GRADES
K–adult

TIME
20 minutes

GROUPING
tribes

MATERIALS
markers,
large paper

Suggested Reflection Questions

CONTENT/THINKING
+ Why is brainstorming fun?
+ How do the "DOVE" rules help you to brainstorm?

SOCIAL
+ What would have happened if we had judged, commented, or discussed ideas as they were offered?
+ How could you tell that your tribe members were enjoying themselves?
+ How well did your tribe members follow the "DOVE" rules?

PERSONAL
+ How much did you participate?

Appreciation

INVITE STATEMENTS OF APPRECIATION:
+ "I liked it when you said..."
+ "Your suggestions helped me to..."

Options

Brainstorm possible endings to a story, a list of "meaningful sentences," or multiple examples of a theme. Use for classroom issues or decisions.

Building a Time Machine

Objectives

1. To encourage tribe members to create something together
2. To have tribes present their creations to the community
3. To experience influence

Instructions

1. Ask the students if they have ever read any books or seen any movies about time machines.
2. Call on a few students to share what they know about time machines.
3. Let the students know that their tribes will have an opportunity to build a time machine.
4. Have the community meet in tribes. Give each group equal amounts of "junk" to build their time machine.
5. Give the tribes the next twenty minutes to construct their time machines.
6. Have the tribes take turns presenting their time machines to the class.
7. Have each student write a letter to someone in another time that could be delivered by his or her tribe's time machine.

GRADES
3–adult

TIME
45 minutes

GROUPING
tribes

MATERIALS
assorted junk

Suggested Reflection Questions

CONTENT/THINKING

+ What decisions did your tribe have to make?
+ Why is it important to use your imagination?
+ What did you learn by doing this strategy?

SOCIAL

+ How did your tribe make its machine?
+ What did you do to help?
+ How can your tribe work together better?

PERSONAL

+ How did you help your tribe build the time machine?
+ How did you feel while you were working?

Appreciation

INVITE STATEMENTS OF APPRECIATION:

+ "[Name], you helped when..."
+ "I liked it when..."

Options

Use this experience as a writing prompt. Have students write answers to reflection questions, the pros and cons of time travel, or a time they would like to travel to and why.

Bumper Sticker

Objectives
1. To present something special about oneself
2. To build inclusion
3. To encourage attentive listening

GRADES
2–adult

TIME
30 minutes

GROUPING
community, tribes

MATERIALS
colored paper
strips, crayons or
markers

Instructions
1. Review agreements.
2. Give each student a long strip of paper and a marker or crayon with which to create a "bumper sticker" that he or she would enjoy displaying on his or her automobile bumper (wagon, bicycle. etc.).
3. Have each student in turn share his or her bumper sticker with the community. Remind everyone to give their full attention to the speaker.
4. Tell the students they may ask questions, and express mutual feelings and concerns after everyone has shared.

Suggested Reflection Questions
CONTENT/THINKING
+ What similar kinds of things did you put on your bumper stickers?
+ What's one special thing you learned about another student?

SOCIAL
+ How well did everyone listen when you shared your bumper sticker?

PERSONAL
+ How did you feel as you shared?
+ What can you do in the future to help others feel more comfortable when they share?
+ Would you really want to put your sticker on your car or bicycle? Why or why not?

Appreciation
INVITE STATEMENTS OF APPRECIATION:
+ "I liked it when..."
+ "I admired you for..."

Options
Use subject area topics, such as "Why study Social Studies?"

Campaign Manager

Objectives
1. To build inclusion
2. To foster positive feelings in the community
3. To build self-esteem

Instructions
1. Have students meet in their tribes.
2. Pass out paper circles, cards, and a small bag to each tribe.
3. Instruct each tribe member to write his or her name on a slip of paper and drop it into a bag. Then have each member draw a name out of the bag (making sure he or she doesn't draw his or her own).
4. Tell the students that each is to be the "campaign manager" for the person whose name he or she drew a person who has been nominated for "Wonderful Person of the Year."
5. Explain that each student will design a campaign button on the circle of paper, and list three good campaign statements on the card to promote his or her nominee. The campaign manager may inter-view their candidate if they need more information on special qualities.
6. Have the campaign managers deliver the campaign speeches (using the cards) and present their nominees with their campaign buttons. Lead applause and cheering.

GRADES
3–adult

TIME
60 minutes

GROUPING
tribes

MATERIALS
small circles with 6-inch diameter, 3 x 5-inch cards, pencils, small bags

Suggested Reflection Questions
CONTENT/THINKING
+ What similarities did you notice between the campaign buttons and the presentations?
+ Why is it important to make a good campaign speech?

SOCIAL
+ What social skills did you need to make this activity successful?

PERSONAL
+ How did you feel when your manager was presenting your campaign?
+ How did you feel when you were presenting your candidate's campaign?
+ Would you ever like to manage a campaign for someone?

Appreciation
INVITE STATEMENTS OF APPRECIATION:
+ "I liked it when..."
+ "I felt good when..."

Options
Use characters from literature, history or current events, or study candidates in a current election.

Career Choices

Objectives

1. To help the students make choices and honor each other's choices
2. To give the students an opportunity to share some of their career views
3. To experience influence

Instructions

GRADES
2–12

TIME
40 minutes

GROUPING
community

MATERIALS
career signs

1. Make two signs with a career choice such as "chemist" and "marine biologist" (or use two other occupations) written on each of them and put them up on different sides of the room.
2. Tell your students that they are going to be asked to make a choice about occupations related to the field of science or health.
3. They will make their choice by moving to one side of the room or the other, to stand under the sign of the occupation of their choice.

   Example: Point out the sign "chemist" on one side of the room and "marine biologist" on the other side of the room.
4. Have students discuss in groups of 3 or 4 why they chose the occupation.

Suggested Reflection Questions:

CONTENT/THINKING

- ✦ Why is it important to make choices?
- ✦ What other occupations did you consider?

  SOCIAL

- ✦ How well did the community honor the agreements?
- ✦ Which agreement might be the most important in an strategy like this?

PERSONAL

- ✦ Why did you make the choice you did?
- ✦ How did you feel about making your choice public?

Appreciation

INVITE STATEMENTS OF APPRECIATION:

- ✦ "I appreciated it when..."
- ✦ "It was great when..."

Options

Use current social issues (in school, society, the world). Use scientific hypotheses. Use as reflective practice (for example, choose a mathematical concept that you can explain thoroughly and correctly).

Celebrity Sign-In

Objectives

1. To structure a cooperative learning experience for a history topic
2. To enhance communication skills
3. To experience influence

Instructions

1. Give each tribe the name of a celebrity or historical character, and allow time for each tribe to learn as much as it can about the person.
2. Set up a row of chairs in front of the room facing the class.
3. Ask each tribe to select a tribe member to "be" their celebrity.
4. Have each celebrity sign in on the chalkboard and then take a seat in the row of chairs ("interview panel").
5. Ask each character to tell the other panel members about his or her prominence in history. After they have all done so, call time out and let tribe members huddle with their character to remind them of more data to present. After several huddles, invite the audience to ask questions of the "celebrity." Allow tribe members to help answer.
6. Lead rounds of applause after each character's performance.

GRADES
4–adult

TIME
varies

GROUPING
community, tribes

MATERIALS
rows of chairs in front of room

Suggested Reflection Questions

CONTENT/THINKING

✦ What did you learn about the different celebrities?

✦ Why is this an interesting way to learn new information?

✦ What values were reflected by the characters?

✦ In what other ways can you use this activity?

SOCIAL

✦ What did tribe members do to support their celebrity?

PERSONAL

✦ How did you feel while you were portraying your character?

Appreciation

INVITE STATEMENTS OF APPRECIATION:

✦ "[name], I respect you for..."

✦ "[name], I liked the way you portrayed..."

Options

Use people in the news, history, and literature. Use content standard topics, inviting students to choose a tribe member to explain the topic.

Chain Reaction

Objectives

1. To build inclusion and influence
2. To increase communication skills
3. To share personal interests, opinions and ideas
4. To ask each other questions about subject matter

GRADES
K–adult

TIME
15–30 minutes

GROUPING
community, tribes

MATERIALS
none

Instructions

1. Have the community meet in tribes.
2. Remind the students of their right to pass and to honor the other agreements. Remind tribe members to give full, caring attention.
3. Have one tribe member begin by asking a question of a second tribe member. Have the second tribe member answer the question and then ask another question of a third tribe member. Instruct the tribes to continue the chain until each tribe member has answered and then asked a question. In large tribes have students ask the persons directly across from them. This helps the students to speak loudly enough.
4. Explain that questions may be autobiographical or deal with curriculum or a number of issues (politics, hobbies, education, friendship, family interests). (This is a good activity for students to help each other prepare for a test.)

Suggested Reflection Questions

CONTENT/THINKING
+ What did you learn about your tribe members?
+ Why is this a good way to find out information about each other?

SOCIAL
+ How could you tell whether your tribe was honoring the tribal agreements?
+ How do the agreements protect you?
+ How well did you give full, caring attention?

PERSONAL
+ How did you feel when it was your turn?
+ What do you feel about your tribe members now?

Appreciation

INVITE STATEMENTS OF APPRECIATION:
+ "I liked it when…"
+ "I admired your honesty when…"

Options

Practice spelling words, story sequence (retelling), how to construct a simple paragraph (pre-writing activity), steps in solving quadratic equations.

Client-Consultants

Objectives
1. To encourage active listening
2. To experience group support for a concern
3. To assist a peer, colleague, or friend to resolve a problem
4. To promote influence

Instructions
1. Have the class sit in their tribes.
2. Tell the students that each will have a turn expressing a concern or a problem that he or she may be experiencing at school. Each person will have a turn at being a "client" while the other tribe members are listening as "consultants." Explain that the consultants:
   + are to be non-judgmental
   + are not to tell the client what to do
   + are to offer alternative suggestions to the client for solving the problem
   + and may ask for additional information if it seems helpful or necessary.
3. Review or remind the students about their caring listening skills (especially paraphrasing).
4. Allow approximately 10 minutes for each client's turn.

GRADES
3–adult

TIME
30 minutes

GROUPING
tribes

MATERIALS
none

Suggested Reflection Questions
CONTENT/THINKING
+ What solutions did the consultants find for your problem?
+ Why is having a consultant helpful to you sometimes?

SOCIAL
+ What social skills did you need to be a good consultant?
+ How well did the consultants listen? How could you tell?
+ How does this activity affect the feeling tone in your tribe?

PERSONAL
+ How does it feel to share your own concern with others?

Appreciation
INVITE STATEMENTS OF APPRECIATION (TO TRIBE MEMBERS):
+ "I felt [*feeling*] when you..."
+ "I cared a lot when you said..."
+ "I feel I would like to help you..."

Options
Use for problems such as current events, general school issues, or social issues that are relevant to students (for example, dating, peer pressure).

Community Circle

Objectives

1. To build inclusion and community
2. To teach social skills

Instructions

1. Have the community sit in a large circle.
2. Review the Tribes agreements.
3. Ask a "Question-of-the-Day."

   Example: "I feel happy when…"

   See more suggested questions on the next page.
4. Have everyone respond in turn to the question. Allow time at the end for those who passed to respond if they desire.

Suggested Reflection Questions

CONTENT/THINKING

+ What's one new thing you learned in the community?
+ Why is it sometimes difficult to find something to say in a large group?

SOCIAL

+ How does sharing this way help our class?
+ How well did the community listen when you shared?

PERSONAL

+ How did you feel about sharing with the community today?

Appreciation

INVITE STATEMENTS OF APPRECIATION:

+ "I liked it when…"
+ "I feel like you when…"

Options

Use questions to review material before a test, to practice answering in complete sentences, or to practice using vocabulary words in context.

GRADES
K–adult

TIME
20 minutes

GROUPING
community

MATERIALS
none

Community Circle

Suggested Questions-of-the-Day

1. I feel happy when...
2. I feel sad when...
3. I feel angry when...
4. I feel scared when...
5. The scariest thing is...
6. The biggest thing in the world is...
7. I'm bigger than...
8. I'm smaller than...
9. The smallest thing is...
10. My favorite toy is...
11. My favorite pet is...
12. My favorite food is...
13. My favorite T.V. show is...
14. My favorite song is...
15. My favorite story is...
16. My favorite color is...
17. My favorite weather is...
18. Rain makes me feel...
19. Wind makes me feel...
20. Sunshine makes me feel...
21. Snow makes me feel...
22. Fog makes me feel...
23. When I think of blue, I think of...
24. When I think of red, I think of...
25. When I think of green, I think of...
26. When I think of yellow, I think of...
27. When I think of orange, I think of...
28. When I think of black, I think of...
29. When I think of brown, I think of...
30. Today I feel...
31. What is something scratchy?
32. What is something soft?
33. What is something sharp?
34. What is something smooth?
35. What is something sour?
36. What is something sweet?
37. What is something cold?
38. What is something cool?
39. What is something warm?
40. What is something hot?
41. If I were an animal, I would be...
42. If I were a building, I would be a...
43. The first thing I want to do when I grow up is...
44. When I grow up, I want to be...
45. When I daydream, I usually think about...
46. Someday I want to...
47. Friends are...
48. Put downs make me feel...
49. When I am doing math I am most like what animal?
50. Relate to the curriculum:
    ✦ The best/worst thing about this science project is...
    ✦ The main character in the book we are reading is like/not like me when...
    ✦ These math problems make me feel...

Note

The best questions are those most relevant to the participants' experiences, interests and cultures.

Community Circle Metaphor

GRADES
2–adult

TIME
40 minutes

GROUPING
community, pairs

MATERIALS
sentence strips for
younger students

Objectives
1. To build community inclusion
2. To share feelings about an aspect of school

Instructions
1. Begin with everyone in a community circle. Explain that the students will be completing the following sentence:

   "When I am working on [*name a subject, such as math, writing, reading, art, music*] I am most like a [*name an animal*] because I [*name a behavior or quality*]."

2. After brief thinking time, have the students form pairs. Ask the partners to face each other and discuss their answers to the question. Give the partners two to five minutes to share.

3. Ask several pairs to share their answers with the community.

Suggested Reflection Questions
CONTENT/THINKING
+ What did your answers have in common?

SOCIAL
+ Why is sharing with a partner easier than sharing with the community?

PERSONAL
+ Did you share a fully as you could? Why or why not?
+ How did you help your partner?
+ How did you feel about sharing with your partner?

Appreciation
INVITE STATEMENTS OF APPRECIATION:
+ "It felt good when..."
+ "One thing I liked about what you said was..."

Options
Use for conflict resolution (bullying). Use with content topics, such as "During the Renaissance, (*person*) was like (*animal*) because..." Instead of animals, use geographical features, natural disasters, or inanimate objects.

Confrontation

Objectives

1. To provide a way to work out problems
2. To enhance self-awareness
3. To reduce tattling by teaching communication skills
4. To encourage influence

Instructions

1. One day when a problem between two students comes to your attention, invite the community to sit in a community circle. Ask the two students for permission to share the problem.
2. State the problem or have the two students involved describe it. Example:
   Tanya: *"Dawn keeps moving ahead of me when we are supposed to take turns."*
   Dawn: *"No, I don't. Tanya is always pushing people."*
3. Review the agreements carefully, and ask everyone to listen attentively without comment.
4. Have the two students involved sit facing each other in the center of the circle.
5. Ask each to tell the other what he or she is feeling about the problem by using "I-Messages;" help them phrase the "I-Messages" if needed.
6. Ask each to repeat exactly what the other has stated.
7. Then ask each what he or she could do to help resolve the problem.
8. If they have difficulty, turn to the rest of the community for suggestions. Tell the students not to judge who is right or wrong.
9. If the discussion wanders, ask leading questions to redirect the students to the problem. If the problem cannot be solved, set a time to work with the pair privately.
10. When a solution is reached, have the two students write a contract with each other.

GRADES
K–adult

TIME
15–40 minutes

GROUPING
whole community

MATERIALS
none

Suggested Reflection Questions

CONTENT/THINKING
+ Why is it important to tell someone you are upset with him or her?
+ What do you think will happen now?

SOCIAL
+ What kind of listeners were you?
+ Why is listening important when you're involved in a conflict?

PERSONAL
+ How do you feel right now?
+ What feelings did you have as the discussion was going on?

Appreciation

INVITE STATEMENTS OF APPRECIATION:
+ "I admire you for..."
+ "I learned..."

Options

Use school or social issues pertinent to students' lives. Use to determine persuasive writing topics.

Consensus-Building

Objectives

1. To reach a consensus or agreement on shared concerns, ideas, or priorities
2. To build tribe cohesiveness
3. To experience influence

Instructions

GRADES
3–adult

TIME
25–40 minutes

GROUPING
tribes, pairs

MATERIALS
5 x 7-inch
file cards

1. Have the students meet in tribes, and distribute 5 x 7-inch cards to each person.
2. Discuss the importance of groups having a way to make decisions together so that every member can contribute his or her ideas.
3. State a question that students will try to come to an agreement on through discussion. Example: What field trip sites would be most interesting for our class?
4. Ask each student to write down five answers to the question.
5. Have two tribe members get together, compare lists and agree on four ideas eliminating all others.
6. Have two pairs get together, compare lists, agree on 4 out of their 8 combined ideas and eliminate the others.
7. Have the tribes report their four final ideas to the class. Keep a list on the chalkboard of all ideas.
8. Have the class discuss all of the ideas and eliminate those that seem unworkable or less possible. Then use "sticker voting" to give each student an opportunity to choose his or her three preferred ideas. (See "Group Problem Solving.")
9. Add up the value of the stickers to determine the final choice of the class. The value of the stickers are: Blue=15 points, Red=10 points and Yellow=5 points.

Suggested Reflection Questions

CONTENT/THINKING

✦ What four ideas did your group come up with?

SOCIAL

✦ Why might making decisions this way be easier/difficult sometimes?
✦ How did your group come to a consensus?

PERSONAL

✦ How did you feel when your tribe made their final choices?
✦ How did you influence your tribe's decision?

Appreciation

INVITE STATEMENTS OF APPRECIATION:

✦ "I like our choices because..."
✦ "Our tribe is cool because..."

Options

Have tribes research an important event in history and then build consensus on a question related to the topic. Have tribes use this strategy to decide how to research or present a curriculum topic to the class.

Cooperation Squares

Objectives
1. To encourage cooperation
2. To help students become aware of their own behaviors that may help or hinder community effort
3. To build inclusion and influence

Instructions
1. Begin the strategy with a community circle discussion of the meaning of cooperation. List on the chalkboard the requirements for cooperation as generated by the community.
   Example: Everyone has to understand the problem.
   Everyone needs to believe that he or she can help.
2. Ask the community to meet in tribes. Describe the activity as a puzzle that only can be solved through cooperation.
3. Hand out one puzzle set (see next page for instructions) to each tribe.
4. Read or state the following instructions aloud:
   "Each tribe should have an envelope containing pieces for forming five squares of equal size. Each square contains three puzzle pieces. Each tribe needs to select five students who each get three puzzle pieces; the other tribe members can be observers. The strategy is complete when each of the five tribe members has formed a perfect square. While doing this, the five tribe members may not speak or signal for puzzle pieces, but they may give puzzle parts to others in the tribe if they think they might help them complete their squares."
5. Now ask each tribe to distribute the puzzle pieces equally among its five chosen members.
6. Have the observers share their observations after the puzzles are completed.

Suggested Reflection Questions
CONTENT/THINKING
+ What did you learn about nonverbal cooperation?
+ Why did you do this strategy without talking?

SOCIAL
+ What social skills did you need to make this activity successful?
+ Why is "giving" a social skill?

PERSONAL
+ How did you feel when someone finished his or her square and then sat back without helping others solve their puzzles?
+ How did you feel when someone held a puzzle piece and did not know you needed it or did not see the solution?

Appreciation
INVITE STATEMENTS OF APPRECIATION:
+ "I liked it when..."
+ "I felt good when...

GRADES
4–adult

TIME
30 minutes

GROUPING
tribes

MATERIALS
puzzle sets (see next page for directions)

Cooperation Squares

Options

Use only one set of shapes (duplicate one square per tribe), but use words or phrases that determine a complete square (for example, attributes of a character in literature or history, numbers to form an equation that equals 10, synonyms for vocabulary words). For a real challenge, have the students design the shapes and what is written on each piece.

Directions For Making A Puzzle Set

A puzzle set consists of one envelope containing fifteen cardboard pieces that are cut in the design below. When properly arranged they form five separate squares of equal size. Each square contains three pieces. Prepare one puzzle set for each group of five persons.

To prepare a puzzle set:

1. Cut out five six by six-inch cardboard squares.
2. Line them up in a row and mark them as illustrated below, penciling the letters a, b, c, etc. lightly, so that they can be easily erased later.
3. Cut each square as marked.

4. Mark 5 envelopes A, B, C, D and E.
5. Place the 15 cardboard pieces, a-j, on top of the five envelopes as follows:

   A: pieces i, h, e
   B: pieces a, a, a, c
   C: pieces a, j
   D: pieces d, f
   E: pieces g, b, f, c

6. Before inserting the pieces into the envelopes, erase the penciled letters and write the appropriate envelope letter on each piece. This will make it easy to return the pieces to the envelopes so that the activity may be used again.

Creative Storytelling

Objectives

1. To encourage listening
2. To promote the expression of fantasy
3. To develop inclusion and influence

Instructions

1. Tell the community, "We are going to make up a group story."
2. Give instructions as follows: "The leader will start by saying a few sentences, then we'll choose someone to continue the story where the first person left off. That person will do the same until the story goes around the circle two or three times."
3. Choose a setting for the story that involves the students themselves yet leaves lots of room for fantasizing.

   Example: "Once there was a group of kids named [name], [name], [name] and [name] who wanted to find a place to go swimming together. They came upon a big water hole that looked very inviting. But as soon as one person jumped in, a funny animal reared its head out of the water and..."
4. Encourage the students to listen to each other, and have them continue the story however they want to.
5. Review the "right to pass" and other agreements.

GRADES
K–6

TIME
15–30 minutes

GROUPING
community

MATERIALS
none

Suggested Reflection Questions

CONTENT/THINKING

+ Why is creating a group story fun?
+ How is it different if just one person creates a story for everyone to hear?

SOCIAL

+ How can you improve the way you worked together on your story?

PERSONAL

+ How did you feel as a storyteller/listener?

Appreciation

INVITE STATEMENTS OF APPRECIATION:

+ "I like your part of the story because..."
+ "I felt good when..."

Options

Practice with content standard topics, such as elements of plot, literary devices (metaphor, symbolism, irony), elements of a business letter, resume, etc.

Current Events Debate

Objectives
1. To enable students to express their views
2. To encourage discussion of current events
3. To enhance the student's ability to see different sides of an issue
4. To provide a structure for learning or reviewing the curriculum
5. To experience influence

GRADES
4–adult

TIME
30 minutes

GROUPING
community

MATERIALS
none

Instructions
1. Arrange six chairs in a circle.
2. Tell the community that you would like to have five volunteers sit in the circle to express their views on [*topic*]. Explain that the extra chair is for anyone who wants to come in briefly and add information to the debate (facts, dates, etc.), after which he or she must go back to his or her seat.

   Examples:
   + Should skateboards be allowed at school?
   + How important is it for people to learn to use computers?
   + How can people resist peer pressure to use cigarettes, alcohol, or other drugs?
3. Say that the remaining community members are to be silent until all the students in the circle have been heard.
4. After the circle members have debated the topic, invite the community to direct questions to the circle members.

Suggested Reflection Questions
CONTENT/THINKING
+ What did you learn about the topic?
+ Why is the debate circle a good way to learn about a topic?

SOCIAL
+ What social skills did you need to be good debaters?
+ How did it help to have the "open" chair in the circle?
+ How well did you listen to others?

PERSONAL
+ How did you feel being inside/outside the circle?

Appreciation
INVITE STATEMENTS OF APPRECIATION:
+ "I felt good when you said..."
+ "I liked it when..."
+ "I am glad you said..."

Options
Use "historical" rather than "current" events, or create "future" events and debate with facts and opinions, acknowledging which is which.

Dear Abby

Objectives

1. To encourage active decision-making
2. To build appreciation for another's point of view
3. To share a concern or problem anonymously, and have peers suggest solutions
4. To promote influence

Instructions

1. Have the community meet in tribes, and give each tribe a pile of cards on which you have previously written a concern or problem (real issues) appropriate to your students' age level.
2. Ask tribe members to each take a turn at reading a problem out loud from a card to rest of the tribe. Then have them say, "If I were Dear Abby I would suggest this person [*advice*]."
3. Later (that day or a different one), distribute blank cards to the tribes and ask each tribe member to write one real concern or problem on the card, addressing it to the fictitious news columnist, "Dear Abby."
4. Collect the cards and redistribute the cards back to tribe members to suggest what they, as "Dear Abby," would advise the person to do.

GRADES
4–adult

TIME
30–45 minutes

GROUPING
tribes

MATERIALS
5 x 8-inch cards

Suggested Reflection Questions

CONTENT/THINKING

+ What type of problems seemed to be the most frequent?
+ Why is being able to solve problems an important skill?

SOCIAL

+ How well did your tribe members listen? How could you tell?
+ What is the link between good listening and good solutions to problems?

PERSONAL

+ What did you feel when you listened to other students' concerns?
+ How did you feel when you were giving a solution?

Appreciation

INVITE STATEMENTS OF APPRECIATION:

+ "[*name*], you were a good listener..."
+ "[*name*], I liked it when you said..."

Options

Write about historical issues or events in literature, or practice as a letter-writing lesson (content standard).

Dream Quilt

GRADES
3–adult

TIME
40 minutes

GROUPING
community, pairs

MATERIALS
squares of paper: a
size which works
for your room and
age group

Objectives
1. To build community inclusion
2. To share a personal goal for the year

Instructions
Note: This is an excellent strategy to start the year or the semester.
1. Have the community sit in a circle.
2. Ask each student to think of a goal for the year, something he or she wants to accomplish.
3. Ask students to choose a partner and take turns sharing their goals.
4. Now pass out squares of paper to the students and ask them to write or illustrate their goals.
5. In a community circle, ask the students to share their goals with the class.
6. After all the students have shared their goals, have them decorate their square, sign their name, and post all the squares together on a bulletin board in the form of a quilt.

Suggested Reflection Questions
CONTENT/THINKING
+ What did you learn?
+ What type of goals did most of you have?
+ Why are goals important?

SOCIAL
+ What could you do to improve this strategy?

PERSONAL
+ How did you feel about putting your goal down on paper?
+ What other goal didn't you put down that you might want to share?

Appreciation
INVITE STATEMENTS OF APPRECIATION:
+ "Thanks, [name] for..."
+ "I appreciated your sharing..."

Options
Make a dream quilt of "what we learned" in any subject (for example, for Math, each square is a different math problem that is designed and solved by a student).

Extended Nametags

Objectives
1. To promote inclusion
2. To share personal history, interests, beliefs
3. To enhance communication skills

Instructions
1. Distribute 5 x 8-inch cards.
2. Ask each student to print his or her first name or nickname in the center of the card, and directly under it the quality he or she most values in people.
3. Then have each student write the following in the corners:
   + upper left—a place where he or she spent his or her happiest summer
      option: his or her favorite place on earth
   + lower left—the name of a person who taught him or her something important
      option: the name of his or her best friend
   + lower right—the year he or she last spent three great days in a row
      option: the year he or she went on a big trip
   + upper right—three things he or she does well
      option: a goal that he or she has for the future
4. Have the students meet in triads. Explain that the triad will talk about the upper left corner of their cards for three minutes, which means each person has one minute to talk. Ask them to keep track of their time and to share equally.
5. After three minutes, have the triads give statements of appreciation. Allow two minutes for the statements. Examples:
   + "I liked it when..."
   + "You're a lot like me when..."
6. Have the students form new triads three more times, sharing the other three corners and giving statements of appreciation after each round. Use the same time periods as suggested in steps four and five above.
7. Form a community circle and invite each student to share some-thing special he or she learned about a class member.

GRADES
3–adult

TIME
15–25 minutes

GROUPING
community, triads

MATERIALS
5 x 8-inch cards, pencils, clock

Suggested Reflection Questions

CONTENT/THINKING
+ Why is it important for the members of a community to have opportunities to share information about themselves?
+ Are there other good questions we could ask?

SOCIAL
+ How did you know that others were listening well when you spoke?

PERSONAL
+ What were your feeling when you were speaking? What were you feeling when you were listening?
+ How did this activity help our class community get better acquainted?

Extended Nametags

Appreciation

SUGGEST PEOPLE MAKE STATEMENTS OF APPRECIATION:

✦ "I liked hearing..."

✦ "I admire your..."

Options

Use as a prewriting outline (topic sentence, transition words, detail sentence, conclusion). Use as a review for a test, with students asking questions of each other, or using teacher-designed questions. Use as a reflective practice after introducing new material. Collect and review, or have students share.

Family Camp Trek

Objectives

1. To promote critical thinking
2. To learn to assess and set priorities
3. To have students share special things about themselves
4. To promote respect for individual differences
5. To experience influence

Instructions

1. Ask the community to meet in tribes, and pass out the "Family Camp Trek" worksheets to each student.
2. Tell the students that they are to imagine that each of their families has been invited on a special three-month camping trek next summer in Canada. Tell them that each person may carry one backpack. All the other supplies (food, medicines, tents, sleeping bags, etc.) are being provided. Say that each trek group will consist of three families (about twenty people) and an experienced guide. Explain that each student is to make a list of important or satisfying things to have in his or her backpack, because he or she will be away from home for such a long time.
3. Allow the students ten minutes to make their lists. Then have them share their lists with their tribes.
4. Next have each student decide which three items would be the most important and note them with a star.
5. Again have the students share their lists with their tribes, explaining why these items are more important to them than others.

Suggested Reflection Questions

CONTENT/THINKING

+ What were some of the things you took in your packs?
+ What was similar/different?
+ Why is it important in life to set priorities?

SOCIAL

+ What social skills do you need when a group is setting priorities?

PERSONAL

+ What did you learn about yourself during this activity?
+ How did you feel about having to leave some things out of your pack?

Appreciation

INVITE STATEMENTS OF APPRECIATION:

+ "I liked it when..."
+ "Thank you, [name], for..."

Options

Use this strategy within the context of history (such as an evacuation), social issues (such as a conflict), essentials of a story, or elements to include in a checklist or rubric.

GRADES
2–8

TIME
45 minutes

GROUPING
tribes

MATERIALS
"Family Camp Trek" worksheets

Family Camp Trek

Family Camp Trek Worksheet

1.

2.

3.

4.

5.

6.

7.

8.

9.

10.

Family Changes—Comparing/Contrasting

Objectives
1. To give students an opportunity to share something about their parents
2. To have students compare and contrast the differences between their parents when they were younger and now

Instructions
1. Ask each student to find two pictures of one of their parents—one as a child and one current. Ask him or her to mount the photos together on cardboard and bring them to school. Give the students a few days to gather the photos.
2. Have the community meet. Have each student share his or her parents' photos with the community.
3. When everyone has shared, explain the meanings of compare and contrast (compare is to look for the similarities, contrast is to look for the differences). Then ask for a volunteer to compare and contrast his or her parents' photos.

GRADES
3–adult

TIME
2 class periods

GROUPING
community

MATERIALS
photos of parent mounted on cardboard

Suggested Reflection Questions:
CONTENT/THINKING
+ What did you learn about comparing and contrasting?
+ What did you learn about your parents or someone else's parents?
+ Why is this strategy difficult?

SOCIAL
+ What social skills were important during this strategy?
+ How can you improve this strategy?

PERSONAL
+ How did you feel sharing your parents' pictures?
+ How did you feel listening to others as they shared?

Appreciation
INVITE STATEMENTS OF APPRECIATION:
+ "It helped me when..."
+ "I liked it when..."

Options
Use pictures from history (compare and contrast). At the end of the school year, use student photos (one from the start of the year, one taken recently) as a reflective writing opportunity. Have students demonstrate understanding of mathematical concepts, such as linear equations and corresponding graphs.

Find the Word

Objectives
1. To introduce a unit's vocabulary words and their meanings
2. To build inclusion and influence

Instructions
1. Give each student a card with a word printed on it from the social studies, history, science, or language unit. (If the words have been only recently introduced, writ e a work dist on the chalkboard.) Have kindergarten students do this activity with pictures rather than printed words.
2. Have each student pin his or her card on the back of another students without that student seeing it.
3. Tell the students to move around the room and ask each other questions that can be answered "yes" or "no" until each students determines what is written on the card on his or her back. Explain that they may ask each students only one question and then must move along to the next student.

GRADES
K–adult

TIME
20–30 minutes

GROUPING
community

MATERIALS
Animal Triads sets

Suggested Reflection Questions

CONTENT/THINKING
+ What kind of questions did you ask?
+ Why might this be a fun way to learn new vocabulary words?

SOCIAL
+ What social skills did you need to make this activity work?

PERSONAL
+ How did you feel when you found how what or who you were?
+ How did you enjoy this activity?

Appreciation

INVITE STATEMENTS OF APPRECIATION:
+ "I enjoyed it when…"
+ "I liked it when…"
+ "I'm similar to [*name*] because…"

Options
Use vocabulary words, review key concepts (people, places, events), demonstrate feeling words; act out or role play.

Finding All We Have In Common

Objectives

1. To give students an opportunity to introduce themselves
2. To give students an opportunity to work in pairs and find commonalities
3. To build inclusion

Instructions

1. State that we are a unique group about to start an exciting journey together, and that, like any people coming together, we need to learn about each other.
2. Have each student find a partner he or she does not know at all or does not know very well. Say "In the next five minutes find out all the things that you have in common with your partner (likes, dislikes, qualities, skills, goals or whatever)."
3. Have the community sit in a circle. Have each partner introduce himself or herself and tell what he or she discovered.

Suggested Reflection Questions:

CONTENT/THINKING

✦ What are things many of you have in common?

SOCIAL

✦ Why is finding out what you have in common a good way to get to know somebody?

✦ Why is attentive listening so important for this strategy?

PERSONAL

✦ How did you feel about finding out all that you and your partner had in common?

✦ How did you feel about sharing what you and your partner have in common?

Appreciation

INVITE STATEMENTS OF APPRECIATION:

✦ "I really liked..."

✦ "It was great when..."

Options

Have students share common facts from the day's lesson. Compare attributes or characteristics. Review what "I know," or share what "I hope to learn…"

GRADES
2–adult

TIME
35–45 minutes

GROUPING
community, pairs

MATERIALS
none

Five E's

GRADES
3–adult

TIME
depends on
material

GROUPING
tribes

MATERIALS
academic theme/
information

Objectives

1. To enhance the abilities of students to think constructively by developing the capacity to investigate, analyze, solve-problems and construct meaningful knowledge
2. To enable students to take responsibility for their own learning
3. To practice the collaborative skills of team planning, project management and assessment
4. To enable students to discover and believe in their own unique abilities

Instructions

Pre-class preparation: Select an academic theme or topic for group exploration and assemble a list of resources applicable to the investigation or project to be carried out by student groups. Define the objectives and outcome tasks for the learning groups.

1. **Engage (teacher leadership)**: Define an inclusion question or strategy that links the topic to students' interests or personal experiences. Connect the topic to past learning. State the objectives, task and the time for the tribes to accomplish their explorations or projects. Describe your role as a "guide on the side" who is available to suggest resources, to clarify the process as necessary and to review the tribes' progress.

2. **Explore (student leadership)**: Transfer responsibility to the tribes to review the four Tribes TLC agreements, and then to discuss and list several questions about the topic that they would like to explore. Each tribe selects one question and informs the class community what they will research. Each group decides how they will research their selected question (interviews, Internet, library, videos, books, articles, conduct experiment, etc.). Each tribe makes an action plan (who will do what) and initiates their investigation.

3. **Explain (student leadership)**: The tribes discuss their discoveries, plan presentations (how they will teach the class); they confer with the teacher-guide and present their discovery to the class community. They share their action steps and justify conclusions from researched information.

4. **Elaborate (student leadership)**: The tribes involve the class (other tribes) to expand on concepts, connect to real-world issues and think of questions for further exploration.

5. **Evaluate (student leadership)**: Each tribe asks reflection questions they have prepared. They complete assigned individual or group reports.

Suggested Reflection Questions:

CONTENT/THINKING

+ What was the most important thing that your tribe learned?
+ How can your tribe's discovery be applied elsewhere?

SOCIAL

+ What was difficult for your group to do?
+ What was most interesting?

PERSONAL

+ What feelings did you have during your tribe's presentation?
+ What makes this a good way to learn about a topic?

Five E's

Appreciation
INVITE STATEMENTS OF APPRECIATION:
+ "I liked it when…."
+ "I appreciated the way our group…."

Options
Role play this process and reflect or discuss to help students refine and monitor for success. Introduce content standards, such as including a business letter in the "explore" stage of discovery learning.

Five Tribles

Objectives

1. To build inclusion
2. To share current feelings
3. To help build a feeling vocabulary

Instructions

1. To prepare for this strategy, duplicate the "Five Tribles" worksheet, one for each student.
2. Have community sit in a circle.
3. Talk about how they all arrived today with different feelings: some of them are happy and excited; some of them are feeling sad, tired, or angry; and some of them feel kind of in between in their own emotions: not happy, not sad, just here.
4. Pass out the "Five Tribles" worksheet.
5. Ask people to look at the five Tribles and decide which face looks most like they feel right now.
6. Review the Tribe agreements.
7. As the teacher, share first to model the activity. Be honest. Share which face you feel like and why.
8. Go around the circle, giving each student an opportunity to share or pass. If many pass, go around again until you feel that all who wish to share have done so.

GRADES
K–adult

TIME
15 minutes

GROUPING
community, tribes

MATERIALS
"Five Tribles"
worksheet

Suggested Reflection Questions

CONTENT/THINKING

✦ Why is it important to share how you are feeling with others?
✦ What were some of the feelings you shared?

SOCIAL

✦ How does sharing our feelings help us to know each other better?
✦ What's the mood of the community now?

PERSONAL

✦ How did you feel as your turn came closer?
✦ What did you learn as a result of this activity?

Appreciation

INVITE STATEMENTS OF APPRECIATION:

✦ "I felt like you when..."
✦ "I liked it when..."

Options

Use as a reflective practice to show feelings about a particular idea or lesson.
Use shapes, colors, or content-related images instead of Tribles, if appropriate.

A Trible is a warm, fuzzy, loving creature that first appeared from outer space in the television program "Star Trek."

Five Tribles

Flies On the Ceiling

Objectives
1. To identify the dynamics of group interaction
2. To process a sequence of learning activities and behaviors
3. To practice reflecting on systems and situations
4. To experience influence

GRADES
2–adult

TIME
35 minutes

GROUPING
tribes

MATERIALS
paper, pencils

Instructions
1. After students have been working together on a task, have them set aside their books and papers.
2. Ask the students to close their eyes and pretend they had been flies on the ceiling watching their tribe work together during the last few minutes or hours. Tell them to "run the movie backwards now" and think what the flies saw happening.
   - ✦ Who did what to get you started?
   - ✦ What did you do while your tribe was working together?
   - ✦ What did other tribe members do?
   - ✦ What helpful things happened?
   - ✦ Who did them?
   - ✦ Did everyone participate?
   - ✦ How did you help each other?
3. After a few minutes, have the tribe members share what they as flies saw happening. It is helpful to have each tribe choose a recorder to make a list of behaviors, positions, acts, interactions, etc.
4. Have the tribes give their report to the community.
5. Then ask each tribe to make a list of "things what we could do to have our tribe work better next time."

Suggested Reflection Questions:
CONTENT/THINKING
   - ✦ These questions were handled in #2 above.

SOCIAL
   - ✦ Why is it important to look at how groups are working together?

PERSONAL
   - ✦ How could you use this strategy in other groups and relationships?
   - ✦ How can you help your tribe to work together better?

Appreciation
INVITE STATEMENTS OF APPRECIATION:
   - ✦ "Thanks for..."
   - ✦ "It helped me when..."

Options
Use the strategy as a written reflection or assessment. Have students summarize (in writing or orally) a sequence of events in history or literature, or even steps in an equation.

Folding the Line Reading

Objectives

1. To build interdependence
2. To practice reading with a partner
3. To experience influence

Instructions

1. Have the students get some identical reading (history, social studies, or other).
2. Ask the students to line up (without talking) across the room according to their birth dates, beginning with January on one side of the room.
3. Starting on one side, have each student in turn state his or her birth month and date.
4. Create two lines by leading the last person, so that each student is facing a partner. Have the partners stand an arm's length apart.
5. Have one partner read the first paragraph of the text. The other partner paraphrases what was read.
6. Next have the other partner read the next paragraph. Partners alternate reading and paraphrasing until they finish reading the selection you assigned.

GRADES
3–adult

TIME
30 minutes

GROUPING
community line-up and pairs

MATERIALS
textbook or handout reading material

Suggested Reflection Questions

CONTENT/THINKING

✦ What did you learn from the material you just read?

SOCIAL

✦ Why is reading together helpful?
✦ Why is choosing partners using a lineup fun?

PERSONAL

✦ How did you help make this strategy successful?
✦ How do you feel reading to another person?

Appreciation

INVITE STATEMENTS OF APPRECIATION (TO PARTNERS):

✦ "I liked your reading because..."
✦ "Thanks for helping me..."

Options

Review school discipline policy, classroom procedures, or have students edit and assess one another's work in progress.

Funeral for Put-Downs

GRADES
K–adult

TIME
35 minutes

GROUPING
community, tribes

MATERIALS
2-inch paper slips,
pencils

Objectives
1. To promote awareness and sensitize the students to the hurt of put-downs
2. To involve the students in eliminating put-downs (good strategy for secondary students)
3. To create a positive community climate and inclusion

Instructions
1. Give each student a slip of paper.
2. Have each student write a hurtful put-down remark or behavior he or she never wants to hear or see again. (Have the teacher, aide, parent, or student helper write the slips for younger students.)
3. Have each tribe put their slips in a community box and ask three to four students to take turns reading the slips to the class.
4. Invite several students to share how they felt when put down by another person in the school.
5. Take the class outside and light a fire within a metal wastebasket or trashcan. Throw the box of slips into the fire. (Other options are to bury the slips or put them into a dumpster.)
6. Invite statements of good-bye to the put-downs.
7. Ask the students what they could do to help each other keep the painful statements dead.

Suggested Reflection Questions:
CONTENT/THINKING
+ What did you do?
+ Why is it important to "burn, bury, or trash" the put-downs?
+ What can the community do to keep the put-downs buried?

SOCIAL
+ What can your tribe do to keep those put-downs buried?

PERSONAL
+ What can you do to keep those put-downs buried?
+ How did it feel to burn or bury the put-downs?

Appreciation
INVITE STATEMENTS OF APPRECIATION:
+ "I appreciated..."
+ "It was great when..."

Options
Use the strategy as a reflective process (what not to do on the next report, project, etc.).

Fuzzyland Map

Objectives
1. To build tribe inclusion
2. To understand the importance of kindness to others
3. To learn to work cooperatively on tasks

Instructions
1. Ask the community to meet in tribes.
2. Read, or preferably tell, the story "Fuzzyland."
3. Discuss and clarify the meaning of the story. Ask questions such as:
   ✦ What is a warm fuzzy? A cold prickly?
   ✦ Why did people in the story need warm fuzzies?
   ✦ Why did people stop giving warm fuzzies freely after the witch cast her spell?
4. Give each tribe a large sheet of paper and colored markers or crayons.
5. Review the agreements. Ask each tribe to create a map of Fuzzyland, with each tribe member drawing some part of the map.
6. Visit each tribe to make sure the instructions are clear.
7. Ask each tribe to share its map with the community. Encourage each student to share what he or she has contributed.

GRADES
K–3

TIME
40 minutes

GROUPING
tribes, subgroups

MATERIALS
24 x 36-inch paper, markers, crayons

Suggested Reflection Questions

CONTENT/THINKING
   ✦ What did you learn from the story of Fuzzyland?
   ✦ Why did I have you create maps?

SOCIAL
   ✦ Name two things your tribe did well while working together.
   ✦ How well did you share ideas, materials, etc.?
   ✦ Did everyone participate?

PERSONAL
   ✦ Would you like to give something nice to someone in your family? To whom? What would it be?

Appreciation
INVITE TRIBE MEMBERS TO GIVE EACH OTHER WARM FUZZIES, SUCH AS:
   ✦ "I liked it when you said..."
   ✦ "You're neat because..."
   ✦ "I'm like you when..."

Options
Use the terms (warm fuzzy, cold prickly) and apply to content, or have students create new words or descriptions that are more age-appropriate or applicable.

Fuzzyland

Once upon a time, a long time ago and far from here, there was a place called Fuzzyland. People were very happy in Fuzzyland because in those happy times everyone at birth was given a small, soft, fuzzy bag. Any time a person reached into this bag he was able to pull out a warm fuzzy. Warm fuzzies were very much in demand because whenever somebody was given a warm fuzzy, it made him feel warm and good all over. People who didn't get warm fuzzies regularly were in danger of developing a sickness called "Fuzzy Deficiency Anemia." Their backs would shrivel up, and they would shrink up so much in size that they would hide from people.

In those days it was very easy to get warm fuzzies. Anytime you wanted a warm fuzzy, all you had to do was walk up to someone and say, "I'd like a warm fuzzy, please." The person would then reach into his bag and pull out a fuzzy the size of a little girl's hand. As soon as the fuzzy saw the light of day, it would smile and blossom into a large, shaggy warm fuzzy. The person would then lay it on your shoulder or head or lap and it would snuggle up and make you feel good all over. Fuzzies were always given freely, and getting enough of them was never a problem. Fuzzyland was a happy place because everyone felt so friendly and kind to each other.

One day, a bad witch came to Fuzzyland and tried to sell people her strange potions and salves. When no one wanted to buy them, she became very angry and cast an evil magic spell on the people of Fuzzyland. The spell made the people believe that warm fuzzies were getting scarce and that eventually the supply would run out. So people reached less and less into their fuzzy bags and became very stingy. Everyone began to notice the lack of warm fuzzies, and newspapers carried stories about the "great fuzzy shortage." People started to feel that they were shrinking, so they went to the witch to buy her potions and salves, even though they didn't seem to work at all.

The bad witch didn't really want people to shrink and hide. Who then would buy things from her? So she devised a new scheme. She gave everyone bags that were very similar to fuzzy bags, except these were cold instead of warm. Inside the bags were cold pricklies. These cold pricklies did not make people feel warm and fuzzy but made them feel cold, prickly, and crabby. From then on, people who would not share warm fuzzies would give away cold pricklies.

A lot of people were unhappy, feeling very cold, prickly, and crabby. Remember, it really all began with the coming of the bad witch, who made people believe that there was beginning to be a shortage of warm fuzzies in their land.

Finally, on one sunny day, a good witch arrived in Fuzzyland. She had not heard about the bad witch and wasn't worried about running out of warm fuzzies at all. She gave them freely to everyone. The kind witch knew that cold pricklies were bad for people. She never ever would give anyone a cold prickly. Many people disapproved of her because she

Fuzzyland

was giving children the idea that they really should never worry about running out of warm fuzzies. And then a new wonderful magic began to happen! Each time the good witch gave a child one of her warm fuzzies, the bad witch's evil spell was broken, and that child could break the evil spell again by giving someone else a warm fuzzy. Many people, children and grown-ups alike, were so used to exchanging cold pricklies that at first they refused to accept warm fuzzies. But the children whom the good witch had befriended kept giving warm fuzzies freely until everyone in Fuzzyland was once again feeling good and warm and fuzzy all over—everyone, that is, except the bad witch. They say that she just sneaked out of Fuzzyland one dark night, hoping to peddle her potions and crabbiness elsewhere.

This story was adapted from *A Fairy Tale* by Claude Steiner, Sacramento, CA: JALMAR Press, Inc. 1977. Mr. Steiner gave permission for the adaptation and its use.

Gallery Walks

GRADES
K–adult

TIME
30 minutes

GROUPING
community and
triads

MATERIALS
student art work
or lesson topic

Objectives
1. To build communication skills
2. To build self-esteem and pride in work
3. To build inclusion and influence

Instructions
1. Invite several students to stand next to projects on which they have been working. Refer to them as "Artists of the Day."
2. Have the remaining students form triads.
3. Invite the triads to take a "gallery walk" around the room to view articles on display, projects-in-making, etc.
4. Have each student artist stand by his or her work and share the origin of his or her ideas, materials used, personal objectives, feelings about finished work, etc.

Suggested Reflection Questions
CONTENT/THINKING
+ What kind of things did the artists mention?
+ What different talents do people have?
+ How did the artists seem to feel about their work?

SOCIAL
+ What social skills did "gallery walkers" and artists need to use to make this activity successful?

PERSONAL
+ How did you feel when you shared your work?
+ What did you do best when you presented your work?
+ What did you do to keep the focus on the artist?

Appreciation
INVITE STATEMENTS OF APPRECIATION:
+ "I liked it when you said..."
+ "Some of your talents are..."
+ "I like your masterpiece because..."

Options
Use this strategy for a "work in progress," to help students reflect on their own work for improvement or achievement.

Give Me a Clue

Objectives

1. To demonstrate understanding geometric vocabulary terms
2. To use spatial reasoning to think in three dimensions
3. To learn that accomplishing a group task depends upon each member contributing their skills and knowledge.

Instructions

1. Have students meet in tribes or small groups of four to six members.
2. State the objectives and the task: to build a three dimensional figure with colored cubes, using the information on the "Build It" clue cards.
3. Distribute eight colored cubes (two blue, two green, two red, and two yellow) to each tribe. Have each tribe member draw one clue card.
4. State the rules:
    + the clue card is theirs alone and no one else may touch it
    + the blocks may be touched only when it's a member's turn
    + students share their clue by reading its information aloud
    + help may be asked in reading the information
    + if a question arises, ask tribe members before asking the teacher
5. Tell students to:
    + read the clues on their cards to their tribe
    + share their thinking to help the tribe come to an understanding of each vocabulary term
    + analyze the clues until a solution seems to have been found
6. Tell the students that they will recognize the correct solution when everyone agrees that the three dimensional figure matches with the clues.
7. Have the tribes record their solution by drawing it.

Suggested Reflection Questions

CONTENT/THINKING
+ Which vocabulary words needed to be clarified by your tribe?

SOCIAL
+ What did tribe members do to help your tribe be successful?
+ What did tribe members say or do that opened up your thinking?

PERSONAL
+ What did you do that was helpful?

Appreciation

INVITE STATEMENTS OF APPRECIATION:
+ "I liked it when..."

Options

Have students make clue cards for solving equations, identifying historical figures, or determining scientific classifications. Then have tribes exchange clue cards and solve.

GRADES
4–12

TIME
20–30 minutes

GROUPING
tribes, subgroups

MATERIALS
clue cards, color cubes, colored pencils or crayons

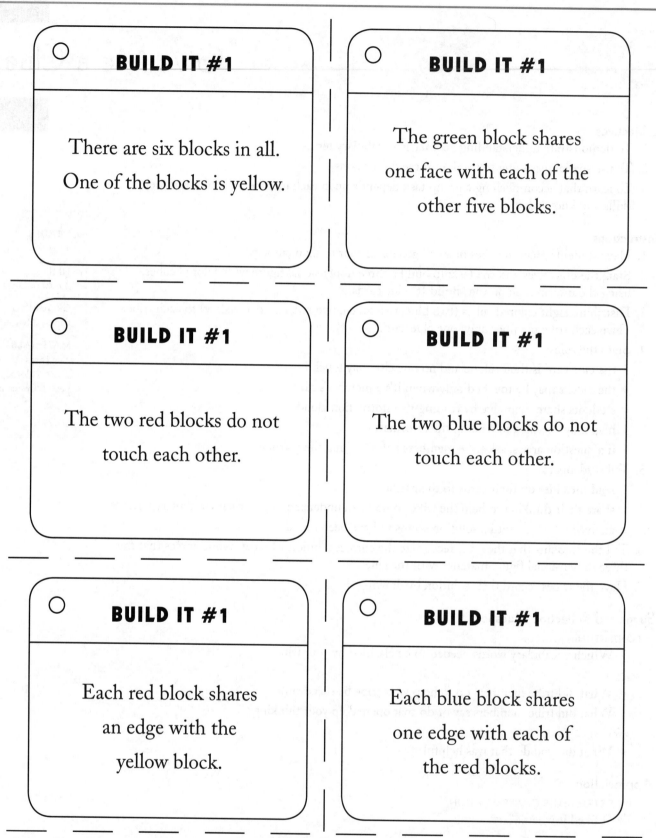

BUILD IT #1

There are six blocks in all. One of the blocks is yellow.

BUILD IT #1

The green block shares one face with each of the other five blocks.

BUILD IT #1

The two red blocks do not touch each other.

BUILD IT #1

The two blue blocks do not touch each other.

BUILD IT #1

Each red block shares an edge with the yellow block.

BUILD IT #1

Each blue block shares one edge with each of the red blocks.

This strategy is adapted from Get It Together—Math Problems for Groups 4–12. *Lawrence Hall of Science, Berkeley, 1989. Permission to use granted. © 1989 The Regents of the University of California, from* Get It Together—EQUALS, *Lawrence Hall of Science.*

This page may be duplicated for classroom use.

Goal-Storming

Objectives

1. To enable a large group to identify shared goals and concerns
2. To structure interest-related work groups
3. To experience influence

Instructions

1. Decide upon a relevant question for the full community to address: Example: "Where would we like to go on a field trip?"
2. Ask the community to form small groups or meet in tribes.
3. Review the rules for "Brainstorming:"
   D defer judgment **O** offbeat, original **V** vast number **E** expand, elaborate
4. Ask each tribe to choose a recorder and then brainstorm for five minutes, listing all ideas.
5. Ask the recorders to read all the ideas to the community. Discuss consensus and how to form a consensus. (See "Consensus-Building")
6. Instruct each tribe to form a consensus on three ideas.
7. Record the three ideas from each tribe on a single sheet of paper or the chalkboard.
8. Discuss the ideas as a full community. Combine and/or eliminate ideas that are similar or repetitive.
9. At this point choose among several options:
   + Form task or interest groups around listed concerns
   + Sticker vote as individuals to determine highest priority

GRADES
3–adult

TIME
60 minutes

GROUPING
community, tribes

MATERIALS
large paper, markers, tape

Suggested Reflection Questions

CONTENT/THINKING
+ Why is this a good way to find out what a group wants?
+ What makes goal-storming difficult?
+ Why are the DOVE brainstorming guidelines important?

SOCIAL
+ What social skills did you need to make brainstorming successful?
+ How could you tell if your tribe worked well together?

PERSONAL
+ How do you feel about the group's priority?

Appreciation

INVITE STATEMENTS OF APPRECIATION:
+ "I liked it when you..."
+ "I felt good when..."

Note: "Goal-Storming" is a variation of "Brainstorming." The group should first become familiar with the Brainstorming process.

Options

Use in combination with the "Five E's" to help students refine goals for each "E" stage. Use the strategy to solicit student input on classroom procedures or expectations, both social and academic.

Graphing Who We Are

Objectives

1. To graph and review information gathered by tribes
2. To develop an appreciation of differences
3. To develop a sense of community
4. To experience influence

GRADES
4–12

TIME
30–60 minutes

GROUPING
tribes

MATERIALS
wall graph formats, large paper, tape measures, rulers, maps

Instructions

1. Prior to initiating this strategy, select some different types of graphs (Venn diagram, bar graph, line graph and/or picture graphs) to teach the recording of statistical information. Sketch the graph models on newsprint or the blackboard. Set aside large sheets of paper, one for each tribe.
2. Have the students meet in their tribes, and explain that each tribe will graph information on the large sheets of paper about the members of their tribes (heights, eye colors, numbers of siblings, distance from school, shoe sizes, head circumferences, etc.).
3. Have tribe members choose roles: recorder, reader, measurer, taskmaster. Review the responsibilities of each role.
4. Ask each tribe to discuss and choose which graph model they will use.
5. Invite a tribe to use you as an example, measuring your height and recording the information.
6. Have the tribes present their graphs when completed to the community.

Suggested Reflection Questions:

CONTENT/THINKING
+ Why is it important to be able to read graphs?
+ What did you learn about graphing in this strategy?

SOCIAL
+ What social skills did you need to be successful in this strategy?

PERSONAL
+ How did you help your tribe?
+ What else might you have done to help your tribe?

Appreciation

INVITE STATEMENTS OF APPRECIATION:
+ "I appreciated..."
+ "It was great when..."

Options

Once students are successful with various graphs, invite students to graph (any content) information and then assess one another's graphs.

Adapted from "All About Us," by Nan and Ted Graves, *Cooperative Learning*, Vol. 11, No. 2, December, 1990

Group Inquiry

Objectives

1. To practice constructive thinking skills (assessing information, interpreting, synthesizing and applying)
2. To practice collaborative team skills
3. To transfer responsibility to students

Instructions

1. **INCLUSION:** Build inclusion within the tribes by using the structure, write/pair/share. Ask people to take 5–10 minutes to write down the skills, talents and abilities that they bring to the group. You may want to list and discuss the various collaborative skills (See chapter 5 for Tribes collaborative skill list). Have people share their lists first in pairs. Then share with the tribe.

2. **CONTENT AND OBJECTIVES:** Discuss the general subject content and sub-content areas to be researched by the tribes. It is optional whether the class or teacher defines the sub-content areas. List the objectives to be learned from the experience. Have the tribes choose or randomly draw slips of content areas. (See option.)

3. **RESOURCES:** Detail resources they can use for their inquiry or research (books, articles, computer info, library, interviews, films, etc.)

4. **TASK:** Detail the task to be accomplished (group report, presentation, role play, article, etc.) within a specific time; inquiry projects can run from one hour to several weeks or months.

5. **ROLES:** You may want to use roles within elementary tribes (facilitator, encourager, materials manager, recorder, etc.) If so, have people those their roles according to the skills and resources they believe they bring to the group.

6. **ACCOUNTABILITY:**

    ✦ For presentations to the whole class, a peer evaluation sheet may be used.

    ✦ Your own observations of individual performance can be made by taking notes.

    ✦ Group and individual reports can be made and graded.

GRADES
4–college

TIME
varies

GROUPING
tribes

MATERIALS
dependent upon content resources and extent of research

Suggested Reflection Questions

CONTENT/THINKING

✦ What was the most important content (theory, information, etc. that can be applied to _____ today? Or help people to understand _____?

SOCIAL

✦ What was the value for our community in using this teaching method?

✦ What collaborative skills were demonstrated?

PERSONAL

✦ What would you like to know more about?

✦ What skills did you notice in others that you would also like to learn?

Appreciation

Invite oral or written statements of appreciation to individuals or the tribes.

Options

Instead of using sub-topics within tribes, use the "Jigsaw" method to have individual tribe members research the subject in expert groups. Then ask students to return to teach the content to their tribe.

Group Inquiry

PEER EVALUATION OF GROUP PRESENTATION				
GROUP NAME:				
EVALUATION CRITERIA	OUTSTANDING	GOOD	IMPROVEMENT NEEDED	POOR
1. Content				
2. Organization				
3. Cooperation of tribe members				
4. Use of aids: handouts, video, etc.				
5. Involvement/Interest for class				

Specific Suggestions for Improvement:

I Appreciated Learning:

This chart is an adaptation of one in the article "Using Jigsaw Groups for Research and Writing in High School," by Glory-Ann Drazinakis, Cooperative Learning, Vol. 13, No. 2. Winter 1993.

This page may be duplicated for classroom use.

Group Problem Solving

Objectives
1. To teach a group problem-solving process
2. To analyze alternatives
3. To experience influence

Instructions
1. Have the class community meet in tribes.
2. Give each tribe five minutes to come up with three typical problems that a student might have with another student—or that a student might have with someone else at the school.
3. Have each tribe read their problem to the class. Make sure that the problems are well-defined.
4. Explain that each tribe will have ten minutes to brainstorm and list possible solutions. Review the "Brainstorming" strategy and post the brainstorming rules. Give each tribe a large sheet of paper, a felt pen and three colored stickers (red, blue and yellow).
5. Write the "Group-Problem Solving" process on the board.
   + Brainstorm for ten minutes. Have one person record all ideas.
   + Each person selects three top choices with colored stickers (1st choice blue=25 points; 2nd choice red=15 points; 3rd choice yellow=5 points).
   + Add up the total points for each idea.
   + Present your top solutions to the community.
6. If this strategy is used for real-time problems, you may want to teach the tribes how to make a "Tribe Action Plan" that will identify tasks, responsibilities and completion dates. See chapter 9 for the plan format.

GRADES
2–adult

TIME
40 minutes

GROUPING
tribes

MATERIALS
large paper, markers, colored stickers

Suggested Reflection Questions
CONTENT/THINKING
   + What is the value of this process?
   + What other ways can decisions be made in the tribe?

SOCIAL
   + How well did your tribe honor our tribe agreements?
   + What social skills did your tribe use when doing this strategy?

PERSONAL
   + How do you feel about your tribe's work together?
   + How do you feel about your participation?
   + How do you feel about your action plan?

Appreciation
SUGGEST PEOPLE MAKE STATEMENTS OF APPRECIATION:
   + "Thanks for your help..."
   + "You made a positive difference when..."

Options
Use in literature study (character, plot line).
Use with complex equations, word problems, and in science labs.

I Sit In a Chair with My Friend

Objectives

1. To build inclusion
2. To learn names
3. To practice agreements

GRADES
K–8

TIME
20 minutes

GROUPING
community

MATERIALS
none

Instructions

1. Have the students sit in a circle, leaving one chair in the circle empty.
2. Have students move into the empty chair in succession as follows:
   - student #1 says, "I sit" (and moves into the empty chair)
   - student #2 says, "in a chair" (and moves to the empty chair left by student #1)
   - student #3 says, "with my friend" (and moves to the empty chair left by student #2)
   - student #4 says the name of anyone in the circle (and moves to the empty chair left by student #3).
3. Now, the student whose name was said, gets up and walks to the empty chair and simply sits down.
4. The new empty chair is now the one left by the "named" student.
5. Those sitting on either side of the newly emptied chair race to move into it while saying "I sit." The succession begins, according to who gets to the empty chair first.

Suggested Reflection Questions

CONTENT/THINKING
- What names did you learn?
- How did we honor the agreement of "mutual respect"?

SOCIAL
- What did we have to do to make this activity successful?
- How could you tell that others were being good observers and listeners?

PERSONAL
- How did you feel while you were participating in the activity?

Appreciation

INVITE STATEMENTS OF APPRECIATION
- "I liked it when..."
- "Thank you for..."

Options

Use the strategy to act out any sequence, such as mathematical equations, facts, vocabulary definitions, or prewriting sentence examples.

I Used to Be; We Used to Be

Objectives
1. To give the students an opportunity to look at personal changes
2. To give tribes an opportunity to look at how they have changed
3. To share personal and tribal changes
4. To experience influence

Instructions
1. Have the community meet in tribes.
2. Ask each student to (silently) compare the following things about himself or herself today, and his or her old self in the past: physical appearance, favorite things to do, behavior, hobbies, beliefs, fears, friends, etc.
3. Have each tribe member write a poem, using the following format:

   I used to be...   But now I am...
   I used to be...   But now I am...

4. Ask the tribe members to share their finished poems.
5. While students are still in their tribes ask each tribe member to create a poem about his or her tribe, using the following format:

   We used to be...   But now we are...
   We used to be...   But now we are...

6. Ask the tribe members to share their finished poems.
7. Ask each tribe to share one or two of its "we" poems with the community.

Suggested Reflection Questions:

CONTENT/THINKING
+ What did you find out about your tribe members?
+ What changes have your tribe members made?

SOCIAL
+ How well did your tribe honor the agreements during this strategy?
+ How do your tribe members feel about each other now?

PERSONAL
+ How do you feel about how you have changed?
+ What other changes do you want to make?

Appreciation

INVITE STATEMENTS OF APPRECIATION:
+ "I appreciated it when..."
+ "Thank you, [name] for..."

Options
Use as a reflective practice in assessing group or project development after a period of time. Assess development in a scientific, historical, or social context (for example, geology, countries in Africa, civil rights).

GRADES
2–adult

TIME
45 minutes

GROUPING
tribes

MATERIALS
paper, pencils

I'm Proud Appreciation Circle

Objectives
1. To encourage sharing good feelings about oneself
2. To encourage acceptance and appreciation of others
3. To build inclusion

Instructions
1. Discuss the difference between stating appreciation of oneself and bragging.
2. Invite one person of the community or one person in each tribe to sit in the middle as the focus person.
3. Have the focus person make an "I'm proud" statement.
   Examples:
   + "I'm proud that I am..."
   + "I'm proud that I am able to..."
   + "I'm proud that I..."
4. Have the other tribe members give positive feedback or make statements of appreciation to the focus person.
5. Continue the process until each person takes a turn being the focus person.

Suggested Reflection Questions

CONTENT/THINKING
+ How did you choose your "I'm proud" statement?
+ What did you learn about your tribe members?

SOCIAL
+ Why is it important to be able to acknowledge what we are proud of?
+ How supportive was the tribe when you made your "I'm proud" statements?

PERSONAL
+ How did you feel when you made your "I'm proud" statements?
+ How did you feel when you gave/received statements of appreciation?

Appreciation
INVITE PEOPLE TO MAKE STATEMENTS OF APPRECIATION:
+ Is there anyone who would like to make a statement to anyone else in the class?

Options
Use the strategy in a community circle. Share or reflect on academic achievements.

GRADES
2–adult

TIME
30 minutes

GROUPING
community, or tribes

MATERIALS
none

Ideal Classroom

Objectives
1. To involve students in defining class agreements
2. To alter the climate from negative to positive
3. To transfer responsibility to students
4. To experience influence

Instructions
1. Draw a large circle on the board and label it "The Ideal Classroom."
2. Ask the students to think about the following question: How would people act and interact in an ideal classroom?
3. Have student divide up into pairs.
4. Ask the partners to discuss and make a list of what an ideal classroom would be like. After ten minutes have them share their ideas with their tribe.
5. Have the tribes save the lists. Ask everyone to think about the question until the next day.
6. On the following day, use the strategy "One, Two, Three" or "Group Problem-Solving" to have the community select one to three ideas that they consider most important for their classroom.
7. Post the ideas in a prominent place.
8. Ask, "How many of you want to make these agreements that the whole community respects for the next [week, month or year]?" Invite students to stand and say, "That's me!"
9. Ask, "Who will help to remind others to respect our agreements?"

GRADES
K–adult

TIME
40 minutes

GROUPING
tribes, pairs

MATERIALS
paper, pencils

Suggested Reflection Questions:
CONTENT/THINKING
+ What is the ideal classroom like?
+ What would have to change to make this classroom an ideal classroom?

SOCIAL
+ What social skills would be needed in your ideal classroom?
+ Why is working together in pairs a good idea?

PERSONAL
+ How can you make our classroom better?
+ How can these rules apply to other areas of your life?

Appreciation
INVITE STATEMENTS OF APPRECIATION:
+ "It felt good when..."
+ "One thing I liked about what you said was..."

Options
Use the strategy to reflect on or synthesize information (for example, have tribes design a country with an "ideal" democracy, a "Bill of Rights" for teens, the "ideal" meal plan for health).

Interview Circle

Objectives

1. To build inclusion and influence
2. To enhance communication skills
3. To share personal beliefs, feelings, and interests

Instructions

1. Ask the community to sit in a large circle.
2. Explain that we will interview one student who will sit in the center of the circle and answer three questions. The person will choose the questions from people who raise their hands. He or she has the right to "pass" on any questions that she or he chooses not to answer.
3. Model the activity first by being in the center and responding to three questions yourself.
4. Suggest that questions may be autobiographical or may relate to issues, curriculum, politics, hobbies, friendship, sports, etc.
5. Have the community interview a few students each day until every-one has had a turn.

Suggested Reflection Questions

CONTENT/THINKING

✦ What did you discover about a community member?

✦ Why is it difficult to answer some of the questions?

SOCIAL

✦ Which social skills did community members use to make this activity successful?

✦ Did the community use good listening skills? How could you tell?

PERSONAL

✦ How did you feel about being interviewed?

✦ What did you learn about yourself from this activity?

Appreciation

INVITE STATEMENTS OF APPRECIATION:

✦ "I liked it when..."

✦ "I admired your honesty when..."

Options

Use in tribes to review subject matter or as an actual assessment.

Encourage substitute teachers to introduce themselves to your class with this strategy.

GRADES
K–adult

TIME
15–30 minutes

GROUPING
community, tribes

MATERIALS
none

Jigsaw

Objectives

1. To structure team learning/team teaching in tribes
2. To build the academic self-image of students
3. To develop tribe spirit and pride
4. To help each student feel valuable to others
5. To experience inclusion and influence

Instructions

1. Select a lesson that you consider appropriate for the following process.
2. Divide it into equal parts (or the number of members per tribe) and define study questions. Prepare sufficient materials for the study groups.
3. Explain the Jigsaw process to your class. Then ask the students to meet in their tribes.
4. If you have not already done so, engage them with an activity on the personal feeling level to awaken interest about a topic.
5. Give each tribe one set of lesson materials. Ask each tribe to decide who will become an "expert" for each part of the lesson.
6. Ask people responsible for Part 1 to move to a jigsaw study group; do the same for the other parts.
7. Tell the groups what their specific task is and the amount of time that will be allowed. Move from group to group, helping only as needed.
8. When all have finished, ask people to return to their own tribes.
9. Beginning with Part 1, ask the "experts" to share the material that they prepared in their Jigsaw group; prepare a format for sharing if you think it will help them.
10. After each segment has been shared, take time for a full group discussion and in tribes to reflect on the experience.

GRADES
K–adult

TIME
varies depending on lesson task

GROUPING
tribes

MATERIALS
vary

Suggested Reflection Questions

CONTENT/THINKING

- ✦ What did you learn?
- ✦ Why is this a good way to learn a lot in a short time?

SOCIAL

- ✦ What social skills did you need to make this activity successful?
- ✦ Why do you need good listening skills for this activity?

PERSONAL

- ✦ How did you feel to have other students teaching you?
- ✦ How did you feel teaching others what you had learned?

Appreciation

INVITE STATEMENTS OF APPRECIATION:

- ✦ "I liked it when..."
- ✦ "I want to thank [*name*] for..."

Jigsaw

Options
Use with any content material. Expert groups need not have great amounts of information or text to be successful. Combine this strategy with a reflective practice (such as, Group Inquiry, Flies On The Ceiling, Two Truths and A Lie).

Acknowledgment is made to Elliot Aronson's work (see Bibliography).

Joy

Objectives

1. To give each person an opportunity to share something special with others
2. To practice listening skills
3. To build inclusion

Instructions

1. Ask each student to think of three things that he or she would like to share. Use the letters of the word "joy" to structure what is to be shared:

   J: something in your life that *just* happened

   O: *one* thing you would like to do for yourself

   Y: a part of *you* that makes you a very special person

   Point out that the key words say, "just one you!"

2. Urge the students to listen attentively as each student takes a turn sharing.

Suggested Reflection Questions

CONTENT/THINKING

✦ Why is it helpful to share information about yourself?

SOCIAL

✦ How well were people listening?

✦ What can we do to help each other to be better listeners?

PERSONAL

✦ How did this activity make you feel?

✦ What did you find out about yourself?

Appreciation

INVITE STATEMENTS OF APPRECIATION:

✦ "It helped me when…"

✦ "I appreciated…"

✦ "Thank you for…"

Options

Choose any two or three letter word and use the letters to invite purposeful responses, both personal and academic (for example, NOW: something New you learned, One question you have, Write a 10 word sentence summarizing…).

GRADES
2–adult

TIME
20 minutes

GROUPING
community
or tribes

MATERIALS
none

Kitchen Kapers

Objectives

1. To build inclusion and influence
2. To experience the creative power of brainstorming as a problem-solving technique
3. To promote creativity and fun

Instructions

1. Prepare packets containing two 3 x 5-inch cards, two paper clips, four toothpicks, and one pencil in a sealed business-sized envelope.
2. Have the community meet in tribes or form subgroups. Review the agreements.
3. Give each tribe a packet. State that they will have twelve minutes to invent and build "one kitchen utensil every household simply must have." Encourage bizarre, zany, and unique ideas. State that all tribe members need to participate.
4. Stop the "inventors" at twelve minutes.
5. Ask each tribe to then prepare a short, three minute commercial advertising its product. All members need to take part in the commercial.
6. Have each tribe present their commercial to the community.

Suggested Reflection Questions

CONTENT/THINKING

✦ What inventions did the tribes create?
✦ How did the purpose of the utensil change as you built it?
✦ What did you learn from this activity?

SOCIAL

✦ How did leadership in your tribe evolve?
✦ How can building project like this help build tribe spirit?

PERSONAL

✦ How did you feel before your tribe knew what it would build?
✦ How did you feel when you completed the invention?

Appreciation

INVITE STATEMENTS OF APPRECIATION (TO TRIBE MEMBERS):

✦ "I felt good when..."
✦ "I liked it when..."

Options

Use the "invention" theme and have students develop an invention to accompany a unit of study (for example, a way to move a heavy stone using materials common in Ancient Egypt). Have students write an expository description of the finished product.

GRADES
3–adult

TIME
25–30 minutes

GROUPING
tribes, subgroups

MATERIALS
3 x 5-inch cards,
paper clips,
toothpicks,
pencils, envelopes

Life Map

Objectives

1. To build inclusion
2. To create a visual illustration of one's life
3. To encourage attentive listening

Instructions

1. Ask the community to meet in tribes.
2. Give each student a piece of paper and crayons or markers and have him or her draw a visual illustration of "my life to date," the significant trends and patterns in the form of a map.
3. Invite each student to share his or her "Life Map" with his or her tribe members, explaining the rationale for "road signs," "place names," ups and downs, and so on.
4. Ask the students to give their full, undivided, caring attention to the speakers; after each student's presentation ask his or her tribe members to draw out more details, ask questions, and express their mutual feelings or concerns.

Suggested Reflection Questions

CONTENT/THINKING

+ Why is it important to be able to draw a "Life Map?"
+ How were the maps in your tribe the same?

SOCIAL

+ How could you tell if your tribe members were being good listeners when others shared their "Life Maps?"

PERSONAL

+ How did you feel as you made your "Life Map"/as you shared with your tribe?

Appreciation

INVITE STATEMENTS OF APPRECIATION:

+ "I felt good when..."
+ "I like it when..."

Options

Make a plot map, story map, unit map, historical timeline, or scientific life map (for example, at age two I had an ear infection, at age ten I broke my finger...).

GRADES
3–adult

TIME
30 minutes

GROUPING
tribes

MATERIALS
large paper, crayons or markers

Live Wire

Objectives

1. To create a visual illustration of one's life
2. To encourage attentive listening
3. To promote inclusion

Instructions

1. Have the community form tribes or triads.
2. Give each student a three-foot-long piece of wire with which to construct a visual illustration of his or her "life to date:" the significant trends, patterns, and events of his or her years thus far.
3. Invite each student to share his or her "Live Wire" with other tribe members, explaining the rationale for its design.
4. Review the agreements. After one student shares, the others may ask questions, express their mutual feelings or concerns.

Suggested Reflection Questions

CONTENT/THINKING

+ What did you learn in this activity?
+ What similarities/differences were there among your experiences?

SOCIAL

+ Why is the right to pass important for this activity?
+ How well did your group members listen to/help each other?
+ How can you improve your listening skills?

PERSONAL

+ How did you feel as you *made/shared* your lifeline?

Appreciation

INVITE STATEMENTS OF APPRECIATION:

+ "I felt good when..."
+ "I like it when..."

Options

Use as a plot line in literature. Review what was read, and exchange "live wires." Write or create a plot that matches the "live wire."

GRADES
4–adult

TIME
15 minutes

GROUPING
community, tribes, triads

MATERIALS
wire

Look At Me!

Objectives

1. To build inclusion
2. To give students an opportunity to create visual illustrations of themselves from four time perspectives

Instructions

1. Ask the community to meet in tribes.
2. Give each student a "Look at Me!" worksheet, a pencil, and crayons or markers. Have each student draw himself or herself as a baby, as a small child, now, and five years from now. (Use your own worksheet to illustrate.)
3. Ask the tribe members to share their four drawings, explaining any anecdotes or details that seem appropriate.
4. Remind listeners to give full, undivided, caring attention to the speakers.

Suggested Reflection Questions

CONTENT/THINKING
+ What similarities/differences did you notice in your "Look at Me!" worksheets?

SOCIAL
+ How could you tell that tribe members were using good listening skills when your tribe shared?

PERSONAL
+ How did you feel as you drew yourself?
+ What did you learn about yourself?

Appreciation

INVITE STATEMENTS OF APPRECIATION:
+ "I felt good when..."
+ "I understand how you felt when..."

Options

Have students use pictures from magazines. Describe or identify any that illustrate the Tribes agreements. Post throughout the classroom or school as reminders.

GRADES
4–6

TIME
45 minutes

GROUPING
tribes

MATERIALS
"Look At Me!" worksheets, crayons or markers, pencils

Look At Me!

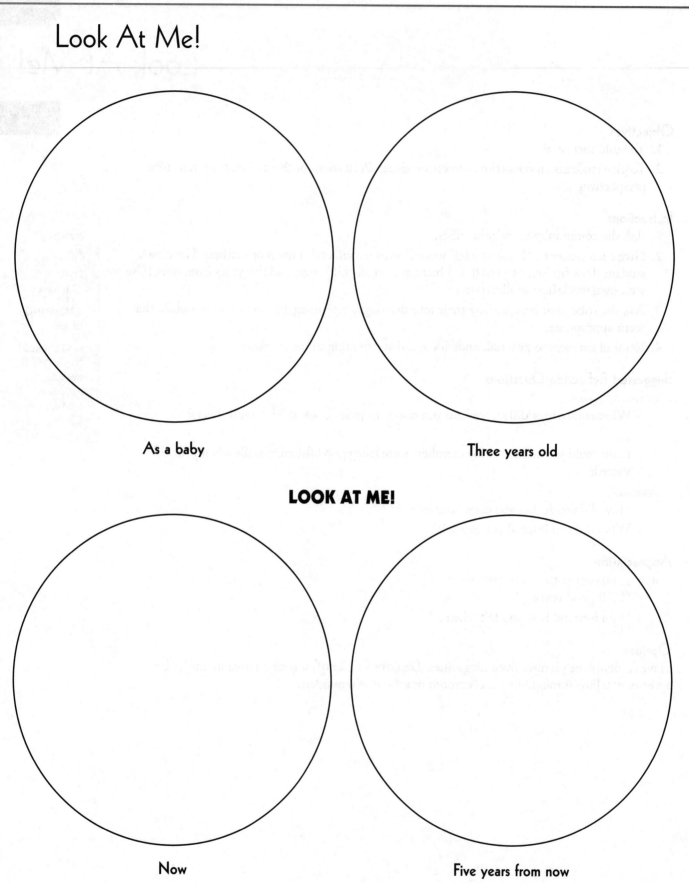

As a baby

Three years old

LOOK AT ME!

Now

Five years from now

Making A Choice

Objectives

1. To learn how to use a point system for evaluating choices
2. To involve students in evaluating choices
3. To create a positive decision-making process
4. To experience influence

Instructions

1. Have the students meet in tribes, and give each tribe the handout "Making A Choice."
2. Have tribe members read the problem aloud, discuss the advantages and disadvantages of the alternatives and make a choice.
3. Tell them to rate the criteria for each alternative by writing one, two or three in the appropriate boxes. Then add up the totals in each column. The tribe choice is the alternative with the highest rating.
4. After the tribes have made their choices, have them present their choice to the class. Point out how often people can have the same information and come up with different solutions.

Suggested Reflection Questions:

CONTENT/THINKING
+ What have you learned about making choices?
+ How could a "weighted" point system help you or your tribe made a choice?

SOCIAL
+ How did your tribe members help each other?
+ What social skills did you need to make a choice this way?

PERSONAL
+ How did you feel when your tribe came up with your solution?
+ How did you help your tribe?

Appreciation

INVITE STATEMENTS OF APPRECIATION:
+ "I appreciated it when..."
+ "You helped when..."

Options

Use a historical event, a school issue, or a current event.

GRADES
4–adult

TIME
45 minutes

GROUPING
tribes

MATERIALS
"Making A Choice" handouts

Making A Choice Handout

INTRODUCTION

When we have a problem, we have a choice between alternative ways to solve it. One aspect of making a choice is to identify and compare the advantages and disadvantages of the alternatives. A systematic approach can be used to make the comparison. Study and complete the model chart below so that you can learn to use it to make good choices.

PROBLEM

You are a playground equipment committee for a brand new elementary school, grades K–6. You have been given the task of deciding which piece of playground equipment you will put in first. Your total budget for this year is $500. The money must be spent within the next two months. You want good quality and something that will have the widest possible use. It must also be attractive and you want students to be able to use it as soon as possible. There is no chance of more money this year.

ALTERNATIVES	ADVANTAGES	DISADVANTAGES
Three tetherball poles	Cost would be within budget	Contractor can't do it for seven weeks
Two basketball poles, backboards, and hoops	Several students can play at a time	It might cost a bit more than $500
Large sandbox	Younger students have been asking for one; it would cost $400	Uncertain if older children would use it
Two swings	Everybody likes swings and contractor could install within two weeks	Only two students at a time could use them

Rate the criteria for each: 3=good or high, 2=medium, 1=low or poor

CRITERIA	TETHERBALL	BASKETBALL	SANDBOX	SWINGS
Low cost to install				
Low maintenance				
In use soon				
Attractive				
Appeals to all ages				
TOTAL				

This page may be duplicated for classroom use.

Me Book

Objectives

1. To build inclusion
2. To build self-esteem and self-awareness
3. To reinforce the relationship between oral and written language
4. To experience working on a long-range project

Instructions

1. Explain to the community that each student will be making a "Me Book" during the next ten days. Tell them they will work on one statement each day.

   Examples:

   - I feel great when...
   - I feel angry when...
   - I feel sleepy when...
   - My mom thinks I'm...
   - My dad thinks I'm...
   - I feel my brother is...
   - I feel my sister is...
   - My favorite toy is...
   - My favorite food is...
   - The place I like best to be is...

2. Have the students form tribes.
3. Have each tribe member draw a picture that illustrates the statement and then describe or write an explanation of his or her drawing.
4. Form the completed drawings into books.
5. Have students share completed books in tribes.

   Note: For very young children, have them dictate statements and explanations to an aide or an older student.

Suggested Reflection Questions

CONTENT/THINKING

- What is your favorite food, toy, etc.?
- What did you learn about a tribe member?

SOCIAL

- Who would like to share his or her "Me Book?"
- How did this activity help you get to know your classmates?

PERSONAL

- Why is it difficult to think of things to draw?
- Did you discover anything new about yourself?

Appreciation

INVITE STATEMENTS OF APPRECIATION:

- "What I like about your 'Me Book' is..."
- "I liked it when..."

Options

Make a "character" book for a historical or fictitious person. Use as a book report format.
Use as a reflective practice or self-evaluation.

GRADES
K–3

TIME
20 minutes per day, 11 consecutive days

GROUPING
community, tribes

MATERIALS
paper, pencils, felt pens, crayons

Meet Someone Special

Objectives
1. To introduce individuals to a community
2. To build community inclusion
3. To build self-esteem and appreciation for uniqueness

Instructions
1. This is a good activity to help new students introduce themselves to each other. Have the community sit in a circle while you give directions.
2. Review the Tribe agreements.
3. Ask each student to stand up, look about for someone he or she does not know well, invite that person to be his or her partner.
4. Have one partner interview the other one for three to ten minutes (depending on age), listening attentively so he or she will remember important unique qualities and details about the person; at the end of three to ten minutes, have the partners switch roles.
5. After the stated time, call the pairs back to the community circle and ask each student to introduce his or her partner and share the special things he or she learned.

Suggested Reflection Questions
CONTENT/THINKING
+ What new things did you learn from your partner?
+ Why did you do this activity?

SOCIAL
+ Why don't people take this type of time to get to know each other in other settings? In business and social organizations? In community meetings?
+ What important social skills did you use during this activity?

PERSONAL
+ How well did you listen to your partner?
+ How did you feel to have this much time to share about yourself?
+ What did you learn about yourself that surprised you?

Appreciation
INVITE STATEMENTS OF APPRECIATION:
+ "I appreciated it when…"
+ "I liked it when…"

Options
Use as a class appreciation by introducing "someone special" at the beginning or end of each day. Have tribes write questions to ask characters from literature or history.

GRADES
K–adult

TIME
20–30 minutes

GROUPING
community, pairs

MATERIALS
none

Milling to Music

Objectives

1. To build community inclusion
2. To review a curriculum topic

Instructions

1. Pre-prepare for each student a slip on which there are four numbered questions. Example:
   + Describe three cities or towns in which you have lived.
   + Share your favorite way to relax or spend vacation time.
   + Describe what your house, apartment, or living space is like.
   + If you were given $100,000 tomorrow, what would you do with it?
2. Give the students their slips with the four topics and ask them to stand up.
3. Explain that when the music starts they are to begin milling around silently but greeting each other as they pass by.
4. Explain that when the music stops (or when you give the hand signal), each student is to stop and discuss question #1 with a student standing close by for 1 minute. Explain that when the music begins again, they are to repeat the process until they have discussed all four questions.

GRADES
3–adult

TIME
15–25 minutes

GROUPING
community

MATERIALS
slips with numbered topics, cassette tape player and lively music

Suggested Reflection Questions

CONTENT/THINKING
+ What kind of greetings did you use?
+ What similar things did you share?

SOCIAL
+ What skills did you have to use in this activity? (Suggest some: listening, speaking clearly, sharing time, respecting differences.)

PERSONAL
+ What do you feel now?
+ How has the atmosphere changed in the room?

Appreciation

INVITE STATEMENTS OF APPRECIATION:
+ "I liked it when..."
+ "I appreciated the sharing that [name] did.

Options

Use content information to create sharing groups.

Mirror...Mirror

Objectives

1. To build inclusion
2. To facilitate sharing feelings
3. To build respect for diversity

Instructions

1. Have the community stand in one large circle and pass around a hand mirror.
2. Point out that mirrors reflect how people all look different in special ways (color of hair, eyes, skin, smiles, etc.) but that mirrors do not show what people think and feel, which is also very important.
3. Pass out "Hand Mirror" worksheets and ask the students to divide into tribes. Ask the students to write "I think" and "I feel" statements on their "Hand Mirror" worksheets. Have aides or older students help the nonreaders if necessary.
4. Have the students share their "Hand Mirror" worksheets in either tribes or the community.

Suggested Reflection Questions

CONTENT/THINKING

+ What do mirrors reflect to us?
+ What do mirrors not reflect?
+ Why is it important to know the difference between what mirrors reflect/don't reflect?

SOCIAL

+ How can sharing your mirrors help you get along better?
+ What social skills were used when mirrors were shared? (Remind the students of skills: listening, sharing, appreciation)
+ Why is it important to use good listening skills when others share?

PERSONAL

+ What did you do to make others feel OK when they shared their mirrors? Why is that important?
+ What is one thing you can do to listen better?

Appreciation

INVITE STATEMENTS OF APPRECIATION:

+ "I liked it when..."
+ "I liked Joel's mirror because..."
+ "I think you are neat because..."

Options

Have tribes write feelings or attributes for historical figures or characters from literature.
Have the community brainstorm attributes for mathematical patterns and concepts.

GRADES
K–4

TIME
45 minutes

GROUPING
community, tribes

MATERIALS
hand mirror,
"Hand Mirror"
worksheets,
crayons

Mirror...Mirror

My Favorite People and Things

Objectives

1. To build inclusion
2. To encourage verbal ability, especially with ESL (English as a second language) students
3. To express likes and dislikes, and promote respect for diversity
4. To learn shapes (circle and triangle)

Instructions

1. Have the community stand in a large circle and have the students take turns stating their favorite colors.

2. Tell the students to form triads, and have the triad members tell each other what their favorite toys may be. Then have the students form new triads, and have the triad members tell each other what their favorite foods are. For grades 2 and 3, have the students form triads one more time, and have triad members share something they dislike.

3. Then have the community form a circle and join hands. Have the students sing or recite the rhyme below:

   "I like you, I like me

   Special people one, two, three,

   Different colors, different eyes

   Each of us is quite a prize!"

   (Lead a big cheer after this.)

4. Have the students again form triads.

5. Pass out "Circle/Triangle" worksheets; tell each student to draw in the spaces around the triangle:

   + his or her favorite color
   + his or her favorite toy
   + his or her favorite food

6. Have students draw a picture (in the middle of the triangle) of a person they really admire or like. (Vary the content so that it is appropriate for the age level and culture of your class.)

7. Have the students share one or all sections of their circle/triangles with their triads or the community.

Suggested Reflection Questions

CONTENT/THINKING

+ What new things did you learn about your classmates?

SOCIAL

+ Why is sharing what we like with others important?
+ How well did we do at taking turns?
+ What can be done to help everyone take a turn?

PERSONAL

+ How did you feel sharing your likes with others?

GRADES
K–3

TIME
30 minutes

GROUPING
triads

MATERIALS
circle/triangle
worksheets,
pencils, crayons

My Favorite People and Things

Appreciation

INVITE STATEMENTS OF APPRECIATION (TO TRIAD MEMBERS):

+ "I like you because..."
+ "I liked it when..."

Options

Use the graphic as a Venn diagram to classify information.

My Favorite People and Things

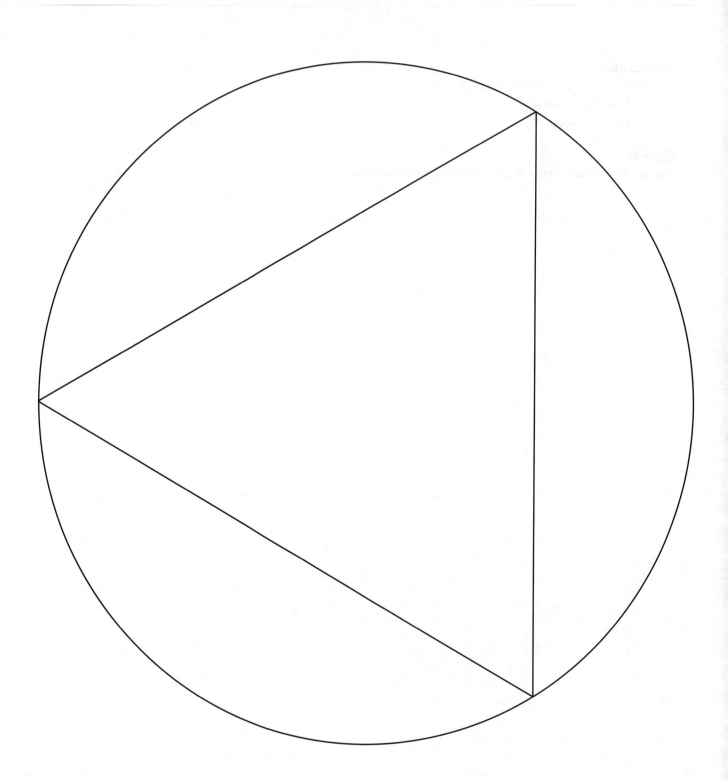

My Name In Print

Objectives
1. To promote appreciation of personal qualities
2. To encourage respect for others
3. To build inclusion

Instructions
1. Have the community meet in tribes.
2. Distribute the materials.
3. Have each student write his or her first name in big colorful letters going down the left side of the paper.
4. Then have each student draw or cut out adjectives (words or phrases that describe special qualities) that begin with the letters of his or her first name. Example:

   P playful, powerful

   A active

   T talkative, tidy

   T terrific

   I interesting

5. Ask each student to share their "Names in Print" with the rest of the tribe or community.
6. Remind listeners to give full attention to the speaker. Say that questions or comments may be posed at the end of each presentation.
7. After asking reflection questions point out how well everyone listened. Give examples.

GRADES
2–6

TIME
30–60 minutes

GROUPING
community, tribes

MATERIALS
9 x 12-inch paper, magazines, scissors, glue, markers

Suggested Reflection Questions

CONTENT/THINKING
- How difficult/easy was it to find adjectives to describe yourself?
- Why is it important to use positive adjectives to describe yourself?

SOCIAL
- How did this activity help you learn more about each other?
- How well did your tribe members listen to each other?

PERSONAL
- How did you feel when you shared your adjectives?
- What did you do to make others comfortable when they shared?

Appreciation
INVITE STATEMENTS OF APPRECIATION:
- "[name], I liked it when you said…"
- "[name], I learned that you are…"
- "[name], I'm glad that we both have [quality] in common."

Options
Use vocabulary words. Have students create positive descriptions of each other or the teacher.
Use as a reflective practice at the end of a study unit.

Name Game

Objectives
1. To help learn first names
2. To build inclusion

Instructions
1. Have the community sit in one large circle.
2. Have one student begin the activity by stating his or her name.
3. Have a second student repeat the first student's name and then state his or her own.
4. Have the third student repeat the first two names and then state his or her own.
   Example:
   "I'm Todd."
   "You're Todd, I'm Scott."
   "You're Todd, you're Scott, and I'm Karen."
5. Continue around the circle by having each student say the names of the previous three people, and then have the community chant the earlier names.

Suggested Reflection Questions
CONTENT/THINKING
+ Why do you like being called by your first name?
+ Why is this a good way to learn people's names?

SOCIAL
+ Which social skills did we use in this activity?
+ How did you help each other during this activity?

PERSONAL
+ How did you feel as your turn came closer?
+ What's the mood of the community now compared to before starting this activity?

Appreciation
INVITE STATEMENTS OF APPRECIATION:
+ "I felt good when..."
+ "I like the way..."

Options
Use alliterative adjectives ("Terrific Todd"), favorite foods ("Ice Cream Todd"), activities ("Football Todd"), etc.
Instead of names, use examples of nouns, multiples of 5, etc.

GRADES
K–adult

TIME
varies

GROUPING
tribe or community

MATERIALS
none

Newspaper Scavenger Hunt

Objectives

1. To learn how to find information in a newspaper
2. To work together to find the needed information
3. To experience influence

Instructions

1. Explain to the students that they will have ten to twenty minutes to find all the items in the paper described on the "Newspaper Scavenger Hunt" sheet, circle them in the newspaper with their colored pencil, and write the page numbers next to the items on the sheet. Say that everybody in the tribe is expected to participate and locate items.
2. Have the community meet in tribes. Assign roles in each tribe:

   TASKMASTER: gets the materials and monitors the time

   FACILITATOR: ensures that each tribe member works his or her section of the paper

   SPOKESPERSON: reads the page numbers to the community when called upon
3. Have each taskmaster pick up one copy of the newspaper, one worksheet for his or her tribe, and a different colored pencil or pen for each tribe member.
4. Have each tribe divide the newspaper up between tribe members.
5. When time is up, ask the spokesperson from each tribe to share how many items his or her tribe was able to find. Randomly ask tribes to share what they found for various items on the worksheet.

GRADES
3–12

TIME
45 minutes

GROUPING
tribes

MATERIALS
a newspaper for each tribe, "Newspaper Scavenger Hunt" worksheets, colored pencils

Suggested Reflection Questions:

CONTENT/THINKING

   ✦ What did you learn about using a newspaper?

   ✦ What are the sections of a newspaper?

SOCIAL

   ✦ How did you participate during this strategy?

   ✦ Which agreement is the most important in an strategy like this?

PERSONAL

   ✦ How did you help your tribe members?

   ✦ How did you feel when you found your items in the newspaper?

Appreciation

INVITE STATEMENTS OF APPRECIATION:

   ✦ "I liked it when..."

   ✦ "Thanks, [*name*] for..."

Options

Use appropriate curriculum topics or themes.

Adapted from "Lesson Plan: Scavenger Hunts," by John Myers, *Cooperative Learning,* Spring, 1992

Newspaper Scavenger Hunt

Look through your newspaper and locate the information asked for below. Circle the item in the paper with a colored pencil. Write in the page number where you found the information. When you are finished, fold the newspaper back into its original condition.

1. a comic where two people are arguing _____
2. an ad for a job in local or state government _____
3. a map _____
4. a picture of a famous person _____
5. the word "business" _____
6. an editorial article criticizing local, state, or federal government _____
7. an article about an environmental problem _____
8. the word "conflict" _____
9. an article about a conflict in sports _____
10. an advertisement for a used car made in 1987 _____
11. news about some aspect of education _____
12. a cartoon making a political statement _____
13. a letter to the editor about local government _____
14. an ad for a movie related to law enforcement _____
15. an article about a foreign country _____
16. a story which has to do with children _____
17. the word "defense" _____
18. an article relating to guns _____
19. a birth or death notice _____
20. the circulation (number of papers sold daily) _____

What strategy did your tribe use?

Make up four more questions:

Adapted from "Lesson Plan: Scavenger Hunts," by John Myers, *Cooperative Learning*, Spring, 1992

Novel in an Hour

Objectives

1. To comprehend a novel, story or chapter of a book
2. To work cooperatively in small groups to retell the story by using drama, pictures, storytelling or other multiple intelligences
3. To practice listening, respecting and working together creatively

Instructions

1. Divide the chapters of a novel or short story into 5–10 sections, numbering each section.
2. Divide the class into the same number of groups.
3. Introduce the novel with an appropriate personal *inclusion question* for discussion.
4. Create interest in the novel by sharing something about the characters, theme or dilemma.
5. Describe the structure and process of Novel in an Hour:
   - the novel has been divided into sections (same number as groups);
   - everyone is actively involved;
   - everyone takes turns reading the material aloud;
   - the group plans multiple ways to share their part of the material with the whole community by using their multiple intelligences (drama, music, illustration, etc.).
6. Have each group appoint a time keeper (example: planning—20 minutes, and presentation—30 minutes).
7. Have the groups make their presentations to the community in the order of the sections of the novel.

Suggested Reflection Questions

CONTENT/THINKING
   - Which character was most important in how the story ended?
   - What do you think the author's message is?

SOCIAL
   - What was difficult for your group in planning your presentation?
   - What was most helpful?

PERSONAL
   - What feelings did you have during your group's presentation?
   - What makes this a good way to learn about a novel or story?

Appreciation

INVITE STATEMENTS OF APPRECIATION:
   - "I liked it when…"
   - "I appreciated the way that our group…"

Options

Use science or social studies curriculum or text.

GRADES
3–adult

TIME
depends upon material

GROUPING
tribes

MATERIALS
a short story or novel

Now I Am

GRADES
K–5

TIME
20 minutes

GROUPING
community

MATERIALS
none

Objectives
1. To recognize and identify feelings
2. To introduce the relationship between oral and written language
3. To develop observation skills
4. To build inclusion

Instructions
1. Have the community sit in a circle; review the agreements.
2. Whisper a different feeling or emotion in each student's ear one at a time. Examples:

fear	frustration	surprise	rage
nervousness	hope	soreness	love
dreaminess	anger	uncomfortable	wild
unhappiness	tired	embarrassed	weird
itchiness	stubborn	excitement	sleepy

3. Ask the students to act out their words nonverbally.
4. Have the community guess what each student is acting out.

Suggested Reflection Questions
CONTENT/THINKING
+ Which feelings were the easiest/most difficult to act out?
+ How did you figure out what feeling was being represented?

SOCIAL
+ How can you help each other discover the feelings you have at different times?

PERSONAL
+ When did you have one of the feelings that was represented?
+ How difficult was it for you to act out your word?

Appreciation
INVITE STATEMENTS OF APPRECIATION:
+ "I liked the way you acted it out because..."
+ "I feel a lot like you when..."

Options
Print feeling words on cards, and have people act them out.
Have students draw feelings using colors that match the feelings or make a face of "how you feel this minute."
Have students write a story about a person who always acts the same.
Have tribes write a story and then act out the feelings associated with a historical or social event.
Follow with the strategy "Five Tribles."

On My Back

Objectives
1. To build self-esteem
2. To encourage giving statements of appreciation
3. To build inclusion

Instructions
1. Give each student a large piece of paper, a felt marker, and two pieces of masking tape.
2. Ask each student to print his or her name at the top of the paper.
3. Have the students attach the papers to each others' shoulders so that they hang down like capes on their backs.
4. Have the students stand and circulate so that each person in the group can write statements of appreciation on other people's paper capes. Emphasize that the statements need to be positive.
5. When each student has several written statements on his or her cape, ask the community to sit in a circle or have them form tribes. Have the students read their statements aloud or have them exchange papers and read to each other.
6. Encourage people to save their papers, perhaps to use as posters for their bedroom walls.

GRADES
3–adult

TIME
20 minutes

GROUPING
community, tribes

MATERIALS
large paper,
tape, markers

Suggested Reflection Questions
CONTENT/THINKING
- What were some of the neat things people wrote?
- What similarities did you see in what people wrote?
- How did the fact that this activity was anonymous help you to be honest?

SOCIAL
- How did you take care of each other?
- How did you take turns?
- Why don't you offer positive statements to others more often?

PERSONAL
- What feelings did you have when people were writing on your paper cape?
- What feelings did you have while your statements were being read aloud or while you were reading your statements?

Appreciation
INVITE STATEMENTS OF APPRECIATION:
- "I like it when…"
- "I felt good when…"

Options
Use as a learning strategy for well known-characters in history, politics, current events, or literature.

One Special Thing About Me

Objectives

1. To give students an opportunity to introduce themselves
2. To give students an opportunity to work in pairs before sharing
3. To promote inclusion

Instructions

1. Have the community sit in a circle. State that we are a unique group about to start an exciting journey together and, like any people coming together, we need to learn about each other.
2. Say: "Think about yourself and something about you that people would remember. Think about something that makes you special. It doesn't have to be something big, but it needs to say something about you. It can be silly, fun, sentimental, or kind."
3. State that there will be one minute of quiet time before sharing with a partner.
4. After the minute, ask each student to share with a partner for two to three minutes.
5. After the students have shared with their partners, ask them to re-form the community circle.
6. Then go around the circle, inviting each student to state his or her name and what makes him or her special. Start with yourself to provide good modeling.

Suggested Reflection Questions:

CONTENT/THINKING
- ✦ Why is it difficult to think of something that makes you special?
- ✦ What type of things makes you feel special?

SOCIAL
- ✦ Why is it easier to share with a partner?
- ✦ What social skills did you need to use to be successful in this strategy?

PERSONAL
- ✦ How did you feel sharing with one other person?
- ✦ How did you feel sharing in the community circle?

Appreciation

INVITE STATEMENTS OF APPRECIATION:
- ✦ "I liked it when you said..."
- ✦ "Thank you for sharing..."

Options

Share: One thing I learned; one question I would ask of a historical figure or a character from literature; one thing I don't understand.

GRADES
K–adult

TIME
25–45 minutes

GROUPING
community, pairs

MATERIALS
none

One, Two, Three

Objectives

1. To make choices between competing alternatives
2. To allow students to affirm and explain their choices
3. To practice decision-making
4. To promote influence

Instructions

1. Ask the students to meet in tribes, form groups of four to six, or meet as a community.
2. State that you will ask a question and then offer three alternative answers. Tell the students that you will be asking them to make some choices by ranking the three alternatives in the order of their importance or preference. Tell each student to write down the three alternatives and then put a number 1, number 2 or number 3 after each item according to his or her first, second and third choice.

   Examples:

   Where would you rather be on a Saturday afternoon?
   + at the beach?
   + in the woods?
   + window shopping downtown?

   Which do you consider most important in a friendship? •honesty?
   + loyalty?
   + generosity?

3. Have the students share their choices with each other and explain why they made the selections.

Suggested Reflection Questions

CONTENT/THINKING
+ How did your choices compare to choices made by others?
+ Why are some choices harder to make than others?

SOCIAL
+ What choices might be more difficult/easier to make?
+ Why is being able to make a choice an important skill?

PERSONAL
+ What feelings did you have when you had difficulty choosing?
+ What have you learned about yourself?

Appreciation

INVITE STATEMENTS OF APPRECIATION:
+ "I liked it when..."
+ "I appreciated your dilemma when..."

Options

Use classroom or social issues. Introduce possible study or assignment topics. Use the "multiple choice" format to reflect or assess the "best answer."

GRADES
3–adult

TIME
10–15 minutes

GROUPING
community,
tribes, subgroups

MATERIALS
pencils, paper

One Minute History

GRADES
2–adult

TIME
20–30 minutes

GROUPING
community,
tribes, triads

MATERIALS
none

Objectives
1. To give each student an opportunity to share his or her background
2. To build inclusion

Instructions
1. Have the community sit in a circle or meet in tribes or triads.
2. Instruct the students that each student will have one minute in turn to tell his or her personal history. Remind the listeners to give full attention without interrupting.

Suggested Reflection Questions

CONTENT/THINKING
+ What did you learn about someone else?
+ Why is it important to be able to summarize your life?

SOCIAL
+ How could you tell that others were using good listening skills?
+ Why was a minute enough/not enough time to share?
+ Did the students who shared later in the activity share more or less? Why?

PERSONAL
+ How did you feel about sharing?

Appreciation

INVITE STATEMENTS OF APPRECIATION:
+ "I liked it when you said..."
+ "I felt good when..."
+ "I was particularly interested when you..."

Options
Review a historical topic and invite students to summarize the content in one minute. Use as a pre-writing strategy.

Open Forum

Objectives

1. To encourage acceptance of diverse feelings, beliefs, and cultures
2. To build inclusion

Instructions

1. Have the community meet in tribes or subgroups.
2. Tell the students that you will write a discussion question on the chalkboard, and each tribe member is to take a turn responding to the question. Discussion or questions are not allowed until each tribe member has had an opportunity to respond to the question. After all tribe members have had a chance to speak, students may ask one another follow-up questions and ask for clarification of what was said.
3. Remind the groups about the tribe agreements, especially "attentive listening."
4. Examples of inclusion questions:
   + What is the best book you ever read? Why did you like it?
   + How do you select your friends?
   + What guides your life?
   + If you could be an animal for a day, what would you be? Why?
   + What goal do you have for your future?

GRADES	3–adult
TIME	30 minutes
GROUPING	tribes, subgroup
MATERIALS	none

Suggested Reflection Questions

CONTENT/THINKING
+ What was something you learned from your discussion?

SOCIAL
+ What social skills did you use to make this activity successful?
+ How could you tell that your tribe members were being good listeners when you shared?

PERSONAL
+ Why would you be uncomfortable answering some of the questions?
+ How did you feel when it was your turn?
+ How did you participate? Are you happy with the way you participated? Why?

Appreciation

INVITE STATEMENTS OF APPRECIATION:
+ "I liked it when..."
+ "I'm a lot like you when..."
+ "You're a lot like me when..."

Options

Use questions about current events or social issues.
Use the strategy for questions related to academic content.

Our Treasury

GRADES
3–6

TIME
60 minutes

GROUPING
tribes

MATERIALS
none

Objectives
1. To allow for individual influence
2. To practice group decision-making

Instructions
1. Ask the community to meet in tribes.
2. Give each group a fictitious sum of money (or paper money), which is to be its tribe treasury.
3. Tell each tribe to brainstorm about the best uses of this money. (Review the brainstorming process if necessary.) Have the tribes make a list of their ideas.
4. Have each tribe decide what four things on its list it would spend its treasury on.
5. Ask each tribe to report its decision to the community.

Suggested Reflection Questions

CONTENT/THINKING
- What were some of the things you listed?
- What did you learn about making choices?
- Why is deciding how to spend money often difficult?

SOCIAL
- How did you resolve differences of opinion among tribe members?
- What are the most important social skills you need when making decisions as a tribe?

PERSONAL
- How do you feel about the decisions you made?
- What have you learned about yourself?

Appreciation
INVITE STATEMENTS OF APPRECIATION:
- "I appreciated it when..."
- "I knew what you meant when you said..."
- "I liked it when..."

Options
Have tribes use the fictitious money to "spend" on charity or public service.
Have students make a personal budget in order to teach life skills.

Our World Is Changing

Objectives

1. To create a tribe list of changes in the world
2. To give individuals an appreciation of change
3. To practice brainstorming

Instructions

1. Have the community meet in tribes and have the tribe members greet each other.
2. Review the rules for brainstorming (see "Brainstorming" strategy).
3. Have each tribe select a recorder. Have the recorders raise their hands so you can be certain each recorder is ready.
4. Have the tribes brainstorm and write lists of how the world has changed since their parents (or grandparents) were born. Give the tribes five minutes to brainstorm.
5. Have the community meet. Have tribes report one or two changes that have made an impact on their lives. (Suggestion: Ask the student with the shortest hair in each tribe to report.)

Suggested Reflection Questions

CONTENT/THINKING

✦ What do you feel are the most important changes that have happened?

✦ Why is it important to know how the world has changed?

SOCIAL

✦ Why is brainstorming a good strategy to use?

✦ What social skills did your group need to be successful at this strategy?

PERSONAL

✦ How did you feel sharing the changes you recognized?

✦ What did you do to help your tribe?

Appreciation

INVITE STATEMENTS OF APPRECIATION:

✦ "I liked it when you said..."

✦ "Thank you for..."

Options

Have the tribes cut pictures from magazines and make collages that show how the world has changed since their parents were born. Expand and elaborate on a single issue, such as how the world has changed. Follow-up with a writing experience, Venn diagram, graph or research project.

GRADES
3–adult

TIME
45 minutes

GROUPING
community, tribes

MATERIALS
paper, pencils

Outlines

Objectives
1. To build inclusion
2. To practice communication and listening skills
3. To discuss academic topics

Instructions
1. Have the students meet either in their tribes or the community circle.
2. Explain the objectives, and pass out "T-shirt Outline" worksheets.
3. Tell students how to fill in the outline:
    + in area #1 write an alliterative adjective that goes with your first name. (Example: "Vivacious Vicki")
    + in area #2 write or draw two to three things you enjoy doing
    + in area #3 name a real or pretend place you would like to visit
    + in area #4 write a word you'd like people to say when they describe you
    + in area #5 write a wish you have for yourself
4. Sharing: First review the Tribes agreements, and ask the students to share the time equally so that each student has an opportunity to speak during each round.

    ROUND 1: each student shares his or her name and alliterative adjective with another student, telling why he or she chose the adjective (three minutes).

    ROUND 2: each student finds two other people and shares the information he or she wrote in area #2 (four minutes).

    ROUND 3: each student finds two other people and shares the information of area #3 (four minutes).

    ROUND 4: each finds three to four others and shares area #4 (four minutes).

    ROUND 5: each Round 4 group combines with another Round 4 group. Names and alliterative adjectives are shared again with students telling why they chose their particular adjectives.

Suggested Reflection Questions
CONTENT/THINKING
+ What did you learn about your tribe members?
+ What were the similarities among your tribe members' wishes?

SOCIAL
+ How well did you listen to each other? How could you tell?
+ How many students do you feel you know better now?

PERSONAL
+ What was the best/most difficult thing for you about this activity?
+ What did you learn about yourself?

GRADES
3–adult

TIME
30–40 minutes

GROUPING
community, tribes

MATERIALS
"T-Shirt Outline"
worksheet, colored
pens or pencils

Outlines

Appreciation

INVITE STATEMENTS OF APPRECIATION:
- ✦ "I like it when..."
- ✦ "I'm glad you're..."

Options

There are endless other fine questions for this activity: someone you admire, a quality you like in a friend, something you want to learn, a favorite subject, book, or academic material. Select those most appropriate for the group's age and culture.

Use the outline for a fictitious character or a well-known person.

Have students design other outlines to use for subject content.

T-Shirt Outline

Pantomime

Objectives
1. To build self-esteem
2. To build inclusion
3. To experience communication without words

Instructions
1. Have the students form two groups. Have each group take a turn doing expressions and movements.
2. There is no discussion until both groups have finished.
3. The following are suggestions of expressions and movement:
   + facial expressions: funny, scared, sad
   + feeling walks: walk angrily, walk sadly
   + weather walks: walk in the rain
   + people walks: robber, clown
   + animal walks: dog, cat, duck
   + characters and situations: an acrobat on a tightrope
   + exploring senses: taste a lemon, smell a skunk
   + handling imaginary objects: play with a yo-yo
   + experiencing different environments: you are on the moon

GRADES
K–3

TIME
20 minutes

GROUPING
community

MATERIALS
none

Suggested Reflection Questions

CONTENT/THINKING
+ Why was it easy/difficult to demonstrate your feelings?
+ What did you find out about yourself and others?

SOCIAL
+ What did we have to do to make this activity successful?
+ How could you tell that others were being good watchers and listeners?

PERSONAL
+ How did you feel while you were participating in the activity?

Appreciation

INVITE STATEMENTS OF APPRECIATION:
+ "I liked it when..."
+ "I'm like you when..."
+ "I felt good when..."

Options
Use the strategy to act out or draw vocabulary words or concepts relevant to content.

Paraphrase Passport

Objectives

1. To follow up on the "Reflecting Feeling" strategy
2. To practice listening
3. To practice paraphrasing while discussing a topic

Instructions

1. Review the strategy "Reflecting Feelings" with the community. Have the students discuss how they felt when they played the roles of speaker, feeling reflector, and observer.

2. Tell students they will be discussing topics by using "paraphrasing passports," which is a way to learn how to be a good listener. In "Paraphrase Passport" no one has permission to speak until he or she correctly restates (paraphrases) the idea of the previous speaker.

   Example:

   John: "I am concerned that violence is increasing in many cities, and believe that unemployment is a major cause."

   Sarah: "John, you are concerned about the increase in violence and attribute it to unemployment."

3. Have students again form the triads they were in for "Reflecting Feelings" and choose who will be the first speaker. Explain that the first student contributes an idea and the second student must restate it correctly before contributing his or her idea.

4. Topic to discuss:

   Older students: "How does good listening help to develop caring and learning in a community?"

   Younger students: "How does good listening help our tribe?"

GRADES
2–adult

TIME
20 minutes

GROUPING
community, triads, tribes

MATERIALS
none

Suggested Reflection Questions:

CONTENT/THINKING
- What did you learn from your discussion about listening?
- Why is listening an important social skill?

SOCIAL
- How well did you paraphrase what the person before you said?

PERSONAL
- How might "Paraphrase Passport" help you to listen to others?
- How could good listening help you to be a better friend?

Appreciation

INVITE STATEMENTS OF APPRECIATION:
- "I liked it when you said.."
- "It felt good when..."

Options

Use to check for understanding, review content, state opinions (perhaps as a pre-write for a persuasive paragraph or essay), or role play historical or social issues.

*This structure is from *Cooperative Learning: Resources for Teachers,* by Spencer Kagan

Paraphrasing

Objectives
1. To build inclusion and influence
2. To teach and practice paraphrasing

Instructions

VERSION A:

1. Have the community stand or sit in a large circle.
2. Turn to the student on your left and ask a question.

   Examples:

   "What is your favorite color?"

   "What is your favorite holiday?"

   "What is your favorite fruit?"
3. The next student answers, and the first student who asked the question repeats back the answer. Example:

   Student #1: "What's your favorite color?"

   Student #2: "Red."

   Student #1: "Shawn's favorite color is red."
4. Have students continue the sequence around the circle.

VERSION B:

1. Give all the students colored paper strips prepared as follows:

   "_____'s favorite_____ is _____."
2. Have tribe members pair up and decide who is #1 and who is #2.
3. Have partner #1 ask a question and partner #2 give the answer.
4. Then have partner #1 fill in the blanks on his or her strip.
5. Have partners switch so that partner #2 now asks the question.
6. After all the students fill in the blanks on their colored strips have the tribes staple the strips together and display them.

Suggested Reflection Questions

CONTENT/THINKING
   + What similarities did you notice in people's answers?
   + Why are we learning about paraphrasing?

SOCIAL
   + Why is it important to take turns in this strategy?
   + How could you tell people were cooperating during this activity?

PERSONAL
   + How did you like working with a partner?
   + What did you contribute during this activity?

GRADES
K–adult

TIME
30–45 minutes

GROUPING
community, tribes

MATERIALS
colored
paper strips

Paraphrasing

Appreciation
"I liked working with you, [*name*], because..."

Options
The strategy can be used for various combinations of curriculum material. A variation on Version A is to have students ask each other across the circle or to integrate the strategy with the "Spider Web" strategy. In Version B, older students can work in groups of three or four, asking and recording things that they have learned about a lesson or topic.

Partner Introduction

Objectives

1. To give students an opportunity to introduce themselves
2. To give students an opportunity to work in pairs before sharing
3. To experience inclusion

Instructions

1. State that we are a unique group about to start an exciting journey together, and, like any people coming together, we need to learn about each other.
2. Have each student find a partner he or she does not know at all or very well. Have the partners decide who will be the interviewer and who will be the interviewed. For one minute the interviewer will tell his partner all the things that he does not know about him. The interviewee is only to listen and not respond. For example, an interviewer might say, "I don't know your name," "I don't know how many people are in your family," etc.
3. The partner being interviewed then responds for two minutes giving information that they would be willing to have shared with the whole community.
4. Have the partners switch roles and repeat the strategy.
5. Have the community form a circle and have each student introduce his or her partner to the community, and share one thing they learned about their partner.

Suggested Reflection Questions

CONTENT/THINKING
+ What did you learn about your partner?
+ What are the most common things you shared?

SOCIAL
+ Why might interviewing be a good way to get to know somebody?
+ Why is attentive listening so important for this strategy?

PERSONAL
+ How did you feel to interview your partner?
+ How did you feel to have your partner share what you said?

Appreciation

INVITE STATEMENTS OF APPRECIATION (TO PARTNERS):
+ "One thing I liked was..."
+ "Thank you for..."

Options

Use this strategy to preview or review a unit of study, concepts, or actual content standard material (for example, have students share everything they know about writing conventions).

GRADES
2–adult

TIME
35–45 minutes

GROUPING
community, pairs

MATERIALS
none

Peer-Response Huddle

Objectives

1. To structure a cooperative learning experience
2. To develop energy and interest in curricula
3. To build pride
4. To promote influence

GRADES
K–adult

TIME
15 minutes

GROUPING
tribes

MATERIALS
none, or
5 x 7-inch cards

Instructions

1. Have the community meet in tribes.
2. Have the tribe members count off, beginning with the number one, or pass out numbered cards so that each tribe member has a number.
3. Tell the students that you will call out a question, and that each tribe has thirty seconds to huddle and decide upon one answer. Say you will then call out a number, and that each tribe member with that number will quickly stand up. Say you will ask one of the students standing to give the answer.
4. Keep the questions, huddle time, and responses going as rapidly as possible so that the energy takes on a "popcorn" effect. Don't call on the first person who pops up unless you intend to promote competition. After an answer is given, lead the applause.

Suggested Reflection Questions

CONTENT/THINKING
- What did you learn that you didn't know before?
- Why is this a good way to review information?

SOCIAL
- What social skills did you need to be successful?
- How can your tribe improve the way it worked together?

PERSONAL
- How did you feel when your number was called?
- How do you feel about your tribe now?

Appreciation

INVITE STATEMENTS OF APPRECIATION:
- "I liked it when..."
- "I want to thank you, [*name*] for..."

Options

This strategy is easily used for a spur-of-the-moment check for understanding or reflection on learning. It can also be used to review an entire unit of study by inviting students to write or define questions.

Acknowledgment to Spencer Kagan's structure, "Numbered Heads Together"

People Hunt

Objectives
1. To promote community inclusion
2. To introduce oneself to others
3. To encourage sharing information

Instructions
1. Give one third of the students worksheet I, one third worksheet II and one third worksheet III.
2. Have the students circulate around the room, stopping to introduce him or herself, and asking different students the questions listed on his or her worksheet. Tell them to write down the names of those who fit the descriptions.
3. After ten to fifteen minutes, ask the community to meet in tribes or form groups of five for reflection questions.

Suggested Reflection Questions
CONTENT/THINKING
+ What did you learn that impressed or surprised you?

SOCIAL
+ How well were group members participating in this task and how could you tell?
+ What social skills were used to be successful with this task?

PERSONAL
+ How did you approach this task, did you go to people or did you wait for people to come to you?
+ Do you feel any different now from when you first walked into the room?

Appreciation
INVITE STATEMENTS OF APPRECIATION:
+ "I liked it when you..."
+ "I felt good when..."
+ "I'm like you when..."

Options
Personalize the "People Hunt" by using statements that you know apply to students.
Use the strategy to review academic content by writing appropriate questions (for example, create a "fraction hunt").

GRADES
3–adult

TIME
40 minutes

GROUPING
community

MATERIALS
"People Hunt" worksheets, pencils

People Hunt Worksheet 1

FIND:

1. A person who does not own a TV

   His or her name is _____

2. A person whose birthday is within a month after yours

   His or her name is _____

3. A person who can cross his or her eyes

   His or her name is _____

4. A person who traveled over 2,000 miles last summer

   His or her name is _____

5. A person who lives in a house where no one smokes

   His or her name is _____

6. A person who owns a horse

   His or her name is _____

7. A person who is new to this school

   His or her name is _____

8. A person who likes brussels sprouts

   His or her name is _____

9. A person who is an artist

   His or her name is _____

10. A person who has more than six brothers and sisters

    His or her name is _____

People Hunt Worksheet II

FIND:

1. A person who can speak two languages

   His or her name is_____

2. A person who has been to a concert

   His or her name is_____

3. A person who has two different colored eyes

   His or her name is_____

4. A person with a new baby in his or her home

   His or her name is_____

5. A person whose birthday is the same month as yours

   His or her name is_____

6. A person who can roll his or her tongue

   His or her name is_____

7. A person who has been ice skating this past year

   His or her name is_____

8. A person not born in this country

   His or her name is_____

9. A person who has more than four animals in his or her home

   His or her name is_____

10. A person who woke up with a smile this morning

    His or her name is_____

People Hunt Worksheet III

FIND:

1. A person not born in California (New York, Texas, etc.)

   His or her name is_____

2. A person who stayed home last summer

   His or her name is_____

3. A person whose birthday is one month before yours

   His or her name is_____

4. A person who is the oldest child in his or her family

   His or her name is_____

5. A person who can touch his or her nose with his or her tongue

   His or her name is_____

6. A person who likes to invent things

   His or her name is_____

7. A person who jogs for exercise

   His or her name is_____

8. A person who has four dogs in his or her home

   His or her name is_____

9. A person who has been horseback riding in the past three months

   His or her name is_____

10. A person who has planted a tree

    His or her name is_____

People Puzzles

Objectives
1. To build inclusion
2. To form or assign membership in tribes

Instructions
1. Pre-prepare one puzzle for each group or tribe. Cut each puzzle so that the number of pieces matches the number of people in each group or tribe.
2. To build random groups, put all the pieces of all the puzzles in a box and have each person take a piece. To assign tribes put the name of one person on each piece of puzzle.
3. Before having the students form their tribes, have a discussion about what possible put-downs could occur and how to avoid them.
4. Ask the students to circulate and find the puzzle pieces that match the ones they are carrying. Tell them they are not to talk while doing this. Tell them they may talk when their group's puzzle has been completed.
5. Once all of the puzzles have been completed, you may choose to have each tribe make up a story relating to the picture its puzzle has formed. Have each tribe select one member to be a storyteller and tell the tribe's story to the community.

Suggested Reflection Questions
CONTENT/THINKING
- ✦ What made this task difficult/easy?
- ✦ Was this a fun way to find students who would be in your tribe?

SOCIAL
- ✦ How did you react to students whose puzzle pieces didn't fit yours?
- ✦ How did you help each other during this activity?

PERSONAL
- ✦ How did you feel when you first started this activity?
- ✦ How did you feel at the end?

Appreciation
INVITE STATEMENTS OF APPRECIATION:
- ✦ "I'm a lot like you when..."
- ✦ "I admire you for..."

Options
Create puzzle sets, each containing related historical events, mathematical or scientific concepts. Have students circulate to find the related concepts, and then review with each other.

GRADES
K–adult

TIME
20 minutes

GROUPING
tribes

MATERIALS
picture, puzzles

Perception and Transmission

Objectives

1. To promote inclusion and influence
2. To promote an understanding of different points of view
3. To demonstrate how perceptual limitations can affect communications

Instructions

1. Have the community meet in tribes.
2. After an inclusion activity, hand out copies of the young girl/old woman drawing to each tribe. Instruct the tribe members to glance at the drawings briefly, without discussion. Then collect all copies immediately.
3. Ask people to share what they saw in the drawing. Emphasize the concept that people perceive differently; ask questions such as "would you talk to this person on the bus?" or "who in your family does this person remind you of?"
4. Give copies of the drawing to each tribe member and have the tribes continue the discussion.
5. Assist students who have difficulty identifying both aspects of the drawing.
6. Have the tribe members expand their discussions to other areas in their points of view might be limited by their perception of information.

GRADES
5–adult

TIME
40 minutes

GROUPING
community

MATERIALS
copies of young
girl/old woman
drawing

Suggested Reflection Questions

CONTENT/THINKING

✦ Why do some of you see a young girl while others see an old woman? Is there a correct way to see the picture?

✦ Why is this an important activity to do?

SOCIAL

✦ Why do conflicts arise between individuals who perceive information differently?

✦ How can you resolve conflicts based on different perceptions?

PERSONAL

✦ What did you feel towards the students who saw the drawing the same way you did/differently than you did?

✦ How did you feel when you "discovered" the other aspect of the drawing?

Appreciation

INVITE STATEMENTS OF APPRECIATION:

✦ "I am a lot like you when..."

✦ "I felt good when you said..."

Options

Use prior to history curricula concerning warfare, debates, constitutional rights, or different political views. Explore social topics, such as the viewpoint of parents versus teenagers.

Perception and Transmission of Information

Personal Contract

Objectives
1. To reflect upon personal situations
2. To commit to new attitudes, behaviors or achievements
3. To experience support from peers
4. To build influence

GRADES
4–adult

TIME
15 minutes

GROUPING
tribes

MATERIALS
5 x 8-inch index cards, pencils

Instructions
1. Have the community meet in tribes. Ask each tribe member to identify a personal behavior, attitude or achievement they would like to accomplish.
2. Explain how writing a "personal contract" makes change easier. Explain that a contract is a commitment that is specific, believable, and attainable in a certain period of time.
3. Give students time to consider, then have each write a personal contract as follows:
   "I, [name], will [describe specific commitment or action] by [specific date].
   Signed:_____
   Witnessed:_____
   Witnessed:_____
4. Have each student ask two tribe members to sign as witnesses and be supportive of the change to be made.
5. Suggest each student ask tribe members to check on progress of the contract's completion.
6. Keep contracts in tribe envelopes for periodic review.

Suggested Reflection Questions
CONTENT/THINKING
+ For what personal behavior, attitude, or achievement did you write a contract?
+ Why is developing a personal contract difficult?
+ How can a personal contract help you make the change you want to make?

SOCIAL
+ What role did the witnesses play in this contract?
+ What support did you get from your tribe members?

PERSONAL
+ How does having a contract make you feel?
+ How did you feel as a witness?
+ How will this help you change?

Appreciation
INVITE STATEMENTS OF APPRECIATION (TO TRIBE MEMBERS):
+ "I felt good when..."
+ "I like my contract because..."

Options
Teach life skills using real contracts. Have students study historical contracts. Compare and contrast social contracts and laws.

Personal Journal

Objectives

1. To allow time and privacy for reflecting on personal learning
2. To provide a method for noting personal goals, commitments, hopes, and growth
3. To facilitate sharing of personal observations
4. To build inclusion

Instructions

1. Plan regular time throughout the week for students to write about personal learning and school experiences. Tell the class that personal journals are a way to reflect on their own progress, hopes and goals; and that no one has access to another's journal without permission.
2. Urge the students to periodically review and compare their recent entries with former ones, and to congratulate themselves for signs of growth or learning. Suggest that they write "I Learned" statements.
3. Have tribe members share things from their personal journals when they choose to do so.

Suggested Reflection Questions

CONTENT/THINKING

 ✦ What sort of information do you imagine most of you are writing in your journals?
 ✦ Why is keeping a personal journal good for you?
 ✦ How can keeping a journal show you your personal growth?

PERSONAL

 ✦ How does it feel to have a personal data bank?
 ✦ What changes have you noticed in yourself?
 ✦ What are you learning about yourself through your journal?

Appreciation

INVITE STATEMENTS OF APPRECIATION:

 ✦ "I appreciate your need for privacy because..."
 ✦ "I liked it when you..."
 ✦ "I think it's neat that you..."
 ✦ "I value who you are because..."

Options

Have students write a journal for a historical event or person or a literary character.
Have students keep a personal journal as a reflection for a discovery learning experience.

GRADES
3–adult

TIME
ongoing

GROUPING
tribes, individuals

MATERIALS
notebooks

Poem By Our Tribe

Objectives

1. To write a tribe poem using individual member contributions
2. To demonstrate synergism and inclusion within the tribe
3. To develop an appreciation of individual contributions to a tribe effort and to experience influence

Instructions

1. Have the community meet in tribes. Tell the students they will be writing a tribe poem.
2. Assign roles for each tribe member:

   TASKMASTER: gets materials and monitors the time

   RECORDER: makes a final copy of the poem

   FACILITATOR: ensures that each tribe member's ideas are heard and respected

   READER: reads the final version of the poem to the community
3. Have the taskmasters obtain three cards for each tribe member and a different colored felt pen for each.
4. Write on the chalkboard the following sentence starters for use in the tribal poem:
   + I wish...I dreamed...
   + I used to be...But now I am...
   + I seem to be...But really I am...
5. Tell your students: "Here are a number of ways to start a tribe poem. Put your heads together in your tribes. Choose the sentence starter you like best or make up your own."
6. Ask each tribe member to take a piece of scratch paper and write as many versions of the completed sentence as possible during the time available (five to ten minutes).
7. Ask each tribe member to choose his or her two best lines and write one line on each of two cards.
8. Explain that each tribe will put together its poem as follows (*steps may be written on the chalkboard*):
   + each tribe member reads his or her two cards to the tribe
   + the tribe gives positive feedback (feelings, words, etc. that they liked) after each tribe member shares

   When all the tribe members have shared, the tribe cooperates to:
   + pick at least one card from each tribe member
   + decide in what order the lines should go in the tribe poem (the tribe may decide to modify lines only with the consent of the author)
   + decide on a one- or two-word title
9. When the tribe members have agreed on the order of the lines and the title, have the Recorder make a final copy and have all the tribe members sign the poem.
10. Ask the tribes to post their poems, and have each tribes' Reader take turns reading their poem to the class.

GRADES
2–12

TIME
50 minutes

GROUPING
tribes

MATERIALS
scratch paper,
3 x 5-inch cards,
felt pens

Poem By Our Tribe

Suggested Reflection Questions

CONTENT/THINKING
- ✦ What did you learn about writing poetry?
- ✦ Why would you like to express your feelings using poetry?

SOCIAL
- ✦ How were your ideas encouraged and honored?
- ✦ Which agreement is the most important in an strategy like this?

PERSONAL
- ✦ How do you feel about how you helped your tribe?
- ✦ How did you encourage other tribe members to contribute?

Appreciation

INVITE STATEMENTS OF APPRECIATION:
- ✦ "Thank you, [*name*], for..."
- ✦ "It was great when..."

Options

Use text from a content area with these modifications (or make your own):
- ✦ I think...I learned
- ✦ I understand...I wonder
- ✦ I didn't know...I'm curious about...

Adapted from "Writing a Group Poem," by Nan and Ted Graves, *Cooperative Learning*, Vol. 11, No. 4, July, 1991

Problem Solving Through Appreciative Inquiry

Objectives

1. To improve group effectiveness and pride by looking for what the group is doing well and what the group values rather than identifying a problem to correct
2. To empower and give groups a sense of competency and pride
3. To encourage positive approaches to innovation and creativity

GRADES
4–adult

TIME
varies

GROUPING
community
or tribes

MATERIALS
none

Instructions

1. Ask the community or tribes to discuss and report back their conclusions on the question: "What do people usually do to solve a problem when a group of people (a team or organization) is not working well together?" Ask for a report back in 5 minutes.
2. Acknowledge their responses (such as, people blame others, make new rules, or try to analyze and fix the problem). State that a very positive way for groups to improve is to look at what they are doing well instead of what is wrong. "Let's try this different way of problem solving."
3. Give the tribes 5–10 minutes to discuss one of the following questions:
   - Describe a time when you felt your group performed really well. What were people doing?
   - Describe a time when you felt proud to be a member of your tribe. What was happening?
   - What do people in your group do that you value and that contributes to success?
4. You may want to have the tribes list their responses before reporting to the class community.
5. Group members can also summarize their learning from the strategy or possible use of the approach to problem solving by writing in their journals.

Suggested Reflection Questions

CONTENT/THINKING
- Why is it helpful to look at the positive side of a situation or problem?
- How could appreciative inquiry be used to study or research a topic in history or literature?

SOCIAL
- How did this approach help your tribe or the community?
- What do you intend to do differently together?
- What hopes do you have for your group now?

PERSONAL
- What did you learn about yourself?
- What creative or positive contributions are you making to your tribe?
- How can appreciative inquiry be helpful to you in other groups?

Appreciation

INVITE STATEMENTS OF APPRECIATION:
- "I appreciate how you..."
- "It's so helpful when you..."

Options

Have tribes design role-plays using history or literature content to show how characters might have handled a situation in a different way to solve a people problem.
Have tribes brainstorm "what if..." questions.

Put Down the Put-Downs

Objectives

1. To build community inclusion
2. To list put-downs and the feelings they cause
3. To share the personal experience of receiving a put-down
4. To practice brainstorming

Instructions

1. Have students meet in tribes.
2. Lead a brief discussion about put-downs (hurtful names and behaviors).
3. After reviewing the rules for brainstorming, have each tribe select a recorder.
4. Ask the tribes to brainstorm put-downs that people use in the class or school.
5. Then have each tribe make a list of the feelings they have when they receive a put-down. Give each student time to share a time when a put-down really was hurtful.
6. Ask the tribes to brainstorm: "What could we do to help each other put-down the put-downs?"
7. Have each tribe present their list to the class, and ask reflection questions.

Suggested Reflection Questions

CONTENT/THINKING
- What were some of the "feeling words" you shared?
- What were some of your solutions for dealing with people who use put-downs?

SOCIAL
- Why do put-downs hurt your feelings?
- What are some important social skills to use when you brainstorm?

PERSONAL
- How did you feel when you remembered getting a put-down?
- How do you feel when you put-down another person?
- How do you feel about your solutions?

Appreciation

INVITE STATEMENTS OF APPRECIATION:
- "Thanks for..."
- "One thing I liked about what you said was..."

Options

Have the community select two or three ideas for ending put-downs. Use sticker voting (Group Problem-Solving) to prioritize.

Approach the cause and effect of put-downs from a historical perspective.

Identify statements and discuss how they may or may not be put-downs.

Encourage students to research how and why certain terms are derogatory.

Watch a sit-com and have students tally put-downs; then discuss.

GRADES
2–adult

TIME
40 minutes

GROUPING
tribes

MATERIALS
paper, pencils

Put Yourself on the Line

Objectives

1. To practice taking a stand among peers
2. To build appreciation for the different opinions
3. To use a structure to promote critical thinking on curriculum topics and issues
4. To experience influence

GRADES
2–adult

TIME
15 minutes

GROUPING
community, tribes

MATERIALS
none

Instructions

1. Ask the community to stand up.
2. Describe an imaginary line down the center of the room. Say the imaginary line may be called a "continuum." Identify the two positions at either end of the line as "strongly agree" and "strongly disagree." State that the middle position is for those who have no opinion, choose to pass, are non-risk-takers, or are "moderates."
3. Tell the students to move to places on the line that express their feelings or opinions when you call out statements. Examples:
   + It's OK to talk to strangers on the street.
   + It's important to always please the teacher.
   + One should never climb dangerous mountains.
   + Always do what your friends do so you won't be left out.

   Have students suggest topics; use for lesson topics and current events.
4. When the students take their place on the line have the ones near each other discuss why they are there. Pick one representative from each area of the line to report to the community.
5. Have the community meet in tribes to share feelings on a particularly controversial topic.

Suggested Reflection Questions

CONTENT/THINKING
+ Why is making your opinion public sometimes important?
+ Why is recognizing individual opinions important?

SOCIAL
+ Why is it important not to put down other people's opinions?
+ Why might you not want to "take a stand" on a topic?

PERSONAL
+ How did you feel about publicly taking a stand?
+ Why might you have been tempted to change your position after you looked around you?

Appreciation

INVITE STATEMENTS OF APPRECIATION:
+ "I felt good when..."
+ "One thing I like about this group is..."

Options

Use current events, social or historical issues. Have students, in tribes, select a representative to put on the line and speak for the group.

Reasons and Alternatives

Objectives
1. To explore motives and alternatives concerning the use of cigarettes, alcohol, or drugs
2. To develop peer support for non-use of alcohol and other drugs
3. To build inclusion and influence in tribes

Instructions
1. Have the community meet in tribes. Ask each tribe to appoint a recorder. Pass out two large sheets of paper and a marker to each tribe.
2. Tell the students that they will be brainstorming; review the rules of brainstorming.
3. Ask the tribes to brainstorm for five minutes on the subject: "Why do people smoke, drink alcohol, or use drugs?" Ask each recorder to jot down all ideas as quickly as they are called out.
4. After five minutes, stop the brainstorming and have the recorders take new sheets of paper. Ask the tribes now to brainstorm about another subject: "What are some alternatives to using cigarettes, alcohol, or other drugs?"
5. Stop the brainstorming after five minutes. Have the recorders report back to the tribe or community.
6. Ask the students to write in their personal journals what they intend to do about using chemical substances and how they would like to live their lives. Have them share their commitments with their tribe members.
7. Next ask the tribes to discuss what they are willing to do to help friends say "no" to the use of cigarettes, alcohol, or other drugs. Have each tribe make a list and report back to the community.

GRADES
4–adult
TIME
45–60 minutes

GROUPING
tribes

MATERIALS
large paper, markers

Suggested Reflection Questions
CONTENT/THINKING
- ✦ What did you learn about substance abuse?
- ✦ Why was this an important activity to do today?
- ✦ How can this knowledge change your behavior?

SOCIAL
- ✦ Why is brainstorming a good structure for this lesson?
- ✦ How can your tribe have improve its brainstorming process?

PERSONAL
- ✦ How do you feel about your tribe members?
- ✦ What will help you to live the commitment you have made?

Appreciation
INVITE STATEMENTS OF APPRECIATION:
- ✦ "It helped me when…"
- ✦ "I appreciated…"

Options
Use a social, historical, or literature-based issue or dilemma. Explore a scientific hypothesis. This strategy can also be used as a pre-writing exercise.

Reflecting Feelings

Objectives
1. To build community inclusion
2. To teach and practice listening skills
3. To share ideas and feelings about a given topic

Instructions

GRADES
4–adult

TIME
40 minutes

GROUPING
triads

MATERIALS
"Feeling Statements" worksheets

1. Discuss with the community how person's feelings can be identified by the tone of his or her voice (harsh, friendly, concerned), body language (leaning forward, withdrawn), or words.
2. Ask the students to form triads and decide which triad members will be A, B, or C. Ask for a show of hands of all A's, all B's and all C's to avoid confusion.
3. The triad members will play the following roles in each round (post a chart, if necessary):

	A	B	C
ROUND 1	Speaker	Feeling Reflector	Observer
ROUND 2	Feeling Reflector	Observer	Speaker
ROUND 3	Observer	Speaker	Feeling Reflector

4. Distribute a set of three feeling statements to each triad, and have each member draw one slip.
5. Have the speaker first state the type of character that will be speaking, and then role-play the statement with much feeling. The reflector will rephrase the statement back to the speaker, again with feeling. Example:

   SPEAKER: "A father is speaking to his son. He says, 'I am delighted that we can go fishing together on Saturday.'"

   REFLECTOR: "You feel very excited that we will be able to fish together all day on Saturday."

   OBSERVER: then tells the Speaker and Reflector what he or she heard and saw.
6. Rotate the roles so that everyone has a turn in each of the three roles.

Suggested Reflection Questions

CONTENT/THINKING
   ✦ What did you learn about reflecting feelings?

SOCIAL
   ✦ Why is listening such an important skill?
   ✦ Why is the observer's role important?

PERSONAL
   ✦ How well did you play the different roles?
   ✦ How are you going to use this information tomorrow?

Appreciation

INVITE STATEMENTS OF APPRECIATION:
   ✦ "Thanks for..."
   ✦ "I liked it when..."

Options
For older students, create more challenging statements that relate to social, historical or current event issues. The discussion can be very valuable. Use as a pre-writing exercise.

FEELING STATEMENTS

Friend: Just because I don't wear name brand clothes, the other kids treat me like I don't exist!

Friend:

- -

Student: I don't get this assignment. I don't see how this is going to help me.

Teacher:

- -

Mom: Your room is a mess! This is driving me crazy!

Son/Daughter:

FEELING STATEMENTS

Friend: My mother won't let me talk on the phone for more than five minutes. She's even making me pay part of the phone bills.

Friend:

- -

Student: I never say anything in class because it doesn't come out right.

Friend:

- -

Friend: My mother dragged me to a discount store and made me buy three outfits! I'm not going to wear them anyway!

Friend:

FEELING STATEMENTS

Student: I wish you wouldn't make me wait when I want your help. You are always helping somebody else.

Teacher:

- -

Friend: My parents always complain about what I don't do, but they never notice when I do something right!

Friend:

- -

Friend: I wanted to go to the movies with all of you Friday night, but my parents just told me I'm grounded.

Friend:

- -

Resentment/Appreciation

Objectives
1. To practice "I-Messages"
2. To develop oral language skills
3. To learn to express feelings and give feedback on behavior

Instructions
1. Have the community sit in a circle.
2. Explain the terms resentment (negative feelings concerning something that happened) and appreciation (positive feelings concerning person or event).
3. Review the "I-Message" framework for expressing either negative or positive feelings. Write the sentence framework on the blackboard.

   I am [*name the feeling*] when [*name the behavior or event*].

   Examples: "I am angry, when I cannot have my turn."

   "I appreciate Cary's thoughtfulness in making hot chocolate for all of us."
4. Review the Tribes agreements.
5. Ask for volunteers who wish to express an appreciation or resentment.

Note: It is important to follow up with a student privately if any statements of resentment are expressions of a serious concern; handle statements concerning the whole class with the community. Lead the class to solve problems that may pertain to all by using problem-solving strategies.

Suggested Reflection Questions

CONTENT/THINKING
- ✦ What appreciations/resentments did you share?
- ✦ Why might sharing resentments/appreciations be positive for you?

SOCIAL
- ✦ Why does trust need to be developed before people will share resentments?
- ✦ How could you tell that students were listening?
- ✦ Why is sharing feelings helpful to a community?

PERSONAL
- ✦ How do you feel now that you were able to say what you felt?

Appreciation
INVITE STATEMENTS OF APPRECIATION:
- ✦ "I admire you for..."
- ✦ "I learned..."

Options
Start by giving some examples of resentments in historical or social context. In response, have tribes develop appreciation statements. Discuss the reality and application to life events.
Use the strategy, "Confrontation," as a possible follow-up.

GRADES
K–adult

TIME
10 minutes

GROUPING
community

MATERIALS
none

Roles People Play

Objectives

1. To promote an awareness of helpful group roles
2. To learn how the accomplishment of group tasks depends upon helpful behaviors
3. To learn to use collaborative skills

Instructions

1. Discuss the objectives of the strategy and ask students to review the Tribe agreements.
2. Distribute the handout on "Roles That People Play In Groups."
3. Ask the students to study the cartoon and decide which role (or roles) they usually play when working with others in their tribe.
4. Ask the students to write answers to the questions on the bottom of the handout. Allow five to ten minutes time.
5. Have them share their responses with a partner.
6. Ask the students to share with their tribe a new role that he or she will try for the day (or week).

OPTION #1: A ROLE PLAY

+ Have each tribe plan and present a brief role play in which one person is playing an unhelpful role.
+ Ask the class to guess which role is being demonstrated.

OPTION #2: FOR ADULT AND/OR MULTICULTURAL GROUPS

+ Delete the "What People Say" right hand column on the role description handout before distributing it to the tribes.
+ Have the groups to brainstorm and list all the things that people of their own peer group culture may say.
+ Then proceed with steps three to six in the instructions above, or use role play option #1.

Suggested Reflection Questions

CONTENT
+ What happens in a group when even one person is acting in an unhelpful role?

SOCIAL
+ What helpful roles do people play in your tribe?
+ How do those roles make working together easier?
+ Do people in your tribe always play the same roles? How helpful is that?

PERSONAL
+ What feelings did you have during this strategy?
+ What did you learn about yourself?

Options

Choose roles that apply to historical or social situations. Try a "headband" approach, where the role is worn as a headband; the person wearing it has no knowledge of what role it is, and has to figure out the role, based on the behavior and statements of others.

GRADES
3–adult

TIME
20 minutes

GROUPING
community, tribes

MATERIALS
handout on roles

Roles People Play

DESCRIPTIONS OF HELPFUL ROLES	WHAT PEOPLE SAY
Encourager: Tells group positive things and keeps energy going well.	Right on! Good job! Yes! Let's do it. Keep going. Brilliant!
Organizer: Helps group stay on task and time; encourages management of materials and resources.	File the papers. We have one bottle of glue. First we should…
Peace Keeper: Helps members to solve problems, make decisions, express feelings and understand each other.	Time out. Let's talk about this! You both have a good point.
Idea Person: Gives and seeks helpful ideas. Initiates action and clarifies.	What if we looked at it this way? Another idea would be to… What ideas do you have? Let's brainstorm more ideas.
Helper: Is supportive and friendly, willing to listen and help others.	We need to hear from everyone. I'll help you. Let's work on it together.

UNHELPFUL ROLE DESCRIPTIONS	WHAT PEOPLE SAY
Joker: Claims attention by interrupting, goofing off, distracting and trying to be funny.	There's a spider on your head. At recess I'm going to… Look at this! Want some gum?
Boss: Takes charge. Knows it all. Tells people what and how to do things. Usually doesn't listen well.	Do it my way! That's not right. The best way is to…
Sitter: Doesn't participate. Sits on the side. Always claims the right to pass. Will not help others. Can seem judgmental.	I pass. Don't count me in.
Put-Downer: Ridicules others and their ideas.	That's stupid. You're so dumb. We tried that once. How can you be so oblivious?
Talker: Goes on and on talking. Ignores others also wanting time. Controls by not pausing between sentences.	Blah, blah, blah. And then he said to me… I also know that… Stop interrupting me.

This page may be duplicated for classroom use.

Roles People Play In Groups

Encourager • Joker • Organizer • Boss • Peace Keeper • Talker • Idea Person • Sitter • Helper • Put-Downer

QUESTIONS

1. Which role do you usually play in a group?

2. Why do you think that it's the easiest role for you to play?

3. What other role or roles would you like to play to help your group?

4. How willing are you to try out a new helpful role today?

Self-Esteem Cards

Objectives
1. To build self-esteem
2. To reinforce the concept of appreciation
3. To foster positive feelings among tribe members
4. To build inclusion

GRADES
3–adult

TIME
15 minutes

GROUPING
tribes

MATERIALS
3 x 5-inch cards

Instructions

Note: This strategy should not be used until tribe members know one another fairly well.

1. Have the community meet in tribes; pass out cards.
2. Instruct each tribe member to write his or her first name in an upper corner of the card.
3. Tell the tribe members to place all their cards in a center pile. Have each tribe member draw a card (not divulging whose card he or she has), and write a thoughtful, warm statement on the card about the student whose name is on the card.
4. Have the students return all of the cards to the central pile when done writing and repeat the process of drawing and writing four or five additional times. If anyone draws his own card, begin the drawing again or have the students exchange cards.
5. After the final writing, return all cards and draw again. This time have each tribe member read the remarks on the card to the student whose name is on the card, delivering the tribe's message as warmly and sincerely as possible while the rest of the tribe listens.

Suggested Reflection Questions

CONTENT/THINKING
+ What did you learn by doing this activity?
+ How did you choose the statements you wrote for your tribe members?

SOCIAL
+ How does making thoughtful, warm statements to each other bring your tribe closer together?
+ Why is it important to receive positive statements from others?

PERSONAL
+ How did you feel while your card was being read to you?
+ How do you feel about your tribe now?

Appreciation

INVITE STATEMENTS OF APPRECIATION:
+ "I felt good when..."
+ "Thank you for..."

Options

Use to enable students to reflect on what they have learned about a topic. Students can also suggest "test questions," or write "I learned" or appreciation statements regarding an assignment.

Shaping Up With Blocks

Objectives

1. To develop observation and communication skills
2. To practice following directions
3. To understand spatial relationships
4. To learn geometric shapes
5. To experience influence

Instructions

1. Have the students meet in tribes.
2. Invite two members in each tribe to sit back to back in the center of the tribe. Give each partner the same number and colors of blocks.
3. Tell the tribes that the two members will be moving their blocks into a pattern, taking turns being the "director." The director gives instructions to the other member, the listener. They will switch roles when the pattern has been completed.
4. Tell the director to move one block and describe the placement of the block to the listener.

   Example: "Put the blue triangle in front of you pointing away from you." Tell the listener to place his or her colored block in the same position.
5. Have the director continue adding six to ten blocks and describing their positions until a pattern he or she is pleased with is completed.
6. Have the two partners compare patterns and see how similar or dissimilar they are.
7. After the partners' discussion, have other students in each tribe reflect what they saw/heard.
8. Invite other tribe members to take turns doing this strategy.

Suggested Reflection Questions

CONTENT/THINKING

✦ What did you learn about giving directions to others?

✦ Why is this a difficult activity?

SOCIAL

✦ Why is listening and following directions important?

✦ How did the director and the listener work together?

✦ How can they improve working together?

PERSONAL

✦ How did you feel about having to follow directions without seeing your partner's pattern?

✦ How do you feel about the importance of clear directions?

Appreciation

✦ "It was neat working with you because..."

✦ "You two were a good team because..."

Options

This strategy can be used for older students while studying various subject areas, such as geography, science, and art; give the director different materials to use for the partner to assemble (such as maps, patterns, or diagrams).

GRADES
1–5

TIME
20 minutes

GROUPING
tribes, subgroups

MATERIALS
colored blocks of various geometric shapes

Sharing From a Sack

GRADES
K–adult

TIME
20–50 minutes

GROUPING
community, tribes

MATERIALS
each student
brings an object
in a paper sack

Objectives
1. To give each student an opportunity to share something special or meaningful about herself or himself
2. To build inclusion
3. To practice active listening

Instructions
1. Several days before this activity, ask each student to choose a special object to bring from home. The object may represent a hobby, interests, award, or symbol of a personal quality. Tell the students to bring the objects concealed in paper sacks.
2. Have community form one large circle or meet in tribes.
3. Going around the circle, ask each student to share his or her object by removing it from the sack and talking about it, telling why the object is important or symbolic.

Suggested Reflection Questions
CONTENT/THINKING
+ How did you choose what object you would bring?
+ What did you learn about others?
+ How did having your object in a sack before sharing make this activity more enjoyable?

SOCIAL
+ Why did this activity help you get to know one another better?
+ How well did you listen?

PERSONAL
+ How did you feel when you shared your object?
+ How did you feel as you listened to others?

Appreciation
INVITE STATEMENTS OF APPRECIATION:
+ "[name], you seem to love your hobby. May I do it with you sometime?"
+ "[name], I liked it when you said..."
+ "[name], thank you for listening..."

Options
Place materials in a sack that pertain to a curriculum topic or that have meaning in historical or scientific context; have students talk about the item pulled from the sack. Put vocabulary words in a sack, and ask students to give definitions or create sentences.

Shoe 'n Tell

Objectives
1. To build inclusion
2. To practice active listening
3. To have fun

Instructions
1. Ask each student to bring a pair of his or her shoes from home in a paper sack. (Allow a few days.)
2. Have full group or tribe sit in circle(s).
3. Explain that sharing from the sack could take on any of these forms:
   + how these shoes help me to do things that I like to do
   + sharing from the point of view of the shoe (what it's like being the shoe that belongs to the person sharing)
   + sharing from the point of view of the shoe (how I'd like to be taken care of if I could have it my way)

Suggested Reflection Questions
CONTENT/THINKING
   + How did the shoes tell you about the students who shared?
   + How did you go about choosing the shoes you shared?

SOCIAL
   + How did tribe members show they were interested?

PERSONAL
   + How did you feel sharing your shoes?

Appreciation
INVITE STATEMENTS OF APPRECIATION:
   + Going around the circle, ask each student to give a statement of appreciation to the student on left.
   + "[name], I liked it when..."

Options
Have students discuss and write about a shoe belonging to a person in history or a shoe that is related to an occupation. Students can read to a partner or tribe while listeners figure out "whose shoe" it might be.

GRADES
K–6

TIME
50 minutes

GROUPING
community, tribes

MATERIALS
each student brings a pair of shoes in a paper sack

Silhouettes

GRADES
K–4

TIME
60 minutes
or more

GROUPING
pairs

MATERIALS
paper, pencils,
scissors, glue,
magazines,
envelopes

Objectives

1. To build self-esteem
2. To promote inclusion
3. To encourage positive statements towards one another

Instructions

1. Have the community form pairs.
2. Have the pairs place construction paper on the wall. Darken the room and place a bright light close to the wall.
3. Have one partner sit between the light and wall, making a profile shadow on the paper.
4. Tell the other partner to outline the shadow with a pencil.
5. Have the partners switch roles and repeat the activity.
6. After both silhouettes have been traced, the partners cut out and mount the silhouette.
7. Have each partner clip out magazine pictures that represent how he or she sees himself or herself, and glue a collage on his or her silhouette.
8. Display the silhouettes. Under each, attach an envelope with the name of the student drawn in big letters.
9. Explain that the envelopes are for appreciation statements that will be written during the year.
10. Ask the students to draw names and have them place written appreciation statements in the appropriate envelopes. Writers are to remain anonymous.

Suggested Reflection Questions

CONTENT/THINKING

✦ How do the magazine pictures represent you?
✦ What did you learn?

SOCIAL

✦ How does this activity help you get to know other students?
✦ How well did you work with your partner?

PERSONAL

✦ How did you feel when you finished your silhouette?
✦ What is one thing you can do to work better with a partner?

Appreciation

INVITE STATEMENTS OF APPRECIATION:

✦ "I liked it when..."
✦ "I am a lot like you because..."

Options

Have students find or draw pictures of historical characters or people; ask the students to write statements of appreciation citing the characters' contribution to people or nations. Use silhouettes of objects or events; have students write paragraphs using various writing styles or genres.

Singing the Blues

Objectives
1. To promote commonality and inclusion
2. To introduce sharing of concerns in a nonthreatening, enjoyable way
3. To channel community energy

Instructions
1. Ask the community if they know what "the blues" are. State that in this activity, having "the blues" means feeling badly about something.
2. Ask if anyone has the blues and why.
3. Sing or strum a melody that is simple and fun.

   Example: A seven-year-old boy says his dog was hurt. Words could be: "I've got the blues, I've got the blues, I've got the my-dog-was-hurt-blues."
4. Ask everyone to join in singing.
5. Share one of your own blues first. Lead the singing on it.
6. Invite the students to tell their blues and lead the singing.
7. Discourage the students from making fun of another's blues. Help them to understand it's a put-down to do so.

GRADES
K–3

TIME
20–30 minutes

GROUPING
full group

MATERIALS
none or a guitar

Suggested Reflection Questions

CONTENT/THINKING
- ✦ What did you learn about "the blues" today?
- ✦ How were your "blues" similar?

SOCIAL
- ✦ How did the singing make it easier to share?

PERSONAL
- ✦ How did you feel when you first started "singing the blues?"
- ✦ Do you feel different after "singing the blues?"
- ✦ How would you feel to sing about "good times?"

Appreciation

INVITE STATEMENTS OF APPRECIATION:
- ✦ "I enjoyed singing because..."
- ✦ "I feel like you do when..."

Options
Have students create songs, raps or poems about historical, social, literary or school events.

Slip Game

Objectives
1. To build inclusion
2. To promote personal sharing

Instructions

1. Pre-prepare a bag for each tribe containing slips of paper with questions on them. Examples:
   + "When are you really happy?"
   + "What is the most special positive quality about you?"
   + "When have you felt very proud?"

   (See more sample questions on the next page.) Make sure each bag contains the same number of question slips as the number of tribe members, plus a few extra.

2. Instruct the community to meet in tribes. Review the agreements. Pass out bags.

3. Everyone has the "right to pass" if they do not like the question that they draw and may select an alternative one from those that remain in the bag. They must put the original slip back after taking an alternative one. Ask tribe members to each draw a slip with their eyes closed; tell them about right to pass and option for drawing alternative questions.

4. Have tribe members take turns reading and answering their questions.

Suggested Reflection Questions

CONTENT/THINKING
+ What's one thing someone shared that you found interesting?

SOCIAL
+ Why is "right to pass" such an important agreement for this activity?
+ How did having the opportunity to choose another question slip help you and your tribe be successful?
+ Did you feel more comfortable about sharing as the activity progressed?

PERSONAL
+ Why could it be difficult for you to share?
+ How did you feel when you were answering the question you drew?

Appreciation

INVITE STATEMENTS OF APPRECIATION:
+ "I'm a lot like you when..."
+ "I admired you for..."

Options

Use the strategy for discussion of lesson topics. Have tribes develop questions and exchange with other tribes to answer.

Slip Game Sample Questions

What makes you angry?

What makes you happy?

What makes you sad?

What do you do for fun?

Do you have any pets?

What is your favorite food?

What is your favorite place?

What is your favorite animal?

What is your favorite sport?

What is your favorite song?

What is your favorite TV program?

What do you and your friends do for fun?

If you could have one wish, what would it be?

What famous person would you like to be?

In what period of time, past or future, would you choose to live in?

What foreign country would you like to visit?

What would you like to be really good at?

What is your favorite story?

What is one food you don't like?

What do you do when you feel lonely?

What would you do with one million dollars?

Would you rather be rich, famous or happy?

What would you do if you were the president?

What would you do to improve school?

What qualities do you look for in a friend?

Who is the best person in the world?

What do you do when you get really angry?

Snowball I-Messages

GRADES
2–adult

TIME
45 minutes

GROUPING
community, tribes

MATERIALS
paper and pencils

Objectives

1. To create community inclusion and energize the class
2. To give individuals practice in writing I-Messages

Instructions

Note: Use the strategy "Teaching I-Messages" prior to using this one.

1. Ask each student to bring one piece of paper, a pencil and something firm to write on and sit in a community circle.
2. Review the elements of an "I-Message" and the difference between an "I-Message" and a "You-Message."
3. Give examples of an "I-Message" and a "You-Message" and ask the students to think of an example of each.
4. Ask several students to model an "I-Message" and then a "You-Message."
5. Ask each student to draw two lines that divide the paper into four squares, and to write a "You-Message" in one square.
6. After the students have done so, tell them you will give them two commands: "crumple" and "toss." Explain that when you say "crumple," they will crumple their papers into "snowballs," and when you say "toss," they will toss the "snowballs" into the center of the circle.
7. Then have the students pick up a "snowball," read the "You-Message," and change it into an "I-Message." Have the students write the "I-Message" in another square.
8. Repeat the process one more time.
9. Have each student take a snowball back to his or her tribe, and have the tribes critique the messages.

Suggested Reflection Questions

CONTENT/THINKING
+ Why is it important to know the difference between a "You-Message" and an "I-Message?"
+ What kind of messages do you get/give in "You-Messages?"

SOCIAL
+ Why is this strategy a good way to learn about "I-Messages?"

PERSONAL
+ How did it feel to change a "You-Message" into an "I-Message"?
+ How can you use "I-Messages" in your life?

Appreciation

INVITE STATEMENTS OF APPRECIATION:
+ "I liked..."
+ "I enjoyed it when..."

Options

Use examples from history or social situations; have students write "I Messages" and discuss possible responses.

Something Good

Objectives
1. To build inclusion
2. To encourage sharing of positive feelings

Instructions
1. Have the community sit in a large circle.
2. Ask each student to share one positive experience that happened during the previous week or recent past. Say that there will be no discussion until all have shared.

Suggested Reflection Questions

CONTENT/THINKING
+ Were there any similarities about the "good things" you shared?
+ When was the last time you told someone about a positive experience?

SOCIAL
+ How can you tell if others are using good listening skills?
+ Did you share more freely as the activity progressed? Why?
+ How did this activity help the community?

PERSONAL
+ How did you feel while sharing with the community?

Appreciation

INVITE STATEMENTS OF APPRECIATION:
+ "I liked it when..."
+ "I'm like you when..."
+ "I felt good when..."

Options
Invite statements about the day's lesson, project or content standard. Have students role play historical or social situations in terms of "something good."

GRADES
K–adult

TIME
varies

GROUPING
community

MATERIALS
none

Something I Cherish

GRADES
2–adult

TIME
20 minutes

GROUPING
community, tribes

MATERIALS
none

Objectives
1. To increase communication skills
2. To build inclusion

Instructions
1. Ask the community to meet in tribe.
2. Ask each tribe member to take a turn sharing "one thing that I cherish," explaining why it is so special or why she or he wants others to know, etc.
3. To draw the tribes back into the community, have each tribe member share with the community one item that another member of his or her tribe cherishes. Make sure each tribe member speaks of and is spoken about by another member of his or her tribe.

Suggested Reflection Questions
CONTENT/THINKING
+ What type of things do your tribe members cherish?
+ Why is it important to share what you cherish with each other?

SOCIAL
+ How well did your tribe members listen when others shared?

PERSONAL
+ How did you feel about sharing something you cherished?
+ How can this type of sharing help your own family?

Appreciation
INVITE STATEMENTS OF APPRECIATION (TO TRIBE MEMBERS):
+ "I liked it when..."
+ "I felt good when..."
+ "I was interested when..."

Options
Use to role play curriculum content. Invite students to create statements about their own learning, such as "I cherish my ability to read because..." Use as a pre-writing exercise.

Space Pioneers

Objectives

1. To give practice in assessing different qualities and opinions
2. To encourage sharing
3. To encourage understanding and acceptance of others' perspectives
4. To provide an opportunity to look at evolving styles of communication and leader-behavior within the group
5. To encourage influence

Instructions

1. Tell "Space Pioneers" story (on next page) while students are seated in tribes.
2. Write the list of "Advisors" (or a similar list of your own selection) on the blackboard for all to see.
3. Ask each participant to identify the five advisors they would want to help settle the newly discovered planet.
4. Discuss the difference of a group of people making a decision by consensus in contrast to voting.
5. Announce that the tribes have fifteen minutes to reach a consensus on which five advisors to take into space.
6. Ask the tribes to appoint a recorder to take notes.
7. After fifteen minutes have the recorders report the final consensus lists to the community.

   Note: Use the strategy "Consensus Building" prior to having the whole class community do this strategy.

Suggested Reflection Questions

CONTENT/THINKING

+ What do you see as the main purpose of Space Pioneers?
+ Why would you want to, not want to, go on this trip?

SOCIAL

+ What did you have to do to reach consensus on who you would take? Was it an effective way to come to an agreement?
+ How did different group members provide leadership for this activity?

PERSONAL

+ How did you feel about your tribes choice?
+ What did you contribute to help your group make the selection?

Appreciation

INVITE STATEMENTS OF APPRECIATION:

+ "I liked it when..."
+ "I admired you for saying..."
+ "I'm much like you when..."

GRADES
4–adult

TIME
35 minutes

GROUPING
tribes

MATERIALS
pencils, paper

Space Pioneers

Space Pioneers

A new planet has been discovered in our solar system. This planet resembles Earth in every way, except that there are no human beings living there. Our government wants the students of this class to be the first pioneers to settle on the newly discovered planet. They want you to select five adult advisors who you think would be valuable on the new planet. Select from the following list of ten space pioneer advisors:

1. Zelda Learner, age 45, elementary school teacher.
2. Oroville Oates, age 41, farmer.
3. Clara Kettle, age 34, cook.
4. Dr. Margarita Flowers, age 27, botanist.
5. Woodrow Hammer, age 56, carpenter.
6. Flo Nightingale, age 37, registered nurse.
7. Irma Intel, age 32, engineer.
8. Melvin Melody, age 24, musician.
9. Reverend Adam Goodfellow, age 51, minister.
10. Tiger Forest, age 24, golf pro.

Options

HAVE THE STUDENTS...

+ agree on a name for the new planet
+ share one personal possession each would take on the trip
+ brainstorm and agree on what supplies and equipment they would need

USE THE STRATEGY TO EXPLORE ACADEMIC TOPICS

+ advisors to design a model city
+ advisors to work on a national policy for children

Special Friend I Know

Objectives
1. To build community inclusion
2. To share feelings about an aspect of school
3. To experience the "Think-Pair-Share" structure*

Instructions
1. Have the community meet in tribes. Ask the students to think silently for a moment about the following questions:
   + When were you a special friend to someone?
   + What made you a special friend?
   + What did you do or say?
2. Invite each student to turn to a tribe and share his or her special qualities by speaking in the present tense.
   Example:
   "Margery, I would like you as my special friend because [*two or three of her special qualities*]."

Suggested Reflection Questions:
CONTENT/THINKING
   + What qualities did you share that were similar?
   + Why is friendship important?

SOCIAL
   + Why is being a good listener important in being a good friend?
   + How did this strategy help you as a tribe/community?

PERSONAL
   + What would you change about yourself if you wanted to be a better friend?

Appreciation
INVITE STATEMENTS OF APPRECIATION:
   + "I liked it when..."
   + "It helped me when..."
   + "I admired you when..."

Options
The "special friend" can be an object of study (such as "I appreciate the first amendment because…," "Adjectives are important because…"). Practice re-stating or elaborating on statements shared.

GRADES
3–adult
TIME
30 minutes
GROUPING
community, tribes
MATERIALS
none

*This is a structure from *Cooperative Learning: Resources for Teachers*, by Spencer Kagan

Spider Web

GRADES
K–adult

TIME
varies depending
on group size

GROUPING
community

MATERIALS
ball of
colored yarn

Objectives

1. To build inclusion and a sense of community
2. To practice attentive listening

Instructions

1. Ask the community to sit in one large circle.
2. Explain that during this activity each student will have an opportunity to share his or her name and something special about himself or herself. Give the students a minute to think of something special.
3. Have one student begin the activity by stating his or her name and something about himself or herself.

   Example: "My name is Sue, and I am wonderful at organizing things." Then, have the student hold onto the end of the yarn and roll the yarn ball to someone across from him or her in the circle. Have the students continue this process until everyone has either shared or passed and a "spider web" pattern has been created.
4. It is fun to "play" with the web before rolling it up. Have everyone pick up the web, stand, hold it up overhead. Have them hold it waist high and shake it.
5. If time permits, have the students re-roll the web one by one in reverse order. (Students below fifth grade have a hard time re-rolling a ball of yarn.)

Suggested Reflection Questions

CONTENT/THINKING

✦ How can you symbolically interpret this "spider web?" Note symbolism, design, community involvement, etc.

✦ Why is this a good community-building activity?

✦ What did you learn as a result of this activity?

SOCIAL

✦ How does "Spider Web" bring you closer together as a community?

PERSONAL

✦ How did you feel before it was your turn/right after your turn?

✦ How do you feel right now?

Appreciation

INVITE STATEMENTS OF APPRECIATION:

✦ "I liked it when you said..."

✦ "I'm a lot like you when..."

✦ "I admire you for..."

Options

Make a statement of appreciation to someone in the circle; continue until each student has received a statement. Toss the yarn up and into the center, see where it goes, and then give that person a statement of appreciation. Paraphrase what the previous person said before giving a statement of appreciation. Use "I learned..." statements.

Student-Developed Lesson Plans

Objectives

1. To promote tribal influence
2. To have students develop their own lesson plans

Instructions

1. Have tribes meet for two or three minutes and create their own inclusion.
2. Give each tribe a copy of the "A Tribes Learning Experience."
3. Discuss the elements that make up the plan:
   + an inclusion activity to awaken interest or connect to previous experiences
   + an academic learning goal
   + a social learning goal
   + a tribal strategy or cooperative learning structure (or a sequence of the same)
   + instructions
   + reflection questions
   + time for statements of appreciation
4. Have each tribe plan a twenty-minute lesson on a theme or academic topic for younger students or the community.
5. When finished, the lessons can be presented or taught to the class by the tribes.

Suggested Reflection Questions

CONTENT/THINKING
+ What was the most difficult thing about this strategy?
+ What did you learn by doing this strategy?

SOCIAL
+ How well did your tribe work together?
+ What can your tribe do to work together even better next time?

PERSONAL
+ How do you feel about developing lesson plans now?
+ What could you do to help your tribe be even more successful next time?

Appreciation

INVITE STATEMENTS OF APPRECIATION (TO TRIBE MEMBERS):
+ "I liked it when..."
+ "I appreciated..."

Options

Use this strategy as an alternative to homework assignments for various units of study. Students may choose to develop and teach a lesson.

GRADES
4–adult

TIME
90 minutes

GROUPING
tribes

MATERIALS
copies of "Tribes Lesson Plan"

Suggestion Circle

Objectives

1. To encourage attentive listening
2. To experience group support for a concern
3. To assist a peer, colleague, or friend to resolve a problem
4. To experience individual problem-solving in the influence stage

GRADES
2–adult

TIME
30 minutes

GROUPING
community

MATERIALS
none

Instructions

1. Have the community form a circle.
2. Review the agreements. Choose a recorder who will write down the suggestions made by the community.
3. Ask for a volunteer to share a concern or problem that he or she is experiencing and for which he or she would like some suggestions for resolving.
4. Tell the community that they are to listen without judgment or comment while the problem is being shared, but they may ask for additional information, if necessary, when the student has finished sharing.
5. Invite the students to make a suggestion, one at a time, to the person who shared. Encourage them not to repeat what someone else has already suggested.
6. Have the recorder give the list of possible solutions to the person who shared the problem.

Suggested Reflection Questions

CONTENT/THINKING

+ Why did we do this strategy?
+ What type of suggestions were offered?

SOCIAL

+ Why is it important to get ideas for solving problems from others?
+ Which social skills did you use during this strategy?

PERSONAL

+ How did you feel to give suggestions?
+ How could this type of a process help you?
+ Where else could this strategy be used?

Appreciation

INVITE STATEMENTS OF APPRECIATION:

+ "Thanks for..."
+ "What made a difference for me was..."

Options

An excellent strategy to use for classroom, social or school issues; this will ultimately save time as well as teach and model valuable life skills.

Taking a Closer Look

Objectives

1. To explore individual attitudes about the use of alcohol or other drugs
2. To practice attentive listening skills
3. To build peer support and influence

Instructions

1. Have the community divide up into pairs, and have each partner decide whether he or she will be an "A" or a "B." Pass out pre-prepared question slips (see following page), or generate your own questions appropriate for the culture and age level of your students.
2. Suggest that the partners move to a comfortable place where they can hear each other well. Explain that partner A will begin by answering the questions while B listens, and that at the end of five minutes, the partners will switch roles.
3. Review the agreements, particularly attentive listening.
4. Give the signal to switch after five minutes, and call the partners back to the community circle after the additional five minutes.
5. Have the community discuss and reflect on the experience.

Suggested Reflection Questions

CONTENT/THINKING
- ✦ What kind of messages did you get about using substances?
- ✦ How did this activity stretch your own thinking about drugs?

SOCIAL
- ✦ Why did we work in pairs rather than as a community?

PERSONAL
- ✦ Did you make any new decisions as a result of this experience? What were they?

Appreciation

INVITE STATEMENTS OF APPRECIATION
- ✦ "I really appreciated it when..."
- ✦ "[name], you are special because..."
- ✦ "Thank you, [name] for..."

Options

Modify the questions to role play a social dilemma, historical event, or even the writing process (for example, How will you begin your essay?).

GRADES
5–adult

TIME
30 minutes

GROUPING
tribes, pairs

MATERIALS
question slips

Taking a Closer Look Question Slips

1. What kind of messages did you get about cigarettes, alcohol, or drugs when you were younger (right or wrong to use/OK for men, but not for women/beer and wine don't hurt you)?

2. Where did these messages come from (school/family/media/church/friends)?

3. What was the first decision you ever made about choosing to use or not use cigarettes, alcohol or drugs? How old were you? What happened? What process did you use to make a decision?

4. Describe what your life would be like if you did not use any of these substances. **Option:** What might it be like if you did use? Ask people to think about over-the-counter or prescription drugs they may use. Coffee?

5. What have you learned about chemical substances that you would want your brother, sister or child to know?

6. Would you feel comfortable with your child using cigarettes, drugs, or alcohol as much as you do?

Teaching Agreements

Objectives

1. To have each tribe create a lesson to help teach an agreement to the community
2. To transfer responsibility to tribes for lesson development
3. To experience influence

Instructions

1. Review the agreements of attentive listening, right to pass, no put-downs, and mutual respect (and any others you've created for your class).
2. Explain to the students that you are looking for new and creative ways to teach these agreements and would like their help.
3. Have each tribe choose (or assign) one of the agreements. Explain that each tribe will create a lesson to teach that agreement to the community. Explain that they can use butcher paper, felt pens, and paint (or other art media you have available) to make any posters or signs needed to teach the lesson. Emphasize that you want them to be creative. Let them know they will have the rest of the period and one other period to create their lessons and share them with the community.
4. When the tribes are finished, have them present their lessons to the community.

GRADES
2–adult

TIME
two class periods

GROUPING
tribes

MATERIALS
large paper, felt pens, poster paint

Suggested Reflection Questions

CONTENT/THINKING
+ What did you learn about creating a lesson?
+ Which agreement do you think is the most important? Why?

SOCIAL
+ What social skills did your tribe need to be successful at this strategy?

PERSONAL
+ What did you contribute to your tribe to help it be successful?
+ How did you feel when your tribe presented its lesson?
+ What would you have done differently?

Appreciation

INVITE STATEMENTS OF APPRECIATION:
+ "You helped a lot when…"
+ "I liked…"

Options

Use the strategy with any content topic. For example, have tribes choose math concepts to teach to the class while applying the concepts to real-life problems. Assign chapters in a textbook and have tribes develop a creative lesson to teach to others.

Teaching I-Messages

Objectives
1. To give tribes practice in brainstorming and to introduce words to express feelings
2. To show the link between "feeling words" and "I-Messages"
3. To practice giving "I-Messages"

Instructions

Note: Teach this strategy before using "Snowball I-Messages."

1. Have the community sit in tribes and explain that they will be brainstorming (see "Brainstorming" strategy).
2. Have each tribe select a recorder.
3. Discuss various "feeling words" (happiness, anger, upset, love). Ask the tribes to brainstorm as many "feeling words" as they can in five minutes. Have the recorder write them down.
4. After five minutes, ask the tribes to take turns calling out the "feeling words" they wrote down. As teacher, record the words on the blackboard. Discuss how sharing feelings is important for clear communication.
5. Then ask, "Why is it also important to have a way to let people know how their behavior affects us?" Explain that "I-Messages" are a way to share feelings but not blame.
6. Use the formats in chapter five to write three to four examples of "I-Messages" and "YOU-Messages" on the board. Explain the difference between an "I-Message" and a "YOU-Message." Ask the class to contrast the impact the two different types of messages have.
7. Have each tribe member write four "I-Messages" using the feeling words they listed earlier. Each person should write to a friend, a relative, a classmate and a teacher. Allow ten minutes work time.
8. Then have the tribes review the "I-Messages" written by their tribe members. Have them help each other change any statements that are "YOU-Messages" to "I-Messages."
9. Ask the students to practice using "I-Messages" during the next few days, and to report back to their tribe on what happened.

GRADES
3–adult

TIME
20 minutes

GROUPING
tribes

MATERIALS
large paper and felt pens

Suggested Reflection Questions

CONTENT/THINKING
+ Why is it important to use "I-Messages?"

SOCIAL
+ How can "I-Messages" help you to lessen conflict with friends?

PERSONAL
+ How does it feel to receive a "YOU-Message?"/"I-Message?"

Appreciation
SUGGEST PEOPLE MAKE STATEMENTS OF APPRECIATION
+ "It helped me when..."
+ "It felt good when..."

Options
Use current events or characters from literature as the "recipients" of the "I-messages."

Teaching Listening

Objectives

1. To practice components of attentive listening:
   - ✦ Attending
   - ✦ Paraphrasing
   - ✦ Reflecting feelings
2. To share ideas and feelings about any given topic
3. To build inclusion

Instructions

1. Discuss and demonstrate attentive listening skills. Write components on chalkboard.
2. Ask the students to form triads, and designate each triad member as an A, B, or C. Ask for a show of hands of all A's, all B's and all C's to avoid confusion.
3. Explain that each triad member will have an opportunity to play each role; in round 1, A will observe, B will be the speaker, and C will be the listener. Post this chart:

	A	B	C
ROUND 1	Observer	Speaker	Listener
ROUND 2	Speaker	Listener	Observer
ROUND 3	Listener	Observer	Speaker

4. Give the speakers a topic of your choice (depending on age) to speak on for two to five minutes. Example: "Should students be allowed to vote?"
5. Ask the listeners to practice one or two components of attentive listening.
6. Ask the observers to pay attention to the interaction and after two to five minutes give feedback to the listeners. Ask them to include what they saw the listener doing both verbally and nonverbally, and their observations of how the speakers responded.
7. Have the triads repeat the process until all three members have had an opportunity to be observers, speakers, and listeners.

Suggested Reflection Questions

CONTENT/THINKING
- ✦ Why was it important to have an observer?
- ✦ How can you be a good listener, speaker, or observer?

SOCIAL
- ✦ How can you tell if someone is being a good listener?
- ✦ Why is listening such an important social skill?

PERSONAL
- ✦ How did it feel to be listened to in that way?
- ✦ How well did you attend, paraphrase, and reflect feelings?

Appreciation

INVITE STATEMENTS OF APPRECIATION
- ✦ "I liked it when..."

Options

This strategy can be used to review, discuss or assess any academic topic. It may also be extended into a written reflective practice exercise.

GRADES
2–adult

TIME
30 minutes

GROUPING
tribe

MATERIALS
none

Teaching Paraphrasing/Reflecting Feelings

Objectives

1. To build community inclusion
2. To teach and practice the listening skills paraphrasing and reflecting feelings
3. To share ideas and feelings about a given topic

Instructions

1. Have the students form pairs and have the partners decide who is #1 and who is #2.
2. Have the partners sit "knees to knees" and "eyes to eyes."
3. Demonstrate how to paraphrase a statement.
   Example: Heidi says, "Sometimes I think I'd like to be an airline pilot."
   Paraphrase response: "Now and then you wonder about becoming a pilot."
4. Ask the #1 partners to speak briefly on the topic: "A time when I listened carefully." Partners #2 are to listen and then paraphrase the statement they heard. After three minutes have the partners switch roles.
5. Ask the community, "What is the importance of paraphrasing?"
6. Demonstrate how to reflect feelings along with paraphrasing.
   Example: Heidi says, "Becoming a airline pilot would be exciting because there still are not many women pilots."
   Paraphrase: "You feel excited whenever you imagine being one of the few women pilots."
7. Ask the #2 partners to speak briefly on the topic: "A time that I found my work a challenge." Partners #1 are to listen and then paraphrase the key statement and feelings. After three minutes have the partners switch roles.
8. Have the partners share what each felt during the activity.

GRADES
4–adult

TIME
30 minutes

GROUPING
pairs

MATERIALS
none

Suggested Reflection Questions

CONTENT/THINKING
  ✦ What listening skills did you use during this strategy?
  ✦ How does good listening help to build community?

SOCIAL
  ✦ How does reflecting feelings help you communicate better?

PERSONAL
  ✦ How would you feel if someone listened to you like this?
  ✦ How can you use these skills?

Appreciation

SUGGEST PEOPLE MAKE STATEMENTS OF APPRECIATION
  ✦ "I could tell you were listening when..."
  ✦ "I appreciated your..."

Options

Using any academic topic, develop (or have students develop) discussion questions designed for application, synthesis, and evaluation. For example, discuss the long-term implications of a national event.

That's Me—That's Us

Objectives
1. To build community inclusion
2. To help the students identify personal or community skills, interests, or achievements

Instructions
1. Tell the students that you will call out a series of questions, and those who identify or agree are to jump up and say, "That's me!"
2. Start with a few simple topics that are appropriate to the students' age level and interest.

   Examples:
   + How many people have moved in the last two years?
   + How many people have green eyes?
   + How many people like broccoli?
3. Use this strategy to learn how the tribes are working together. Ask the tribes to stand and say, "That's us!"

   Examples:
   + Which tribes had no put-downs today?
   + In which tribe did everyone participate on the task?
   + Which tribe figured out why the rain forest in the Amazon is threatened?

GRADES
2–adult

TIME
40 minutes

GROUPING
community, tribes

MATERIALS
none

Suggested Reflection Questions

CONTENT/THINKING
+ What did you find out about your tribe members/community members?
+ What's one more question you might add?

SOCIAL
+ Why was listening important?

PERSONAL
+ How did you feel about jumping up?
+ How could you tell that your entire tribe would stand up?

Appreciation

INVITE STATEMENTS OF APPRECIATION
+ "It helped me when..."
+ "Thanks for..."

Options
Use teacher or student designed questions for review or assessment. Ask one of the students who responded "That's me!" to answer or explain. Invite students to ask for help from another person standing.

Third-Party Mediation

GRADES
K–adult

TIME
varies

GROUPING
community, tribes

MATERIALS
none

Objectives

1. To provide a process for conflict resolution that helps both parties arrive at a mutually agreeable solution
2. To model a third-party-mediator role as one who does not make judgments or take sides
3. To develop trust and acceptance of individual differences
4. To build inclusion yet allow influence (a sense of value)

Instructions

1. Call together two students who are in conflict and tell them that it is likely a mutually agreeable solution can be worked out. Ask if they would like that to happen. Make it clear that you will not take sides or set yourself up as a judge.
2. Ask each student, one at a time, to describe the conflict; say the other is not to interrupt. Encourage each student to focus on what is going on now rather than list past grievances. If they try to interrupt each other or are not listening, ask each to summarize the other's position.
3. Ask each student in turn to state how the situation makes him or her feel. Encourage use of "I-Messages." Reflect back their feelings. Have each person rephrase the other's feelings.
4. Have both students in turn state what they would like as an outcome to the conflict. As mediator, encourage both to modify their "ideal states" and decide what they would be willing to give up and work toward. Help them look at alternatives.
5. Have both students acknowledge what changes they each are willing to make in a specific period of time.
6. Have the students draw up a list of the steps each agrees to take and have them make an appointment to check back with the mediator.

Note: This method can be used with groups as well as individuals.

Suggested Reflection Questions

CONTENT/THINKING
+ What specific steps did the mediator use to help the two students resolve their conflict?
+ Why is having a third-party mediator helpful in some conflicts?

SOCIAL
+ What social skills did you use as you observed the conflict?

PERSONAL
+ What did you feel as we worked through your conflict?
+ Observers: What were you feeling for the students in conflict?
+ How can this help you in the future? At home?

Appreciation

INVITE STATEMENTS OF APPRECIATION
+ "It was helpful when you..."
+ "I appreciated..."

Options

Use this strategy to role play social or historical situations.

This Is Me

Objectives
1. To build self-esteem
2. To build inclusion

Instructions
1. Explain to the community that they will be introducing themselves positively to each other by using "This Is Me" posters which they will create themselves.
2. Give each student a copy of the "This Is Me" poster worksheet (see following page), a straight pin, and pencil.
3. Allow five to ten minutes for everyone to complete their posters. Remind them to write positive things. Tell them that no self-put-downs are allowed.
4. Have the students help each other pin the posters to their own backs; then tell everyone to circulate and read each other's posters and share their own.
5. Have the community sit in a circle.
6. Discuss and reflect upon the activity.

Suggested Reflection Questions
CONTENT/THINKING
+ What did you learn about your tribe members?
+ Why is sharing personal information sometimes important?

SOCIAL
+ How did the poster theme of the activity help you to participate?
+ How did you help others to feel OK about their posters?

PERSONAL
+ What section of the poster was the most difficult for you to complete? Why?
+ How did you feel milling around the room?
+ How do you feel about yourself now?

Appreciation
INVITE STATEMENTS OF APPRECIATION:
+ "I liked it when..."
+ "I appreciated that..."

Options
Use this strategy with curriculum content by having students create posters. Change the qualifiers to fit the topic or person.

GRADES
4–adult

TIME
30 minutes

GROUPING
community

MATERIALS
"This Is Me" poster worksheet, pins, pencils

"This Is Me" Poster

NAME

I AM ALWAYS

I NEED

I VALUE

A SLOGAN I LIVE BY

Thumbs Down

Objectives
1. To encourage active decision-making
2. To encourage the expression of opinions
3. To accept individual differences
4. To encourage influence

Instructions
1. Have the community sit in a circle.
2. Demonstrate three different ways the students can vote or express their opinions on an issue:
   - thumbs up—agree
   - thumbs down—disagree
   - thumbs sideways—no opinion or pass
3. Then, in rapid-fire sequence, ask controversial questions appropriate to the age level and interests of the community and have students vote.

   Examples:

   "How do you feel about eating at McDonalds?"

   "Playing soccer? Skateboards? Jumping rope?"

   "People helping each other in tribe learning groups?"

Suggested Reflection Questions
CONTENT/THINKING
- What other issues could you vote on?
- How did this type of voting differ from other voting you've done?
- Why is discovering different ways to vote important?

SOCIAL
- How is this type of voting helpful to our community?

PERSONAL
- How did you feel about making your opinions known in public like this?
- Why might you have been tempted to change your vote as you looked around?

Appreciation
INVITE STATEMENTS OF APPRECIATION
- "I felt good when..."
- "One thing I like about this group is..."

Options
This strategy can be related to lesson topics by having the students vote on decisions made by characters in books or history, or by having the students express their opinions on lessons or activities.

This strategy is easily used as a quick check for understanding before, during, or after a learning event. Add a challenge by inviting students to volunteer questions.

GRADES
K–adult

TIME
5–10 minutes

GROUPING
community

MATERIALS
none

Tower-Building

GRADES
K–adult

TIME
20–30 minutes

GROUPING
tribes, subgroups

MATERIALS
8½ x 11-inch
paper,
masking tape

Objectives

1. To promote an awareness of influence issues
2. To explore nonverbal communication
3. To build tribe cohesiveness

Instructions

1. Have the community meet in tribes. Pass out fifteen to twenty pieces of paper and one roll of masking tape to each tribe.
2. Tell the tribes that they are to nonverbally construct a tower or castle using only the given supplies, and that they will have ten minutes to complete the task.
3. At the end of the ten minutes, stop the action.
4. Have all the tribes view each others' buildings.
5. Ask tribe members to return to their tribes for discussion and reflection.

Suggested Reflection Questions

CONTENT/THINKING

✦ What was the purpose of this activity beyond building a tower?

✦ Why might nonverbal communication be as important as verbal communication?

SOCIAL

✦ What social skills did you need to successfully build your tower?

✦ How did leadership in your group develop while you were building your castle? Did all your tribe members participate?

✦ What were the feelings among tribe members?

PERSONAL

✦ What did you learn about yourself?

✦ Is this your usual style of working with others?

✦ How would you change the way you work in a group?

Appreciation

INVITE STATEMENTS OF APPRECIATION

✦ "I appreciated it when..."

✦ "I thought that [*name*] was very..."

✦ "Our tribe is..."

Options

Use index cards, folded either lengthwise or in half.

Give the tribes five minutes to plan their towers before they start building. Then stop the action and let the tribes talk for thirty seconds. Have them continue nonverbally for the last five minutes.

"Handicap" the students: someone cannot see, someone is only one handed, only one person can speak, one person must sit in one place and not move, etc.

Require the towers to be connected by roads, bridges, or some other fashion.

Tribal Peer Coaching

Objectives

1. To help slower learners understand or learn subject matter
2. To provide peer support for learning
3. To structure a cooperative learning experience
4. To build inclusion and encourage kindness
5. To experience influence

Instructions

1. Have the community meet in Tribes. Ask tribe members to share which of them are very sure that they understand the concept or material from a lesson topic or unit.
2. Ask if those tribe members would be willing to be "coaches" for a short time to the other tribe members who are not quite as sure.
3. Have tribe members form pairs or triads, with one coach in each subgroup.
4. Tell the coaches that their goal is to have their students be able to repeat back or explain to them the information or concept being learned. Suggest some ways that the coaches can be helpful.
5. Tell the students how much time will be allowed, and remind them of their attentive listening skills.
6. When time is up, ask those who were "students" to explain to their whole tribes what they learned from their coaches.

Suggested Reflection Questions

CONTENT/THINKING
- ◆ What did you learn about coaching/being coached?
- ◆ Why is peer coaching a powerful way to help you learn?

SOCIAL
- ◆ What social skills does a peer coach need?
- ◆ What recommendations do you have for a peer coach?

PERSONAL
- ◆ How did you feel as a coach/being coached?
- ◆ How did you help others during this activity?

Appreciation

INVITE STATEMENTS OF APPRECIATION
- ◆ "I appreciated it when..."
- ◆ "[name], you really helped me when..."
- ◆ "Thank you, [name], I think you are..."

Options

Use this strategy for the development of student projects. Use to help students edit their writing, review for assessment, or create portfolios.

GRADES
K–adult

TIME
varies

GROUPING
tribes, triads, pairs

MATERIALS
vary

Tribe Graffiti

Objectives

1. To encourage the sharing of feelings and beliefs
2. To gather and appreciate many points of view
3. To review subject matter in cooperative learning groups
4. To build inclusion and promote influence

GRADES
2–adult

TIME
60 minutes

GROUPING
tribes

MATERIALS
large paper,
crayons or
felt pens

Instructions

1. Ask the community to meet in tribes.
2. To each tribe, distribute pens and a large piece of paper (at least 2 x 6-feet long) labeled with one of the following subjects (or an academic topic) on each:

   ◆ pet peeves   ◆ favorite moments
   ◆ what I wonder about   ◆ things that scare me a lot
   ◆ ambitions   ◆ things that excite me

3. Invite the tribes to write "graffiti" on their paper for three to five minutes, all tribe members writing at once.
4. At the end of three to five minutes, ask the tribes to stop writing and exchange papers. Have the tribes now write on their new graffiti papers for the next three to five minutes. Repeat this procedure until all the tribes have had a chance to write graffiti on all the papers.
5. Return original papers to tribes and allow the members time to read the graffiti and discuss similarities in what people wrote.
6. Have each tribe report its findings back to the community.

Suggested Reflection Questions

CONTENT/THINKING
   ◆ What general things did the community write?
   ◆ Why did you exchange papers?

SOCIAL
   ◆ How did your tribe members cooperate?

PERSONAL
   ◆ What did you write that told something about yourself?
   ◆ How did you feel during this activity?
   ◆ Which graffiti topic meant the most to you?

Appreciation

INVITE STATEMENTS OF APPRECIATION
   ◆ "It was helpful when you..."
   ◆ "I liked it when you wrote..."

Options

Use prompts about content topics such as: What I know…, What I would like to know…, I wonder…. Be sure that students understand the agreements so that the "graffiti" is productive, appropriate, and content-rich.

Tribe Mimes/Role Play

Objectives
1. To build self-esteem
2. To promote inclusion and influence
3. To act out or role-play dilemmas or problem situations

Instructions
1. Have the students meet in their tribes.
2. Ask if anyone knows what a "mime" is or how circus clowns communicate with an audience. Explain that "mime" means acting out a message or image without speaking any words.
3. Give each tribe a written message or image to act out. Examples:
   + harnessing a horse
   + baking a cake
   + fixing a bicycle tire
4. Have each tribe decide how they will portray the message or image without speaking.
5. Have each tribe present its mime. Have other students guess what is being portrayed.
6. Then explain "role play" which means adding speech to what is being acted out. Give the tribes prepared cards that contain problem situations that may be confronting students. Example: Terry and Aaron are approached by two friends who ask them to go with them after school to smoke cigarettes they just found. Act out how Terry and Aaron could handle the situation so that they feel proud of themselves.
7. Give the tribes time to plan and then present their role plays of the problem cards.
8. Be sure to follow all presentations with reflection questions.

GRADES
2–adult

TIME
45 minutes

GROUPING
tribes

MATERIALS
none

Suggested Reflection Questions
CONTENT/THINKING
+ What did you learn from the mime presentations?
+ Why is acting out a situation using mime a good way to learn?

SOCIAL
+ What social skills did you need to do mime?
+ How did leadership in your tribe develop during this activity?

PERSONAL
+ How did you feel while you were acting your part?
+ How did you feel as you watched others acting their parts?

Appreciation
INVITE STATEMENTS OF APPRECIATION
+ "I really liked it when..."
+ "I enjoyed most seeing..."

Options
Have the tribes define problem situations, write them on cards, and exchange them with other tribes to act out.

Tribe Portrait

GRADES
K–adult

TIME
varies

GROUPING
tribes

MATERIALS
paper, felt pens,
pencils, erasers

Objectives

1. To develop self-awareness
2. To develop awareness of spatial relationships
3. To develop cooperative skills
4. To practice observation skills
5. To build inclusion and influence

Instructions

1. Explain to the community that each tribe will draw a self-portrait and that the portrait will include individual drawings of each tribe member.
2. Ask the community to meet in tribes, get their materials, and find a space to work.
3. Discuss possible put-downs that could occur and how to avoid them.
4. Each tribe member asks one other member to do a sketch of him or her.
5. "Artists" draw their subjects using pencils.
6. After completing portraits, artists check with subjects for additions or corrections.
7. After corrections and additions have been made, the artists use marking pens on portrait.
8. When the portraits of all the tribe members are finished, the tribe decides how to present their portraits to the rest of the class.

Suggested Reflection Questions

CONTENT/THINKING

+ Why did you draw a tribal portrait?
+ Why was it easy/difficult to draw a tribal portrait?

SOCIAL

+ How did this task require you to work together?
+ How well did you work together?
+ Did every member of your tribe participate in this activity?

PERSONAL

+ How did you feel when your portrait was being done?
+ How did you feel when you saw your portrait?

Appreciation

INVITE STATEMENTS OF APPRECIATION (TO "ARTISTS" AND TRIBE MEMBERS)

+ "I like what you drew because..."
+ "When I look at our tribal portrait I feel..."

Note: This project can best be done over a period of two to five days. Also, the teacher may move from tribe to tribe giving some instruction.

Options

Excellent opportunity to bring in an outside art resource person to work with small groups.
Have tribes create portraits illustrating what they learned about a topic.

Two On a Crayon

Objectives
1. To demonstrate the power of nonverbal communication
2. To promote cooperation and fun
3. To build inclusion and influence

Instructions
1. Have the community form pairs.
2. Give each pair one crayon and one piece of construction paper.
3. Explain that both partners will hold the crayon simultaneously and draw a picture together while a three- or four-minute song is played in the background. Tell the students that partners may not decide before the activity what kind of picture they will draw together, and that they may not talk to each other while they are drawing.

Suggested Reflection Questions
CONTENT/THINKING
+ What did you draw?
+ What does it represent?

SOCIAL
+ Was it difficult to not talk to your partner?
+ How did this activity help you get to know your partner?
+ How did you decide who would lead and who would follow?

PERSONAL
+ Did you discover anything new about yourself?

Appreciation
INVITE STATEMENTS OF APPRECIATION TO PARTNERS
+ "I liked it when..."
+ "I felt good when..."
+ "I like your picture because..."

Options
Use topics to illustrate scenes from a story or novel.

GRADES
K–6

TIME
20 minutes

GROUPING
pairs

MATERIALS
paper, crayons, music

Unfinished Fantasies

Objectives

1. To promote inclusion
2. To develop greater self-awareness
3. To encourage the development of imagination

Instructions

1. Have the community meet in tribes or triads.
2. Present an unfinished fantasy.

   Examples (or create one of your own):

   + You are eating lunch in a school cafeteria. You get your lunch and walk into the lunchroom. The lunchroom is crowded and noisy with lots of students laughing and shouting and having a good time. Off in a corner is a boy sitting all alone at a table. What do you do? What happens?

   + You are sitting in a class. Several students in the class are making belittling comments to another student. That student is obviously having her feelings hurt. She catches your eye and looks at you. What do you do? What happens?

   + You are sitting in a classroom. A student whom you don't know has constantly bugged the teacher and caused trouble ever since the class began several months ago. Although he is often funny, everyone is fed up with his behavior. He comes into the room and takes a seat next to you. What do you do? What happens?

3. Have each tribe member think about her or his ending to the fantasy situation and then share it.
4. Have the tribe decide which endings would be the kindest, most helpful, or most positive.

GRADES
2–adult

TIME
30 minutes

GROUPING
tribes, triads

MATERIALS
none

Suggested Reflection Questions

CONTENT/THINKING

+ What choices do you have when your feelings are hurt by others?
+ Which endings were the kindest, most helpful, or most positive?
+ Why is finishing a fantasy a powerful tool for learning?

SOCIAL

+ How well did group members participate in this activity? How could you tell?

PERSONAL

+ How do you feel about the way you ended your fantasy?
+ How do you feel about the others in your tribe or triad?

Appreciation

INVITE STATEMENTS OF APPRECIATION

+ "I liked it when..."
+ "I'm like you when..."

Options

Use in writing assignments to practice dialogue, use of adjectives, narrative or expository genres.

Urgent!

Objectives
1. To build inclusion and influence
2. To provide students an opportunity to think of significant other persons in their lives
3. To encourage communicating with a special person
4. To promote caring and acceptance for the concerns of others

Instructions
1. Have the community sit in a circle. Review the agreements.
2. Invite each student who cares to participate to send a verbal message to a person in his or her life with whom he or she feels an urgent need to communicate. Messages can involve suggestions for change in a person's life, a reaffirmation of caring and friendship, and so on.
3. Explain that the format for a message is: "Dear [*name*], I urge you to..." Have each student end his or her message by saying: "Your [*adjective*] friend, [*name*]." Model a message yourself.
4. There is no follow-up discussion after this activity. All messages are sent in an atmosphere of total acceptance.

Appreciation
INVITE STATEMENTS OF APPRECIATION
+ "I liked it when..."
+ "I felt good when..."
+ "I appreciated it when..."

Options
Students can write statements addressed to characters in literature. Use as a prewriting exercise for persuasive writing; follow the "I urge..." statements with opinions and facts.

GRADES
4–adult

TIME
varies

GROUPING
community, tribes

MATERIALS
none

Warm Fuzzies

Objectives
1. To build inclusion
2. To express positive feelings towards others

Instructions
1. Ask the community to meet in tribes.
2. Demonstrate how to create a warm fuzzy. (Instructions are on the next page.)

Suggested Reflection Questions

CONTENT/THINKING
- ✦ What is a warm fuzzy?
- ✦ What did you learn in the story about warm fuzzies?
- ✦ What can you do with the warm fuzzies you made?

SOCIAL
- ✦ How did you help each other make your warm fuzzies?
- ✦ How can your tribe work together better?

PERSONAL
- ✦ How did you feel while making your warm fuzzy?

Appreciation

INVITE STATEMENTS OF APPRECIATION
- ✦ "I like the warm fuzzy you made because..."
- ✦ "I feel good when..."

Options
Students can create other forms of appreciation statements, such as "thumbs up" cut-outs.
Statements can be written to parents and/or former teachers as well as classmates.
Designate an "appreciation" spot or receptacle and have a specific time to review and share.

GRADES
K–3

TIME
30 minutes

GROUPING
tribes

MATERIALS
leftover yardage of yarn, felt, pipe cleaners, glue, scissors, pencils, cardboard

INSTRUCTIONS FOR MAKING A WARM FUZZY

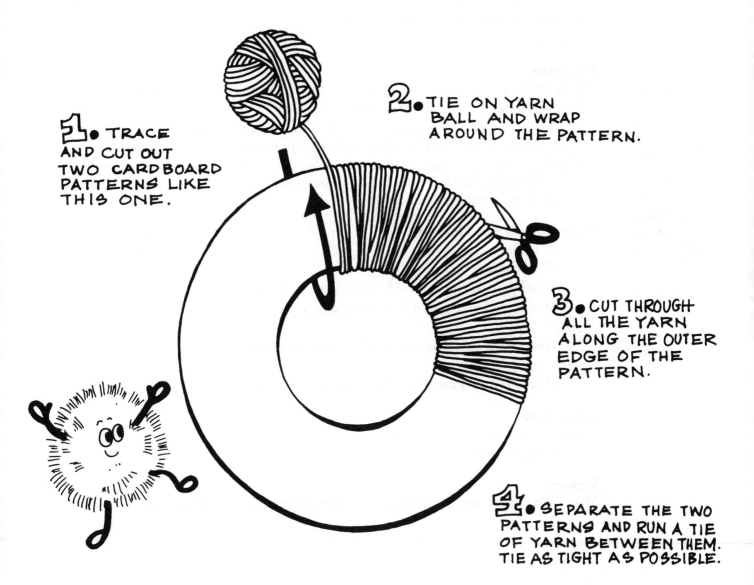

1. TRACE AND CUT OUT TWO CARDBOARD PATTERNS LIKE THIS ONE.

2. TIE ON YARN BALL AND WRAP AROUND THE PATTERN.

3. CUT THROUGH ALL THE YARN ALONG THE OUTER EDGE OF THE PATTERN.

4. SEPARATE THE TWO PATTERNS AND RUN A TIE OF YARN BETWEEN THEM. TIE AS TIGHT AS POSSIBLE.

5. PULL OUT PATTERNS, AND GIVE YOUR WARM FUZZY A "HAIRCUT" TO EVEN THE FUZZ.

6. DECORATE WITH FELT EYES, MOUTH AND PIPE CLEANER ARMS AND LEGS.

Warm Fuzzy Bag

Objectives

1. To build group inclusion
2. To reinforce the concept of appreciation
3. To build self-esteem

Instructions

1. Have each person make a small bag out of poster paper, and print his or her name on it.
2. Have the students hang their bags around the room.
3. Ask each student to write a warm fuzzy statement for each member of his or her tribe or one for each member of the class, and place them in the warm fuzzy bags.
4. Tell the students that they can place additional warm fuzzies in the bags anytime throughout the month (or school year). Set aside time once a week for students to open their bags and read the messages they have received.

Suggested Reflection Questions

CONTENT/THINKING

 + What did we learn during this activity?
 + Why is it important to know how to give warm fuzzies?
 + How might your our world be a better place if people gave away more warm fuzzies?

SOCIAL

 + How has the class climate changed as a result of this activity?

PERSONAL

 + How did you feel about receiving such nice messages?

Appreciation

INVITE STATEMENTS OF APPRECIATION

 + "I liked it when..."

Options

Make collections of appreciation statements after guest speakers, field trips or presentations.

GRADES
2–4

TIME
two 20-minute periods

GROUPING
tribes

MATERIALS
felt bags or envelopes, pencils, pens, paper

Week In Perspective

Objectives

1. To give each student an opportunity to reflect on recent experiences
2. To increase communication skills and sharing
3. To build inclusion and influence

Instructions

1. Ask the community to form triads or pairs.
2. Tell the students that they will take turns interviewing each other. Ask them to decide who will be the first person to be interviewed, the second, and the third (if using triads).
3. Urge the students to listen attentively to the person being inter-viewed and not discuss anything he or she is saying.
4. Provide the students with questions to ask.
   Examples:
   ✦ "What new and good thing happened to you this past week?"
   ✦ "What was hard about your week?"
   ✦ "Is there something you meant to do this week but put off?"
   ✦ "What one thing did you do that you enjoyed?"

GRADES
4–adult

TIME
10–15 minutes

GROUPING
triads, pairs

MATERIALS
none

Suggested Reflection Questions

CONTENT/THINKING
   ✦ What did you learn by doing this activity?
   ✦ Why is answering questions about your week easy/difficult?

SOCIAL
   ✦ Why is interviewing a difficult skill to master?
   ✦ Why are being the interviewer and the interviewee both important skills?

PERSONAL
   ✦ How did you feel while you were being interviewed?
   ✦ How do you feel as a community now?
   ✦ What did you learn about yourself in this activity?

Appreciation

INVITE STATEMENTS OF APPRECIATION (TO PARTNERS)
   ✦ "I liked it when you said..."
   ✦ "I felt good when..."

Options

Use this strategy for current events, to review content, or to define learning goals. Invite students to reflect on their goals by writing in their journals.

What Feelings Do You Have?

Objectives
1. To build inclusion
2. To encourage the expression of feelings

Instructions
1. Begin by discussing the importance of being aware of our feelings.
2. List some feelings and expressive colors.
   Examples:

FEELING	THREE COLORS THAT SEEM TO FIT THE FEELING
Happy	Yellow, Pink, Orange
Angry	Black, Red, Brown
Sad	Blue, White, Black

3. Ask reflection questions (use think/pair/share structure with grades 2 and 3).

Suggested Reflection Questions
CONTENT/THINKING
   ✦ Which colors represent happy/angry/sad?
   ✦ Why do colors seem like feelings?

SOCIAL
   ✦ How can a friend's choice of colors tell you how he or she feels?
   ✦ How well did we listen to each other?

PERSONAL
   ✦ How did you feel when you chose your colors?

Appreciation
INVITE STATEMENTS OF APPRECIATION
   ✦ "I liked it when you..."
   ✦ "I appreciated..."

Options
Have students discuss or write about feelings related to study topics (for example, their own feelings or feelings of persons portrayed historically or literarily). A nice follow-up strategy is "Abstract Painting of Feelings."

GRADES
K–3

TIME
30 minutes

GROUPING
community

MATERIALS
chalkboard, chalk,
chart, paper, pens

What Will Happen Next?

Objectives
1. To encourage critical thinking skills
2. To build inclusion and influence

Instructions
1. Have the students meet in their tribes.
2. Begin to read, or have students read, a story stopping at an interesting or suspenseful point.
3. Have each tribe discuss what they think will happen next. Each tribe can share their version by illustrating it on one large piece of paper, or they can role play it.
4. Ask the tribes to present their versions to the class.
5. Lead much applause after each tribe's presentation.

Suggested Reflection Questions
CONTENT/THINKING
+ How did your tribe go about writing your version together?
+ How did your tribes' stories differ from one another?

SOCIAL
+ How did you decide which ending to use?
+ How could your tribe have improved getting everybody involved in deciding about the story ending?
+ What's happening in your tribe now?

PERSONAL
+ How did you feel about your tribe's story?

Appreciation
INVITE STATEMENTS OF APPRECIATION
+ "I'd like to thank [*name*] for listening to me."
+ "I felt good when..."
+ "I was excited when..."

Options
Invite students to write their own stories or episodes to be finished by a writing partner or their tribe.

GRADES
K–adult

TIME
20–30 minutes

GROUPING
tribes

MATERIALS
paper, pencils, crayons

What's In a Name?

GRADES
4–adult

TIME
45–60 minutes

GROUPING
tribes

MATERIALS
large paper,
colored pens

Objectives
1. To build inclusion and influence
2. To learn information

Instructions
1. Have the community meet in tribes.
2. Have each tribe choose the name of a well-known character who may be the subject of a history, social studies, or science lesson.
3. Have each tribe write the name vertically with colored pens on the left side of a large piece of paper.
4. Challenge each tribe to research and write a phrase or fact about the character's life after each letter of the name.

    Example:

    W as president from 1789 to 1797

    A lways told the truth, it is said

    S uffered at Valley Forge in 1778

    H ad 3,000 of his men die at Valley Forge

    I n no political party as the president

    N ever stopped drilling his soldiers in the winter

    G oing on for six years of war, the British were tired of it

    T wo years after Yorktown, British and Americans signed a treaty

    O n October 19, 1781, was surrendered to by Cornwallis

    N ever gave up in the Revolutionary War

Suggested Reflection Questions
CONTENT/THINKING
- What did you learn about your character?

SOCIAL
- How did your tribe organize itself for the activity?
- How well did all your tribe members help in the research?
- How did you encourage all your tribe members to participate?

PERSONAL
- How do you feel about your tribe now?

Appreciation
INVITE STATEMENTS OF APPRECIATION
- "I appreciated [*name*]'s help and cooperation."
- "I liked it when..."

Options
This strategy can be used to learn academic content material from most subject areas, for example, "What are the characteristics of Mammals?"

What's In My Name?

Objectives
1. To initiate tribe inclusion
2. To encourage tribe members to share feelings
3. To practice attentive listening

Instructions
1. Ask each student to complete the following "homework" assignment: Find out from your parents how you were named. Were you named after someone? How was your name picked? You may want to send home the instruction sheet for younger students (see next page). Allow a few days for the students to complete the assignment.
2. Have the students meet in tribes or the community circle.
3. Ask the students to take turns sharing how their names were selected, what nicknames may have happened, and how they feel about their names or nicknames.

Suggested Reflection Questions

CONTENT/THINKING
+ What similarities did you notice about how people's names were selected?
+ Why is it important to know how you got your name?

SOCIAL
+ How well did your tribe members participate in this activity?
+ Why can this type of activity help tribe members feel better about each other?

PERSONAL
+ How did you feel when you learned how your name was selected for you?
+ Would you consider changing your name? Why?

Appreciation

INVITE STATEMENTS OF APPRECIATION
+ "[name], I liked what you said about your name because…"
+ "[name], I like your name because…"
+ "[name], I felt that you understood when I said…"

Options
Use as a pre-writing assignment to organize thoughts. Use in a study of heritage or ethnicity.

GRADES
3–adult

TIME
20 minutes

GROUPING
tribes

MATERIALS
"What's In My Name?" worksheets

What's In My Name?

Name_____

Instructions:
Answer the following questions about your name. Interview your parents if you do not know all the answers.

1. Why did your parents choose your name?

2. If you were named after someone, who was it?

3. What nicknames do you have, and how did you get them?

4. Do you like your name? Why, or why not?

5. If you could choose another name, would you, and what would it be?

What's In Your Wallet?

Objectives
1. To create tribal inclusion
2. To give the students an opportunity to share something of themselves

Instructions
1. Remind the students of the agreements.
2. Ask each student to select something from his or her desk, wallet, purse, or backpack that is special and symbolic of him or her.
3. Ask the students to meet in their tribes to share their special items.

Suggested Reflection Questions:

CONTENT/THINKING
+ What was the value of this strategy?
+ What did you learn?

SOCIAL/INTERPERSONAL
+ How well did your tribe members listen to each other?
+ What could you do to help each other listen better?

PERSONAL
+ Was it hard for you to select something special to share? Why?
+ How did you feel after sharing your special object?

Appreciation

INVITE STATEMENTS OF APPRECIATION
+ "I liked it when..."
+ "I appreciated..."

Options
Use the strategy to discuss what people from different periods of history might carry with them.
Use as a pre-writing exercise.

GRADES
2–adult

TIME
30 minutes

GROUPING
tribes

MATERIALS
personal items

What's the Tint of Your Glasses?

Objectives

1. To build understanding that our different backgrounds give us different perspectives
2. To show that seeing things differently is O.K.
3. To experience how different viewpoints help us to see the whole picture
4. To promote multicultural awareness, acceptance and understanding
5. To experience influence

GRADES
6–adult

TIME
45 minutes

GROUPING
tribes

MATERIALS
poster paper and colored pencils/ pens for each tribe

Instructions

1. Have the community meet in tribes.
2. Have each student draw a pair of eyeglasses on a sheet of paper.
3. Ask each student to draw small designs or symbols on his or her glasses in response to the questions you will read.
   Examples:
   + What is your country of birth?
   + How many sisters and brothers do you have?
   + What language do your parents speak other than or in addition to English?
   + Have you ever lived on a farm or ranch? In a big city?
4. Have the tribe members compare glasses. Ask "Do any look that same?"
5. Discuss how different experiences give people different perspectives and opinions.
   Example: City person versus country person looks at pigs in a pen (pigs are dirty/pigs are great).
6. Ask each tribes to make a list of three other examples.
7. Have each tribe report their list to the community. Ask "What can happen when people believe everyone sees things the same way?" Discuss perceptions, assumptions, conflict, or respect for differences.

Suggest Reflection Questions

CONTENT/THINKING
+ What did you learn about how different people see the same thing?

SOCIAL/INTERPERSONAL
+ How well did your tribe work together during this activity?

PERSONAL
+ How did you feel when someone had a different point of view?
+ How can you help others see your point of view?

Appreciation

INVITE STATEMENTS OF APPRECIATION
+ "Thanks, [name] for..."
+ "I appreciate your..."

Options

Use the strategy to study a historical perspective. Have students paraphrase responses before adding their own, as described in the strategy "Paraphrase Passport."

What's Your Bag?

Objectives
1. To build inclusion
2. To present uniqueness of oneself

Instructions
1. Have the community meet in tribes.
2. Give each tribe a pile of magazines, scissors and glue, and one bag per member.
3. Instruct the students to use pictures and phrases from magazines to create personal collages, using the outside of the bag for public image and interests and the inside for private world or less shared world.
4. Tell the students that they may staple their bags shut if they want to ensure privacy for their inside worlds.
5. Invite tribe members to take turns sharing with each the outside of their bags and offering the rationale for some of their choices. Tribe members may choose to share a part of the inside world at the time of activity, or this could be done in a separate activity.

Suggested Reflection Questions

CONTENT/THINKING
+ What type of things did you share about your outside worlds?
+ Why is it important to have both an outside (public image) world and an inside (personal beliefs) world?

SOCIAL
+ What social skills did your tribe members use during this activity?
+ How did you help each other during this activity?

PERSONAL
+ How did you feel while making your bag?
+ What did you learn about yourself/your tribe?

Appreciation

INVITE STATEMENTS OF APPRECIATION
+ "I felt good when..."
+ "I like your bag because..."

Options
Make bags for characters in literature, people in history, or subject areas. Use as an authentic assessment for a content standard by writing clues on the outside of the bag and putting examples inside the bag.

GRADES
3–adult

TIME
60 minutes

GROUPING
tribes

MATERIALS
paper bags, glue, magazines, scissors, stapler

Where Do I Stand?

Objectives
1. To encourage sharing
2. To encourage respect for individual differences
3. To experience inclusion and influence

GRADES
3–adult

TIME
15–40 minutes

GROUPING
community, tribes

MATERIALS
animal signs,
string, tape

Instructions
1. On large cards, print four animal names: lion, deer, fox, dove; or use alternate signs such as: mountain, river, ocean, meadow; piano, trumpet, drum, flute; or have students suggest signs.
2. Suspend the animal signs from the ceiling in four areas of the classroom.
3. Ask each student to stand under the sign for the animal that they are most like when in their tribe. Encourage people to talk among themselves while they are deciding where to stand.
4. When all the students have chosen animals and have taken their places under the signs, ask them to share why they placed themselves where they did.
5. Continue the activity by repeating steps 3 and 4 with other situations. Examples:
   + How you are with your friends?
   + How you are with your family?
   + How are you by yourself?
   + How are you in a social situation with people you don't know?
6. Ask the students to meet in tribes and talk about their choices—why they stood where they did.
7. Have all write in their Personal Journals what they learned.

Suggested Reflection Questions
CONTENT/THINKING
   + What are the qualities of a lion/fox/dove/deer?
   + What did you learn about other students in the community/yourself?

SOCIAL
   + Why would you find it difficult to take a stand?
   + How is taking a stand an important skill for all of us?

PERSONAL
   + How did you feel when you took your stand?
   + What did you learn about yourself?

Appreciation
INVITE STATEMENTS OF APPRECIATION
   + "I was interested when..."
   + "I felt good when you said..."

Options
Use four different metaphors that apply to a theme or topic. Have students move to the metaphor most meaningful to them.

Why Is This Word Important?

Objectives
1. To practice group decision-making skills
2. To study and learn the meanings of words
3. To build group inclusion and influence

Instructions
1. Have the community meet in tribes; give each student a card from "Find The Word" strategy. Have each student write down what he or she thinks is the significance or importance of the particular word in relation to the unit being studied.
2. Then have tribe members pass the cards to each other and add additional comments on the importance of the word or concept.
3. After all the tribe members have written their comments, have the tribe members read the cards aloud.
4. Ask the tribe members to decide on one sentence that best represents the significance of the word or concept on each card (by using voting, stickers or a point system).
5. Have the students read the cards to the community and display them so that others may review them.

GRADES
4–8

TIME
60 minutes

GROUPING
tribes

MATERIALS
paper, pencils

Suggested Reflection Questions

CONTENT/THINKING
- ✦ What vocabulary words did you learn?
- ✦ Why do you have different ideas about the importance of a word?

SOCIAL
- ✦ Why is building a consensus difficult sometimes?
- ✦ How well did your tribe work together?

PERSONAL
- ✦ How did you feel when you had to write a comment about the importance of the word?
- ✦ What have you learned about yourself?

Appreciation
INVITE STATEMENTS OF APPRECIATION
- ✦ "I liked it when..."
- ✦ "[name] really helped us when..."
- ✦ "Our tribe is..."

Options
Use for both individual and peer assessment of learning.

Wishful Thinking

GRADES
K–adult

TIME
varies

GROUPING
tribes, community

MATERIALS
none

Objectives
1. To provide the opportunity to express a wish
2. To build inclusion

Instructions
1. Have the students sit or stand in a community circle or in tribes. Instruct them that no discussion is allowed during this activity.
2. Ask each student in turn to make a brief statement beginning with "I wish..." related to personal life, feelings about politics, school, the community, etc.
3. If possible, take turns around the circle more than once.

Suggested Reflection Questions
CONTENT/THINKING
+ How easy/difficult was it for you to think of wishes to share?
+ Why are wishes important?
+ What wishes do you have in common?

SOCIAL
+ How well did your tribe members listen to each other's wishes? •How do you know they listened?
+ How did tribe members help each other share?

PERSONAL
+ How did you feel while you were sharing your wish/listening to others share?

Appreciation
INVITE STATEMENTS OF APPRECIATION
+ "I liked it when..."
+ "I felt good when..."
+ "I admired your honesty when..."

Options
Use the strategy to share concerns about current events, school issues or content related topics. The strategy can be expanded for problem solving and/or decision making.

Zoo Stories

Objectives
1. To build inclusion
2. To encourage sharing

Instructions
1. Have the community or tribe sit in a circle.
2. Each person takes a turn at answering the question: "What kind of animal do you feel like today?"

Suggested Reflection Questions

CONTENT/THINKING
+ What animals were in your tribe today?
+ What were the similarities/differences between the animals?

SOCIAL
+ How well did your tribe members participate in this activity?
+ How did this activity help you get to know each other better?

PERSONAL
+ What was difficult about this activity for you?
+ When was the last time you felt like this animal?
+ What animal did someone else think of that you also liked?

Appreciation
INVITE STATEMENTS OF APPRECIATION
+ "I liked your animal because..."
+ "I'm like your animal when..."

Options
Ask tribes to select an animal or character and then to create a story by going around the circle.

GRADES
K–3

TIME
20 minutes

GROUPING
community, tribes

MATERIALS
none

ENERGIZERS FOR PAIRS

Mirrors

Partners face one another. One student begins the activity by moving his or her arm slowly enough so that the partner can "mirror" the action. The objective for the leader is not to trick the follower, but to enable his or her partner to follow successfully. The partners then change roles and repeat the activity. Once the students get the idea, let them move their knees, feet, legs, heads, etc., as well. Follow with reflection questions on being a leader and a follower.

Stand Off

Stand facing each other, one arm's length from your partner. Place open hands up and out a little from your shoulders. The object is to make your partner lose footing by pushing or hitting his or her hands only. Reflect, emphasizing the agreement of "mutual respect."

Stand Up

Sit on the ground back to back with your partner with knees bent and elbows linked. Now stand up together. Try it in threes and fours.

Trust Walk

Have everyone find a partner. One person of the pair volunteers to be led with his or her eyes closed or blindfolded. The other member of the pair leads the person for five minutes, taking very good care of the blind partner. After five minutes, switch roles.

Traffic Jam

Students are in partners, standing one behind another, as if in line. The person in front is the car, the person behind is the driver. Cars have eyes closed. One car has a roll of tape, or other object, and they are the ones to be avoided; they are not "reckless", but they try to "hit" other car/drivers. Then that duo becomes the "snowplow". Use lots of metaphors in your instructions, students will enjoy this. Great energizer to reaffirm trust in the classroom, working together on challenges, etc.

ENERGIZERS FOR SMALL GROUPS

Paper Toss

Have students in groups of four or five – each student takes a number. All students have crumpled paper balls. Establish an order/pattern of who tosses to whom, so that the paper balls are just being "passed". All except the student with number "1" place their paper balls under their thigh, or in a place that they can easily reach. Once the group is proficient in successfully tossing one paper ball, then the number "2" person adds their paper ball to the pattern. The goal is to get all paper balls going at the same time. Use music to help students focus, and to get them to stop when you want to reflect. This is a great energizer to use to reflect to students "how well they just worked together"…or not?!

Knots

Stand in a circle shoulder to shoulder. Ask everyone to reach out and grab two other hands. (You cannot have both hands of one person, and you cannot have the hand of persons on each side of you.) If possible, try not to criss-cross. Now untangle so that all are standing in a round circle again. After a successful un-entanglement, be sure to reflect to your students what effective problem-solvers they just were…and now you can expect that skill in today's lesson!

Wink

Have the students stand in a circle with their eyes closed. One person walks around the circle and quietly taps the back of one person who will be the "winker." Everyone opens their eyes and begins to mill around the room. If a person has been winked at, she or he must count to ten silently and then make a scene to let others know she or he is out of the game. The object is to catch the winker before everyone loses. If a person suspects the winker's identity, she says "I have an accusation!" However, there must be two accusers to stop the game. When someone else becomes suspicious, she or he shouts "I have an accusation!" Then both accusers count to three and point to the player they think is the perpetrator (no discussion is allowed). If they both point to someone who is innocent or to different people, they are automatically out of the game. If, however, they both point to the true winker, the game is over.

Bubble Gum

Each group has a pair of mittens and a pack of bubble gum. From the pack, each member must open a piece of gum with the mittens on and then pass the gum and mittens to the next member to do the same. To incorporate curriculum, discuss how bubble gum often has pictures of famous people in it, (sports figures, musicians, etc.). Each group should choose a famous person from the unit being studied and prepare a report or project to present to the class.

Alligators

As many students as possible stand on a bench or in a marked area. They are told they are in a lifeboat and there are alligators in the water. If any of them fall in, the alligators will know they are there and they will all die. Their job: line themselves up in order of height, by birthdates, etc.

Alligator Attack

Each tribe or team is given a piece of cardboard just big enough for all group members to stand on. All teams are at one end of the field or gym. All members must have a hand in carrying the cardboard (their "boat"). The leader will have a choice of two commands: "Go" means the teams may advance forward, holding their boat, at any speed; "Attack!" means that the team must place their boat on the ground and all members must get aboard and stay there. If one member should fall off the boat, the whole team is a goner. The last team on their boat is eliminated or must take a chunk out of their boat before the next "Go" command. See how many teams make it to the end of the field or gym!

People Patterns

Discuss types of patterns (A B A B, A B C A B C, A B B A B B). Have the members of a tribe or small group establish themselves in a pattern and stand in front of the class in that order. For example, an A B A B pattern might be "stripes on shirt, no stripes on shirt" or "earrings, no earrings." The people pattern should tell the audience what type of pattern they are demonstrating (A B A B, etc.) Members of the class must try to guess who can go next in the pattern; they may not guess the pattern until they have named a person to stand next in the people pattern. The person to correctly identify the pattern will join his or her tribe or small group to establish the next pattern. Pattern criteria should be clearly visible to all.

ENERGIZERS FOR LARGE GROUPS

Zoom, Zoom, Brake!

Have everyone stand in a community circle, facing in, shoulder to shoulder. Introduce the sound "zoom" and say that the sound goes zooming around the circle whenever you say it. When you say it, look to your right. That person immediately says "zoom" while looking to their right and this continues quickly around the circle. After going around the circle once, say that the car was only in first gear. Shift up into second and then third gear, the "zoom" going faster each time with more power. Now introduce the "brake" by demonstrating a screeching noise along with a hand signal of pulling back the brake. Have everyone try it with their own screeching brake sound. Now the group is ready to play. The rules are that you only get to brake once. When someone "brakes" the zoom reverses direction and goes the opposite way around the circle. Eventually everyone will get a chance to "brake" or the facilitator can call an end to the noise. It's a lot of fun, especially for younger kids.

Three Ball Pass

This is a mini "group juggle." Using something that is easy to catch, establish a pattern around the room as follows: Leader says someone's name and tosses them the ball; they choose another person, say that person's name, and toss them the ball; continue in this manner until each person has caught and tossed the ball once. The ball will end the pattern in the hands of the leader. Repeat the pattern until it can be done quickly. Begin again, and after several people have caught and tossed the ball, throw in the second ball, using the same pattern sequence; then throw in the third ball. This is a great energizer for learning names. After the group has mastered "Three Ball Pass," have them reverse the pattern! For a real challenge, have your group try it silently (after the pattern is established). This energizer can also be used to review content in any subject, or as a reflection at the end of the day or week.

Two Truths and a Lie

This energizer is great for building inclusion and re-entry after a school vacation. Have each person write down three things about themselves, what they did over vacation, etc. Of these three statements, two must be true and one must be a lie. Suggest that the lie should not be very obvious; it can even be a small detail. The rest of the class (or small group) must guess which one is the lie.

Lineup

Have students line up in order of birthdate, height, number of family members, number of the bus they ride to school, alphabetical order of middle name, etc. Have them do this without talking. This is a good energizer for getting your group focused, settled, and silent. The line-up is also a handy way to get your class into random cooperative groups.

Fork and Spoon

This is a hilariously confusing exercise in communication. Have everyone seated in a circle. The leader has a fork in the right hand and a spoon in the left hand. The leader turns to the person on the right and, holding up the fork, says, "This is a fork." The person being spoken to says, "A what?" The leader repeats, "A fork" and hands the fork over. The person with the fork says, "Oh, a fork!" Now, the person with the fork turns to the person on their right and says, "This is a fork." The person being spoken to says, "A what?" The person with the fork turns to the leader and asks, "A what?" The leader says, "A fork." Then the person turns to their right and says, "A fork" and hands over the fork to the next person. That person says, "Oh, a fork," turns to the person on the right and begins again with "This is a fork." When the person replies, "A what?" each person must go back up the line, one at a time, asking "A what?" until the leader tells them "A fork." Then "Oh, a fork" is said down the line until it reaches the person holding and then handing over the fork, beginning again with "This is a fork." Now that the fork is flowing smoothly to the right, start the process to the left with the spoon! The leader must now be alert for responding in both directions to the "A what?" questions, saying "A fork" to the right and "A spoon" to the left. Watch the fun when both the fork and the spoon reach the same person at once, usually midway around the circle. This energizer is very effective in foreign language classes, or with difficult vocabulary, as the word or phrase (substituted for "fork" and "spoon") is repeated.

Ali Baba

Participants stand in a circle. The facilitator begins the chant, "Ali Baba and the Forty Thieves", to be repeated over and over, to establish a rhythm. Up to five gestures are performed, one for each "Ali Baba…". Watch the group try to send the gestures, in order, around the circle. Variation (difficult version!) of Fork and Spoon.

Zap

Have all participants stand in a circle. The leader has everyone "create some energy" by rubbing their hands together, quickly, back and forth. Next the leader has everyone take a deep breath in, hold for two to three seconds, and breathe out. Do two more deep breaths, while continuously rubbing hands. Now the leader instructs, (while all are still rubbing hands), that on the count of three, everyone will make a sweeping point with their right arm to the center of the circle and yell "zzzzzzaaaappp!" This energizer really creates some energy, while at the same time allowing for the expenditure of energy. Try zapping a person (only if they ask to be zapped), or even social issues such as classroom put-downs.

Shuffle Your Buns

Have all participants seated in a circle with chairs pushed in tight. (All chairs should be of equal height.) The leader stands and moves to the center of the circle, leaving one empty chair. Model the directions by saying, "Shuffle to the right." Only the person with the empty chair to his or her right may "shuffle their buns" into the chair to the right. As each person moves, they vacate their chair for the next person to "shuffle their buns." This begins to move around the circle quite rapidly. Now the leader may say, "Shuffle to the left." At this command, the person that just completed a shuffle to the right must reverse and "shuffle their buns" into the empty chair to their left. The procession then follows; each time a chair is vacated, someone is shuffling into it. It must be understood that one cannot "shuffle their buns" unless they are moving into an empty/vacated seat. Once the group has mastered shuffling their buns, the leader speeds up the process by reversing commands frequently enough so as to confuse the action. The object now is for the leader to shuffle his or her buns into an empty seat. Having interrupted the flow, the person now in the middle giving the "shuffle" commands is the person who failed to shuffle fast enough and lost his or her seat to the leader. To really get things rolling, give each person in the group a one-time-only opportunity to automatically reverse the shuffle by slapping the empty chair next to them instead of shuffling into it. This "confusion" allows the person in the middle a better opportunity to find a seat, and keeps anyone from having to be the middle person for too long.

Changes

Have students get in pairs, or do in a full group by having five people come and stand in the front of the room. Instructions are to look at your partner or class volunteers and notice and remember as much as you can about their appearance. Partners turn back to back (volunteers leave the room) and change three noticeable things about their appearance. Students must guess what changes have been made. This energizer is easy to repeat, because as time goes on, the changes can be more subtle, specific, even scientific! (Change three things involving color, quantity, your torso, etc.)

Clap-Slap

Get a rhythm going: two claps, two slaps on lap. Go around the circle filling the blanks to the following chant: My name is (Karen), I come from (Kuwait), and I sell (Kleenex). The first sound must match the beginning sound in your name.

Hagoo

Divide into two teams and form two lines. Have people stand shoulder to shoulder facing a person on the other team. Stand a yard apart. One person from each team will volunteer to walk past each person in the row of the opposite team. The people on the team try to make the volunteer from the other team smile as he/she walks by. No touching is allowed. If the volunteer cracks up he/she must join the opposite team. If he/she makes it to the end straight faced, he/she goes back in the row with his/her original team.

Hug Tag

Play this in the same way people play any game of tag, except that when two people are hugging they are safe from getting tagged by the person who is "it."

I Like My Neighbors

Have all members seated on chairs in a circle, with one person standing in the middle as "it." The person in the middle makes a statement such as "I like my neighbors, especially those who are wearing running shoes" (wearing glasses, are over twelve, have a birthday in September, etc.). All those people who are wearing running shoes must jump up from their seats and scramble to find a chair; the person in the middle also scrambles for an empty chair. The one person left standing becomes the new "it."
Extension: Two or more people seated away from each other may make eye contact and nonverbally "plot" to change places. When they make the dash to each others' seats, the "leader" may try to beat them to it.

I Love You, Honey

Have everyone stand in a large circle. One person in the middle walks up to one person in the circle and says, "I love you, honey." The chosen "victim" is to respond, "I love you too, but I'm not allowed to smile," without smiling. It can be said twice to the same person in the same way. Guess what happens. They smile! Right! The smiler may then trade places with the person in the center or join the person in the center in tempting others to smile. The second option is generally easier on individuals in the group than the first option.

Lap Game

Everyone stands in a long line behind each other and puts their hands on the waist of the person in front of them. On the count of "three" everyone sits down on the lap of the person behind them. This can also be done in a big circle.

Rain

Have everyone sit in a circle, facing the center. Ask all to close their eyes, pausing for a moment or two to become quiet while each person gets ready to hear the sound the person on the right will be making. Keep eyes closed as the rainstorm begins with the leader rubbing her palms together, back and forth. The person to the left joins her, and then the person to her left, and so on, around the circle. When the leader hears the drizzle sound being made by the person on the right, she starts snapping her fingers. When the snapping action has been picked up by everyone around the circle, the leader switches to hand clapping, then to thigh slapping, and finally to foot stomping. After foot stomping, the leader reverses the order of sounds, introducing thigh slapping, hand clapping, finger snapping and finally palm rubbing. For the last round, the leader stops rubbing her palms and takes the hand of the person on her left. Each person follows suit around the circle until there is silence once again.

Do After Me

Sit in a large circle. One person begins by entering the circle and making a gesture, sound, or movement (the more ridiculous, the more fun), and then points to someone else in the circle to succeed him. This person makes the same gesture, sound, or movement as the preceding person made, and then adds her own performance. She then chooses the next person, and this person need only repeat the preceding action and add one before choosing someone new. The game is over when everyone has had a chance in the circle.

Monkey, Elephant, Palm Tree

Form a large circle with one person standing in the middle as "it." The person in the center first demonstrates positions for people to take when he/she calls out one of the animals or the palm tree. They are illustrated below:

MONKEY

ELEPHANT

PALM TREE

The person in the center then twirls around and points his or her finger at one of the people in the circle and shouts out: "Monkey," or "Elephant," or "Palm Tree." The person pointed to and the two people on either side of her take the appropriate positions with their bodies. The member of the trio that flubs up becomes the new "it" and goes into the center of the circle to continue on with the game.

Skin the Snake

Have people line up one behind the other. Reach between your legs and with your left hand grab the right hand of the person behind you. The person in front of you needs to reach back to grab your right hand with their left hand. Once the chain is formed, you're set to go. The last person in line lies down on his back. The person in front of him backs up, straddling his body and lies down behind him. Continue until the whole group waddles back.

People Machine

One person begins the activity by assuming a strange position and making a repetitive movement with a repetitive sound. The next person connects physically in whatever creative way he or she chooses, making a different movement and sound. People keep adding themselves to the machine. The result is a huge people machine making a lot of noise.

Electricity

Have everyone sit down in one large circle, cross-legged and knees touching. Hold hands. One person starts a squeeze on one side and the next person quietly passes it on around the circle. Variation: start it off by squeezing both sides. Watch it explode. Variation: send an "ooh" or an "aah" the other way.

Bumpety-Bump-Bump

Form a circle standing up, with a chosen "it" in the center. The "it" walks up to you and stands in front of you and says one of the following:

"Center, bumpety-bump-bump"

"Self, bumpety-bump-bump"

"Right, bumpety-bump-bump"

"Left, bumpety-bump-bump"

You must say his or her name, your name, or the person's name to the right or left of you before "it" completes saying "bumpety-bump-bump;" otherwise you become "it."

Name Wave

All stand in a circle. One person says their name and at the same time makes a motion or gesture. (Example: Beth, as she waves her hand.) The person to the right says "Beth" and waves her hand as Beth did. The name and motion spread around the circle in a "wave." When the circle is complete, the next person says their name and a different motion and that "waves" around the circle. Continue until all names are said and activated.

Snowball

Each student places his/her name on a piece of paper and wads it up. Students line up, half on either side of the room. At a signal they begin a snowball fight. At the end each gets a snowball, learns new information about the person whose snowball they found, and shares it with the class. For content, use any sequence; student #1 writes an equation, then snowball, the person who picks it up writes the next step, and so on.

Pen Pals

Give each participant a 3 x 5 index card and tell them to write a little known fact about themselves on the card, something they won't mind the group eventually knowing. State that they are not to write their name on the card. Collect all cards, shuffle and redistribute. If someone gets his/her own card back, it is exchanged for another. When everyone has an unfamiliar card, have all stand and circulate, asking one another questions about the information on the card. For example, "Did you barrel race horses as a child?" When the person answering the description is found, he/she signs the card and puts it on a designated wall space. When you are finished, the community has an instant bulletin board of people and their accomplishments. This is a good full group inclusion energizer, good for parents on back-to-school night, too!

"10"

Establish an order…this works best with students standing at their desk. Students, in order are to count to 10; each student may say one or two numbers in counting. The student who has to say "10" sits down. That last student standing in the "winner."

What Are You Doing?

In pairs, one student mimes an action that is familiar (and appropriate). The other student asks, "What are you doing?" The student performing the familiar action (such as brushing teeth) states another action that has nothing to do with what he/she is doing (such as riding a bicycle). Now the "asker" has to perform the action (in this case, riding a bicycle). The partner who was brushing teeth, stops and asks the bicycle rider, "What are you doing?" The bicycle rider names another action and the asker performs that action. And so on. This is a great energizer, and doesn't need to last more that 2 minutes. The energizer is from the book, *The Laughing Classroom* by Diana Loomans and Karen Kolberg.

Vehicle

Have four chairs in the center of the circle. Designate which is the driver's seat, and where the "hitch-hiker" will sit, as well as the rotation. Fill all four seats with students. The "hitch-hiker" names a vehicle (any mode of transportation) and all in the "vehicle" act out what their interpretation of being in/on that vehicle would be like. The driver says "hitch-hiker!" and leaves the car so that the new "hitch-hiker" can enter the vehicle and name a new "vehicle" to be acted out.

14

Resources

14 Resources

THE HISTORY OF TRIBES AND TRIBES TLC®

The initial version of the Tribes process began to evolve in the early seventies, a time when concerned educators and parents began groping for ways to motivate children's learning, to manage behavior problems, and to stem the tide upon which many good åteachers were leaving the profession. National surveys were alerting the general public and industry leaders that the majority of high school students did not have the knowledge or skills to do well in the world of work and social complexities that they would face in life. Twenty years ago? Or is it today?

Jeanne Gibbs had observed that children's achievement and behavior in school seemed to be influenced by the quality of the classroom and school environment. Being a student at heart, Jeanne began exploring studies on school climate, human development, and the dynamics of organizational systems. In 1973 she was asked to consult with the Contra Costa County Department of Education towards the prevention of substance abuse related problems. There was little research at that time on prevention other than studies which confirmed that informational curricula alone did not deter problems. The author reasoned that since environment influences human behavior, building positive environments within schools and families not only would be preventive, but could be significant in promoting academic learning and social development.

The concept made enough sense to some other visionaries at the California Department of Education who in 1974 funded a grant that would enable elementary school teachers to pilot a group development process that Jeanne had been using for many years within community settings. As the teachers began to experience the caring environment within their own work groups, they began to use the term, "tribe." Repeatedly they said, "We feel like a family... we feel like a tribe."

In 1976, Jeanne published the first instructional manual, titled *TRIBES: A Human Development Process for Educational Systems,* and then in 1978, Jeanne published the first of many copyrighted *Tribes books, titled TRIBES: A Process for Peer Involvement* (CenterSource Publications).

From 1975 through 1985 numerous applications of the group development process were made through a non-profit corporation which Jeanne founded. The "people process" proved to be valuable in alcohol recovery centers, juvenile facilities, daycare centers, and recreational programs. California schools began to request training when they learned that the Tribes group process decreased behavior problems, increased self-esteem, improved cooperation and achievement, and improved teachers' energy and morale.

Based on the extensive research of the cooperative learning field, the book, *Tribes, A Process for Social Development and Cooperative Learning,* was published in 1987. The demand for training accelerated throughout the country, and in 1991 quality materials incorporating new research, concepts and methods were designed by the author and her colleagues. The more comprehensive version of the Tribes process became known as "Tribes TLC®" and resulted in the writing and publication of *Tribes, A New Way of Learning and Being Together* (1994), which has been expanded and revised several times.[1] The most recent edition is titled *Reaching All by Creating Tribes Learning Communities* (2006).[2]

In 1994, the Research Triangle Institute, under a U.S. Department of Education contract, identified Tribes TLC® as an exemplary program to teach social skills to Kindergarten to 12th grade students.[3] The Council of the Great City Schools cited Tribes as a model to prevent violence.[4]

In 2001, the author researched and wrote a middle level book, titled *Discovering Gifts in Middle School: Learning in a Caring Culture Called Tribes,* which emphasizes the need for schools to become responsive to the contextual basis of adolescent development in order to attain both greater achievement and success for students as well as a new spirit, energy and the discovery of gifts throughout the whole school community.[5]

In 2003, the Collaborative for Academic, Social and Emotional Learning (CASEL) identified Tribes TLC an evidenced-based "SELect Program."[6] In 2005, the Office of Juvenile Justice Delinquency Prevention (OJJDP) identified Tribes Learning Communities as an evidence-based Promising Program in their Model Programs Guide.[7] In 2006, CSAP's WesternCAPT (Center for Substance Abuse Prevention's Center for the Application of Prevention Technologies) recognized Tribes Learning Communities as a Promising Practice that addresses both protective and risk factors for the prevention of substance abuse.

In 2005, CenterSource Systems published an important new book, titled *What Is It About Tribes? The Research-Based Components of the Developmental Process of Tribes Learning Communities.* This important book by Bonnie Benard of WestEd, is an in-depth response to questions that educators have been asking for many years: "What is it about the process of 'Tribes' that makes it work so well in so many schools, cultures and countries?" The author brings hundreds of research studies and literature references into enlightening coherence to discover how and why the student-centered active-learning process transforms people, classrooms, and schools.[8]

Application of the Tribes process continues to grow with the publication of the new high school level book by Jeanne Gibbs and Teri Ushijima, Ed.D. titled, *Engaging All by Creating High School Learning Communities* (2008), which is based on current and evolving best practices for the secondary level.[9] As now defined, the primary mission of Tribes TLC® is "to assure the healthy development of every child in the school community so that each has the knowledge, skills and resiliency to be successful in our rapidly changing world." Indeed, this can happen when schools engage all teachers, administrators, students and families in working together as a learning community dedicated to caring and support, active participation, and positive expectations for all.

References: See page 424 in the Appendix.

THE ORIGIN OF "REFLECTION," THE PELICAN

In one way or another, the talkative pelican that flies throughout the pages of this book insisted on becoming a notable character in all of the Tribes books and materials. This occurred, despite author Jeanne Gibbs more or less ignoring the swooping pelican tribes that flew around her houseboat while she lived in Sausalito, California. The big birds would land and perch for long times on the pilings alongside her boat, seemingly to observe the kayaks, sailboats, cruisers and other activity going by.

An important occasion took place one day when ten 4th and a 5th grade students from a Tribes school, a 4th grade teacher, and a parent came to visit. The occasion arose because the teacher of the 5th graders was not using Tribes learning groups, as had been the practice of all of the other teachers the students had been with since 1st grade. They wanted to talk about writing a letter to the 5th grade teacher—a letter that would urge her to have them learning in Tribes.

Lunching on the deck of the houseboat was exciting enough, but the hot dogs, chips and lemonade were quickly forgotten when a friendly pelican landed on top of the boat. People became quiet and spellbound as they observed the big bird—and as she observed them. After a time she flew off.

Mindful of the students' letter writing plan, after lunch and a lot of discussion about pelicans, Jeanne said, "Let's close our eyes for a few minutes. Now imagine that your school has a glass roof and ceilings so that our pelican could look down and see whatever was happening in your two classrooms. What would she see? What are the students doing? What is the teacher doing? Think about it silently."

Three or four minutes later, everyone wanted to talk at once. "In our 4th grade class the pelican would see our desks together in small groups. People would be talking and working together." "Yeah, helping each other figure stuff out." "Some people are sitting on the carpet, designing a building." "They're sharing materials—they're laughing." "And one tribe is planning how to act out the story they read." "People are moving around the classroom to get things and ideas from other tribes." "The teacher is walking around. She's not just asking them a bunch of questions." "No, people are asking for her ideas."

The parent then asked, "And what would the pelican be seeing in the 5th grade classroom?" "Oh, everyone is sitting alone in straight rows." "The new teacher is talking lots, writing stuff on the board and asking lots of questions." "Not many kids are putting up their hands to answer." "Some even have their heads down on their desks." "And two guys are poking each other." "The teacher is passing those fat workbooks down the rows." "The kids look real bored."

The writing club's conclusion was that the next time they met they would write what the pelican may have seen and what they hoped the 5th grade teacher would consider doing.

Some days later the 5th grade students and parent delivered the letter to the teacher and a copy to the Principal. It took awhile, but the teacher took their message to heart. She participated in a Tribes TLC training, enjoyed learning from other teachers, and gradually transformed the classroom into a student-centered Tribes Learning Community.

After reflecting on her experience with the students, Jeanne rather spontaneously named the pelican "Reflection" and began to emphasize the importance of having students reflect on current situations, events and their own learning. The literature is replete with studies on the impact that timely reflection (reflective practice) has on academic learning, behavior, self-responsibility and social competency. Reflective practice is an essential practice to accomplish whole school reform, systems change, productive professional learning communities and authentic assessment.

There are many, many pelicans in the Tribes books, articles and materials. Reflection, the pelican, is a meta-cognitive symbol to remind all of us to introduce and make *reflective practice* an on-going norm in all school systems. If somehow you missed the invitation from Jeanne on page 74 of this book here it is again….

> *Invite the pelican that soars over the Tribes Trail to be your constant companion. Her name is Reflection. She will tell you, rather immodestly, that she makes the Tribes process work well anywhere. At times, you will want to ignore her calls: "timeout," "stop the action, teacher," "time to reflect," or "what's happening now?" Reflection knows that if you watch from the bird's eye view, classroom management goes more smoothly. Reflection is a wise bird who can describe just what she saw or heard while people worked together. You will find her questions on the pages of every Tribes strategy. Reflection clears up confusion and helps everyone soar to greater heights.*

THE IMPACT OF GROUP PROCESSING

Tribes has always emphasized the importance of using reflection or process questions after each group strategy or learning experience. The motto shared among Tribes teachers has been, "The activity alone is not enough!" Throughout the years, CenterSource Systems trainers have been helping teachers define three types of reflection questions (1) about the content [facts and concepts] of a lesson; (2) about the collaborative social and constructive thinking skills used by students within their tribes; and (3) about the personal learning and meaning that a lesson had for the students. Reflection questions were emphasized as a way to develop metacognition (learning about our learning) and responsibility among students to improve their learning groups (tribes). Empirical studies confirm that the time spent with students on "group processing" also leads to the greater retention of subject matter and academic achievement.

The study "The Impact of Group Processing on Achievement in Cooperative Learning Groups" by Stuart Yager, Roger Johnson, David Johnson, and Bill Snider describes three learning conditions assessed in three classes composed of 84 3rd graders. An intensive five-week unit on transportation was taught in all three classrooms but in different processes.

Classroom A used the conventional individualistic learning method whereby students study alone and fill daily worksheets. Classrooms B and C used cooperative learning groups (four students to a group) with students working together and each group completing the worksheets together. In addition, classroom C spent 5 minutes processing their work as a group and setting goals for improvement. A 50-item factual knowledge multiple choice test on the subject was given to all children prior to the unit and three weeks after the unit. A 25-item test was given after twelve instructional days and another 25-item test as soon as the unit was completed.

The graph was constructed from the research data. The first bar graph for each class shows achievement and the second bar graph indicates retention of knowledge after three weeks. Pretest scores for all students had averaged about 50%. In classroom A, using the individualistic approach, marginal gains moved from 50 to 65% in achievement, with retention dropping to 58% three weeks after the unit was completed. In classroom B, using cooperative learning groups and no processing, gains moved from 50 to 78%, with 73% retention. Results in classroom C, using cooperative learning groups with processing are impressive, with higher achievement (87%) and no loss in the retention of knowledge after three weeks.

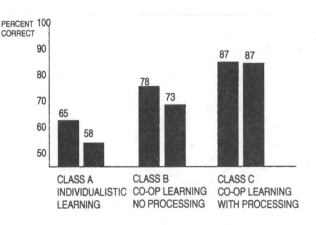

Other studies by the same researchers show comparably dramatic results from the contribution of group processing to learning and individual achievement. Interested readers can learn more by visiting the website of the Cooperative Learning Center at the University of Minnesota (www.co-operation.org), where Drs. David and Roger Johnson continue to document their work and where the following studies can be accessed: Stuart Yager, Roger Johnson, and David Johnson, "Oral Discussion, Group-to-Individual Transfer, and Achievement in Cooperative Learning Groups," *Journal of Educational Psychology,* 77:60-66, 1985. Stuart Yager, Roger Johnson, David Johnson, and Bill Snider, "The Impact of Group Processing: Achievement in Cooperative Learning Groups," *The Journal of Social Psychology,* 126:389-397, 1986.

INITIATING CLASSROOM PARENT TRIBES

Objectives

1. To develop participation and mutual support among the parents of the classroom
2. To provide parents with a satisfying initial experience in the Tribes process
3. To motivate parents to continue meeting throughout the year as a classroom learning community
4. To provide information on the goals of Tribes, its process, and collaborative agreements
5. To help parents learn how to foster resiliency in their children

Instructions

8 min. 1. As parents arrive the teacher and parent facilitators (PFs) invite the parents to sit in small groups of prearranged chairs or desks (four to seven in a group).

2. The teacher welcomes all, gives overview of the hour and tells why the Tribes process is being used within the class or school. He or she introduces the PFs, and briefly describes their role.

4 min. 3. The PFs share their names, students names, and their commitment to having the parents of the class become a supportive learning community.

4. The PFs then describe the Tribes agreements and ask the parents to honor them during their time together. They demonstrate the Tribes hand signal as a way to call attention.

5 min. 5. The parent facilitators discuss the importance of the Tribes agreements and attentive listening, and they demonstrate the skills.

1 min. 6. After asking each group to select a timekeeper, the PFs each ask the parents to share their name and one great quality about their student. Ask the timekeepers in each group to monitor the sharing time.

5 min. 7. The PFs ask the parents to think about, then share with one other person in the group, two things they hope for their child during the year. As one parent shares, the other notes down in one to three words the parent's hopes on a card. When the time is up, the PFs collect the cards.

5 min. 8. The teacher responds to some of the hopes listed, tying them to goals for the year.

5 min. 9. The PFs ask the following reflection questions:

  ✦ How many people enjoyed being able to talk with other parents tonight?

  ✦ How many would like to get together this way again?

5 min. 10. The PFs demonstrate and invite statements of appreciation in tribes.

5 min. 11. They invite everyone to close in a community circle, sharing, "I learned" statements.

TIME REQUIRED
60 minutes

FACILITATORS
2 classroom parents trained by teachers

MATERIALS
Tribes agreements posted on wall, 3 x 5-inch cards, pencils, large pieces of paper, felt tip pens

A TRIBES TLC® LEARNING EXPERIENCE

1. PROVIDE FOR INCLUSION—A YOU QUESTION, ENERGIZER OR STRATEGY:

2. IDENTIFY THE CONTENT OBJECTIVE TO BE LEARNED AND THE COLLABORATIVE/SOCIAL SKILL OBJECTIVE TO BE PRACTICED.
Content Objective (write):

Collaborative Objective:
- ❒ Participating fully
- ❒ Listening attentively
- ❒ Expressing appreciation
- ❒ Reflecting on experience
- ❒ Valuing diversity of culture/ideas
- ❒ Thinking constructively
- ❒ Making Responsible Decisions
- ❒ Resolving conflict
- ❒ Solving problems creatively
- ❒ Working on tasks together
- ❒ Assessing improvement
- ❒ Celebrating achievement

Social Skills:
- ❒ Sharing
- ❒ Listening
- ❒ Respecting
- ❒ No Put-Downs
- ❒ Empathizing

3. IDENTIFY THE STRATEGY(IES).

4. ASK REFLECTION QUESTIONS ABOUT WHAT WAS LEARNED.

5. PROVIDE AN OPPORTUNITY FOR APPRECIATION.

This material may be duplicated for classroom use.

FORM A: TEACHER OBSERVATION
Assessing Collaborative Skills—Listening

Date _____

Lesson _____

_____

_____

Tally each time the behavior is observed

NAMES OF INDIVIDUALS OR TRIBES

	BASIC SKILLS					ADVANCED SKILLS				TOTALS
	FACES SPEAKER, LEANS FORWARD	MAINTAINS EYE CONTACT	NODS, SMILES IF APPROPRIATE	DOES NOT INTERRUPT THE SPEAKER	ENCOURAGES SPEAKER TO CONTINUE TALKING	ASKS RELEVANT QUESTIONS TO CLARIFY AND SHOW INTEREST	PARAPHRASES SPEAKER'S MAIN IDEAS	REFLECTS THE SPEAKER'S FEELINGS	SUMMARIZES FOR THE GROUP	

This form may be duplicated for classroom use.

FORM B: STUDENT ASSESSMENT

PARTICIPATION IN MY TRIBE   Date _____

Name _____ Tribe _____

	NEVER	SOMETIMES	MOSTLY	ALWAYS
1. I listened to people in my tribe.				
2. I helped other people.				
3. I contributed ideas and information.				
4. I helped to clarify and summarize ideas and information.				
5. I encouraged others.				
6. I participated in making decisions.				
7. I expressed appreciation to others.				
8. I helped us to reflect on what we learned.				

NOTES

FORM C: STUDENT ASSESSMENT

OUR TRIBE'S WORK TOGETHER

Tribe Name _____ Date _____

Using the numbers 1 (poorly), 2 (okay), and 3 (great!), rate how well your tribe did the following:

RATING   SOCIAL SKILL OR GROUP INTERACTION

_____   1. We listened to each other.

_____   2. We checked our understanding of the task.

_____   3. We shared ideas and information.

_____   4. We encouraged and helped each other.

_____   5. We stayed on the task and used our time well.

_____   6. Other:

Total Score: _____

This form may be duplicated for classroom use.

FORM C: STUDENT ASSESSMENT

OUR TRIBE'S WORK TOGETHER

Tribe Name _____ Date _____

Using the numbers 1 (poorly), 2 (okay), and 3 (great!), rate how well your tribe did the following:

RATING   SOCIAL SKILL OR GROUP INTERACTION

_____   1. We listened to each other.

_____   2. We checked our understanding of the task.

_____   3. We shared ideas and information.

_____   4. We encouraged and helped each other.

_____   5. We stayed on the task and used our time well.

_____   6. Other:

Total Score: _____

This form may be duplicated for classroom use.

FORM D: STUDENT ASSESSMENT

MY CONSTRUCTIVE THINKING SKILLS

Date _____

Name _____ Tribe _____

INSTRUCTIONS:

Read the descriptions of constructive thinking skills below and estimate how well you do each skill. You can use a different colored pencil or pen each week to evaluate your own progress in using these skills.

	NEVER	SOMETIMES	MOSTLY	ALWAYS
1. I am able to **access information** (using the library, computer, articles, interviewing, and working with others).				
2. I can **organize information** (using graphics, charts, note cards, computer data entry).				
3. I am able to **compare and summarize** facts and ideas.				
4. I can **plan and use** what I learn to solve problems and be creative.				
5. I am able to **reflect and evaluate** how well something is working and make improvements.				

OTHER COMMENTS

This form may be duplicated for classroom use.

PREVENTING CONFLICT THROUGH DIALOGUES OF DISCOVERY

Ron Patrick, M.Ed.

Ron is an ecological/systems psychologist and a Tribes TLC® Trainer. He has worked with school and mental health communities for 33 years, most recently as Director of Psychological and Student Services. He also served as a consultant/coach with the Mid-Eastern Ohio Regional Resource Center where he focused on primary preventive mental health, systems change, and literacy programs. As a Native American, Ron believes that the Tribes TLC® process honors his cultural values and the tradition of deep respect within native spiritual practice.

Have you noticed that every year conflict management programs are multiplying almost as fast as proverbial rabbits? The majority of approaches focus on managing rather than viewing conflict as a symptom in the school environment that can be prevented. Misunderstandings indeed are inevitable, whether in a classroom, school, district or parent organization. However, it became evident during my years of using the process of Tribes TLC® in preschool to university settings, that conflict need not undermine relationships or learning. We have only to shift our focus to creating a caring environment in which people feel safe enough to deal with misunderstandings before they become serious. For students, it means feeling safe enough to ask challenging questions, to learn and listen deeply, and to enter into genuine dialogue until they discover and understand the diverse perspectives, opinions and social values that in time could lead to conflict.

Our culture teaches us that listening is the mechanical act of using our auditory sense, listening to the words someone is saying without hearing the deeper messages under the words. Listening for "discovery" means listening with our hearts as well as our heads. The practice itself helps to create safety in the environment. Moreover, it…

> promotes openness, honesty and trust; clarifies thinking, feelings, perceptions, beliefs and assumptions; develops respect, acceptance and appreciation for individual gifts and resources.

Listening, even in the midst of conflict, is the most important skill we can teach our students and children. If you think of a brick house, listening is like the mortar of that house. If the mortar erodes or is lost, the building begins to crumble. Quality listening is the mortar of communication and learning. How else can we understand the needs, beliefs, values, hopes and dreams of another person?

Peter Senge, author of *The Fifth Discipline,* emphasizes the imperative of deep listening and thinking for learning organizations.[2] By now you are well aware that this is what the systems approach of Tribes TLC® is all about—transforming the

To create a classroom where students feel safe enough to challenge each other—and us—is to give them an enormous gift.[1]

—ALFIE KOHN

whole school community into a caring learning community. It begins by teaching everyone to listen for discovery, which then creates genuine dialogue within a classroom, group, or system. The big payoff is that dialogue allows a group to move beyond any one individual's perception, to build a collective understanding and to develop shared meaning and purpose.

Conflict management simply becomes an anachronism in safe and caring environments that involve students in heartfelt listening and meaningful dialogue. Alfie Kohn is wise when he says, "It is to give them an enormous gift." And I would add, *it's a gift for life*.

References:

1. Kohn, A. (1996). *Beyond discipline: From compliance to community*. Alexandria, VA: Association for Supervision and Curriculum Development.

2. Senge, P. (1991). *The fifth discipline: The art and practice of learning communities*. New York, NY: Double Day/Currency.

TRIBES PROFESSIONAL DEVELOPMENT

BRING YOUR SCHOOL TO LIFE WITH TRIBES TLC® PROFESSIONAL DEVELOPMENT

Tribes is a community building process—a culture and active learning pedagogy best learned by experiencing it. You can make the process come alive for your district or school by scheduling training for your teachers, administration and support staff.

CenterSource Systems has a network of licensed trainers who conduct professional development training in many countries throughout the world. Schedule an overview presentation and classroom demonstration at your school where the key concepts of Tribes are explained and demonstrated through typical training strategies and our videos. Give your administration, school board and staff the information they need to consider whole school training. Schools and districts committed to the full implementation of Tribes TLC® can arrange training and support to teams and faculties through the following staff development opportunities:

Building Community for Learning (Tribes "Basic" Training)
The purpose of this 24-hour experiential training is to prepare teachers, administrators and support staff personnel to develop a caring school and classroom environment, and to reach and teach students through an active learning approach that promotes student development, motivation and academic achievement.

Discovering Gifts in Middle School
The purpose of this 24-hour experiential training is to provide a research-based approach for middle level school educators to focus their schools on the critical developmental learning needs of young adolescents. The training illuminates how to transform the cultures of middle schools into caring learning communities that support the full range of students' growth and development as well as establishing academic excellence.

Engaging All By Creating High School Learning Communities
The purpose of this 24-hour experiential training is to provide the research-based concepts, experience, and strategies that are essential for engaging all by creating high school learning communities. Among the topics to be considered will be: critical indicators of the very different needs of 21st century youth, voices of students themselves, and a consensus of recommendations from the literature and studies, including the National Association of Secondary School Principals

What Tribes can bring to a class is dynamite—what it can bring to a total staff is spectacular!

—LESLIE MCPEAK,
PRINCIPAL
MODESTO CITY SCHOOLS

(NASSP). Participants will understand why and how the research-based developmental process of Tribes Learning Communities, when implemented well, can transform the culture, structures and pedagogy of the whole high school system—particularly one committed to preparing today's students for an entirely different era—the Era of Learning.

Artistry for Learning

The purpose of this 24-hour experiential advanced-level training is to increase the capacity of teachers and administrators within Tribes Learning Community Schools to intensify quality implementation of the research-based developmental process of Tribes – thereby to assure that all students, no matter their diversity and ability, achieve higher social, emotional and academic learning.

Collaboration: The Art Form of Leadership—
Leading for Results in a Tribes Learning Community

The purpose of this 14-hour experiential training is to bring together school leaders and leadership teams who have already been trained in the process of Tribes TLC® so that they can explore and complete authentic leadership tasks and gain a new exciting view of their roles in reculturing the school community. The Tribes collegial team learning experiences will create a professional learning community environment that will support and sustain increased student learning and achievement.

Implementing After-School Tribes

The purpose of this 12-hour experiential training is to prepare after-school educators, youth workers, and community members to develop a caring learning center environment and to reach and teach children and youth through an active learning approach that promotes human development, resiliency, and social-emotional competence. Using multiple intelligences, brain compatible learning and cooperative methods, the community learning center climate and staff awareness will begin to reflect the message of life-long learning, personal development, and social responsibility as the keys to success in the 21st Century.

Multi-Year TRIBES TLC® Training

CenterSource Systems can help you design a multi-year training program to meet the needs of your school by implementing several of the professional development opportunities mentioned above. When integrated into the whole school community, Tribes can effect system-wide change by creating a caring culture and cooperative learning community, which fosters student growth and achievement, strengthens staff relationships and collegiality, and effectively redesigns the learning community.

Training-of-District Trainers

CenterSource Systems has designed a capacity building model for professional development so that your district or school can have your own Certified Tribes TLC® Trainers providing on-going training, coaching and support to teachers, administrators, resource personnel and parent community groups. The CenterSource Systems 40-hour Training-of-District Trainers provides in-depth skills, knowledge, experience and quality training materials to your own qualified personnel. A variety of training modules enable them to facilitate the Basic Tribes Course, support faculty groups, initiate parent community groups and conduct classroom demonstrations.

Summer Institute for District Trainers

The purpose of the Tribes TLC® Summer Institute is to advance the professional capacity of the Tribes Learning Community international network of trainers to lead and accelerate academic, social and emotional learning for all students in their schools and to develop the leadership capacity to sustain and intensify the implementation of Tribes through the development of professional learning communities in their schools and districts.

Follow-up coaching and support at your school site is available throughout the year so that your staff can fully implement the process of Tribes and intensify its use throughout the whole school community.

Tribes TLC is recognized as a Model or Promising Program by:
>   **Collaborative for Academic, Social and Emotional Learning**
>   **Office of Juvenile Justice Delinquency Prevention**
>   **Center for Substance Abuse Prevention's Western CAPT**
>   **Find Youth Info.Gov**

FOR ADDITIONAL INFORMATION, CONTACT:

CenterSource Systems, LLC
7975 Cameron Drive, Bldg 500
Windsor, California 95492

Phone: 800-810-1701 or 707-838-1061
FAX: 707-838-1062
Email: tribes@tribes.com
Website: www.tribes.com

TRIBES LEARNING COMMUNITIES®
A MODEL AND PROMISING PROGRAM

CASEL SELect Program

After an extensive program and evaluation review, Tribes was chosen by the Collaborative for Academic, Social and Emotional Learning (CASEL) as one of 22 SELect Programs. CASEL summarizes the conceptual framework, criteria, and program review results in their publication, *Safe and Sound: An Education Leader's Guide to Evidence-Based Social and Emotional Learning (SEL) Programs.* (www.casel.org)

Tribes TLC® earned recognition as a CASEL SELect Program by demonstrating the following essential requirements:

+ provides outstanding coverage in five essential SEL areas

+ has well-designed evaluation demonstrating effectiveness

+ offers high-quality professional development.

OJJDP Model Programs Guide

Tribes TLC® has been included in the OJJDP (Office of Juvenile Justice Delinquency Prevention) *Model Programs Guide.* OJJDP, an office of the U.S. Department of Justice, created the Model Programs Guide to assist educational practitioners and communities in "implementing evidence-based prevention and intervention programs that can make a difference in the lives of children and communities." (www.dsgonline.com)

The Guide's ratings are derived from four dimensions of program effectiveness:

+ conceptual framework of the program

+ program fidelity

+ evaluation design

+ empirical evidence demonstrating the prevention or reduction of problem behaviors, the reduction of risk factors, and the enhancement of protective factors.

Tribes is recognized as an OJJDP prevention program in the categories of:

+ academic skills enhancement

+ afterschool and recreation

+ classroom curricula

+ conflict resolution and interpersonal skills

+ leadership and youth development.

CSAP's Western CAPT

Tribes TLC® is recognized as a promising practice by the Center for Substance Abuse Prevention's Western CAPT (Centers for the Application of Prevention Technologies). Promising practices are programs and strategies that have quantitative data showing positive outcomes in preventing or delaying substance abuse over a period of time. Tribes Learning Communities is listed as a comprehensive practice that addresses both risk and protective factors in the areas of family, school, individual, peer, and community.

CSAP's WesternCAPT has identified guiding principles as recommendations on how to create effective prevention programs and to gauge the program's potential effectiveness. The guiding principles can also be used to design innovative programs and strategies that are appropriate to the community's needs.

Visit http://captus.samhsa.gov/western/western.cfm

Find Youth Info.Gov

Tribes Learning Communities is recognized in the evidence-based *Find Youth Info Program Directory*. The directory represents a collaborative effort of nine federal departments, including the U.S. Department of Education, Department of Justice, Department of Health and Human Services, Department of Housing and Urban Development, Office of National Drug Control Policy, and National and Community Service. (www.findyouthinfo.gov)

Tribes is recognized as a program that displays "a strong theoretical base and has been demonstrated to prevent delinquency and other child and youthful problems or reduce risk factors and enhance protective factors for them." The rating is based on evaluation studies and identifies the concepts of risk and protective factors as frameworks for effective programs.

Funding Sources for Tribes Implementation

Tribes TLC® has been implemented using a variety of grant and foundation funding sources with a focus on enhancing academic achievement, professional development, mentor teaching, beginning teacher training, developing leadership, safe and drug free schools, comprehensive school reform, alcohol, tobacco and other drug abuse prevention, violence and bullying prevention, conflict resolution and mediation, character education, service learning, small learning communities, alternative education, charter schools, youth development, delinquency prevention, community development, technology in education, English language acquisition, diversity, multi-cultural education, health, wellness and physical education.

Contact CenterSource for additional information and supporting documentation.

EVALUATION OF TRIBES LEARNING COMMUNITIES

Evaluation of Tribes Learning Community Schools has shown that:

- ✦ *Tribes TLC has a positive impact on classroom environment*

- ✦ *teachers spend less time managing student behavior*

- ✦ *students are less likely to be referred for disciplinary problems*

- ✦ *the Tribes process helps teachers address academic standards*

- ✦ *students in well-implemented classrooms score significantly higher on standardized tests than students from comparison groups*

- ✦ *teachers report increased staff collegiality and planning.*

WestEd conducted a 2-year evaluation of Tribes TLC that involved administering surveys in 13 schools and collecting standardized test results for 40 Tribes schools and 80 control schools. The evaluators found that:

- ✦ the Tribes TLC process was fully implemented

- ✦ Tribes was seen as a vehicle for facilitating continuous school improvement

- ✦ there was evidence of improved student inclusion, collaboration, respect for multicultural populations, sense of value, resiliency, and student engagement

- ✦ students and staff enjoyed safe and supportive classroom and school environments

- ✦ teachers and principals reported declines in student referrals and suspensions

- ✦ there was evidence of better classroom management and increased teacher collaboration and planning

- ✦ three-quarters of teachers reported that the Tribes process helped them to address academic standards and helped students master standards

- ✦ 2nd and 5th grade reading and math scores increased more in high-growth Tribes schools than in comparison schools.

The **School District of Beloit** in Wisconsin conducted a 3-year evaluation of the Tribes process that included more than 3,000 elementary and middle school students. Dr. Derick Kiger presented the study at the 2001 American Education Research Association Annual Meeting and earned the First Place Instructional Program Evaluation Award.

Evaluators found that:

+ 4th graders from Tribes classrooms where the program was well-implemented scored significantly higher on the CTBS than students from less well-implemented Tribes classrooms

+ sixty percent of the teachers reported that they spent less time managing student behavior because of the Tribes process.

In **Tulsa, Oklahoma,** Dr. Judith Holt used a randomized design to conduct an evaluation of the impact of Tribes on discipline referrals at a middle school. The study found that:

+ students based in Tribes classrooms were significantly less likely (27%) than non-Tribes students (73%) to be referred to the principal's or counselor's office for disciplinary problems of all types, including disruptive behavior, refusal to work or follow directions, and fighting.

The **Central Oahu School District** in the State of Hawaii conducted a study of 17 elementary schools that implemented the process of Tribes. The evaluators found that:

+ mutual respect was the most common practice for students and faculty.

Fifty-five classroom teachers and their students in **Spring Branch ISD** in Texas participated in a Tribes evaluation survey, which found that in Tribes classrooms:

+ teachers spent less time managing student behavior

+ teachers had more time for creative teaching

+ students saw new learning as "fun"

+ mutual respect was evidenced through behaviors

+ group behaviors changed even at bus stops as students began accepting more responsibility for their behavior.

MATERIALS FOR THE TRIBES LEARNING COMMUNITY

Reaching All by Creating Tribes Learning Communities
by Jeanne Gibbs
Item 100 $39.95

This 30th anniversary edition shows teachers how to reach students by developing a caring environment as the foundation for growth and learning. Material details how to teach essential collaborative skills, design interactive learning experiences, work with multiple learning styles, foster the development of resiliency, and support school community change. 2006.

Discovering Gifts in Middle School: Learning in a Caring Culture Called Tribes
by Jeanne Gibbs
Item 140 $39.95

This comprehensive book supports middle level schools to make adolescent developmental growth and learning the over-riding focus of the whole school community. The author presents a lively synthesis of a wealth of research studies and effective practices. The major emphasis on middle level schools becoming responsive to the contextual basis of adolescent development leads not only to greater achievement and success for students but a new spirit, energy and the discovery of gifts throughout the whole school community. 2001.

Engaging All by Creating High School Learning Communities
by Jeanne Gibbs and Teri Ushijima
Item 115 $39.95

This comprehensive and dynamic book provides the research-based pedagogy, concepts and strategies that are essential for engaging all by creating high school learning communities. The book includes critical indicators of the needs of 21st century youth and recommendations from the literature, including the National Association of Secondary School Principals (NASSP). Readers will explore the *most promising strategy* for substantive school improvement—that of building the capacity of school personnel to function as a *collegial learning community*. Readers will understand why and how to transform the culture, structures and pedagogy of the whole high school system to prepare today's students for the Era of Learning.

What Is It About Tribes? The Research-Based Components of the Developmental Process of Tribes Learning Communities
by Bonnie Benard
Item 110 $19.95

This enlightening book, by Bonnie Benard of WestEd, is an in-depth response to questions that educators have been asking for many years: "What is it about the process of 'Tribes' that makes it work so well in so many schools, cultures and countries? What is it that helps all kinds of students love learning?" The reader will discover why and how implementing the core components of the process of Tribes transforms people, classrooms and schools—not because the approach is a curriculum to be taught or a program to be replicated—but because it is an on-going student-centered active-learning process that everyone in a school lives daily and owns. The book will also prove to be invaluable in the writing of grants, and designing parent, community and district programs. 2005.

Energizer Box
Item 162 $24.95

This colorful desktop card file contains 101 tried and true energizers that are a great way to revitalize students throughout the day.

Guiding Your School Community
by Jeanne Gibbs
Item 130 $19.95
In this 110-page book written with school Administrator's in mind, you will learn why and how the positive Tribes culture will develop community throughout an entire educational system. You will gain an understanding of how to initiate, support and sustain the Tribes process over time. 1999.

Four Tribes TLC Videos on DVD
Item 150 $29.95
All of our most popular videos are contained on this one DVD.
1. Tribes, Learning for the 21st Century
2. Creating Futures of Promise
3. Tribes, A New Way of Learning

plus a FREE bonus video produced by the School District of Beloit, Wisconsin. (You can also view the Beloit video on the Tribes home page.)

Teaching Peace by Red Grammer
Item 154 (CD) $15.00
A delightful set of 10 songs written, sung and played by Red Grammer. This music supports the same caring principles and fun enjoyed in Tribes.

Teaching Peace Songbook and Teacher's Guide by Kathy Grammer
Item 155 $15.00
Features piano, guitar and vocal accompaniment to the Teaching Peace songs and contains activity and discussion ideas for each song. The guide also contains a bibliography of over 100 books that relate to the themes of the songs. 1993, 85 pages.

Tribes Buttons and Magnets
(2 ¼ inches)
Item 165E   English (50 Buttons) $20.00
Item 165H   Hawaiian (50 Buttons) $20.00
Item 165S   Spanish (50 Buttons) $20.00
Item 166   (25 Magnets) $20.00
Assorted Tribes buttons in English, Spanish or Hawaiian. We also put the agreements on a flexi-magnet for your kids to take home for the fridge. Great for the whole school, parent nights, Tribes Celebration days, and just for fun.

The Tribes Assessment Kit: Reflecting on the Tribes TLC® Process
Item 400 $75.00
The Tribes Assessment Kit will help your school strengthen its implementation of the process and assess outcomes. The Kit includes four process assessment instruments and complete directions for use throughout classrooms of the school.

MAIL, FAX, OR PHONE IN YOUR ORDER TODAY! OR ORDER ONLINE AT: WWW.TRIBES.COM

CenterSource Systems, LLC, 7975 Cameron Drive, #500, Windsor, CA 95492
Phone: 800-810-1701   707-838-1061   Fax: 707-838-1062

TRIBES TLC® MATERIALS ORDER FORM

ITEM NO.	DESCRIPTION	PRICE	QTY	COST
Books				
100	*Reaching All by Creating Tribes Learning Communities* by Jeanne Gibbs	$39.95		
110	*What Is It About Tribes?* by Bonnie Benard	$19.95		
115	*Engaging All by Creating High School Learning Communities* by Gibbs/Ushijima	$39.95		
130	*Guiding Your School Community* by Jeanne Gibbs (Tribes Administrators book)	$19.95		
140	*Discovering Gifts in Middle School* by Jeanne Gibbs	$39.95		
142	*Student Journal—Teacher Manual*	$15.00		
143	*Student Journal*	$ 6.00		
145	*Cooperative Learning* by Spencer Kagan	$35.00		
147	*Silly Sports & Goofy Games* by Spencer Kagan	$25.00		
400	*Tribes TLC® Assessment Kit*	$75.00		
A/V: Audio and Video				
150	*DVD—All four Tribes Videos on one DVD*	$29.95		
154	*Teaching Peace* (CD) by Red Grammer	$15.00		
155	*Teaching Peace Song Book & Teacher's Guide* by Kathy Grammer	$15.00		
Fun Stuff: Posters, Buttons, Cards and More				
162	*Energizer Box* (desktop card file with 101 Energizers)	$24.95		
163	*Bookmarks with Agreements*—50 per pack	$ 5.00		
166	*Magnets* (Bag of 25) Agreements on Flexi-Magnets	$20.00		
185	*Poster—Tribes Agreements* (19" x 25")	$ 7.95		
186	*Poster—Tribes Trail* (19" x 25")	$ 7.95		
187	*Posters—Set of Four Agreements Posters—Elementary Design* (19" x 25" each)	$15.95		
188	*Posters—Set of Four Agreements Posters—Middle/High Design* (19" x 25" each)	$15.95		
179	*Lanyards—Tribes Learning Community*	$ 2.00		
175	*Tribes Book Bag* (15" L x 12" H)	$14.95		
165	*Tribes Buttons Assorted* (2¼ inches) Bag of 50 ❏ English ❏ Spanish ❏ Hawaiian	$20.00		
173	*Tribes Postcards* (Pack of 50) ❏ English ❏ Spanish	$10.00		

METHOD OF PAYMENT

Check enclosed for $_____

❏ MasterCard ❏ VISA ❏ Am. Express

#_____

Exp. Date: MM/YY _____ /_____

Purchase Order # _____

Please attach purchase order to this form

SHIPPING RATES:	CONTINENTAL USA	HI, AK & CANADA
Order under $25.00	= $8	= $10
$25.00–$74.99	= $9	= $14
$75.00–$124.99	= $10	= $18
$125.00–$349.99	= 10%	= 15%
$350 or more	= 8%	= 14%

All shipping is via UPS ground or USPS Priority Mail
Call for international or rush shipping rates.

* California residents: include sales tax for your county

SUBTOTAL	
SHIPPING	
SALES TAX*	
TOTAL	

SOLD TO: NAME _____

ORGANIZATION _____

ADDRESS _____

CITY/STATE/ZIP _____

DAY PHONE _____

SHIP TO: NAME _____

ORGANIZATION _____

ADDRESS _____

CITY/STATE/ZIP _____

DAY PHONE _____

15 Appendix

15 Appendix

NOTES

Preface

1. Barth, R. S. (2001). *Learning by heart.* San Francisco, CA: Jossey-Bass, p.xiv.

2. National Institute of Mental Health. (2001). *Teenage brain—A work in progress: A brief overview of research into brain development during adolescence.* Bethesda, MD: National Institute of Mental Health.

   Pert, C. B. (1997). *Molecules of emotion: The science behind body-mind medicine.* New York, NY: Simon and Schuster.

   Taubeneck, A. (2006, Summer). The millennials: Today's students are always on. *Northwestern University Magazine.*

3. Benard, B. (2005). *What is it about Tribes? The research-based components of the developmental process of Tribes Learning Communities.* Windsor, CA: CenterSource Systems. (Available at 800-810-1701 or www.tribes.com.)

Chapter 1: A New Pattern of Interaction

1. The data in this illustration is from:

   Grunbaum, J., Kann, L., Kinchen, S., Ross, J., Lowrey, R., Harris, W. et al. (2004). Youth risk behavior surveillance – United States. *Morbidity and Mortality Weekly Surveillance Summaries, 53* (SS-2), pp. 1–100.

   Handel, M. J. (2005). *Worker skills and job requirements: Is there a mismatch?* Washington, DC: Economic Policy Institute.

   Bridgeland, J., Dilulio, Jr., J., & Morison, K. B. *The silent epidemic: Perspectives on high school dropout students.* A report by Civic Enterprises in association with Peter D. Hart Associates for the Bill and Melinda Gates Foundation.

2. Weissberg, R., Devaney, E., Utne O'Brien, M., Resnik, H., & Keister, S. (2006). *Sustainable schoolwide social and emotional learning (SEL) implementation guide.* Chicago, IL: Collaborative for Academic, Social and Emotional Learning (CASEL), p.11.

3. Grunbaum et al, 2004.

4. Benson, P., Scales, P., & Roehlkepartain, F. (1999). *A fragile foundation: The state of developmental assets among American youth.* Minneapolis, MN: Search Institute.

5. David and Roger Johnson's extensive work has been an immense contribution to the development of cooperative learning and the process of Tribes Learning Communities. The benefits of cooperation in education were initially summarized in their book (1989) *Cooperation and competi-*

tion, theory and research. Edina, MN: Interaction Book Company; and in subsequent publications such as: (1995) Cooperative learning and individual student achievement. In *Secondary schools and cooperative learning: Theories, models and strategies.* New York, NY: Garland Publishing.

6. Johnson & Johnson, 1989.

7. Steele, C. M. (1992, April). Race and schooling of Black Americans. *Atlantic Monthly,* p. 75. According to Steele, Philip Treisman, calculus professor at the University of California, Berkeley, offers evidence that cooperative effort is more likely to achieve excellence than is individual effort. In the typical competitive university setting, Treisman's African American students consistently were at the bottom of every calculus class. After he started using cooperative learning groups in which students had regular opportunity for study together, these same students "reversed their fortunes, causing them to outperform their white and Asian counterparts." In fact everyone's scores became higher.

8. The name "Tribes" has never denoted Native American tribes or any particular indigenous tribe. The term came into usage when teachers began to refer to their experience in the Tribes process as caring and supportive. They connected the sense of community that evolved to what they imagined tribal communities were like.

9. Senge, P. (1991, October). The learning organization made plain. *Training and Development,* p. 38.

10. Kohn, A. (1993, September). Choices for children: Why and how to let students decide. *Phi Delta Kappan Magazine, 75* (1), pp. 8–19. The Shelley Berman side bar quote cited by Kohn is from Berman, S. (1990). The real ropes course: The development of social consciousness. *ESR Journal,* p. 2.

11. Kohn, 1993, p. 12.

Chapter 2: Finding Our Way to the Future

1. Grieder, W. (1992). Stand and deliver: Alternatives within public schools. *Utne Reader,* Nov/Dec, p. 76.

2. Secretary's Commission on Achieving Necessary Skills. (1999). *SCANS report for America 2000: What work requires of schools.* U.S. Department of Labor.

3. SCANS, 1999.

4. Weissberg, R., Devaney, E., Utne O'Brien, M., Resnik, H., & Keister, S. (2006). *Sustainable schoolwide social and emotional learning (SEL) implementation guide.* Chicago, IL: CASEL, p.11.

5. Weissberg et al, 2006, p.12

6. Cited by Hodgkinson, H. (1990) of the Institute for Educational Leadership in a paper titled, *Guess who's coming to work*. Presented at the Education and Work Conference, Northwest Regional Educational Laboratory, Portland, OR.

7. Nakagawa, Mako. (1986). *Cooperative pluralism and public schools*. Olympia, WA: Office of Superintendent of Public Instruction, p. 2.

8. Benard, B. (1991). *Moving toward a just and vital culture: Multiculturalism in our schools*. Portland, OR: Western Regional Center for Drug Free Schools and Communities, Northwest Regional Educational Laboratory, p. 9.

9. The fine phrase "habits of the heart" is credited to Robert Bellah, Professor of Sociology, University of California, Berkeley, author (1985) of *Habits of the heart: Individualism and commitment in American life*. New York, NY: Perennial Library, Harper & Row.

Chapter 3: The Research-Based Components of Tribes Learning Communities

1. Comer, J. (1999). *Child by child: The Comer process for change in education*. New York, NY: Teachers College Press.

2. Comer, 1999.

   Darling-Hammond, L. (1997). *The right to learn: A blueprint for creating schools that work*. San Francisco, CA: Jossey-Bass.

   Meier, D. (1995). *The power of their ideas: Lessons for America from a small school in Harlem*. Boston, MA: Beacon Press.

3. Dewey, J. (1956). *The child and the curriculum and the child and society*. Chicago, IL: University of Chicago Press.

   Johnson, D., Johnson, R. & Smith, K. (1995). Cooperative learning and individual student achievement. In *Secondary schools and cooperative learning: Theories, models and strategies*. New York, NY: Garland Publishing.

   Gay, G. (2000). *Culturally responsive teaching: Theory, research and practice*. New York, NY: Teachers College Press, Columbia University.

   Goodlad, J. (1997). *In praise of education*. New York, NY: Teachers College Press, Columbia University.

   Wheelock, A. (1998). *Safe to be smart: Building a culture for standards-based reform in the middle grades*. National Middle School Association.

4. Fullan, M. (2001). *Leading in a culture of change*. San Francisco, CA: Jossey-Bass.

5. Fullan, M. (1994). *Turning systemic thinking on its head*. U.S. Department of Education.

   Werner, E. & Smith, R. (1989). *Vulnerable but invincible: A longitudinal study of resilient children and youth*. New York, NY: Adams, Bannister and Cox.

   Bruner, J. (1996). *The culture of education*. Cambridge, MA: Harvard University.

   Gay, 2000.

   Meier, 1995.

6. Benard, B. (1991). *Fostering resiliency in kids: Protective factors in families, schools and community*. Portland, OR: Western Regional Center for Drug Free Schools and Communities, Northwest Regional Educational Laboratory.

   Benard, B. (2005). *Resiliency: What we have learned*. San Francisco, CA: West Ed.

7. Bruner, 1996.

   Fosnot, C. (1996). Constructivism: A psychological theory of learning. In *Constructivism: Theory, perspectives and practice*. New York, NY: Teachers College Press.

   Bruner, 1996.

8. Darling-Hammond, 1997.

9. Fosnot, 1996.

10. Gardner, H. (1999). *Intelligence reframed: Multiple intelligences for the 21st century*. New York, NY: Basic Books.

    Jensen, E. (1998). *Teaching with the brain in mind*. Alexandria, VA: Association for Supervision and Curriculum Development.

    Johnson, D. & Johnson, R. (1989). *Cooperation and competition: Theory and research*. Edina, MN: Interaction Book Company.

    Caine, G. & Caine, R. (1991). *Making connections: Teaching and the human brain*. Alexandria, VA: Association for Supervision and Curriculum Development.

Chapter 4: A Perspective on Children's Development

1. Bronfenbrenner, U. (1979). *The ecology of human development: Experiments by nature and design*. Cambridge, MA, p. 9.

2. Halverson, C. & Waldrup, M. (1974). Relations between preschool barrier behaviors and early school: Measures of coping, imagination and verbal development. *Developmental Psychology, 10*, pp. 716–720.

3. This chart is based on a synthesis of stages described by child development theorists Jean Piaget and Erik Erikson. The "implications" column evolved out of many years of many teachers' experience and common sense.

4. Benard, B. (1991). *Fostering resiliency in kids: Protective factors in the family, school and community.* Portland, OR: Western Regional Center for Drug Free Schools and Communities, Northwest Regional Educational Laboratory, pp. 1–20. The primary researchers cited in Benard's documents are Norman Garmezy, Michael Rutter, and Emily Werner.

Some of the source documents are:

Garmezy, N. (1991). Resiliency and vulnerability to adverse developmental outcomes associated with poverty. *American Behavioral Scientist, 34*(4), pp. 416–430.

Garmezy, N. & Rutter, M. (1983, Nov). How and why do some kids flourish against all odds? *Behavior Today,* pp. 5–7.

Rutter, M. (1979). Protective factors in children: Responses to stress and disadvantage. *Primary Prevention of Psychopathology, 3.*

Werner, E. & Smith, R. (1989). *Vulnerable but invincible: A longitudinal study of resilient children and youth.* New York, NY: Adams, Bannister, and Cox.

5. Benard, B. (1993). Resiliency requires changing hearts and minds. *Western Center News,* Portland, OR: Western Center for Drug Free Schools and Communities, Northwest Regional Educational Laboratory, p. 4.

6. Weissberg, R., Devaney, E., Utne O'Brien, M., Resnik, H., & Keister, S. (2006). *Sustainable schoolwide social and emotional learning (SEL) implementation guide.* Chicago, IL: Collaborative for Academic, Social and Emotional Learning.

7. Citing David and Roger Johnson's summary of studies in (1989) *Cooperation and competition: Theory and research.* Edina, MN: Interaction Book Company, pp. 169–179.

8. Miller, R. (1990). What are schools for? *Holistic education in American culture.* Brandon, VT: Holistic Education Press.

9. Wolins, M. & Wozner, Y. (1982). *Revitalizing residential settings: Problems and potential in education.* San Francisco, CA: Health, Rehabilitation and Social Services, Jossey Bass Publishers, p. 10.

10. Bronfenbrenner, 1979.

Chapter 5: How Children Learn

1. *Wall Street Journal.* (1992, Sept 11). Digging for knowledge. *Wall Street Journal.*

2. Hertz-Lazarowitz, R. & Shachar, H. (1990, Dec). Changes in teachers' verbal behavior in cooperative classrooms. *Cooperative learning, 11*(2), pp. 13–14.

3. Hertz-Lazarowitz & Shachar, p. 13.

4. Von Oech, R. (1990). *A whack on the side of the head: How you can be more creative.* New York, NY: Warner Books, p. 24.

5. Schneider, S. (1993, April). A better way to learn. World *Monitor,* p. 32.

6. The article, *Gender gaps: Where schools fail our children,* was commissioned by the American Association of University Women as a follow-up to *How Schools Shortchange Girls* (1991). The updated study was researched by the American Institutes of Research (1998).

7. Miller, R. (1990). *What are schools for? Holistic education in American culture.* Brandon, VT: Holistic Education Press.

8. Gardner, H. (1999). *Intelligence reframed: Multiple intelligences for the 21st century.* New York, NY: Basic Books.

9. David L. (1989). *Seven ways of teaching: The artistry of teaching with multiple intelligences.* Palatine, IL: Skylight Publishing Company, p. 109.

10. Stoddard, L. (1992). *Redesigning education: A guide for developing human greatness.* Tucson, AZ: Zephyr Press.

11. Kotulak, R. (1997). I*nside the brain: Revolutionary discoveries of how the mind works.* Andrews & McMeel.

12. Jensen, E. (1998). *Teaching with the brain in mind.* Association for Supervision and Curriculum Development.

Caine, G. & Caine, R. (1994). *Making connections: Teaching and the human brain.* Addison-Wesley Publishing.

Pert, C. (1997). *Molecules of emotion: The science behind mind-body medicine.* New York, NY: Simon and Schuster.

13. Pert, 1997.

14. The nine principles for student-centered active learning are based on:

Barbara L. McCombs' original work, *Twelve learner-centered psychological principles.* Midwest Center Educational Laboratory.

Learner-Centered Work Group. (1997). *Learner-centered principles: A framework for school redesign and reform.* Board of Education Affairs, American Psychological Association.

Duffy, T. & Jonassen, D. (Eds.). (1992). *Constructivism and the technology of instruction.* Hillsdale, NJ: Lawrence Erlbaum Associates.

Chapter 6: What Tribes Are and How They Work

1. Wells, G. (1996). *Dialogic inquiry in education: Building the legacy of Lev Vygotsky.* Toronto, Canada: Ontario Institute for Studies in Education, University of Toronto.

2. Two significant research reports led to the practice in Tribes of advocating long-term membership groups: Lott, A. & Lott, B. (1966, April). Group cohesiveness and individual learning. *Journal of Educational Psychology, 57,* pp. 61–72.

   Fox, R., Luszki, M. & Schmuck, R. (1966). *Social relations in the classroom: Diagnosing learning environments.* Chicago, IL: SRA, Inc.

   The validity has been sustained repeatedly since then.

3. McKnight, J. (1992, Jul/Aug). Are social service agencies the enemy of community? *Utne Reader,* pp. 89.

4. McKnight, 1992, pp. 89–90.

Chapter 7: Creating The Learning Community

1. Yager, S., Johnson, R., & Johnson, D. (1985). Oral discussion: Group to individual transfer, and achievement in cooperative learning groups. *Journal of Educational Psychology, 77,* pp. 60–66.

   Yager, S., Johnson, R., Johnson, D., & Snider, B. (1986). The impact of group processing on achievement in cooperative learning groups. *The Journal of Social Psychology, 126,* pp. 389–397.

2. We appreciate the permission to use this poem written by Gilbert Rees of Ontario, Canada. The poem is contained in an article by Miller, J. & Drake, S. (1990, Fall). Implementing a holistic curriculum. *Holistic Education Review,* p. 30.

Chapter 8: Building Tribes

1. Senge, P. (1991). *The art and practice of the learning community.* New York, NY: Doubleday/Currency.

2. Kohn, A. (1996). *Beyond discipline: From compliance to community.* Alexandria, VA: Association for Supervision and Curriculum Development, pp. 76–77.

3. The Conflict Resolution Program of the San Francisco Community Board trains students as conflict managers for their schools. Elementary and secondary school curriculum has been published.

Chapter 9: Calling Forth Power and Self Worth

1. Sapon-Shevin, M., & Schniedewind, N. (1991). Cooperative learning as empowering pedagogy. *Empowerment from Multicultural Education,* SUNY Press.

2. Sapon-Shevin & Schniedewind, 1991.

Chapter 10: Designing And Implementing Learning Experiences

1. Zins, J., Weissberg, R., Wang, M., & Walberg, H. (Eds). (2004). *Building academic success on social and emotional learning: What does the research say?* New York, NY: Teachers College Press.

2. Johnson, D., Johnson, R. & Smith, K. (1995). Cooperative learning and individual student achievement. In *Secondary schools and cooperative learning: Theories, models and strategies.* Pedersen, J. & Digby, A. (Eds.). New York, NY: Garland Publishing.

3. Weissberg, R., Devaney, E., Utne O'Brien, M., Resnik, H., & Keister, S. (2006). *Sustainable schoolwide social and emotional learning (SEL) implementation guide.* Chicago, IL: CASEL, p.11.

4. Weissberg et al., 2006, p.18.

5. Weissberg et al., 2006, p.19.

6. Freire, P. (1970). *Pedagogy of the oppressed.* New York, NY: Herder and Herder.

7. Franklin, U. (1996). Introduction to the symposium, Towards an Ecology of Knowledge, University of Toronto. As reported by Gordon Wells (1996) in *Dialogic inquiry in education: Building on the legacy of Vygotsky.* Toronto, Ontario: Ontario Institute for Studies in Education, University of Toronto, p. 16.

8. Brooks, J. & Brooks, R. (1993). *In search for understanding: The case for constructionist classrooms.* Alexandria, VA: Association for Supervision and Curriculum Development.

9. Brooks, 1993.

10. Bybee, R. (1997). Constructivism and the five E's. *The Biological Science Curriculum Study,* Miami Museum of Science. Internet document: www.miamisci.org.

11. Johnson, D. & Johnson, R. (1989). *Cooperation and competition: Theory and research.* Edina, MN: Interaction Book Company.

12. Stoddard, L. (1992). *Redesigning education: A guide for developing greatness.* Tucson, AZ: Zepher Press.

13. Brady, M. (1989). *What's worth teaching? Selecting, organizing and integrating knowledge.* New York State University Press.

14. Brady, 1989.

15. Lazear, D. (1991). *Seven ways of teaching: The artistry of teaching with multiple intelligences.* Palatine, IL: Skylight Publishing.

16. Armstrong, T. (1999). *7 kinds of smart: Identifying and developing your multiple intelligences.* New York, NY: Penguin Putnam.

17. Gardner, H. (1999). *Intelligence reframed: Multiple intelligences for the 21st century.* New York, NY: Basic Books.

18. Yager, S., Johnson, R., Johnson, D., & Snider, B. (1986). The impact of group processing on achievement in cooperative learning groups. *The Journal of Social Psychology, 126,* pp. 389-397.

19. The questions are based on Selma Wassermann's (1992) booklet, *Asking the right questions: The essence of teaching.* Bloomington, IN: Phi Delta Kappan Educational Foundation, pp. 10–17.

20. Wassermann, 1992, pp. 10–17.

21. Duckworth, E. (1997). *The having of wonderful ideas on teaching and learning.* New York, NY: Teachers College Press.

Chapter 11: Working With People Big and Small

1. To the best of the author's knowledge, the Flatland story comes from a small book entitled "Flatland" written in the 1880s by a mathematician named Abbott. It has been used for more than 100 years to illustrate the difficulty of conveying the impact of a meaningful or powerful experience to others who have not as yet lived it.

2. Lounsbury, J. H. (1992). Perspectives on the middle school movement. In *Perspectives and possibilities.* Judith Irvin (Ed.). Boston, MA: Allyn and Bacon.

3. Cited by: Koochan, F. K. (1992). A new paradigm of schooling: Connecting school, home and community in transforming middle school education. In *Perspectives and possibilities.* Judith Irvin (Ed.). Boston, MA: Allyn and Bacon.

4. Beane, J. (1992). Middle school curriculum from rhetoric to reality. In *Perspectives and possibilities.* Judith Irvin (Ed.). Boston, MA: Allyn and Bacon.

5. Carnegie Council on Adolescent Development. (1989). *Turning points: Preparing American youth for the 21st century.* New York, NY: Carnegie Corporation of New York.

6. Johnson, R. & Johnson, D. (1986). Mainstreaming and cooperative learning groups. *Exceptional Children, 52,* pp. 553–561.

7. Johnson, R., Johnson, D., Scott, L., & Ramolae, R. (1985). Effects of single sex and mixed-sex cooperative interaction on science achievement and attitudes and cross-handicap and cross-sex relationships. *Journal of Research in Science Teaching, 22,* pp. 207–220.

8. Alberg, J., Eller, S., Petry, C., Nero, B. (1994). *Resource guide for social skills.* Researched and compiled under the contract, Approaches and choices to developing social competence in students with disabilities. Research Triangle Institute and the U.S. Department of Education. Longmount, CO: Sopers Publishers.

Elementary and Middle Schools Technical Assistance Center. (2001). *Programs that facilitate access for children with disabilities in inclusive settings.* Washington, DC: Elementary and Middle Schools Technical Assistance Center (EMSTAC). http://www.emstac.org/registered/topics/inclusion/productreviews.htm.

Research Triangle Institute. (1994). *Promising classroom interventions for students with attention deficit disorder.* Research Triangle Park, NC: Research Triangle Institute and Office of Special Education Programs, U.S. Department of Education.

9. David Christiano's quote can be found in Olsen, L. (1990). Embracing diversity: Teacher's voices from California classrooms. San Francisco, CA: *California Tomorrow Immigrant Students Project Research Reports.*

10. *Time.* (2006, April). Drop Out Nation. *Time, 167*(16), pp. 30-40.

Orfield, G. (Ed.). (2004). *Dropouts in America: Confronting the graduation rate crisis.* Cambridge, MA: Harvard Education Press.

11. National Association of Secondary School Principals. (2004). *Breaking ranks II: Strategies for leading high school reform.* Reston, VA: National Association of Secondary School Principals.

424   REACHING ALL BY CREATING TRIBES LEARNING COMMUNITIES

Chapter 12: Bringing It All Together

1. Rogers, E. (1988). Diffusion of the idea Beyond War. *BreakThrough: Emerging new thinking.* New York, NY: Walker & Co., pp. 240–248.

2. Senge, P. (1991). *The fifth discipline: The art and practice of learning communities.* Double Day/Currency.

3. Johnson, D., Johnson, R. & Smith, K. (1995). *Cooperative learning and individual student achievement in secondary schools.* Edina, MN: International Book Company.

4. The quote by Marc Tucker of the National Center on Education and the Economy is contained in Edward Fiske's book (1991), *Smart schools, smart kids.* New York, NY: Simon & Schuster, p. 259.

5. Florin, P. & Chavis, D. (1990, May). *Community prevention and substance abuse prevention.* San Jose, CA: Bureau of Drug Abuse Services, County of Santa Clara.

6. These recommendations are from Joyce, B. (1991/1992, Winter). Cooperative learning and staff development: Teaching the method with method. *Cooperative Learning, 12*(12), pp. 10–13.

7. Anne Henderson, an associate with the National Committee for Education has cited forty-nine studies showing a positive correlation between family school collaboration and gains in student achievement. Cited in Edward Fiske's book (1991), *Smart schools, smart kids.* New York, NY: Simon & Schuster, p. 232.

8. The quote by Dr. James Comer is also cited in Fiske, 1991, p. 209.

History of Tribes

1. Gibbs, J. (2001). *Tribes: A new way of learning and being together.* Windsor, CA: CenterSource Systems.

2. Gibbs, J. (2006). *Reaching All by Creating Tribes Learning Communities.* Windsor, CA: CenterSource Systems.

3. Alberg, J., Eller, S., & Petry, C. (1994). *A resource guide for social skills instruction.* Longmount, CO: Center for Research in Education, Research Triangle Institute, Sopers Publishers.

4. Newkumet, M. & Casserly, M. (1994). *Urban school safety: Strategies of the great city schools.* Washington, DC: Council of the Great City Schools.

5. Gibbs, J. (2001). *Discovering gifts in middle school: Learning in a caring culture called Tribes.* Windsor, CA: CenterSource Systems.

6. Collaborative for Academic, Social and Emotional Learning (CASEL). (2003). *Safe and sound: An education leader's guide to evidence-based social and emotional learning programs.* Chicago, Illinois: CASEL, University of Illinois. www.casel.org

7. Office of Juvenile Justice Delinquency Prevention (OJJDP). (2005). *Model programs guide.* Washington, DC: OJJDP, Department of Justice. www.ojjdp.ncjrs.gov

8. Benard, B. (2005). *What is it about Tribes? The research-based components of the developmental process of Tribes Learning Communities.* Windsor, CA: CenterSource Systems. www.tribes.com

9. Gibbs, J. and Ushijima, T. (2008). *Engaging All by Creating High School Learning Communities.* Windsor, CA: CenterSource Systems. www.tribes.com

BIBLIOGRAPHY

Alberg, J., Eller, S., Petry, C., Nero, B. (1994). Resource guide for social skills. *Approaches and choices to developing social competence in students with disabilities.* Longmount, CO: Research Triangle Institute, Sopers Publishers.

American Association of University Women. (1998). *Gender gaps: Where schools fail our children.* American Institutes of Research.

Armstrong, T. (1999). *7 kinds of smart: Identifying and developing your multiple intelligences.* New York, NY: Penguin Putnam.

Barth, R. S. (2001). *Learning by heart.* San Francisco, CA: Jossey-Bass.

Beane, J. (1992). Middle school curriculum from rhetoric to reality. In *Perspectives and possibilities.* Judith Irvin (Ed.). Boston, MA: Allyn and Bacon.

Bellah, R. (1985). *Habits of the heart: Individualism and commitment in American life.* New York, NY: Perennial Library, Harper & Row.

Benard, B. (1991). *Fostering resiliency in kids: Protective factors in families, schools and community.* Portland, OR: Western Regional Center for Drug Free Schools and Communities, Northwest Regional Educational Laboratory.

Benard, B. (1991). *Moving toward a just and vital culture: Multiculturalism in our schools.* Portland, OR: Western Regional Center for Drug Free Schools and Communities, Northwest Regional Educational Laboratory.

Benard, B. (1993). Resiliency requires changing hearts and minds. *Western Center News,* Portland, OR: Western Center for Drug Free Schools and Communities, Northwest Regional Educational Laboratory, p. 4.

Benard, B. (2005). *Resiliency: What we have learned.* San Francisco, CA: West Ed.

Benard, B. (2005). *What is it about Tribes? The research-based components of the developmental process of Tribes Learning Communities.* Windsor, CA: CenterSource Systems.

Benson, P., Scales, P., & Roehlkepartain, F. (1999). *A fragile foundation: The state of developmental assets among American youth.* Minneapolis, MN: Search Institute.

Berman, S. (1990). The real ropes course: The development of social consciousness. *ESR Journal,* p. 2.

Brady, M. (1989). *What's worth teaching? Selecting, organizing and integrating knowledge.* New York State University Press.

Bridgeland, J., Dilulio, Jr., J., & Morison, K. B. *The silent epidemic: Perspectives on high school dropout students.* Civic Enterprises & Peter D. Hart Associates, Bill and Melinda Gates Foundation.

Bronfenbrenner, U. (1979). *The ecology of human development: Experiments by nature and design.* Cambridge, MA.

Brooks, J. & Brooks, R. (1993). *In search for understanding: The case for constructionist classrooms.* Alexandria, VA: Association for Supervision and Curriculum Development.

Brown, J. & Isaacs, D. (Dec 1996/ Jan 1997). Conversation as a core business process. *The Systems Thinker,* Pegasus Communications, Inc.

Bruner, J. (1996). *The culture of education.* Cambridge, MA: Harvard University.

Bybee, R. (1997). Constructivism and the five E's. *The biological science curriculum study.* Miami Museum of Science. Internet document: www.miamisci.org.

Caine, G. & Caine, R. (1991). *Making connections: Teaching and the human brain.* Alexandria, VA: Association for Supervision and Curriculum Development.

Caine, G. & Caine, R. (1994). *Making connections: Teaching and the human brain.* Addison-Wesley Publishing.

Carnegie Council on Adolescent Development. (1989). *Turning points: Preparing American youth for the 21st century.* New York, NY: Carnegie Corporation of New York.

Comer, J. (1999). *Child by child: The Comer process for change in education.* New York, NY: Teachers College Press.

Darling-Hammond, L. (1997). *The right to learn: A blueprint for creating schools that work.* San Francisco, CA: Jossey-Bass.

David L. (1989). *Seven ways of teaching: The artistry of teaching with multiple intelligences.* Palatine, IL: Skylight Publishing Company.

Dewey, J. (1956). *The child and the curriculum and the child and society.* Chicago, IL: University of Chicago Press.

Duckworth, E. (1997). *The having of wonderful ideas on teaching and learning.* New York, NY: Teachers College Press.

Duffy, T. & Jonassen, D. (Eds.). (1992). *Constructivism and the technology of instruction.* Hillsdale, NJ: Lawrence Erlbaum Associates.

Elementary and Middle Schools Technical Assistance Center. (2001). *Programs that facilitate access for children with disabilities in inclusive settings.* Washington, DC: Elementary and Middle Schools Technical Assistance Center (EMSTAC). http://www.emstac.org/registered/topics/inclusion/productreviews.htm.

Fiske, E. (1991). *Smart schools, smart kids.* New York, NY: Simon & Schuster.

Florin, P. & Chavis, D. M. (1990, May). *Community prevention and substance abuse prevention.* San Jose, CA: Bureau of Drug Abuse Services, County of Santa Clara.

Fosnot, C. (1996). Constructivism: A psychological theory of learning. In *Constructivism: Theory, perspectives and practice.* New York, NY: Teachers College Press.

Fox, R., Luszki, M. & Schmuck, R. (1966). *Social relations in the classroom: Diagnosing learning environments.* Chicago, IL: SRA, Inc.

Franklin, U. (1996). Introduction to the symposium, Towards an ecology of knowledge. In Wells, G. (1996) *Dialogic inquiry in education: Building on the legacy of Vygotsky.* Toronto, Ontario: Ontario Institute for Studies in Education, University of Toronto.

Freire, P. (1970). *Pedagogy of the oppressed.* New York, NY: Herder and Herder.

Fullan, M. (1994). *Turning systemic thinking on its head.* U.S. Department of Education.

Fullan, M. (2001). *Leading in a culture of change.* San Francisco, CA: Jossey-Bass.

Gardner, H. (1999). *Intelligence reframed: Multiple intelligences for the 21st century.* New York, NY: Basic Books.

Garmezy, N. & Rutter, M. (1983, Nov). How and why do some kids flourish against all odds? *Behavior Today,* pp. 5–7.

Garmezy, N. (1991). Resiliency and vulnerability to adverse developmental outcomes associated with poverty. *American Behavioral Scientist, 34*(4), pp. 416–430.

Gay, G. (2000). *Culturally responsive teaching: Theory, research and practice.* New York, NY: Teachers College Press, Columbia University.

Goodlad, J. (1997). *In praise of education.* New York, NY: Teachers College Press, Columbia University.

Grieder, W. (1992, Nov/Dec). Stand and deliver: Alternatives within public schools. *Utne Reader,* p. 76.

Grunbaum, J., Kann, L., Kinchen, S., Ross, J., Lowrey, R., Harris, W. et al. (2004). Youth risk behavior surveillance – United States. *Morbidity and Mortality Weekly Surveillance Summaries, 53* (SS-2), pp. 1–100.

Halverson, C. & Waldrup, M. (1974). Relations between pre-school barrier behaviors and early school: Measures of coping, imagination and verbal development. *Developmental Psychology, 10,* pp. 716–720.

Handel, M. J. (2005). *Worker skills and job requirements: Is there a mismatch?* Washington, DC: Economic Policy Institute.

Hertz-Lazarowitz, R. & Shachar, H. (1990, Dec). Changes in teachers' verbal behavior in cooperative classrooms. *Cooperative learning, 11*(2), pp. 13–14.

Hodgkinson, H. (1990). *Guess who's coming to work.* Presented at the Education and Work Conference, Northwest Regional Educational Laboratory, Portland, OR.

Jensen, E. (1998). *Teaching with the brain in mind.* Alexandria, VA: Association for Supervision and Curriculum Development.

Johnson, D. & Johnson, R. (1989). *Cooperation and competition: Theory and research.* Edina, MN: Interaction Book Company.

Johnson, D., Johnson, R. & Smith, K. (1995). Cooperative learning and individual student achievement. In *Secondary schools and cooperative learning: Theories, models and strategies.* Pedersen, J. & Digby, A. (Eds.). New York, NY: Garland Publishing.

Johnson, R.T. & Johnson, D.W. (1986). Mainstreaming and cooperative learning groups. *Exceptional Children, 52,* pp. 553–561.

Johnson, R.T., Johnson, D.W., Scott, L.E., & Ramolae, R.A. (1985). Effects of single sex and mixed-sex cooperative interaction on science achievement and attitudes and cross-handicap and cross-sex relationships. *Journal of Research in Science Teaching, 22,* pp. 207–220.

Joyce, B. R. (1991/1992, Winter). Cooperative learning and staff development: Teaching the method with method. *Cooperative Learning Magazine, 12*(12), pp. 10–13.

Kohn, A. (1993, September). Choices for children: Why and how to let students decide. *Phi Delta Kappan Magazine, 75* (1), pp. 8–19.

Kohn, A. (1996). *Beyond discipline: From compliance to community.* Alexandria, VA: Association for Supervision and Curriculum Development.

Koochan, F. K. (1992). A new paradigm of schooling: Connecting school, home and community in transforming middle school education. In *Perspectives and possibilities.* Judith Irvin (Ed.). Boston, MA: Allyn and Bacon.

Kotulak, R. (1997). *Inside the brain: Revolutionary discoveries of how the mind works.* Andrews & McMeel.

Lazear, D. (1991). *Seven ways of teaching: The artistry of teaching with multiple intelligences.* Palatine, IL: Skylight Publishing.

Learner-Centered Work Group. (1997). *Learner-centered principles: A framework for school redesign and reform.* Board of Education Affairs, American Psychological Association.

Lott, A. & Lott, B. (1966, April). Group cohesiveness and individual learning. *Journal of Educational Psychology, 57,* pp. 61–72.

Lounsbury, J. H. (1992). Perspectives on the middle school movement. In *Perspectives and possibilities.* Judith Irvin (Ed.). Boston, MA: Allyn and Bacon.

McCombs, B. *Twelve learner-centered psychological principles.* Midwest Center Educational Laboratory.

McKnight, J. (1992, Jul/Aug). Are social service agencies the enemy of community? *Utne Reader,* pp. 89–90.

Meier, D. (1995). *The power of their ideas: Lessons for America from a small school in Harlem.* Boston, MA: Beacon Press.

Miller, J. & Drake, S. (1990, Fall). Implementing a holistic curriculum. *Holistic Education Review,* p. 30.

Miller, R. (1990). *What are schools for? Holistic education in American culture.* Brandon, VT: Holistic Education Press.

Nakagawa, Mako. (1986). *Cooperative pluralism and public schools.* Olympia, WA: Office of Superintendent of Public Instruction.

National Association of Secondary School Principals. (2004). *Breaking ranks II: Strategies for leading high school reform.* Reston, VA: National Association of Secondary School Principals.

National Institute of Mental Health. (2001). *Teenage brain—A work in progress: A brief overview of research into brain development during adolescence.* Bethesda, MD: National Institute of Mental Health.

Olsen, L. (1990). *Embracing diversity: Teacher's voices from California classrooms.* San Francisco, CA: California Tomorrow Immigrant Students Project Research Reports.

Orfield, G. (Ed.). (2004). *Dropouts in America: Confronting the graduation rate crisis.* Cambridge, MA: Harvard Education Press.

Pert, C. (1997). *Molecules of emotion: The science behind mind-body medicine.* New York, NY: Simon and Schuster.

Research Triangle Institute. (1994). *Promising classroom interventions for students with attention deficit disorder.* Research Triangle Park, NC: Research Triangle Institute and Office of Special Education Programs, U.S. Department of Education.

Rogers, E. (1988). Diffusion of the idea Beyond War. In *BreakThrough: Emerging new thinking.* New York, NY: Walker & Co.

Rutter, M. (1979). Protective factors in children: Responses to stress and disadvantage. *Primary Prevention of Psychopathology, 3.*

Sapon-Shevin, M. & Schniedewind, N. (1991). Cooperative learning as empowering pedagogy. *Empowerment from Multicultural Education,* SUNY Press.

Schneider, S. (1993, April). A better way to learn. *World Monitor,* p. 32.

Secretary's Commission on Achieving Necessary Skills. (1999). *SCANS report for America 2000: What work requires of schools.* U.S. Department of Labor.

Senge, P. (1991). *The fifth discipline: The art and practice of learning communities.* New York, NY: Double Day/ Currency.

Senge, P. (1991, October). The learning organization made plain. *Training and Development,* p. 38.

Steele, C. M. (1992, April). Race and schooling of Black Americans. *Atlantic Monthly,* p. 75.

Stoddard, L. (1992). *Redesigning education: A guide for developing human greatness.* Tucson, AZ: Zephyr Press.

Taubeneck, A. (2006, Summer). The millennials: Today's students are always on. *Northwestern University Magazine.*

Time. (2006, April). Drop Out Nation. *Time, 167*(16), pp. 30–40.

Von Oech, R. (1990). *A whack on the side of the head: How you can be more creative.* New York, NY: Warner Books.

Wall Street Journal. (1992, Sept 11). Digging for knowledge. *Wall Street Journal.*

Wassermann, S. (1992). *Asking the right questions: The essence of teaching.* Bloomington, IN: Phi Delta Kappan Educational Foundation.

Weissberg, R., Devaney, E., Utne O'Brien, M., Resnik, H., & Keister, S. (2006). *Sustainable schoolwide social and emotional learning (SEL) implementation guide.* Chicago, IL: Collaborative for Academic, Social and Emotional Learning.

Wells, G. (1996). *Dialogic inquiry in education: Building the legacy of Lev Vygotsky.* Toronto, Canada: Ontario Institute for Studies in Education, University of Toronto.

Werner, E. & Smith, R. (1989). *Vulnerable but invincible: A longitudinal study of resilient children and youth.* New York, NY: Adams, Bannister and Cox.

Wheelock, A. (1998). *Safe to be smart: Building a culture for standards -based reform in the middle grades.* National Middle School Association.

Wolins, M. & Wozner, Y. (1982). *Revitalizing residential settings: Problems and potential in education.* San Francisco, CA: Health, Rehabilitation and Social Services, Jossey Bass Publishers.

Yager, S., Johnson, R., & Johnson, D. (1985). Oral discussion: Group to individual transfer, and achievement in cooperative learning groups. *Journal of Educational Psychology, 77,* pp. 60–66.

Yager, S., Johnson, R., Johnson, D., & Snider, B. (1986). The impact of group processing on achievement in cooperative learning groups. *The Journal of Social Psychology, 126,* pp. 389–397.

Zins, J., Weissberg, R., Wang, M., & Walberg, H. (Eds). (2004). *Building academic success on social and emotional learning: What does the research say?* New York, NY: Teachers College Press.

INDEX

1976

1978

1987

As the Tribes Learning Community has grown, so has the Tribes book!

We thought you'd like to see the parade of books that we're celebrating!

1994

1995

2001

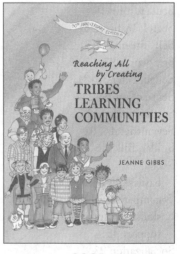

2006

CHECK OUT OUR WEBSITES FOR UP-TO-DATE NEWS, ARTICLES AND RESOURCES! WWW.TRIBES.COM AND WWW.TEACHCOMMUNITY.COM

ABOUT THE AUTHOR

JEANNE GIBBS
Founder and Author
Tribes Learning Communities

Jeanne has spent her professional career studying, writing and implementing systemic processes and programs to support children's development and prevent youth problems. Her perspective on human development is a systems approach that encourages schools, families and communities to create healthy environments in which children can grow and learn. The developmental culture and educational process now known as "Tribes Learning Communities" evolved out of years of studies Jeanne has pursued to synthesize a wealth of literature pertaining to the ecology of human development and learning. She is convinced that well being and success for students is not a result of curriculum, instruction and assessment—nor of intelligence—but the result of a school finally focusing on the growth and whole human development of its students in all aspects of their individual uniqueness and brilliance. The vision takes on reality whenever a school system focuses first on creating and sustaining a caring culture in which children truly are able to discover themselves and succeed.

Jeanne supervised implementations of the community learning process throughout hundreds of schools and youth-serving agencies for more than ten years while managing a non-profit corporation, which she had founded. Though serving as the executive director, she continued to research, refine and author publications—until her first formal retirement. Since then, Jeanne has retired many times—none of which last long due to her to passionate purpose. Ever-growing requests from schools throughout the United States, Canada, Australia and other countries for professional development and quality materials led her to establish CenterSource Systems in 1995 as "the home of Tribes."

Her primary interest now centers on the potential of school reform being achieved through reflective Learning Communities that are responsive to the developmental and learning needs of their students. It is no surprise that people across the country know Jeanne for her warm and generous spirit… and ability to build community wherever she goes.

NOTES